MW01088930

Faith of the Fathers

FAITH
OF THE
FATHERS

THE COMPREHENSIVE HISTORY
OF CATHOLIC CHAPLAINS
IN THE CIVIL WAR

ROBERT J. MILLER
FOREWORD BY JAMES M. MCPHERSON

University of Notre Dame Press

Notre Dame, Indiana

Library of Congress Control Number: 2024947145

ISBN: 978-0-268-20934-6 (Hardback)
ISBN: 978-0-268-20941-4 (WebPDF)
ISBN: 978-0-268-20940-7(Epub3)

GPSR Compliance Inquiries:
Mare Nostrum Group B.V., Mauritskade 21D, 1091 GC Amsterdam, The Netherlands
gpsr@mare-nostrum.co.uk | Phone: +44 (0)1423 562232

CONTENTS

Part 4. From the Vantage Point of History

FOREWORD

One of the more striking monuments at Gettysburg National Military Park is a bronze statue of Father William Corby, chaplain of the 88th New York, standing on a boulder to give absolution to the soldiers of the Irish Brigade as they were about to go into action near the Wheatfield on the afternoon of July 2, 1863. Forty-two men of this skeleton brigade would be killed or mortally wounded in the next couple of hours. Corby's statue is mounted today on the same stone where he stood in 1863.

Corby was the only one of 3,400 Union and Confederate chaplains to be honored by a monument in any Civil War park, while scores of generals and colonels in bronze or stone are scattered around these battlefields. The same disparity exists in the literature about the Civil War, in which a handful of books about chaplains are almost invisible in the shadow of thousands of books about combat officers. And most of the writing about chaplains focuses on the Protestants — perhaps not surprising, since only 4 percent of chaplains were Catholics and probably fewer than 10 percent of Civil War soldiers were Catholics. Nevertheless, the 126 Catholic chaplains described and analyzed in this book were a special breed. Four-fifths of them had been born abroad. They were more thoroughly educated and trained than most of their Protestant counterparts, they served longer than the average Protestant, and worked in a more structured format in the regiments or hospitals where they served. Most of them staffed the "ethnic" regiments (predominantly Irish) where all or a majority of soldiers were Catholics. They had to confront and overcome the legacy of the anti-Catholic and nativist culture of the Know Nothing political party in the 1850s that persisted into and through the Civil War years. Yet as this book makes clear, they won the support and admiration of the top military and political leadership in both the Union and Confederacy. They helped foreign-born Catholic soldiers take the first steps toward acceptance and assimilation into American society. As spiritual counselors to the men they served, they offered a spark of humanity to counter the inhumanity of war.

Robert Miller's thorough research, impeccable scholarship, and lucid writing have filled a large gap in Civil War scholarship with this study. A substantial portion of it consists of biographies of the 126 chaplains, which present much new information that can be found nowhere else. *Faith of the Fathers* is thus an important reference work that is encyclopedic in scope. But like all good history, it is also a true story that will engage its readers and deepen their understanding of this vital period in the American past. It will also help us appreciate why Father Corby, who features prominently in the book, is honored by a statue at Gettysburg and another on the campus of the University of Notre Dame, where he served at president for eleven years after the Civil War.

James M. McPherson

ACKNOWLEDGMENTS

As with any project of this magnitude, *Faith of the Fathers* could not have been written without the support and assistance of many people. In the twenty or so years that have gone into the researching and writing of this book *Faith of the Fathers* (as well as the production of a related documentary film of the same title, released in 2023), many people have assisted me along the way with their wisdom, knowledge, passion, support, encouragement, faith (in myself and this project), and simply their friendship. To these people specifically (many of whom are close friends), I express public gratitude here.

Those who read this manuscript and offered invaluable corrections and comments: Bruce Allardice, for his experienced editorial "nitpicking" of inestimable value; Father David Endres, for information on Father William O'Higgins and the Cincinnati Diocese, and for reading and commenting on the manuscript; Cary Heinz, for doing manuscript reading, review, and "cleanup"; and Katherine Jeffrey, for reading through chapters, and for suggestions, corrections, and historical wisdom.

Those who gave archival, historical, and biographical assistance: Brian Burtka SJ, for Jesuit chaplains research; Jerome Kowalski, for library research on specific chaplains; Will Kurtz, for insights on nineteenth-century history; Mark A. Noll, for insights on American religious history, wisdom, and assistance with the documentary film; Father John Vidmar OP, for Dominican archival sources; and Robert Wooden and Patrick Hayes, for Redemptorist archival, historical, and chaplain information.

Those who helped with individual biographical assistance: Peter Belmonte (Father Leo Rizza OFM); Linda Holley (Father Thomas

Mooney); Linda Kutner (Father Joseph Jarboe OP); Julie Moytka (Father Patrick J. Murphy); and Pat Tuminello (Father Jeremiah Trecy). Thanks also, Pat, for making me feel welcomed in Huntsville, Alabama, during the filming of our documentary *Faith of the Fathers*.

Those who gave special assistance, including: the archivists at the Archdiocese of Cincinnati, University of Notre Dame, Dodge County (Wisconsin) Historical Society, Jesuit Archives and Research Center (St. Louis, Missouri), Georgetown University (Booth Family Center), and the Rod Coddington Collection; Doug Dammann, for support of the vision and value of this research, and for making possible a nine-month exhibit on the *Faith of the Fathers* at the Kenosha Civil War Museum from September 2023 to June 2024; Tim Frakes, for his incredible cinematography and scriptwriting of the documentary film *Faith of the Fathers*, and help with book illustrations; Rachel Kindler, my editor at the University of Notre Dame Press, who picked up this manuscript after unfortunate delays, moving it to completion with her positive support and wisdom; Mary Kay Matthys, for manuscript reading and review, correcting chaplains' biographical errata, and invaluable research assistance; Wayne Wolf, for his support for the project, and crafting the index; and John Urschel, for bringing to my attention Father Henry Clavreul's Andersonville "diary."

To high school teachers like Father Edward Cosgrove CSsR (who first lit the fire of my lifelong love for American history), and to my family and friends (who patiently tolerate and even support my "habit" and love of history).

To all those historians and reenactors who labor to preserve our endangered Civil War battlefields and continue its "living history," and Civil War Roundtable members nationwide who meet faithfully to learn, fellowship, and ensure that memories of our deadliest national combat are always kept alive.

Finally, to our ancestors who lived the history we only write about—the soldiers, civilians, enslaved persons, freedmen, pastors, clergy, theologians, families, and political leaders of mid-nineteenth-century America—and to the awesome Lord of all history who somehow "makes everything work out for good" (Romans 8:28).

INTRODUCTION

In his 1929 book, *Catholic Military and Naval Chaplains—1776–1917*, Dom Aidan Henry Germain published the first work directly focused on Catholics in the American military. In his introduction, Germain wrote that "the contribution made by Catholic priests toward the welfare of the military and naval service of the United States has never been told from the official records of our government." Ninety years later, to the very year (2019), in the opening words of their book, *Soldiers of the Cross*, Will Kurtz and Father David Endres comment that "the story of Catholic chaplains . . . during the Civil War (1861–1865) is generally unappreciated, known mainly to historians of Catholic America."

In the near century between these books, despite the rapidly increased popularity of the Civil War in culture, media, and literature, the topic of religion in the Civil War has remained underappreciated—and the role of Catholic priest-chaplains in that conflict is discussed even less. There is a dearth of "institutional history" about the important role that Catholic clergy played in America's most deadly war, and specifically to identify *who* those clergy were and what they did. Through the collective biographies provided here, I hope to enlighten readers about these clergy, their religious experiences, and the significant impact they made in a broken country which, divided against itself, could not stand.

Thankfully the role of religion in the Civil War itself, through the perspective of wartime chaplains, has begun to be explored, with updated listings, biographies, life summaries, and so on. Most notable are these works: *Faith in the Fight* (Brinsfield, Davis, Maryniak, and Robertson), *Soldiers of the Cross* (Dollar), *For Courageous Fighting and Confident Dying* (Armstrong), *In God's Presence* (B. Miller), and *The Spirit Divided: Memoirs of Civil War Chaplains—The Confederacy* (Brinsfield) and *The Union* (Maryniak and Brinsfield). Some biographies or transcriptions of chaplains' diaries have also emerged, among them accounts of Milton L. Haney (55th Illinois), Joseph Twichell (71st New York, Excelsior Brigade), Louis N. Beaudry (5th New York Cavalry), William E. Wiatt (26th Virginia), Charles Todd Quintard (1st Tennessee) and James H. McNeilly (49th Tennessee).

More narrowly focused works on the Catholic presence in the Civil War have also emerged in recent years. The diaries of two Catholic priest-chaplains are outstanding accounts of wartime ministry—Union chaplain William Corby (*Memoirs of a Chaplain's Life*) and Confederate chaplain James Sheeran (*The Civil War Diary of Father James Sheeran*). In 2019, an 1880s account of fifteen priest-chaplains by David Conyngham was finally published as *Soldiers of the Cross* (Kurtz and Endres). Most notable among the more broadly focused Catholic wartime studies are *Faith and Fury: The Rise of Catholicism during the Civil War* (Connor), *Excommunicated from the Union* (Kurtz), *For the Union and the Church: Four Converts in the Civil War* (Longley), *Catholic Confederates: Faith and Duty in the Civil War South* (Kraszewski), *The Catholics and Mrs. Mary Surratt* (Zanca), and *American Catholics and the Quest for Equality in the Civil War Era* (Curran).

During the horrors of the Civil War, the Catholic priest-chaplains and nun-nurses who served the troops presented the clearest public persona of Catholicism. Far more than soldiers' bishops, superiors, or hometown pastors many miles away, it was the wartime priests and nuns who were the concrete and immediate face of Catholicism, the "contact point" with God and eternity for both Catholics and non-Catholics as well. Inferences and references to priest-chaplains permeate many diaries, letters, and even the *Official Records of the Civil War* (also known as the OR) on occasion.

But obtaining an accurate and comprehensive list of these priest-chaplains has been incredibly elusive ever since Germain wrote his foundational 1929 *Catholic Military and Naval Chaplains*. While there have been Catholic chaplains in the American military since the earliest days of the country, their role has suffered from the overall anti-Catholic overall sentiment of nineteenth-century American culture, and from the more recent lack of interest or focused research by contemporary Civil War or Catholic historians.

PARAMETERS OF THIS WORK

The focused intent of *Faith of the Fathers* is to offer a much-needed, comprehensive update to the list of Catholic priests who served in the Civil War, using the full range of modern research tools. For the first time, an accurate, modern historical record of *all* known Catholic priests who served has been compiled, utilizing new and essential delineations between wartime chaplains—officially recognized and occasional chaplains, full-time and part-time priests who served, and also those bishops who were known to have ministered as well. I will present those whose service was extensive, encompassing many months and even years, but will also highlight (for the first time) many previously unknown priests who served much shorter and more limited terms, for various reasons.[1]

Research in this area has resulted in a far more accurate and greatly expanded listing of Catholic wartime priest-chaplains than has been previously available. One hundred and twenty-six Catholic priests have been accounted for in all, seventy-six of whom were official and full-time, and fifty others who served occasionally (or situationally). Seventy-four of these priests served the Union cause, and fifty-two served in the Confederacy, although this book will outline many unique circumstances surrounding several priests who served.[2]

As a general rule a decision was made not to separate Confederate from Union chaplains with regard to overall historical analysis of Catholic chaplains in the war, although some obvious delineations had to be made (e.g., governmental decisions about chaplains). In the Jesuit religious order, for example, chaplains served on both sides, and nearly every Catholic chaplain ministered to troops on both sides if the need presented itself. When the war ended, the Jesuits' core identity again took precedence over any wartime differences—and indeed almost all Catholic chaplains were really united before, during, and after the war by the beliefs and practices of their Catholic priesthood. In the end all were simply Catholic priests performing vital wartime ministry, and ultimately that religious bond predominated over sectional differences.[3]

For purposes of reference, previous listings of Catholic Civil War chaplains have been less comprehensive and far shorter than the one presented here, although lists from more recent years tend to be similar.

Here is a brief summary of some of the more well-known Catholic chaplain listings given by author:

- Aidan Germain (1929): 79 Catholic chaplains (13 Union hospital, 38 Union regimental, 28 Confederate regimental).
- Benjamin Blied (1945): a simplified verbatim repetition of Germain's 1929 list.
- John Tracy Ellis (1956): "Eventually sixty-seven priests were enrolled as chaplains in the field with the Union and Confederate armies, together with a number of hospital and volunteer chaplains."[4]
- Bernard Maryniak (2003): a comprehensive list of all wartime chaplains, mentioning 85 Catholic chaplains (54 Union, 31 Confederate). However, there are four errors in that list, which results in only 81 total Catholic chaplains (53 Union, 28 Confederate) in actuality.
- William Kurtz (2016): 53 Union chaplains only (13 hospital and 40 regimental).
- Gracjan Kraszewski (2020): 28 Confederate priests only serving as chaplains, out of 278 total priests in the Confederate states.[5]

Thus, the need for an updated listing is obvious, which this book intends to be. *Faith of the Fathers* can therefore be described in several ways: as a reference work of Catholic wartime chaplains now available to others for future research; as a much-needed update to the historical record of the places and people Catholic Civil War chaplains served; and finally, as a collective biography of 126 fascinating men who served in America's most deadly war.

One might describe this book as the retelling of long-forgotten stories, attractively presented, from the admittedly biased view of an author who believes in the worth of his topic and values these men. Author and historian Father David Endres summarized the goal of *Faith of the Fathers* quite well in response to his reading of this manuscript, remarking that "this [book] is not written so much with the goal of making brand-new intellectual contributions or 'arguments' to fields of academic research. . . . rather *Faith of the Fathers* is a resource-gathering tool, a bringing together in one place what has never been brought together before—a comprehensive listing of Catholic priests who served in the Civil War, and the contexts in which they served and ministered during and after the war."[6]

Several other comments on the book's focus and the challenges of compiling historical resources for this manuscript may be helpful. First, no less than 126 Catholic priests (Union and Confederate, hospital and regimental, in all theaters of the war) had to be accounted for and given proper treatment with regard to their wartime ministry, life stories, and ministry contexts. That alone has added to the length of this text—further contextualizing additions (either social or ecclesial) or providing deeper analysis of these men and their work would make this an unwieldy encyclopedic work. Thus, I have chosen a more focused approach of compiling collective biographical portraits of the most important priest-chaplains in the personal arenas of their unique wartime ministries.

Second, *Faith of the Fathers* is not intended to be a primarily academic work, nor is its audience limited to academics or seminary students. From my personal experience and long involvement in local Civil War groups, I can verify that there is a large crowd of Civil War reenactors, roundtable members, and historical afficionados outside of academia who avidly read and study Civil War history. Because *Faith of the Fathers* helps fill a vast gap in the religious history of the war, these accounts of Civil War priest-veterans will have a broad appeal to anyone interested in the war from their own different perspectives.[7]

Third, one cannot tell the story of the Civil War without at least mentioning its core cause, slavery, or speaking at least briefly about the Church and its chaplains' connection in that regard. However, since no Catholic chaplains worked in any significant way with enslaved persons or freed Blacks during the war (though Edward O'Brien did postwar), there is virtually no material archivally to delve into. I would encourage further research and reporting of the stories of enslaved persons and freed Blacks who may have intersected with the Catholic Church in the Civil War era. At the end of chapter 13, I will speak briefly to the role of the Catholic Church historically regarding slavery and comment on the American Church's postwar actions regarding freed Blacks. In short, regrettably the postwar Church neglected to provide much practical support or spiritual "welcoming" to African American believers.

As a pastor who spent more than thirty-five years ministering in that very community, I can verify that much progress has been made since that time, although more awareness and sensitivity by the broader Church is needed.

Finally, an epilogue has been included for the purpose of presenting potential thematic trajectories beyond the scope of this book. The themes presented there are filled with possibilities for expanded development by historians or academics based upon the life stories and experiences of the Catholic wartime chaplains. It is my sincere hope that broader contextualizing of the larger historical, ecclesial, and social aspects which this book raises will indeed result from has been presented, particularly from those in academic settings.

LABOR OF LOVE

Finally, I would be remiss if in closing I did not remark that this manuscript has been a labor of love which has been in compilation mode for two decades now. From even before my previous book (*Both Prayed to the Same God*) was published, I have been researching and gathering data from every corner of the Civil War world—wartime diaries and letters, biographies of soldiers and pastors, Civil War histories of all types, libraries, newspaper articles, church history sites, regimental and Civil War histories, and reliable internet sites and databases. Historians both secular and religious, as well as fellow Civil War afficionados, have assisted me all along the way with their insights, information, and recommendations. I have been blessed beyond what I deserve by the help I have received, by the positive support both for this project, and in my frequent speaking engagements on the topic of chaplains, religion, and the Civil War.

On a humorous note, I have been amused time after time while writing, that just when I was about to close out my formal listing of Catholic chaplains, yet *another* priest's name would appear in a footnote or marginal reference! Once again, further research would ensue, and dusty corners of the historical or religious world delved into anew, to verify the details and status of this new-to-me priest's Civil War service.

Thus, the list of Catholic clergy who served grew far beyond what I had ever expected when this project began.

In the process of completing what has been a decades long passion, I have made 126 new friends. Nearly every one of the priests mentioned in this book has become as familiar to me as next-door neighbors or family members. Some of them are indeed quirky and different, a few might best be admired from a distance, but most are simply warm-hearted, down-home men I would love to share food and a drink with. All 126 are truly deserving of the highest commendation and praise possible for their service, dedication, and ministry at the time of America's greatest crisis. This work is a sincere and loving attempt to tell an over-looked story about oft-forgotten men, and to honor them for their contributions. May the long line of America's dedicated Catholic chaplains never be broken!

PROLOGUE

Catholic Chaplains in America
Prior to the Civil War

Before beginning a study of Catholic Civil War chaplains, a very brief overview of the history of the chaplaincy in America—especially in regard to Catholic priests—is in order. A more developed history of this topic is available in other sources, so there is no need to repeat it here; a list of those sources can be found in the footnote below. However, a brief review of Catholics in American chaplaincy will help set the stage for the remainder of this book.[1]

ORIGIN AND EARLY HISTORY OF CHAPLAINS

The English word "chaplain" comes from the Latin word *cappella*, meaning cape or cloak, and the French word *cappelani*. Traditionally, it is connected to the cloak of St. Martin of Tours (316–397 AD), which he cut in two, giving half to a beggar who was later revealed to be Jesus Christ himself.[2]

Our modern understanding of chaplains as professional religious serving in the military originated in Italy in 1587, when twenty-five army chaplains (all Jesuit priests) were organized into the first official chaplain corps system. By the eighteenth century, all major Western nations had established some form of chaplaincy services for their military. The famed English Duke of Wellington in his Peninsular Campaign (1808–1814) asked for more quality chaplains for his army, men who could handle the harsh life of being on campaign. (A whole thesis was written in 2013 on the failures of English chaplains at that time.)[3]

CHAPLAINS IN EARLY AMERICA

In 1758 Virginia established a militia chaplaincy at the request of then Colonel George Washington, and in July 1775 the Continental Congress officially recognized chaplains and began to pay them monthly. That date has now become the official date that the American Army Chaplain Corps claims as its birth. In July 1776, General George Washington issued an order regarding chaplains, stating that "the blessing and protection of Heaven are at all times necessary, but especially so in times of public distress and danger." That order also stated that colonels and commanding officers should make sure that chaplains were assigned to each regiment to ensure that soldiers regularly attended religious services.[4] Washington did want chaplains to be religious leaders, but also to visit the wounded, write letters home for the illiterate, and give patriotic discourses to prevent soldiers from deserting. The chaplain was intended to be a key link between the commander and the troops. Their initial pay was $20 per month, the same amount paid to captains and judge advocates.

Through the support of General Benedict Arnold, the French priest Louis Eustace Lotbinière (1715–1786) became the first Catholic chaplain connected to the United States military. Unfortunately, most of the wartime communications between Lotbinière and the American Congress dealt with remuneration issues, as Congress was badly remiss in giving him his monthly payments. He was in fact not paid at all from 1784 to 1786, a situation Aidan Germain spoke of presenting "the pathetic figure of an aged priest, seventy-one years of age, in a strange country, in utter poverty, without friends, appealing to the head of the government in a tongue he used with little facility." Of the 218 chaplains who eventually served in the Continental Army, about twenty-five were killed or wounded in the American Revolution—the highest casualty rate ever in America's chaplain corps, even to this day.[5]

At the outset of the War of 1812, thirteen official regular army chaplains served American troops, although many more (over two hundred) were serving as state militia chaplains. However, there is no definite proof that any Catholic priests were among those who served. Catholic diocesan records of the time offer sparse details in that regard, which is somewhat understandable given the predominantly missionary nature of the American Catholic Church at that time. However, Catholic priests did administer the sacraments during the Battle of New Orleans (January 1815). As Germain phrases it, "There are records of Catholic nuns, time-honored angels of mercy, having appeared on the field at that battle. From this we gather that priests were caring for the soldiers at New Orleans, since the nuns generally follow the priests to battle." Nevertheless, the War of 1812 is the only American war in which we have no specific name of any Catholic priest who served in any capacity as a military chaplain.[6]

CONFLICTED CHAPLAINS IN THE MEXICAN-AMERICAN WAR

The Mexican-American War posed a unique challenge for Catholics because Mexico was predominantly Catholic and the United States was mostly Protestant. Many Catholic American immigrants from Ireland and Germany were part of the United States Army. As part of an American religious minority fighting against a Catholic Mexican enemy, they faced unique problems. Many Catholic soldiers were forced to attend Protestant services in camp or were not allowed to practice their faith, and all felt discrimination in some way. This led to some Catholics actually defecting from the United States and fighting for Mexico. The Saint Patrick's Battalion was formed from over 175 US Army "deserters"—a number of them being Irish and German Catholic immigrants, as well as some European expatriates and formerly enslaved persons.

President James Polk recognized this sensitive issue, and as a result, on July 5, 1846, two Jesuit priests joined American troops in Mexico— John McElroy (1782–1877) and Anthony Rey (1807–1847). However, although President Polk had invited and approved of their presence, Fathers McElroy and Rey were technically still not official chaplains of the United States Army. Thus, without official military records to document their "careers," we lack specific details about their work. We do know that they accompanied the American troops into Mexico, with McElroy serving in a garrison for a time, and Rey taking part in the

Battle of Monterrey from September 20 to 23, 1846. At that battle, Rey was on the battlefield caring for over 368 wounded soldiers and giving the last rites to the dying (over one hundred).

However, in January 1847, against the advice of army officers, Rey went outside of the garrison to minister to Catholics in a nearby village, despite warnings of danger. Not long after, he was killed by Mexican guerrillas and his body was found pierced with lances several days later. Though not an official chaplain per se, Rey thus became the first American Catholic priest-chaplain killed in the line of duty.[7]

Following the Mexican-American War, Catholic chaplains were officially appointed to the regular army and became the first such Catholic chaplains since the Revolutionary War: Samuel H. Milley (Monterey, California); succeeded by Ignacio Ramirez (Monterey, California), who served from 1850 to 1852; Michael Sheehan (Fort Belknap, Texas); and we cannot omit the Jesuit Pierre-Jean De Smet, who lived from 1801 to 1873 and served as the near-legendary Indian missionary. Though called in his appointment a "chaplain to the Army of Utah" in 1858, it seems his work with the army was unofficial, involving occasional mediation and negotiation with Native American leaders who trusted him as a result of his missionary work among them. (De Smet later played a significant role in helping Jesuits avoid the Conscription Act in the Civil War.)[8]

THE CIVIL WAR LOOMS ON THE HORIZON

As the North and South began to gear up for a war that initially few thought would last long, the role and need for religious chaplains was appreciated, but unique problems on both sides greatly confused the formalization of these chaplains' roles and activities. The North had an eighty-five-year history of customs pertaining to chaplains, but no clear federal legislation existed to govern the issue.[9]

Beginning in May 1861, an effort was made to begin to convert these informal, often inconsistent customs about religious in the military into some clearer legal guidelines. General Orders 15 and 16 greatly expanded the size of the US Chaplaincy Corps. President Abraham Lincoln ordered the colonels of all regular and volunteer regiments to appoint regimental chaplains to help maintain "the social happiness and moral improvement of the troops" and issue regular reports on the "moral and religious condition" of their units. They were to be elected by field officers and company commanders, and to be "regularly ordained ministers of some Christian denomination."[10]

However, the chaplains' official rank, uniform, and daily duties were not clearly defined. Although they received a captain's salary and horse (thus frequently dressing as officers), the chaplains were not officially identified as captains by the government or provided with uniforms, rations, or forage for their animals.[11]

Lincoln took a personal interest in the "chaplain project," and after July 1861 (Battle of First Bull Run or Manassas), he personally wrote notes to seven clergymen in Washington, DC, and asked for their much-needed assistance in the hospitals. There were two Catholic priests in that group of seven: Matthew F. McGrath OP (1833–1870) and Francis E. Boyle (1827–1882), both of whom will be discussed later. All seven ministers promptly accepted Lincoln's invitation, although it would be sixteen months before Congress named them "hospital chaplains of U.S. Volunteers."[12]

Debates over remuneration for chaplains and their attire then ensued, resulting eventually in policies such as mandatory $100 pay a month, two rations a day on duty, forage for one horse, and uniform guidelines (which were often ignored). Catholic priests, like many other chaplains, would end up wearing a wide variety of garb as they performed their duties. Numerous unofficial chaplains would also serve the Union cause without commissions. But all the War Department statutes, the executive and general orders, and the wartime discussions that ensued did accomplish one valuable thing. Finally, the status, work, and role of chaplains in the United States military had been officially established on a firm foundation for the future.

In the South, the immediate 1861 energies of the Confederacy were organizing themselves as a new national entity and setting up a provisional army. Legislation passed by the Confederate Congress on May 3, 1861, said only that "there shall be appointed by the President Chaplains to serve the armies of the Confederate States during the existing war." It went on to specify that these chaplains were to be "appointed by the president" and assigned by him to "such regiments as he deemed necessary."[13]

The monthly pay for a Confederate chaplain was only $85, far less than many state militia chaplains, and barely enough to buy rations and forage for a horse. There was no description of their duties, nor provisions for uniforms or rank, and no stipulations regarding age, education, or ecclesiastical status. Their pay would later be reduced to a mere $50 a month, though finally in April 1862 it was raised to $80 a month. Later in the war, rations and forage would be provided for as well.[14]

Curiously, the organization of the Confederate army mirrored that of the US Army nearly exactly, with one notable exception. Despite the aforementioned provisions of the Confederate Congress, there were no provisions for chaplains in the Confederate army's first formulation. This was somewhat ironic since the preamble to the Confederate Constitution actually invoked God (unlike the United States' version), saying that they were "invoking the favor and guidance of Almighty God." Yet actually providing for the spiritual welfare and career of their soldiers seemed to never be a high priority for the Confederacy.[15]

Thus, what happened with Confederate troops was that ministers from various denominations began volunteering to be chaplains, and individual state units began looking for ministers willing to serve (or later allowing chaplains to emerge organically from their ranks). Confederate regiments and their commissioned officers also became more active in seeking chaplains. The procedure gradually developed such that regimental commanders, often upon consultation with other officers, would first approve those men who had volunteered to be chaplains. Then the commanders would request a formal commission for the chaplains from the Secretary of War on behalf of President Jefferson Davis. However, blessings and drawbacks accompanied this process.

Since no church endorsements or certificates of training or ordination were ever required, some of the early chaplains were not the most highly trained men theologically. Many were indeed simply soldiers themselves who volunteered for the position due to need (especially true of the Baptist and Methodist traditions). Hence the tradition of "fighting chaplains" became far more prevalent in the Confederacy. John Brinsfield estimates that of the 1,308 Confederate chaplains who were known and commissioned, fully 58 percent were deacons, local preachers, or laymen without full ordination.[16]

Though the pay may have been poor and the job description practically nonexistent, there was a certain glamor for some clergy and laymen to become a commissioned Confederate chaplain. Though not technically an officer, the position of chaplain could bring with it some measure of extended honorary authority and the possibility of wearing a military uniform. As there was immense latitude in what could be worn (more so than for Union chaplains), individual chaplains' attire did run the gamut. Even among the Jesuit chaplains, Hippolyte Gache would insist on wearing a traditional black robe with biretta, while Darius Hubert wore a typical Louisiana captain's uniform, while Joseph Prachensky preferred a dashing major's regalia with sash and a plumed hat! Other non-Catholic chaplains could be found wearing backwoods bearskin attire or, most commonly, civilian clothing. Many chaplains wore simply a plain gray uniform coat with gray trousers and whatever hats, belts, and other accessories that they could find.[17]

"AND THE WAR CAME . . ."

After nearly ninety years of confusion and uncertainty about the role of chaplains in a young America's military, on the eve of the Civil War, the role and position had never been stronger or more accepted. Both the Union and Confederacy would enter the war with at the least the possibility of government support for the religious ministry of chaplains. The actual numbers of chaplains who served, however, would be another story; there was a perpetual, dramatic shortage of chaplains on both sides. Even the legendary Confederate General Thomas "Stonewall" Jackson, devout Presbyterian and Bible-school teacher that he was, had chaplains only in forty-four of his ninety-one regiments. Episcopal Bishop and General Leonidas Polk had even fewer chaplains—only fifteen of his forty regiments were supplied.

But while chaplains on both sides faced many troubles early in the war, particularly regarding issues of pay, status, and role, Roman Catholic chaplains would experience special challenges in providing religious

care and even being appointed as official chaplains. Catholics had been
a religious minority in a predominantly Protestant country, and would
be in both wartime armies as well. The larger societal Catholic struggle
for recognition in America, and the active prejudice that existed, significantly impacted Catholic churches and chaplains on the eve of war.
The chaplains' stories will comprise the remainder of this book.

PART 1

TROUBLED TIMES, WILLING MEN, FAITHFUL WORK

———— •✦• ————

On one occasion, an officer was dying—shot in the face—
blood pouring out. He wrote on a slip of paper: "Chaplain,"
and the slip, red with blood, was carried around by a soldier,
seeking for a chaplain. It was handed to me. I hurried: the man
was conscious—dying fast. "Speak to me," he said, "of Jesus."
He had been baptized—there was no time to talk of the Church.
I talked of the Savior, and sorrow for sin. The memory
of that scene has never been effaced from my mind.
I have not doubted the salvation of that soul.

—FATHER JOHN IRELAND,
5th Minnesota

PART I

TROUBLED TIMES
WILLING MEN
FAITHFUL WORK

CHAPTER 1

PREWAR CHALLENGES TO CATHOLIC CHAPLAINS

The Civil War marked the beginning of the officially authorized presence of Roman Catholic clergy in the United States military. Although two priests had accompanied troops during the Mexican-American War, it had only been by presidential appointment; only three had been employed briefly as post chaplains in the 1850s. Catholic clergy were not allowed to serve in sizeable numbers until the Civil War, and their numbers were even then small compared to Protestant wartime chaplains. This book will identify and introduce the reader to 126 Catholic priests who are recorded as having served in some recognized, official, non-anecdotal capacity as chaplains to Union or Confederate troops. Their service was far-ranging, life-changing, and tumultuous, and marked by resistance, conflict, and challenge from the outset.

Catholic clergy who desired to become chaplains had to first battle the culture of the day, governmental bureaucracy, politics, prejudice, and occasionally even lukewarm support from their own leaders. As mentioned in the prologue, although chaplains had existed in American armies dating back to the Revolutionary War, much about their role and position was still vague, unclear, and confusing as the Civil War era approached. Several major issues (especially with governmental policies) confronted all those who desired to be chaplains, while Catholic chaplains specifically had to deal with even more nuanced issues than those of other ministers.

IMMIGRATION AND CLERGY SHORTAGES

During the first sixty years of the nineteenth century, immigration (overwhelmingly from Europe) changed the face of the United States as the nation's population grew from five to thirty-one million people. An estimate from the first national census of America showed that in 1790 there were only thirty thousand Catholics in a total population of 3.2 million. This increased to 195,000 in 1820 (still an estimate), and to about 1.75 million in 1850, by which time Catholicism had, numerically at least, become the country's largest denomination. The greater majority of those European immigrants were Irish and Catholic, and for most of them, organized religion provided a true sense of belonging in a foreign land. Jesuit historian Michael Perko has described the important role that Catholic clergy played in the spiritual lives of all Catholics, especially the immigrant.[1]

> The speed with which immigrants founded churches is a testimony to the importance religion exercised in their lives. For Catholics, the local parish frequently became the center of their lives, providing an island of safety and comfort in an alien land, while easing their transition into American life. . . . Though poor, the Irish rallied to found parishes [and] tended to rely more heavily on the clergy for direct leadership than some other groups did.[2]

Catholic priests were not only important in the mid-nineteenth century for leadership in parishes and providing an "island of safety," however. They were also essential for ordinary Catholics to even practice their faith. Because of the ritual nature of the Catholic faith of the day, only priests could celebrate Mass, minister forgiveness through confession, anoint the dying, and baptize babies or converts. In a country where the Catholic population had swelled out of all proportion to the number of available priests, there was a desperate shortage of

Catholic clergy on the eve of the Civil War. Understaffed even in peacetime, the Church became even more stressed by the divergent needs of surging ethnic waves of Catholic immigrants—especially in urban areas.

Catholic bishops in the 1860s found it extremely difficult to spare their priests for the military chaplaincy when the Civil War broke out. Aidan Germain comments about the challenges of Catholic leaders had in even allowing small numbers of their priests to volunteer as wartime chaplains. "Since immigration was practically unimpeded ... the Catholic population of all states grew constantly and the need of priests to minister to them increased in proportion. It was next to impossible to determine in advance with what regiments the Catholic soldiers were most numerous, and thus it chanced that now and then a Catholic chaplain was, like Father Titta assigned to a regiment having very few Catholics. Again, as Father Ireland experienced, battle losses and expiration of enlistments diminished the Catholic soldiers of a given regiment to a comparative handful, which made it desirable that the services of chaplains be utilized in spheres of greater need."[3]

Looking at the careers of actual Catholic wartime chaplains, one finds these challenges borne out in their actual military service. Some priests were allowed by their bishops to be named chaplain, but were later recalled to their dioceses or congregations after serving only a short while—such as the above-mentioned James Titta (Gombitelli) (13th Pennsylvania Cavalry) and John Ireland (5th Minnesota), and also George Doane (New Jersey Militia) and Joseph Prachensky SJ (3rd Alabama). At the time of his March 1863 letter of resignation, John Ireland wrote that "my motive for thus resigning is that, within a few days past, I have received a letter from my bishop who, in view of the fact that the clergyman who has taken my place in Minnesota is sick, and totally unable to attend the spiritual wants of a large congregation. ... [He] invites me to return home as soon as the laws and regulations of the army will allow me." (Other sources, though, indicate that Ireland also had health issues affecting him at the time, resulting in him leaving his regiment during the 1863 Vicksburg Campaign.)[4]

The situation of Thomas Quinn (1st Rhode Island), captures the difficulties both priests and bishops faced regarding military chaplaincy. A member of the Hartford Diocese (Connecticut), Quinn served from

April 1861 until his honorable discharge in January 1862. However, his Rhode Island regiment soon found itself without a chaplain again, and they voted for Quinn (who was indeed willing) to rejoin them. But by then he had been assigned to another church in the diocese, and his bishop would not allow him to return. The records of the 2nd Rhode Island Regiment state simply that "another attempt was made to obtain a chaplain. On the evening of the 21st of February, at a meeting of the officers, Rev. Thomas Quinn of Providence, chaplain in the First, Third, and First Light Artillery, from April, 1861 to July, 1862, was elected. Father Quinn was willing to accept the appointment, but his ecclesiastical superiors had already assigned him to other duties, and were indisposed to release him, and the appointment was therefore declined."[5]

The St. Louis priest John Bannon (1st Missouri CSA Infantry) never even sought permission from his bishop to become a Confederate chaplain because he knew his Union-leaning bishop didn't support the Southern cause and would likely not approve such an appointment. (Bannon departed the rectory in the middle of the night, leaving a farewell letter for Bishop Peter Kenrick, which the bishop never opened.) Other priests attempted to balance both their far-reaching parish responsibilities with "informal" chaplain duties; Oscar Sears (Lynchburg), the Dominican John Thomas Nealis (Chattanooga), Thomas O'Reilly (Atlanta), and Innocent Bergrath (eastern Tennessee) are a few examples here, although further research is needed in this area. Aidan Germain's foundational work on Catholic chaplains captures that reality succinctly:

> It was the practice of a considerable number of priests to follow the movements of the troops from place to place, and administer the sacraments on the very battlefields, all without any semblance of official appointment as chaplains. Such priests doubtless appreciated the difficulty experienced by official chaplains in obtaining leave of absence . . . Their work cannot be too highly praised, for they served the Catholics who were without official chaplains, and would have probably gone through the four years' war or fallen on the field without proper spiritual consolation.[6]

Because of clergy shortages, about one-half (49 percent) of the Catholic priests who served "full-time" were only able to do so for a year or less on average. Of all Catholic priests designated in the military records of both sides as official chaplains (seventy-six), forty-three of them (56 percent) served 18 months or less. Only fifteen priests served about three years or more (38.4 months on average); they are designated as full-time chaplains in this book. Numerous priests served unofficially or occasionally ("situationally" is the term that best captures their work) in military hospitals, camps, and prisons in their respective dioceses or geographic areas while at the same time maintaining their ordinary but important pastoral work in their rapidly growing Catholic parishes.[7]

Despite the clerical shortages at the outset of the war, some bishops did realize the desperate need for priests to serve the Catholics in the armies of both sides. Although Bishop William Elder (Natchez) did not want his priests to be named official chaplains by the Confederacy, he directed most of his fifteen priests to serve the troops in their area as diligently as possible, and himself was a very active informal chaplain. Bishop John Purcell, writing in a January 15, 1862, editorial in *The Catholic Telegraph* (Cincinnati's Catholic paper), was one who called for more Catholic chaplains in the army: "We have not a sufficient number of priests to supply destitute congregations, much less as such would be qualified or willing for this very arduous deportment of the ministry. . . . We think that a good priest should be willing, when judged fit for this duty by his bishop, to devote his entire energies to prepare Catholic soldiers, under such circumstances, to appear before their God." A strong supporter of both the Union and emancipation of enslaved persons, Purcell hung the stars and stripes from his Cincinnati cathedral, blessed the colors of troops as they left the city, and sent three chaplains to serve Union troops during the war.[8]

Unfortunately, due to the shortage of priests for the forty-seven dioceses of the American Catholic Church in 1861 (cf. appendix 1), there was a chronic lack of chaplains for Catholic troops. This mirrored the overall lack of chaplains in both armies, but Catholics faced the greatest shortages. A brief statistical review of soldiers and chaplains during the Civil War confirms this reality.[9]

- In the Union, an estimated 2.1 million soldiers served, but only 2,398 chaplains were commissioned (5 percent of available Northern clergy of appropriate age). Thus, less than 1 percent of those commissioned for service in Union armies were chaplains of some denomination, resulting in a ratio of one Union chaplain for 876 Union soldiers.[10]
- Of the 2,398 official Union chaplains, only 51 were official Catholic priest-chaplains—a mere 2.1 percent of all Union Civil War chaplains. Given an approximate number of 200,000 Catholic troops in the Union armies, the ratio of Catholic priests (excluding occasional chaplains) to Catholic Union troops would have been one priest for 3,921 soldiers.[11]
- The ratio of official Catholic priest-chaplains (excluding the occasional chaplains) to Union troops in general would have been one priest for 41,176 soldiers. (Small wonder then that Union chaplains spent a great deal of time on horseback visiting other regiments and corps in the performance of their duty.)

Statistics for the Confederacy are more difficult to determine with precision, but the pattern remains the same, although with a slightly higher percentage of priests to Catholic Southern soldiers.

- It is estimated that between 750,000 and 1 million Confederate soldiers served, with some 1,308 recognized Confederate chaplains having commissions during the war (14 percent of eligible Southern clergy). The percentage of chaplains to troops was less than 1 percent, but the ratio of chaplains to soldiers was statistically better than the Union (one chaplain for 573 to 765 Confederate soldiers). However, only about 2 percent of all Confederate chaplains were Catholic—because only twenty-five priests served at that level.[12]

Determining the number of Catholic troops who fought for the Confederacy is a daunting and ultimately impossible task, especially since the number of Irish who served (a majority presumably being

Catholic) is itself open to debate. However, making a broad supposition that a majority of the estimated 25,000 to 40,000 Irish who served *may* have been Catholic, and given the twenty-five official Catholic priest-chaplains who served the Confederacy, the ratio of official priest-chaplains (again excluding occasional chaplains) to Confederate Catholics would be far lower than for Union Catholic troops. It would be one Catholic priest for every one thousand soldiers (based on twenty-five thousand Catholics), or one priest per every 1,600 soldiers (based on forty thousand Catholics).[13]

It has been estimated that some 200,000 Catholics served in the war, approximately 145,000 of whom were Irish. The predominantly Catholic regiments (e.g., New York's Irish Brigade and Corcoran's Irish Legion) and individual divisions were rarely without priests, but because of shortages, many Catholics in non-Catholic regiments did not see a clergyman of their own faith for long periods of time. As another example, William O'Higgins (10th Ohio) and Edward Corcoran (61st Ohio) were the only Catholics among all Ohio chaplains. They represented 8 percent of the total number of Ohio's regimental chaplains, with the largest denominational group being the Methodist Episcopal Church.[14]

The Cincinnati-based German Catholic paper *Der Wahrheitsfreund* complained in 1862: "There are regiments where one third are Catholic, yet there is no Catholic chaplain in the brigade, or whole division. There are only a few regiments in which there are no Catholic soldiers, and we do not believe that the tenth part of these Catholics can receive the sacraments when they have most need of them." The few but excellent wartime journals of Catholic priests are full of stories of their meeting Catholic families on their travels who had not seen a Catholic priest for long periods. The overall shortage of priests among troops, though, was slightly mitigated by occasional long encampments, which allowed the precious few Catholic chaplains to circulate among the different regiments in the army. Occasionally as well, priests from the local area came into the camps to minister, thus giving greater opportunities for spiritual interactions (such as the sacraments) to those who desired them.[15]

STAYING OUT OF THE ARMY:
THE CONSCRIPTION ACT

On March 3, 1863, President Lincoln signed the controversial Conscription Act for the Union. America's first genuine national conscription law stated that all able-bodied men between the ages of twenty and forty-five were liable to be drafted into the military service for a period of three years, with each state being responsible to fill the quota through enlistment and draftees. However, military service could be avoided by obtaining a substitute or by paying a $300 commutation fee. What resulted was a widespread perception of a highly unfair system, especially for poor immigrants, which was only exacerbated by newspaper headlines reading "$300 or Your Life"—underscoring the fact that the affluent could buy their way out of duty. This Act made it clear that, as James McPherson so aptly observed, the Civil War was a "rich man's war and a poor man's fight."[16]

While the Act was massively unpopular in the North, leading to heavy resistance and deadly Draft Riots in New York (July 1863), especially among the Irish, the other pertinent fact for Catholics was that clergy and religious were *not* automatically exempted from conscription. (Prior to the Conscription Act, they generally had been, usually through individual agreements made with state leadership.) Now Catholic priests and religious were eligible to be drafted into the Union army for fighting and formal military service—a clear contradiction to their primary roles as spiritual leaders. (Catholic canon law of the day forbade clergy from taking up weapons.) Within the next year, members of many Catholic institutions were in fact conscripted, including some priests and even the auxiliary Bishop of Cincinnati Sylvester Rosecrans, though as the Jesuit historian Gilbert Garraghan phrased it, "the authorities did not have the delicacy to pursue [his] case." This raised immediate issues for all Catholic religious leaders, who had many priests, brothers, and students between the ages of twenty and forty-five in their ecclesiastical ranks.[17]

Some Catholic bishops (led by John Timon of Buffalo, New York) attempted to influence political leaders to amend the Draft Law, giving exemptions to "all ministers of the Gospel, who have no secular pursuit . . . who devote themselves exclusively to the holy ministry and to teaching God's word." However, this effort was not successful. All religious dioceses, orders, parishes, and priests affected by the law dealt with the contentious issue in their own ways. Some Catholic leaders sought exemptions based on ill health or citizenship status, while many bishops simply paid the $300 bounty to get exemptions, sometimes taking up collections to do so. Bishop Henry Juncker (Alton, Illinois) appears to be one who did so, writing in June 1863 to Bishop John Purcell (Cincinnati) to say he intended to "take up a collection to buy out any priests who fall under the conscription." In the Pittsburgh and Buffalo parishes run by the Vincentian order, it was parish members themselves who raised the monies needed to pay the commutation fees for their local pastors. In 1864, the parishioners of St. Patrick's in Detroit raised money to furnish a substitute for their priest, Father J. A. Hennesy, who had been drafted.[18]

Many Catholic religious orders contacted political leaders attempting to gain special privileges for their own members from this new draft law. Early in 1864, five Jesuits from Cincinnati were drafted, as were eight from Missouri and two from Bardstown, Kentucky, including the superior of that house. On receiving the news, Father Ferdinand Coosemans (the Jesuit Provincial), telegraphed the prominent and well-connected Jesuit priest Father Pierre-Jean De Smet, then in Washington, DC, requesting his assistance to save the men from federal military service. On September 22 and 29, 1864, De Smet met with Secretary of War Edwin Stanton and achieved a positive resolution. Following a subsequent meeting with the Inspector General Colonel James Hardie to deal with another attempt to draft Jesuits, De Smet's intervention proved effective, and no Jesuits were ever actually pressed into service.

De Smet wrote a letter about the meeting with Stanton, and after thanking God and Mother Mary, remarked that "I was able to obtain their liberty, with the formal promise of the Secretary 'that hereafter he would exempt all of our people who might be called on for military service.' In order to evade the laws, the Secretary orders our conscripts 'to stay at their homes until he calls for them,' and this call, according to his promise, shall not be issued for as long as the war lasts."[19]

Joseph Carrier served as the chaplain of the 6th Missouri. While he was with the troops in Vicksburg in 1863, Carrier worked ardently for exemptions on behalf of his religious order, the Congregation of the Holy Cross (the order which founded the University of Notre Dame). Carrier wrote letters to Secretary Stanton and President Lincoln and followed them up by visiting the two personally in Washington. He too was successful in keeping his religious brothers out of the "fighting" army, although having the support of his two commanding officers in the army of the Tennessee—Ulysses S. Grant and William T. Sherman— may perhaps have been the biggest factors on his behalf. Sherman concurred with the exemption but did not commit to the legal question involved, while Grant wrote a personal note saying, "I would respectfully represent that the order here applying has contributed largely of its services to the support of the war . . . respectfully submitted for the consideration of the President, hoping . . . the favor asked will be granted."[20]

The German-born founder of the first Benedictine abbey in America, Abbot Boniface Wimmer (1809–1887), had written to the War Department in November 1862 to relieve his monks from military duty. Though successful then in obtaining exemptions from military duty, the subsequent government response was to "transfer" them to the Invalid Corps. A letter that Abbot Wimmer wrote three months later detailed the results, also revealing the challenges of being a wartime religious superior caring for the brothers under his authority.

There were four brothers drafted into the military. However, the army sent one back as unfit and two left to join our priests in Canada. The fourth was sent back by the War Department after he had been three months in the field, or actually in the hospital. . . . Father Emmeran Bliemel (who is in Nashville) tried to smuggle medicine to the southerners in Tennessee, but he was caught and imprisoned. Luckily, he was brought before General Rosecrans, who is a good Catholic, and was sent home to his bishop with an admonition that would do him some good.[21]

On June 11, 1863, Wimmer wrote to Stanton again about the new conscription law, unsure of its application to members of his order. In a long, deeply reasoned letter, the insightful abbot explained with both "moral and material points" why the law "strikes a hard blow at religious orders . . . because it is in contradiction with their vows, with their entire condition of life." On receipt of this letter, an order was issued by the War Department exempting the Benedictines from the draft. But Wimmer's thoughtful letter, like others' efforts before his, would not be sufficient to actually amend the 1863 Conscription Act to grant generic clergy exemptions.[22]

Finally, the saintly superior of the Annapolis seminary of the Redemptorist religious order, Father Francis Xavier Seelos (1819–1867), who had more than eighty young members under his authority, traveled to Washington with the permission of his provincial to intervene with leading politicians. Purchasing exemptions would have cost the order more than $25,000. Between July 22 and 24, 1863, he met with President Abraham Lincoln, Postmaster General Francis Blair, William Seward (the son of the Secretary of State), and finally Secretary of War Edwin Stanton. While sympathetic, Lincoln gave no explicit assurance that clergy, religious, or seminarians would be exempt without providing the fee or securing a substitute. Blair and Seward as well welcomed him cordially and placated his concerns with a promise to help. The Secretary of War, however, was still irate over the recent Draft Riots, and was unsympathetic, prompting Seelos to later write: "should the Church ever decide to celebrate the feast of a rude rascal, Stanton would qualify easily."[23]

In the end, Seelos's efforts achieved no more or less than those of other religious superiors. Although their meetings and letters would not change the basic terms of the Conscription Act, nearly all gained private exemptions for their own clergy. (Conscription was only abandoned after the war's conclusion and not to be revived until 1917 during World War I.) Forearmed with that knowledge, all Catholic religious leaders acted on their own to keep their members out of the fight—whether paying the bounty, moving men around, using health exemptions, etc. As for the Redemptorists, they discarded an initial idea to relocate students to Canada, and devised a method to avert the draft by having seminarians register at a location where the draft board had a reputation for fairness. Less than ten Redemptorist priests and brothers from various parishes were ultimately drafted, but all were exempted due to health issues, citizenship requirements, or commutation fees provided.[24]

PREJUDICIAL ATTITUDES AND
CHAPLAIN APPOINTMENTS

At the onset of the Civil War, while Catholics comprised the largest religious denomination in America, they were also the poorest, at the bottom of the social ladder, and the victims of the prejudices of the day. Anti-Catholicism has had a long presence in America's religious history. The original colonies were overwhelmingly Protestant, and America's founding was dominated by the Puritan spirit and expansionist energies of the English Reformation. In his classic work on America's religious history, Sydney Ahlstrom notes that "the American colonies . . . had become the most thoroughly Protestant, Reformed and Puritan commonwealths in the world . . . providing the moral and religious background of fully 75 percent of the people who had declared their independence in 1776." Ahlstrom goes on to elucidate the accompanying spirit of nativism and discrimination which had been carried to the country from England:

> In England, the clergy played a leading role in awakening people to their obligation to carry the gospel to all parts of the earth. . . . There was a strong anti-Roman Catholicism animus to their pleading, as well as a fervent hope that "errors of Popery" would not be sown in areas as yet unclaimed. In fact, a fierce tradition of anti-Catholicism, both visceral and dogmatic, is one of Puritanism's most active legacies to Anglo-American civilization.[25]

Ahlstrom goes on to mention that as the twin forces of anti-Catholicism and nativism came together to make "the first half of the 19th century the most violent period of religious discord in American history."[26] Anti-Catholic histories were produced by Protestant scholars, and literary accounts of fictional sexual improprieties of priests and nuns also appeared. Many Americans, like Samuel F. B. Morse (the inventor of Morse code) believed that immigration was simply part of a papal plot to take over the United States. Few white American Protestants of the time thought it necessary to even question their underlying presumptions about the national loyalties of Catholics, or the subhuman status of Blacks, or the scorn they held toward Irish immigrants, freemasons, or Mormons. Memories remained still fresh in many people's minds of incidents like these:

- The 1834 mob burning of a Charleston Catholic convent and school, which occurred due to the deranged ramblings of a former student, and the promotion of those ramblings by Congregationalist preacher Lyman Beecher.
- The 1836 publication of a lurid but totally fictional "autobiographical" narrative, *Awful Disclosures of Maria Monk* (a Canadian woman who falsely claimed to have been sexually exploited by nuns and priests during her short stay in a Montreal convent).
- The short-lived Know Nothing political party, which arose in the middle of the nineteenth century, having powerful anti-immigrant and anti-Catholic influence, especially in New York.[27]

When the Civil War broke out, these biases were still prevalent in the general population, and led to several issues complicating the appointment of Catholic chaplains. As James McPherson notes, Civil War armies were perhaps the most religious armies of all American history—but the strong evangelistic attitudes of many Protestant churchmen presented a challenge for Catholic clergymen. James Moorhead has written how many Protestant organizations saw the wartime army as a fertile ground to "sheep-steal" from the Catholic fold and "win souls" for Jesus. These efforts led to a flood of Christian literature, Bibles, tracts, and religious-based relief efforts (by such as the United States Sanitary Commission and the Christian Commission). Randall Miller comments that during the war "Catholics chafed at the Protestant prodding of such men as 'the one-wing devil' General O. O. Howard, who wanted to convert their armies into Protestant crusaders."[28]

Another ongoing concern was the adverse attitudes within the army itself. Some Protestant officers simply refused to accept Catholic priests as chaplains for their Catholic men. In March 1862, only twenty-two priests served among the 472 Union chaplains then on duty—when in reality the ratio of Catholic to Protestant soldiers was approximately one to nine. Thus, Catholic chaplains were chosen only for regiments that were nearly exclusively Catholic (e.g., the 69th New York, which was the heart of the Union Irish Brigade, and the 10th Tennessee CSA). It was a rare situation indeed when a Catholic would chaplain a predominantly Protestant regiment. As mentioned earlier, chaplains like future bishop John Ireland (5th Minnesota) and James Titta (13th Pennsylvania Cavalry) both served only very short chaplain stints partially because of the predominantly Protestant nature of their regiments.[29]

Louis Lambert (18th Illinois) is an example of the tensions that Catholicism could inspire in some non-Catholic regiments. Recruited almost entirely from southern Illinois and described by one author as "a study in internal conflict," the 18th Illinois Regiment was destined for trouble from the outset.[30] There were only 90 Catholics in a regiment with 830 Protestants, yet they were commanded by the Catholic Colonel Michael Lawler, a lawyer and friend of the politician-General John McClernand. A Mexican-American War veteran, Lawler clashed with disagreeable officers and unruly troops, and was court-martialed and convicted for his somewhat unorthodox methods. Soon restored to command after an appeal, he decided to appoint the Catholic priest Louis Lambert as chaplain, despite objections from the Protestant majority. It was a choice not destined to succeed.

Within only four months of having been mustered in at Shawnee-town, Illinois, on July 1, 1861, Lambert was confronted with a petition from thirty-one officers for his removal on December 9, 1861. While the ostensible reason was neglect of his duties, some anti-Catholic bias in the charges is clearly perceptible. Among the grievances mentioned by the officers were that Lambert "has never held any kind of religious services . . . never visited the sick . . . nor has he made a single quarterly report showing the moral conditions of this regiment . . . Chaplain and Col. M. H. Lambert are the only officers in the regiment of roman catholic persuasion . . . nine-tenths of the men are Protestant holding strong prejudice against all Catholic priests who would not attend his ministrations without compulsion were he disposed to hold any."[31]

Lambert's life in the regiment after this must have been extremely uncomfortable, but we have no clear idea of his thoughts, for he wrote nothing about the incident (although he became a prolific writer later in life). He resigned in April 1862, apparently never defending himself against the charges made against him, and the only report we have on the incident is the words of the thirty-one officers. General Ulysses Grant and the War Department apparently did not see their grievances as serious enough to respond to, for the charges were left to languish in oblivion and were only found later in the archives. The only real explanation Lambert himself ever gave in his resignation letter was "having greater liberty, I can enlarge the sphere of my usefulness to those of the army who desire my service."[32] Whatever truth behind the changes of his absences and nonperformance of duty, it is clear the priest had to contend with both inner-regimental politics and the anti-Catholic attitudes of officers.

Lambert's short and difficult time with the 18th Illinois did not seem to affect the rest of his long priestly career. He returned to parish ministry in his Alton (Illinois) Diocese, then in 1869 was accepted into the Rochester (New York) Diocese, becoming a philosophy professor, a writer, and an in-demand lecturer. He founded a Catholic paper (the Philadelphia *Catholic Times*), became editor of the New York *Freeman's Journal*, and survived a long controversy with his Rochester bishop (Bernard McQuaid). He received an honorary degree from Notre Dame in 1892, and died in 1910 shortly after celebrating his golden jubilee as a priest. (Lambert's interesting postwar career will be discussed further in chapter 12.)

As Catholic priests labored for recognition early in the war, it would (as with all chaplains) ultimately be their wartime courage, dedication, and hard-won bond with the soldiers that ultimately won the acceptance and even the deep affection of many they served. One such chaplain was the Jesuit priest Joseph O'Hagan, whose story will be told in chapter 5. His own election in the fall of 1861 by the officers of the Union Excelsior Brigade (73rd New York) is a humorous and fitting paradigm of the prewar sentiment of many soldiers and citizens. O'Hagan himself described the results of his election: "Over 400 voted for a Catholic priest, 154 for any kind of a Protestant minister; 11 for a Mormon; and 335 said they could find their way to hell without the assistance of clergy."[33]

POOR IMAGE OF CHAPLAINS
IN ANTEBELLUM AMERICA

O'Hagan's election is a humorous example of the final barrier all chaplains had on the eve of the war. Influenced by the Reformation and the historically dominant role of Catholicism in Europe, the United States was founded upon a separation between church and state, as the Constitution makes clear ("Congress shall make no law respecting an establishment of religion"). American history was shaped by the authority of a *written* document—the American Constitution—not upon the divine authority of a Pope, a church, or an individual religious leader. Thus, America's religious heritage tended toward a less authoritative, more congregational style of leadership, based upon a uniquely American interpretation of the Bible—centered on individuals' ability to interpret Scripture themselves, without the need for clerics or bishops to mediate its meaning. Thus, a strain of somewhat anticlerical and anti-institutional thought had long been a part the American heritage, and this confronted chaplains at the outset of the Civil War.[34]

On the eve of the Civil War, attitudes toward clergymen were far from universally positive. The prewar experiences of America's professional trained military leaders with chaplains, at least in terms of their spiritual role, is a concrete example. The role of chaplain at the military academies was more a title than a military rank, and Congress had justified that presence "with the mental reservation that it was getting a schoolmaster as well as a pastor, an attitude which became so paramount as to divorce the chaplain from his identification with the regiment." Chaplains had no official duties other than teaching, and while chapel attendance at West Point was mandatory beginning in 1818, there was an ongoing confusion and controversy about the position's justification, all of which diminished the importance of chaplains in the minds of many future Civil War officers. As one historian notes succinctly, "the War of the Rebellion found the chaplaincy in an unorganized state . . . the task the military chaplaincy faced in 1861 was that of restoring the image of the chaplain as the spiritual leader of the men in the ranks."[35]

In much of mid-nineteenth-century America, churchmen were generally seen as being petty and conniving people, and did not enjoy universal good opinion. Many would have agreed with the definition of a clergyman given by Ambrose Bierce (9th Indiana) as "a man who undertakes the management of spiritual affairs as a method of bettering his temporal ones." In *Faith in the Fight: Civil War Chaplains*, Bernard Maryniak cites one veteran echoing similar sentiments in his postwar comments. "For most of the soldiers, army chaplains were not as popular as even the sutlers. . . . Of course when a fellow was on his back in the hospital with an arm or leg gone, he was glad enough to have the chaplain come and talk to him if only to take his mind off his troubles, but ordinarily there is a great lack of reverence for the cloth among soldiers." One young soldier awoke in a hospital after having fallen asleep on picket duty, and requested a chaplain in panic expecting execution, but quickly changed his mind when he found out he was safe from arrest. "Forget about that chaplain!" the boy immediately proclaimed.[36]

A fascinating article in the April 3, 1862, *Cincinnati Daily Enquirer* from the anonymous correspondent "Guliemus" speaks to the poor image of chaplains in the Union army, but does praise one Catholic chaplain in the process.

> There is one subject that should occupy the attention of the War Department as soon as possible. I mean the abolition of the office of Chaplain in the Army. . . . Sutlers are absolutely necessary, while chaplains have been permitted to draw large pay without rendering the slightest equivalent.
>
> The only exception that I know of is that of Father [William] O'Higgins, Chaplain of the Tenth Ohio. He is the only Chaplain of my acquaintance who earns his pay, and pays unremitting attention to the regiment. . . . He is so popular that if the office were abolished the men would pay his present salary sooner than lose

his services. . . . Through frost and snow and mud, in sunshine and in storm, he shares the fate of his flock . . . while other Chaplains fain sickness and rush in hot haste to the arms of their wives, to be nursed for months without seeing their regiments, although they generally find the Paymaster to draw their pay.

I know one white choker personally who never said more than three prayers in his life in the regiment, and even these, against the wishes of the men. . . . When in camp he amuses himself hunting with his dog and gun. To this the soldiers have no objection, believing with his Reverence, that a plump partridge has more saving greases [sic] than his eloquent prayers, and that the theology of the rifle is more potent than that of the Synod.[37]

To be fair, there simply were some very poor chaplains early in the Civil War, which exacerbated the prewar negativity about chaplains. In 1865, one doctor expressed that view in a letter to the Secretary of the Interior, remarking that "unfortunately there has been in the service too many chaplains entirely unfit for the honorable and responsible situation." There are those today who would agree with Charles Smith, who opined that "in general, that the quality of the Civil War chaplaincy was poor." Especially at the outset of the war, many chaplains were too old, physically unfit, or cowards. Some were ne'er-do-wells or misfits who had chosen the wrong profession; others were unqualified, sought personal gain, or lacked scruples. James I. Robertson relates a story of one minister who entered a stud poker game with the 2nd Connecticut Heavy Artillery and cleaned out an entire company. Many similar stories exist: one chaplain was court-martialed for stealing a horse, another deserted with ninety dollars from regimental funds, and a third was caught in flagrante delicto with an enslaved female during Grant's Vicksburg Campaign.[38]

In the end, the best and most successful Civil War chaplains were those who were diligent and courageous in doing their jobs, and able to connect with their men. They earned their authority on the job, not because it was given to them de facto. Specifically, this meant a clergyman who "(1) was not neglectful of his duties . . . (2) never failed to observe the highest moral standards, (3) preached sermons appropriate to the battlefield situation, (4) was mindful of his military bearing and dress, (5) adapted his religious faith to the exigencies of battle, and (6) proved his physical courage in battle." As the first year of the war went by, most of the poorer chaplains began to be weeded out; nonetheless, in both armies, there never were enough good chaplains to meet all the soldiers' needs. Thankfully, by 1865, as the war drew to a close, it can be said that a more positive attitude prevailed about the overall role and influence of these religious professionals.[39]

Of the successful chaplains on both sides, it is not an exaggeration to say that Catholic priest-chaplains as a group were the vanguard and elite of all the denominations who served the spiritual needs of soldiers. Negative reports about them are rarely seen in journals of the time, but praise for their work abounds (as will be related in this book). All six of the aforementioned "job descriptions" of the most successful chaplains applied to nearly every Catholic chaplain, particularly those in regiments. With only one noticeable exception (the Jesuit Joseph Bixio, who will be discussed in chapters 5 and 11), none of the 126 Catholic chaplains abused their job or relationship with soldiers or took advantage of it for purely personal reasons. Two anecdotes from Catholic Civil War chaplains will help portray not only the unique status, relationship, and respect won from their wartime ministry, but also some of the ubiquitous religious prejudice existing on all sides.

Richard C. Christy served with the 78th Pennsylvania, which was not an overtly Catholic regiment. When the war was over, Christy was interviewed by the Irish Catholic journalist David Conyngham, who was gathering information about the wartime service of priests and nuns with the intention of promoting the role Catholics had in the war. Based on those conversations, Conyngham summarized the role of Christy and other Catholic chaplains in the Army of the Cumberland in early 1863:

> The religious fervor of the army was much strengthened and quickened by the zeal of these good men [Fathers Christy, Cooney, Trecy, and O'Higgins]. Many careless ones were recalled and not a few converted. . . . Sundays always found hundreds of the latter assembled to attend Mass and listening with the greatest attention to the practical exhortations of the good missionaries.

The few years of the war did more to allay the bigotry of the Protestant mind than fifty years of civil life could have possibly done. The few Catholic chaplains that were in the army were zealous and efficient men. The Protestant soldiers, at first distrustful and suspicious, soon learned to respect and love the priest, [who] knowing no difference labored so faithfully for the comfort and welfare of the sick and wounded.

He found that whilst the Protestant chaplain rarely exposed himself to danger, in order to succor the helpless or wounded, the Catholic priest was always at his post, laboring night and day in the hospital and in the field, with an entire abnegation of self that soon made the Protestant soldiers regard him as their best and warmest friend. This feeling the soldier has carried with him home, and the good seed thus sown in war and pestilence has grown and matured be neath a peaceful sky until it has multiplied itself, and is now scattered into all the hidden nooks and corners of this great country.[40]

Finally, Thomas Scully was chaplain of the 9th Massachusetts for eighteen months in 1861 and 1862, and during that time, he responded to an invitation for a general meeting of all chaplains. He attended, only to discover that Protestant chaplains alone were attending, and the issues discussed were what Scully considered quite nonessential and peripheral, such as rank, pay, insignias on uniforms, and so on. During the long, rambling discussion that ensued, Scully kept silent, despite growing more frustrated by the other chaplains' obsession with petty and personally aggrandizing issues. Finally, when the suggestion arose that these chaplains actually strike to get more pay, the group turned to Scully for what they thought would be a supportive response. Conyngham's later interview with Scully captured his colorful yet intolerant comeback.

During the debate upon the petition many eyes had been turned toward him; every man in the meeting saw in a moment that he was not one of themselves—but they imagined that the almighty dollar had influenced him as well as the other members of that memorable body. The president of the convention finally called upon the Rev. Mr. Scully. . . . Father Tom arose; he spoke as solemnly as if he were addressing his people from the altar:

"Gentlemen: I cannot join you in your movement upon the government. She has enemies without—I am sorry to learn that she has foes within. I have a higher rank than the president or the congress of the United States can give to man! I am a Catholic priest! I labor in the service of God. He is my paymaster. My men will support me, and I need not to trouble the government of this nation—now sadly troubled indeed—to do that which my Church commands me to do without money and without price; but if my vote will be of any use to you gentlemen, for I know you have families depending upon you, I hope that you may be all generals and be paid as such!" And with a quick bow and quizzical smile, Father Tom went from among them.[41]

CHAPTER 2

TOWARD A ROSTER
OF CATHOLIC CIVIL WAR
CHAPLAINS

When attempting to compile a list of Catholic priests who served as Civil War chaplains, one quickly discovers two indispensable books on the topic written long ago. Both were authored by Catholic priests with doctrinal degrees who addressed this topic in groundbreaking and unique ways. The initial and primary source to this day has been *Catholic Military and Naval Chaplains (1776–1917)*—the 1929 doctrinal dissertation of Benedictine priest (and former military chaplain) Aidan Henry Germain, which is based on extensive and detailed research from military archives and records in Washington, DC. It truly is the bible for anyone studying the history and role of Catholic chaplains in America since it ranges from the Revolutionary War up to the eve of World War One.[1]

The second is Benjamin Blied's *Catholics and the Civil War*—a series of ten essays published in 1945 focusing on the role and impact of Catholic groups and individuals in the Civil War era. Among Blied's insightful essays is one entitled "Charity in the Armies," in which the work of several Catholic Civil War chaplains is described in slightly more detail than Germain. However, Blied's list of chaplains is basically a reiteration of Germain's list from sixteen years before.[2]

Both books are wonderful historical studies on the role of Catholicism in America in the late nineteenth century, especially as seen through the opinions and actions of various groups and people. Germain's work was particularly groundbreaking and foundational both in his historical research, and in the compilation of a detailed list of Catholic chaplains who served in the American military though the Spanish-American War. His chaplain's list is consistently cited (occasionally even with its errors) by nearly everyone writing about Catholic Civil War chaplains since its publication. However, both works suffer from a similar drawback—they are dated. Germain's work was published in 1929, and Blied's essays in 1945. Germain's research particularly, though invaluable in its detailed archival content, did not have the benefit of modern scholarship and writings, and of course the far-reaching internet resources of the twenty-first century.

A third book emerged in 2019 that has helped balance the datedness issue, *Soldiers of the Cross*, with fine contemporary research utilized by its editors, David Endres and William Kurtz. However, this work is an edited and annotated version of a post–Civil War manuscript of David Power Conyngham, an Irish Catholic journalist and war veteran who attempted to compile the stories of Catholic nuns and priests serving during the Civil War. Conyngham's original text was limited to discussing only fourteen chaplains and six female religious communities (North and South), although its well-researched footnotes do mention many other chaplains. However, there are far more priests beyond those mentioned in *Soldiers of the Cross* who need to be acknowledged for their Civil War chaplaincy service.[3]

CLARIFYING THE TERM "CATHOLIC CHAPLAIN"

In the decades since Germain's foundational work was published, the word "chaplain" has been freely and loosely used in many books, diaries, and journals that have emerged in the Civil War field. But although the word is much used, very few have ever undertaken a clear and specific definition of who the word refers to. The word "chaplain" most often is simply used in a generic way for *anyone* bringing the mercies of the spiritual life and God to Civil War soldiers. There have been virtually no important distinctions made to help differentiate the many unique elements of the lives, stories, and ministry of Civil War chaplains.

Depending on who you read, and the context of their writing, a chaplain could be a person formally connected by government approval to Civil War troops, but also someone who simply passed through a camp ministering very briefly. A chaplain could be someone ministering during a single event, or for some longer, unspecified period. A chaplain could be someone with extensive seminary and theological training, or a person who simply felt the Lord's "call" and stepped forward to preach. Few distinctions are ever made regarding a chaplain's formal military status, governmental status, tenure of service, place of residence, theological training, and so on. Thus, as with any oft-used but little-defined word in the English language, it is critical to begin to narrow down to exactly who and what the word "chaplain" refers.

The first and obvious distinction that sets this book apart is its sole focus on Catholic priests—men whose ordination status and ecclesiastical connections are virtually never in doubt. The educational and theological training of Catholic priests has, since the late Middle Ages, been quite clearly defined and closely monitored. In the Civil War era, as today, a man could not be ordained without years of specialized training, the approbation of the seminary in which he studied, or the support of a bishop, diocese, or a religious order (who then assigned him to a specific post-ordination ministry).

Thus, very few Catholic priests served as official chaplains without first receiving clear permission from their ecclesiastical superiors. Although most Catholic chaplains would be eventually formally be approved and mustered into military service by a governmental entity (often after an initial period of preliminary ministry), any official term of military chaplaincy service would have been supported first by one's religious superior. To be specific, that "religious superior" would be either the bishop of the diocese the priest was serving in, or the religious order of which he was a vowed member (e.g., Jesuits, Franciscans, etc.).[4]

In their enthusiasm to serve in their unique circumstances, some priests did serve as chaplains without any clear or official support of their superiors. Two fascinating examples of this were John Bannon (St. Louis) and Jeremiah Trecy (Mobile). Bannon was in trouble on two accounts in December 1861: the Federal government wanted to arrest him for his outspokenness, and his bishop, Peter Kenrick, was not allowing priests to become chaplains (despite Bannon having done so informally already). On December 15, 1861, Bannon left a sealed letter for Bishop Kenrick, snuck out the back door of his St. Louis rectory as federal troops were entering the front, and became chaplain for Sterling Price's 1st Missouri Infantry. Jeremiah Trecy was a pastor in Huntsville, Alabama, who informally served the Confederate troops at Fort Morgan until April 1862 when he was captured by Union troops on a trip to get medicine. Although he was not allowed initially to return to his parish, he eventually wound up in the presence of Generals David Stanley and William Rosecrans (Catholic), who welcomed and authorized the chaplain's services for Union troops.

A second necessary distinction to make in a book regarding Catholic chaplains is clearly ascertaining the length of time they truly spent in active Civil War ministry. To adequately understand their work and struggles, one needs to know how long priests were actually in the field by using the records available to determine how many months and years they served specifically. This is a distinction that Germain made in his 1929 work (though Blied did not)—generally by using the words "unofficial" and "official" to distinguish between those authorized or not by either the Confederate or Union governments, whether on national or state levels. However, Germain also states that "only an official chaplain is a true chaplain" and he does not attempt to list in any comprehensive way those who lack the "official" designation (which I do believe is significant, and have begun to do in this book).

In my research on Catholic chaplaincy, I have found it important and insightful to delineate priests' Civil War ministry and service by using two further distinctions—namely, whether a priest was an official or occasional chaplain, and whether he was a full-time or part-time chaplain. Allow me to clearly define what those terms mean in reference to the Catholic priests who served in the war. First, consider the distinction between official and occasional chaplains.

- Official Chaplain = a priest who was recognized and approved in some formal way by a legitimate government authority (state or national), and had approximately three months of sustained chaplaincy service in the Civil War. According to my research, there are seventy-six Catholic official priest-chaplains who fit this category.
- Occasional (Situational) Chaplain = a priest who ministered to troops without formal government recognition as a spiritual need arose in specific areas where they resided. Perhaps using the term "situational" best captures this group, for they ministered in and because of the unique ministry locales and situations they were in at the time. Examples include ministering when troops were encamped in their vicinity, or battles took place nearby, or soldiers were residing in area hospitals or prisons. There was generally little consistency or sustained status to the chaplaincy work of these priests, because their primary responsibility was to the Church-designated positions they held in their diocese or religious order. At present, I have identified at least fifty priests or bishops who fit this category, although many other Catholic clergy served occasionally and situationally but are not clearly identified in accurate historical public or private records. (Research in this area could go on nearly forever.)

Thus, combining the count of "official" and "occasional" Catholic priest-chaplains, I have arrived at the number of at least 126 priests who can be historically accounted for as ministering to Civil War troops between 1861 and 1865. This is a minimum number, and is certainly not exclusive of the many others whose names have not yet surfaced. It is worth noting that Germain's original 1929 list of Catholic chaplains numbered only eighty-five in both the Confederate and Union armies. However, it is my belief that his list (and necessarily Blied's and subsequent others who relied on their numbers) need to be reevaluated based on two prejudgments made by Germain when enumerating who was an official chaplain.

First, Germain does not generally distinguish length of Civil War service as being a major influencing factor in being a chaplain. In essence I agree with that, but clearly clarifying how much time priests spent in actual Civil War ministry does significantly deepen our knowledge of what they struggled with, endured, and accomplished in those difficult years. Thus, I have chosen to make further distinctions about chaplaincy based on length of ministry. Second, Germain intentionally leaves out priests he terms to be "itinerant, outlaw, or occasional." While I agree with many of his judgments, I believe this entire field of Catholic Civil War chaplaincy is only enriched with more clarity, color, and pathos when we study the fuller range of possible names available because of the far greater resources available to us today. Thus, I have chosen to include the names, basic history, and stories (where applicable) of those occasional chaplains who served the troops, even if briefly.[5]

Let me now define a second set of distinctions to help us to go beyond the names and numbers to better understand the stories, commitments, and courage of these nineteenth-century priest-chaplains. Official chaplains can also be separated into groups of full-time or part-time.

- Official and Full-Time Chaplain = a priest who ministered to troops on a full-time basis, with some formal recognition by either a state or national government, for about three years of sustained chaplaincy service. Serving for three years itself was truly a hardship for all Civil War troops, but for Catholic priests, even more so. Because they had completed their education and seminary training, priests were almost always significantly older than the troops they served. They were far less used to challenging manual labor (especially outdoors), and were certainly not used to the deprivations of outdoor encampments and extended campaigns. Of the 126 Catholic chaplains covered in this book, I consider only fifteen priests to be full-time chaplains. In this group are the "legendary" names one hears most about in Catholic circles, including William Corby, P. P. Cooney, Paul Gillen, Joseph O'Hagan, James Sheeran, and Darius Hubert. Not without reason, as will be shown, nine of those fifteen came from religious orders.

- Official and Part-Time Chaplain = a priest who ministered to troops with some formal recognition by either state or national

government, but of no more than approximately three months'
duration. For a wide variety of reasons, many priests were willing
to serve the troops and even approved to do so, but simply were
not able to serve for extended periods of time. This was primarily
due to health issues that arose for the priests, but language troubles, denominational differences, or being called back to their diocese or order contributed as well. In all, sixty-two of the seventy-
six official chaplains are included in this group.[6]

The third and final important distinction to be made is to identify
in what capacity the chaplains served the troops; that is, to what kind
of Civil War ministry specifically were they assigned. This is a relatively simple distinction to make, albeit blurry at times with specific individuals. There really were only three basic places in which any Civil
War chaplain could serve—whether a Catholic priest, Protestant minister, or Jewish rabbi (there were at least three rabbis who served as
Union chaplains in the Civil War).[7]

- Hospital Chaplain = a priest assigned to work in either a Union or
  Confederate hospital. According to Dr. Stanley Burns, "by war's
  end, there were 204 Union general hospitals with 136,894 beds.
  During the war, over one million soldiers received care in Union
  military hospitals, and perhaps a similar number in Confederate
  hospitals." The amount of ministry needed for wounded and dying
  soldiers was obviously great, and in all, nineteen Catholic priests
  were specifically and officially assigned to a Civil War hospital in
  either the North or South (though at least twenty-three others
  served in hospitals at some time). In many ways, these chaplains
  could also be called post chaplains, because their work was connected to a particular locale or hospital. Their stories will be told in
  greater detail in chapter 8.[8]
- Post Chaplain = a priest assigned as chaplain to a military fort or
  troop encampment in a specific location. The post chaplain system
  was inaugurated in 1838 in the American military; the Catholic
  priests who served in these positions in the years prior to the Civil
  War were very few. (Germain mentions only three between 1849

and 1859.) Only ten of the 126 chaplains listed in this book served formally as post chaplains—two for the Union and eight for the South. Arguably, the most well-known may have been Peter Whelan at Fort Pulaski, Georgia, who served there before it was captured by Union forces in April 1862.[9]

- Regimental Chaplain = a priest assigned to specific military unit (regiment, brigade, corps) in the field. Most chaplains served in this way, with sixty of the seventy-six official chaplains listed below being connected primarily (though not exclusively) to a specific regiment or unit. Because Catholic soldiers were scattered in many different military units, Catholic chaplains (far more than Protestants) commonly traveled between different units in the army celebrating the sacraments. The letters, notes, and diaries of priests routinely recount their trips between different companies, regiments, and even corps to perform their ministry, despite their official connection to only one specific unit. In this book, the specific military unit a priest was primarily associated with will be listed immediately after his name.

There is one final but important point to make about compiling any accurate list of Civil War Catholic chaplains based on the military records we now have. As Aidan Germain discovered and expressed in his 1929 book, the regimental rolls we have now are not always reliable sources of information about priests' military careers. Some data simply was not recorded, some pieces are missing, and some was lost through the fortunes of war and time itself. The official military records available now are often exceedingly scanty, particularly when dealing with the Confederacy. The keeping of regimental rolls also differed from state to state.

As a result, we are left with a great amount of information about some chaplains (particularly those who wrote about their chaplaincy later in life or achieved postwar recognition), as well as a fair amount of somewhat hagiographic later accounts, but unfortunately the histories of many are extremely sparse and difficult to track. In my own work of dealing with the challenge of compiling a more contemporary list of Catholic chaplains, I have used sound historical research, Catholic historical records, reliable personal accounts, and available military sources, thus supplementing the gaps in some scanty records with reliable collaborative information.[10]

TOWARD A CONTEMPORARY LISTING OF CATHOLIC CIVIL WAR CHAPLAINS

Using the distinctions outlined above, we can arrive at a modified list of Catholic Civil War chaplains. With the strong caveat that this is not intended to be a thorough or complete list (specifically with regard to those considered occasional or situational chaplains), there are 126 priests who are known to have ministered as chaplains during the American Civil War. This list can be broken down further in this way:

- Seventy-four priests ministered primarily for the Union; fifty-one were official, and twenty-three occasional or situational chaplains are noted.
- Fifty-two priests ministered primarily for the Confederacy; twenty-five were official, and twenty-seven occasional or situational chaplains are noted.
- Only fifteen priests can be called full-time chaplains (officially recognized, with more than three years of full-time chaplaincy). Nine of these were Union (Brady, Christy, Cooney, Corby, Gillen, O'Hagan, O'Higgins, Ouellet, and Trecy), and six were Confederate (Bannon, Gache, Hubert, Sheeran, Smulders, and Turgis).
- Nineteen priests served officially as hospital chaplains, and ten as post chaplains (post chaplains: Lemagie, Fialon, Croghan, O'Connell, Leray, Manucy, Mouton, Pellicer, Whelan, and Patrick Ryan).

Only seventy-six Catholic priests of the 126 listed can be considered official chaplains, meaning that they were formally recognized by either an individual state or the national government, and served as chaplain for approximately three months. Of these seventy-six:

- Fifty-one priests primarily served Union troops.
- Twenty-five priests primarily served Confederate troops.
- Two priests (at least) served both Union and Confederate troops—

one in a formal way (Jeremiah Trecy) and one informally (Innocent Bergrath), and one fascinating priest (Joseph Bixio SJ) "played at" serving both sides in a deceptive way that left a wake of trouble behind.

Where these Catholic priest-chaplains came from before beginning their Civil War ministry is a significant factor in better understanding their unique stories. The vast majority were immigrants; fifteen different countries of birth were represented by the chaplains. Nearly two-thirds of the 126 priests belonged to a diocese as opposed to a religious order.[11]

- Of the official chaplains, Irish immigrant or first-generation priests dominated (44 percent), followed by those born in America (18.3 percent), France (15.5 percent), Italy (6.5 percent), Germany (5.7 percent) and then ten other countries. It is not surprising that fewer priest-chaplains were born in America, because Catholics—though increasing rapidly due to immigration—remained a minority in the country's predominantly Protestant-oriented denominational makeup. Though Irish priest-chaplains were the largest group in both armies, they were more numerous among Northern troops (thirty-one as opposed to fourteen in the Confederacy), whereas far more French priests worked in the Confederacy (fifteen) than the Union (three).
- Forty-three priests belonged to a Catholic religious order (nine of whom were full-time official chaplains), and eighty-three priests (or bishops) were connected to a specific diocese in either the North or the South.

Perhaps the most difficult challenge in writing on Catholic priest-chaplains is enumerating in an accurate way those who were occasional. As has already been said, the numbers of priests who served Civil War troops, particularly in hospitals, prisons, and camps, is impossible to track with any accuracy. Countless local priests whose names were never recorded went out to minister to soldiers who had come into their localities and needed the sacraments. Mid-nineteenth-century Catholic spirituality was heavily sacrament oriented, which required priests to be the official conveyers of baptism, confession, anointing of the sick (called "extreme unction" at the time) and the Catholic Mass (said in Latin). This was true of diocesan priests in areas deeply affected by the war (such as Virginia, Tennessee, and Washington, DC), and also Catholic religious orders, who were frequently called upon to minister to soldiers beyond their normative geographic or ministerial boundaries.

Two examples of this are the Redemptorists of Annapolis, Maryland, and the Jesuits of Grand Coteau, Louisiana. Annapolis was a busy place for the large Redemptorist community there during the Civil War years (some eighty to ninety professed members at times). They were then running a college (St. Mary's College), a novitiate, a school for seminarians, and a parish, all in a divided state under martial law for a time. In 1864, their Archives recorded that "a great deal of good was done to the soldiers" of General Ambrose Burnside's newly formed 9th Corps bivouacked outside the city. "Mass was often said in camp, and also in the Naval School Hospital. Hundreds of the dying received the Last Sacraments. Many of the Fathers spent whole days ministering to the soldiers." Then in December 1864, the Redemptorists were asked to minister to Union troops in New Bern, North Carolina, and three priests from the community responded to that invitation: Henry Giesen (1826–1893), Timothy Enright (1837–1911), and Thaddeus Anwander (1823–1893). No Redemptorist from this community was ever an official Union chaplain, yet their combined work in both places there spanned more than a year (mid-1864 to August 1865), reached numerous camps, hospitals, and churches, and impacted thousands of people (some three thousand alone attended their mission in February 1865). Yet aside from a brief mention in a footnote of Germain's book, the chaplaincy work of the Redemptorists of Annapolis goes unrecognized in history.[12]

It was much the same for the Jesuit community of Grand Coteau, Louisiana. Recruited as instructors for a college planned by the local bishop, the Jesuits began St. Charles College in 1837, and their community comprised about ten Jesuits (the number fluctuated) during the war years. Several priests connected to St. Charles College are recognized as military chaplains (de Chaignon, Nachon, and Usannez), yet the entire community was intimately involved in wartime ministry on a near daily basis. Both Confederate and Union troops (and sometimes both on the same day) occupied their locale. and some students withdrew from school to fight. The Jesuits ministered at local parishes, worked with any troops passing through their area, and gave the sacraments to soldiers who stopped by the college. Several wounded soldiers from both sides recuperated at St. Charles College and became Catholics during the process, being baptized and joining the Church. Several of this community's Jesuits were arrested by Union troops, one while casually strolling Union fortifications in Baton Rouge as he helped out in the local parish. Anselm Usannez began a mission church in a town whose pastor had died in Virginia working as a chaplain (Ghislaine Boheme, 13th Mississippi).

ALL CIVIL WAR CATHOLIC CHAPLAINS

See table 2.1 for a listing of Union chaplains. In comparison to the military records of the Confederacy, Union chaplain records (whether Federal or State) are far better organized and available. Records frequently reveal that a chaplain began ministering to the troops before he was formally "mustered in," a process often occurring within a few weeks after "enrollment." If that date is well established, it will be mentioned, otherwise only more formal "muster-in/out" dates (or formal "retirement" dates) will be noted in Union chaplain files. Some birth and death dates are approximate, based on the best and most accessible research available at this time.

See table 2.2 for a listing of Confederate chaplains. Formal Confederate chaplain military records are more incomplete than Union records, at least partly due to fires that broke out in Richmond in the final days of the war. Many Confederate chaplains began their ministries informally and only received a formal commission at later dates. Exact end dates for their ministry are often highly uncertain or entirely unknown, partly due to their individual situations, lack of reliable record-keeping, or destruction of files and general institutional chaos at the end of the war.

TABLE 2.1. Official Union Chaplains (Fifty-One)

Name and Place of Birth	Life Dates	Diocese(s) or Order	Military Association and Dates of Service, if Known
Boyle, Francis E. (Maryland)	Sep 6, 1827–Mar 13, 1882	Baltimore	Stone Hospital, Washington, DC Jun 13, 1862–Jul 26, 1865
Brady, Thomas (Ireland)	1824?–Sep 10, 1865	Buffalo; Detroit	15th Michigan (Mulligan Regiment) Mar 13, 1862–Aug 13, 1865[1]
Bruehl, James (Saxony, now Hungary)	Mar 26, 1811–Mar 17, 1865	Jesuit (SJ)	Beaufort and New Orleans hospitals Jul 28, 1862–Mar 4, 1863; Apr 22, 1863–May 20, 1863
Butler, Thaddeus (Ireland)	Nov 1, 1833–Jul 1, 1897	Chicago	23rd Illinois (Irish Brigade) Jun 18, 1861–Mar 1, 1863
Carrier, Joseph (France)	Jul 14, 1833–Nov 12, 1904	Holy Cross (CSC)	6th Missouri Infantry Jul 1, 1863–Oct 3, 1863
Christy, Richard (Pennsylvania)	Oct 14, 1829–Oct 16, 1878	Pittsburgh	78th Pennsylvania Infantry Oct 18, 1861–Nov 4, 1864
Cooney, Peter Paul (Ireland)	Jun 20, 1822–May 7, 1905	Holy Cross (CSC)	35th Indiana Infantry Oct 4, 1861–Jun 16, 1865
Corby, William (Michigan)	Oct 2, 1833–Dec 28, 1897	Holy Cross (CSC)	88th New York (Irish Brigade) Oct 26, 1863–Sep 27, 1864[2]
Corcoran, Edward P. (Ohio)	Mar 26, 1832–Dec 29, 1866	Cincinnati	61st Ohio Infantry Dec 14, 1861–Jan 25, 1863 (resigned)[3]
Dillon, James (Ireland)	Nov 18, 1833–Dec 15, 1868	Holy Cross (CSC)	63rd New York and 182nd New York Oct 20, 1861–Oct 18, 1862 (resigned)
Doane, George H. (Massachusetts)	1830–Jan 20, 1905	Newark	New Jersey Militia May 1–Jul 31, 1861 (Feb 17, 1863)[4]

[1] Brady accepted a request to be chaplain on January 1, 1862, but was only formally mustered in on March 13, 1862. He was mustered out in Little Rock, Arkansas, on August 13, 1865. Cf. Germain, *Chaplains*, 59–60.

[2] Corby joined the regiment informally in the fall of 1861 and served unofficially before being formally mustered in October 1863.

[3] There are conflicting dates for Corcoran's resignation. The official records state he was "honorably discharged upon tender of resignation" on January 25, 1863, and the *Ohio in the War: The History of Her Regiments and Other Military Organizations* (by Whitelaw Reid, published in 1868 by Moore, Wilstach and Baldwin), states that "Chaplain E. P. Corcoran, 61st OH" mustered out on May 12, 1862. Cf. Germain, *Chaplains*, 65–66.

[4] There are conflicting reports on the date Doane left his position. His Newark bishop (James Bayley) reported in his diary that "Father Doane returned [from chaplaincy] on Tuesday the 17th [February 1863] much better than I expected to see him." But New Jersey state records note that Doane was honorably discharged July 31, 1861. Cf. Germain, *Chaplains*, 67.

TABLE 2.1. Official Union Chaplains (Fifty-One) *continued*

Name and Place of Birth	Life Dates	Diocese(s) or Order	Military Association and Dates of Service, if Known
Egan, Constantine (Ireland)	1828–Jul 7, 1899	Dominican (OP)	9th Massachusetts Infantry Sep 18, 1863–Jun 21, 1864; Hospital chaplain, City Point, and 5th Army Corps Jul 28, 1864–Jul 1865
Fusseder, Francis (Austria)	Sep 3, 1825– Jul 16, 1888	Milwaukee	17th Wisconsin Infantry Sep 3, 1862–Jul 28, 1863; 24th Wisconsin Infantry Jul 14, 1864–Jul 14, 1865
Gillen, Paul E. (Ireland)	Nov 24, 1810– Oct 20, 1882	Holy Cross (CSC)	170th New York Oct 19, 1862–Jul 15, 1865
Grzelachowski, Alexander (Poland)	1824–May 24, 1896	Santa Fe	2nd New Mexico Infantry Feb 3, 1862–May 31, 1862
Ireland, John (Ireland)	Sep 11, 1838– Sep 25, 1918	St. Paul	5th Minnesota Infantry Jun 22, 1862–Apr 3, 1863
Kelly, Thomas (Ireland)	Aug 15, 1828– May 3, 1864	Chicago	90th Illinois Infantry Sep 23, 1862–Jul 13, 1863
Lambert, Louis (Pennsylvania)	Apr 13, 1835– Sep 25, 1910	Alton, Illinois; Rochester	18th Illinois Infantry Jul 1, 1861–Apr 2, 1862 (resigned)
Lemagie, Charles Louis (France?)	1811/1812–?	Marquette; Detroit; New Orleans; Erie; Green Bay	Post chaplain, Carrolton, Louisiana; 2nd Louisiana Cavalry Sep 9, 1863–Sep 1864
Martin, Michael F. (Ireland)	1819– Feb 18, 1884	Philadelphia	69th Pennsylvania Infantry Oct 31, 1861–Jun 19, 1862
McAtee, Francis (Pennsylvania)	May 1, 1825– Mar 4, 1904	Jesuit (SJ)	31st New York Infantry Oct 30, 1861–Jun 4, 1863[5]
McCarthy, Patrick F. (Ireland)	Oct 4, 1833– Nov 5, 1882	Baltimore	Seminary Hospital, Georgetown Oct 2, 1863–Aug 21, 1865
McCollum, Bernard (Ireland)	?–Mar 22, 1879	Philadelphia; Scranton	116th Pennsylvania Infantry Nov 18, 1864–Jun 3, 1865
McCosker, John (Ireland)	1830–Jun 5 (7?), 1862	Philadelphia	55th Pennsylvania Infantry Oct 28, 1861–Jun 5, 1862

[5] McAtee mustered in February 5, 1863.

TABLE 2.1. Official Union Chaplains (Fifty-One) *continued*

Name and Place of Birth	Life Dates	Diocese(s) or Order	Military Association and Dates of Service, if Known
McGlynn, Edward (New York)	Sep 27, 1837– Jan 7, 1900	New York	US Hospital, New York Apr 22, 1863–Aug 21, 1865
McGrane, Peter (Ireland)	Jun 19, 1815– 1891	Redemptorist (CSsR), Philadelphia; Wilmington	Satterlee Hospital, Philadelphia Oct 1, 1862–Jul 26, 1865
McGrath, Matthew Francis (Ireland)	1833– Dec 15, 1870	Dominican (OP)	Seminary Hospital, Georgetown Jun 13, 1862–Oct 1, 1863
McKee, Edward (Ireland)	Mar 17, 1826– Dec 5, 1891	Philadelphia	116th Pennsylvania Infantry Sep 24, 1862–Dec 21, 1862
McMahon, Laurence (Canada)	Dec 26, 1835– Aug 21, 1893	Boston (bishop postwar)	28th Massachusetts Infantry Jun 28, 1862–May 30, 1863 (resigned)
Miettenger, (Dominic) Gustav (Germany)	1812– Aug 18, 1869	Albany; Ft. Wayne; Cincinnati; Alton (died in Milwaukee)	2nd New York Infantry Jul 14, 1861–Mar 3, 1862
Mignault, Napoleon (Canada)	Sep 17, 1826– Dec 15, 1895	Order of Mary Immaculate (OMI); Quebec	17th Wisconsin Infantry Mar 19, 1862–Feb 9, 1864
Mooney, Thomas (England)	1824– Sep 13, 1877	New York	69th New York Militia May 9, 1861–Aug 3, 1861[6]
Mullen, Daniel (Ireland)	Sep 1834– Mar 3, 1878	Hartford	9th Connecticut Infantry Nov 17, 1861–Aug 26, 1862
Murphy, Patrick J. R. (Ireland)	1824– Aug 31, 1869	Vincennes; Chicago	58th Illinois Volunteers Feb 11, 1863–Jul 4, 1864; Camp Douglas Oct 1864–Aug 1865
Nash, Michael (Ireland)	Nov 1, 1820– Feb 20, 1893	Jesuit (SJ)	6th New York Zouaves Jun 3, 1861–Jun 25, 1863
O'Brien, Edward (birthplace unknown)	Unknown	Chicago (?)	17th Illinois Cavalry Apr 12, 1864–Dec 1, 1865; Freedmen's Bureau Jan–Dec 1865

[6] Mooney was enrolled April 20, 1861, and formally mustered in May 9, 1861. The 69th New York State Militia was all mustered out after the Battle of First Bull Run on August 3, 1861.

TABLE 2.1. Official Union Chaplains (Fifty-One) *continued*

Name and Place of Birth	Life Dates	Diocese(s) or Order	Military Association and Dates of Service, if Known
O'Hagan, Joseph (Ireland)	Aug 15, 1826– Dec 15, 1878	Jesuit (SJ)	73rd New York (Excelsior Brigade) Oct 9, 1861–Sep 1863; Sep 1864?–Apr 1865[7]
O'Higgins, William (Ireland)	Jun 1829– Nov 4, 1874	British Guinea; Cincinnati	10th Ohio (Bloody Tenth) Jun 3, 1861–Jun 17, 1864[8]
Ouellet, Thomas (Canada)	Dec 21, 1819– Nov 26, 1894	Jesuit (SJ)	69th New York Nov 10, 1861–Dec 25, 1862; Feb 14, 1864–Jun 30, 1865; New Bern North Carolina Hospital May 1863–Jan 9, 1864[9]
Quinn, Thomas (Canada)	Feb 18, 1829– Aug 31, 1871	Hartford	1st Rhode Island Infantry (Militia), 1st Rhode Island Light Artillery Apr 17, 1861–Jan 3, 1862[10]
Rizzo (da Saracena), Leoneda "Leo" (Italy)	Aug 8, 1833– Nov 3, 1897	Franciscan (OFM)	9th Connecticut Infantry Jul 15, 1864–Oct 26, 1864[11]
Scully, Thomas (Ireland)	Mar 25, 1832– Sep 12, 1902	Boston	9th Massachusetts Infantry Jun 11, 1861–Dec 4, 1862[12]
Stephan, Joseph Andrew (Germany)	Nov 22, 1822– Sep 11, 1901	Cincinnati; Ft. Wayne; Dakota (Indian Missions)	Post and hospital chaplain, Nashville May 18, 1863–Jul 15, 1865
Taladrid, Damaso (Spain)	1819?– Jun 1869?	Santa Fe	1st New Mexico Infantry Jul 27, 1861–Jul 21, 1863[13]

[7] Germain does not mention O'Hagan's return to the regiment in 1864 after he had completed his required Jesuit tertianship (final formation) training.

[8] O'Higgins was enrolled on May 10, 1862, at Camp Denison, Ohio, and mustered in on June 3, 1861, at Memphis. Germain, *Chaplains*, 92.

[9] Ouellet rejoined the 69th New York when it was reorganized in February 1864 and was unanimously reelected chaplain; he had served in the New Bern Hospital in the interim. Germain spells his name Willett (or Ouellett). See Germain, *Chaplains*, 104–7.

[10] Though Quinn is officially and clearly recognized as a Union chaplain, Germain admits that his case is "one of those tangling problems whose course of unraveling stretched out for months and months." I also found that archival materials on Thomas Quinn were very few and extremely confusing because of the commonality of his name. The 1870 Federal Census and 1871 Catholic Almanac are the only two reliable sources for the partial vital data we have on Quinn's birthplace and death. Further specific details on this man have proved difficult to ascertain, although what we know is summarized briefly in chapter 7.

[11] Belmonte, *Rizzo*, 54–58.

[12] Scully enlisted on April 15, 1861, with the 9th Massachusetts Infantry at age forty, but was only mustered in June 11, 1861. Due to sickness after his capture during the Peninsula Campaign, he was issued an honorable discharge on December 4, 1862, dated from October 31, 1862. Cf. Germain, *Chaplains*, 94–95.

[13] Taladrid was appointed chaplain by the territorial governor on July 27, 1861, and was formally mustered in at an unknown date the following month; his resignation letter was submitted on July 21, 1863, and was accepted August 17, 1863.

TABLE 2.1. Official Union Chaplains (Fifty-One) *continued*

Name and Place of Birth	Life Dates	Diocese(s) or Order	Military Association and Dates of Service, if Known
Tissot, Peter (France)	Oct 15, 1823– Jun 19, 1875	Jesuit (SJ)	37th New York Infantry Jun 26, 1861–Jun 22, 1863
Titta (da Gombitelli), James (Italy)	1831– Mar 11, 1877	Franciscan (OFM)	13th Pennsylvania Cavalry Dec 23, 1862–Jun 7, 1863
Vahey, John William (Ireland)	Jun 1830– Jun 27, 1903	Chicago; Milwaukee	Alton, Illinois, Union Hospital Nov 2, 1863–Jun 30, 1864
Wiget, Bernardin F. (Switzerland)	Apr 5, 1821– Jan 2, 1883	Jesuit (SJ)	Stanton, Douglas, Finley, and Eckington Hospitals (Washington, DC) Oct 9, 1862–Nov 20, 1865

Chaplain for Both Union and Confederate Troops

Name and Place of Birth	Life Dates	Diocese(s) or Order	Military Association and Dates of Service, if Known
Trecy, Jeremiah F. (Ireland)	1822– Mar 6, 1888	Dubuque; Mobile	Confederate States of America: Huntsville, Alabama, and Mobile Bay forts Apr 1861–about Sep 1862;[14] United States of America: 4th US Cavalry May 2, 1863–Dec 1865

Chaplain with No Official Union Record

Name and Place of Birth	Life Dates	Diocese(s) or Order	Military Association and Dates of Service, if Known
Truyens, Charles (Belgium)	Feb 11, 1813– Dec 14, 1867	Jesuit (SJ)	12th Kentucky Infantry Jan 2, 1862–(mid-)Mar 1862

Chaplain in Massachusetts State Records with No Official Service

Name and Place of Birth	Life Dates	Diocese(s) or Order	Military Association and Dates of Service, if Known
O'Brien, Nicholas (Massachusetts)	1818– Apr 25, 1876	Boston	28th Massachusetts Infantry Jan 7, 1862–May 5, 1862[15]

[14] Tracking Trecy's records is extremely difficult since he regularly traveled all through Alabama between 1861 and 1862. He was clearly ministering (albeit informally) to Confederate soldiers, but then received a pass from the Union commander of the occupied Huntsville in May 1862 to minister to wounded Union troops. Once the Union troops withdrew, Trecy was again traveling when he was captured, then taken to General William Rosecrans, where he ministered for two weeks in late September 1862. Trecy returned to Huntsville briefly on September 28, 1862. In November, Rosecrans asked Trecy to become a Union chaplain, which he did without a formal commission until May 2, 1862, when one was finally issued to him. Though Trecy took a leave of absence in December 1865, he only formally resigned his Union chaplain's commission in August 1866.

[15] Nicholas O'Brien enrolled but never mustered in.

TABLE 2.2. Official Confederate Chaplains (Twenty-Five)

Name and Place of Birth	Life Dates	Diocese(s) or Order	Military Association and Dates of Service, if Known
Bannon, John (Ireland)	Dec 29, 1829– Jul 14, 1913	St. Louis; Jesuit (SJ) postwar	Missouri State Guard, 1st Missouri Confederate States of America Brigade December 15, 1861–Jul 1863
Bliemel, Emeran (Germany)	Sep 29, 1831– Aug 31, 1864	Benedictine (OSB)	10th Tennessee and 4th Kentucky Oct 6, 1863–Aug 31, 1864[1]
Browne, Henry Vincent (New York)	1816– Apr 14, 1870	Nashville	10th Tennessee and 4th Tennessee Nov 1861–Feb 1862[2]
Carius, Anthony (Germany)	Dec 31, 1821– Sep 15, 1893	Ft. Wayne; New Orleans; Mobile	1st Louisiana Infantry (Strawbridge's) Mar 1, 1863–1865?
Coyle, Patrick Francis (Ireland)	Unknown birth– unknown death	Mobile; Nashville	Post chaplain, Pensacola May 21, 1861–Jan 14, 1862; Corinth Hospital Apr 1862–Jan 1863?[3]
Croghan, Charles Joseph (Ireland)	Nov 4, 1822– Jun 28, 1880	Charleston	Post and hospital chaplain, Montgomery White Sulphur Springs, Virginia (and 17th Tennessee?) Apr 25, 1863–Apr 1865?[4]
De Chaignon, Anthony (France)	Jan 8, 1806– Oct 15 (17?), 1867	Jesuit (SJ)	Corinth, 18th Louisiana Regiment Feb 2, 1862–Aug 1862?[5]
Dicharry, Pierre Felix (France)	1827– Jul 28, 1887	Natchitoches	3rd Louisiana Regiment May 17, 1861–Aug 22, 1862[6]

[1] Bannon's credentials to become a chaplain were presented to Colonel William Grace (10th Tennessee) on October 6, 1863, and approved by the local bishop (Verot) on November 1, 1863. However, the officers and men of the 10th Tennessee had to formally apply to the Secretary of War for Bannon's commission, which was only accepted formally on March 3, 1864.

[2] Browne was formally dropped from the roll on February 11, 1864.

[3] Coyle's commission was negotiated and delivered on May 21, 1861, from the War Department in Montgomery, Alabama, prior to the formal establishment of the Confederacy under Jefferson Davis. He resigned that position on January 14, 1862, then became a chaplain (informally, it seems) at a Corinth hospital staffed by the Daughters of Charity in spring 1862. Cf. Gache, *Frenchman*, 30 and 59.

[4] There is uncertainty as to when Croghan's chaplaincy ended, but best reports indicate he served to the end of the war, arriving back in Charleston in July 1865. There also are conflicting death dates, but the date of July 28, 1880, appears more reliable than the date given in the 1881 *Sadliers' Catholic Almanac* (August 3, 1880).

[5] Like other Confederate chaplains, de Chaignon's records are somewhat confusing. He mustered in at Camp Moore (Tangipahoa Parish, Louisiana) on October 5, 1861, but was only formally enrolled as a chaplain by the Confederate Congress on February 22, 1862. He is on the muster rolls for July and August 1862, but the final formal reference to him was a ten-day leave of absence beginning August 23, 1862. It appears he was no longer a chaplain after that.

[6] Germain found two certificates in Confederate archives for Dicharry. He apparently was first a Louisiana state chaplain from May 17, 1861, to June 24, 1862, and then a chaplain for the Confederacy from June to August 1862.

TABLE 2.2. Official Confederate Chaplains (Twenty-Five) *continued*

Name and Place of Birth	Life Dates	Diocese(s) or Order	Military Association and Dates of Service, if Known
Gache, Hippolyte (France)	Jun 18, 1817– Oct 8, 1907	Jesuit (SJ)	10th Louisiana Regiment; Danville Hospital Jul 19, 1861; Aug 29, 1862–Apr 14, 1865[7]
Hubert, Darius (France)	Jul 19, 1823– Jun 14, 1893	Jesuit (SJ)	1st Louisiana Regiment (Nelligan), Richmond hospitals May 2, 1861–Apr 1865
Jarboe, Joseph Thomas (Kentucky)	Jun 26, 1806– Mar 27, 1887	Dominican (OP)	2nd Tennessee Volunteers Jul 1, 1861–Apr 1862?[8]
Leray, Francis Xavier (France)	Apr 20, 1825– Sep 23, 1887	Natchez (bishop postwar)	Post and hospital chaplain, Oxford, Mississippi; Shelby Springs, Alabama; Jackson, Mississippi Nov 26, 1862–May 1864?[9]
Manucy, Dominic (Florida)	Dec 20, 1823– Dec 4, 1885	Mobile (bishop postwar)	Post and hospital chaplain, Montgomery Jan 13, 1865–Jun 1865?[10]
Mouton, John Baptiste (France)	Mar 7, 1831– Oct 22, 1878	Natchez	Corinth, hospitals along Mobile–Ohio Railroad in eastern Mississippi Aug 4, 1862–1865?[11]
O'Connell, Laurence Patrick (Ireland)	Sep 26, 1826– Apr 18, 1891	Charleston; North Carolina; Vicariate Apostolic	Post and hospital chaplain, Montgomery White Sulphur Springs, Virginia September 26, 1862–Apr 18, 1863[12]
O'Reilly, Thomas (Ireland)	1831– Sep 6, 1872	Savannah (now Atlanta)	Post and hospital chaplain, Atlanta; ministered at the Battle of Chickamauga Feb 9, 1864–Apr 1865[13]

[7] From April to June 1861, Gache was chaplain informally to Confederate troops assembling in the Pensacola area (under General Braxton Bragg), then on July 19, 1861, he received a formal appointment, being assigned three days later to the 10th Louisiana Regiment.

[8] In May 1861, shortly after the war began, Dominican records report that "J. T. Jarboe" was authorized to leave his Zanesville, Ohio, parish to go to Memphis, where the 2nd Tennessee Volunteers (Walker) were forming. A formal appointment came in July 1861, but the end of his chaplaincy is unclear, though it appears to be after the Battle of Shiloh, where Jarboe was briefly captured and nearly shot.

[9] Leray had clearly been functioning as a chaplain before his formal appointment, as a May 19, 1862, request for a leave from a Confederate hospital (Shelby Springs, Mississippi) indicates.

[10] Manucy began working in the hospital shortly after his predecessor (Anthony Pellicer) had left but was only formally appointed a month later.

[11] Although Mouton began serving immediately after the Battle of Shiloh, he was only appointed by Secretary of War George Randolph on October 4, 1862, to take rank from August 4. Cf. Germain, *Chaplains*, 125.

[12] O'Connell's unofficial service began on November 16, 1861.

[13] O'Reilly began ministering in the many wartime hospitals which sprang up in Atlanta in mid-1862, long before he was formally appointed on March 16, 1864 (to date from February 9, 1864).

TABLE 2.2. Official Confederate Chaplains (Twenty-Five) *continued*

Name and Place of Birth	Life Dates	Diocese(s) or Order	Military Association and Dates of Service, if Known
Pellicer, Anthony Dominic (Florida)	Dec 7, 1824– Apr 14, 1880	Mobile (bishop postwar)	Post and hospital chaplain, Montgomery September 6, 1862–December 30, 1864
Pont, Francis (France)	1831?– Sep 27, 1867	Natchez	Corinth; 10th Mississippi; 13th Louisiana; Mississippi hospitals May 22, 1861–May 1862[14]
Prachensky, Joseph (Germany)	Jun 22, 1822– Jul 8, 1890	Jesuit (SJ)	3rd Alabama Regiment September 5, 1861–Feb 5, 1862
Ryan, Patrick (Ireland)	1824– Jan 13, 1887	Charleston, Baltimore	Post and hospital chaplain, Charleston Apr 13, 1864–Apr 1865[15]
Sheeran, James (Ireland)	1819– Apr 3, 1881	Redemptorist (CSsR), Newark (postwar)	14th Louisiana Regiment September 2, 1861–Apr 14, 1865[16]
Smulders, Egidius Wilhelm (Holland)	Sep 1, 1815– Apr 2, 1900	Redemptorist (CSsR)	8th Louisiana Regiment Jun 19, 1861–Mar 20 (Apr?), 1865
Turgis, Isadore Francis (France)	Apr 12, 1813– Mar 3, 1868	New Orleans	Corinth, Orleans Guards Militia, 30th Louisiana, and 4th Louisiana Mar 1862–Apr 1865

Recognized Chaplains with No Official Confederate Record (Two)

Name and Place of Birth	Life Dates	Diocese or Order	Military Association
Boheme, Ghislaine (Belgium)	Apr 3, 1803– Jun 27, 1862	Bardstown, Detroit, Natchez	13th Mississippi Apr 25, 1862–Jun 27, 1862[17]
Whelan, Peter (Ireland)	1802– Feb 6, 1871	Savannah	Fort Pulaski Jul 1861–May 1862; Andersonville Prison Jun 16, 1864–September 1864

14 Pont's records are confusing. In May 1861, he departed from his parish with the 10th Mississippi to follow them into service. In April 1862 he is mentioned as being at Shiloh ministering to the 13th Louisiana, but it appears he also became a pastor again in Jackson. It seems he accompanied some wounded from there to Vicksburg, then went to Florida in 1864 to escort the Sisters of Charity there from Mobile.

15 Patrick Ryan's unofficial service began in 1861.

16 Sheeran worked with the gathering Confederate troops in New Orleans in August 1861 before his formal assignment to the 14th Louisiana.

17 Conflicting records indicate that Boheme died either on June 23 or 27, 1862, in Virginia.

Occasional (Situational) Chaplains[13]

Union (Twenty-Three Chaplains)

BOURGET, JULIAN PROSPER (Holy Cross at Notre Dame)
(France, 1831–1862) Bourget worked at the Mound City, Illinois, Union Hospital, where the Holy Cross sisters were as well. Unfortunately, he was only there a few months after his arrival from France until he died from malaria on June 12, 1862.

BRADY, ROBERT (JESUIT)
(Maryland, 1825–1891) Brady ministered to wounded soldiers in the various hospitals around Washington, DC, while living with Bernardin Wiget at St. Aloysius Church there. During his life, this multitalented priest served as a parish priest, jail chaplain, and three-time president of Jesuit colleges.

BURKE, THOMAS (Vincentian)
(Ireland, 1808–1877) While ministering in St. Vincent's Church in St. Louis parish, Burke developed a personal ministry to the sick and wounded soldiers in the hospitals there. It was said of him that "he wore a long grey beard and is known in all the hospitals, especially with the military men." He died and was buried in St. Louis.[14]

BURLANDO, FRANCIS JACOB (Vincentian)
(Italy, 1811–1873) Burlando was in residence in Emmitsburg throughout the war years as the provincial of his order and formal director of Mother Seton's Sisters of Charity. Mentioned frequently as accompanying groups of nuns on their assignments to various military hospitals, he himself with twenty nuns traveled with medical supplies to Gettysburg two days after the battle. They worked primarily out of St. Francis Xavier Church there, which had been hastily converted into a makeshift hospital, though they served elsewhere as well.

FIALON, JOSEPH (Santa Fe Diocese)
(France, 1834–1910) Fialon was a post chaplain from October 29, 1863, to May 5, 1864, at Fort Sumner, New Mexico Territory, which housed Native Americans from the Navajo and Mescalero Apache tribes from 1863 to 1868.

GIBBONS, JAMES (Baltimore Diocese)
(Maryland, 1834–1921) After his 1861 ordination and while pastor of St. Bridget's in Baltimore, Gibbons ministered to troops at Fort McHenry. He later became the first bishop of North Carolina (then comprising the entire state), and later the cardinal archbishop of Baltimore. (Cf. chapter 12.)

LEVEQUE, JOSEPH ZEPHERIN (Holy Cross at Notre Dame)
(France, 1800–1862) Leveque was asked by Father Sorin to be chaplain but ministered only a few months before dying of exhaustion on February 13, 1862. The troops of Company K, 12th Regiment, New York State Militia were invited to attend his New Jersey funeral.

MCCROSSIN, BERNARD (possibly New York Diocese)
(possibly Ireland, dates unknown) McCrossin is in the Federal records as chaplain from 1 July to October 6, 1864, for the 69th Regiment, New York State Militia. But any further records on this priest, aside from an oblique reference to his priestly and immigrant statuses, have not yet been discovered.

MCQUAID, BERNARD (Newark Diocese)
(New York, 1823–1909) Representing his bishop, McQuaid went to Fredericksburg in May 1864 to ascertain the spiritual care available for the troops. Finding no priest, he wrote requesting one and remained there until a priest came, "assisting nobly at taking care of the wounded."[15] In 1868 he was named the first bishop of Rochester, New York, and served until his death in 1909.

MOORE, DANIEL DELACY (Buffalo and Rochester Dioceses)
(Ireland, 1828–1871) An Irish immigrant and patriot, Moore resigned his parish in mid-1861 to recruit a Western New York Irish Brigade. When the three hundred recruits were taken and consolidated into the 105th New York, he was out of a job, and returned to pastoring in October 1862.

NEALIS, JOHN THOMAS (Dominican)
(New York, 1832–1864) A Dominican priest based out of St. Rose Priory in Kentucky, Nealis was a pastor in the Nashville Diocese during the

Civil War years, and ministered to troops from both sides as they passed through. He was an outspoken pro-Union man, and in mid-1862, he was assaulted in Chattanooga by a "rebel bushwhacker" and never completely recovered, dying in 1864 from a fainting spell brought on by the attack.

O'CALLAGHAN, JOSEPH (Jesuit)
(Massachusetts, 1824–1869) A Jesuit teacher and college president from the Maryland Province, O'Callaghan ministered very briefly (little more than thirty days) to the 69th New York Militia in the summer of 1863. O'Callaghan died tragically on a January 1869 trip back from Rome when a storm wave swept over the boat, killing him and two others.

O'REILLY, BERNARD (Quebec Diocese, Jesuit, New York Diocese)
(Canada, 1820–1907) O'Reilly's interesting life story includes being ordained for the Quebec Diocese, becoming a Jesuit, then a postwar member of the New York Diocese, and achieving great notoriety as a historian and writer. He was chaplain of the 69th New York Militia for three months in the summer of 1861 after Thomas Mooney was removed by Archbishop John Hughes for "baptizing" a cannon. O'Reilly's "courageous presence" at First Bull Run is mentioned in one Civil War diary.[16]

ORENGO, JAMES ALOYSIUS ("Luigi") (Dominican)
(Italy, 1820–1909) An Italian Dominican and a pioneer missionary of Tennessee's Catholic community between 1850 and 1875, Orengo (like his compatriot John Nealis) ministered to troops of both sides as they passed through the Nashville area. He founded at least twelve parishes, and his name is on several historical markers in Tennessee.

PACCIARINI, BASIL (Jesuit)
(Italy, 1816–1884) A member of the Jesuits' Maryland Province, Pacciarini was pastor at St. Inigoe's in Maryland (America's oldest continually operating Catholic church). After 1863 he frequently ministered at the newly opened Camp Lookout nearby. His unique ministry touched both Blacks and whites in the church, as well as Confederate and Union troops in the camp.

ROCCOFORT, ALOYSIUS (Jesuit)
(France, 1819–1904) Having entered the Jesuit order at Avignon, France, in 1839, Roccofort came to St. Aloysius and Holy Trinity Churches in Washington in 1856. Despite being named in some internal Jesuit files as a hospital chaplain, he was never officially named one, although he assisted Bernadin Wiget with his official chaplaincy duties in the area.

RYAN, JOHN PATRICK (St. Louis)
(Ireland, 1831–1911) While a pastor in St. Louis, Ryan served informally as chaplain to Confederate prisoners at the Gratiot Street Prison there during the war years. Ryan turned down an appointment for Union hospital chaplaincy out of sensitivity to the Confederates he was ministering to. He became archbishop of Philadelphia in 1884, and served there until his death in 1911.[17]

SMITH, EDWARD M. (Vincentian)
(Ireland, 1835–1896) After coming to America and being ordained in July 1860, Smith had a well-traveled career, founding churches in Chicago and Brooklyn. During the Civil War, he was a situational chaplain who ministered with the Sisters of Charity after the Battle of Antietam at seven hospitals in nearby Boonesborough, Kentucky.

Northern Catholic Bishops Known to Have Ministered to Troops

HUGHES, JOHN, Archbishop of New York
(Ireland, 1797–1864) A strong supporter of the Union, and promoter of Catholic recruitment, Hughes is known to have conferred the sacrament of confirmation upon Union troops at Staten Island in 1861. The mainly Irish troops had been prepared by their own Catholic chaplain beforehand. In late 1861, Hughes made possible the publishing of a *Manual for Christian Soldiers*, which became the most disseminated Catholic publication of the war.[18]

PURCELL, JOHN, Bishop of Cincinnati
(Ireland, 1800–1883). A staunch pro-Union Republican and abolitionist who sent three priests to be chaplains, Purcell often went to Union encampments to meet his priests, preach, and administer the sacraments.[19]

Rosecrans, Sylvester Horton, Bishop of Columbus (Ohio) (Ohio, 1827–1878) The youngest of four sons, and the brother of Union General William Rosecrans, while an auxiliary bishop to John Purcell (Cincinnati), he too visited Union camps, preached, ministered the sacraments, and visited the chaplains there.

Timon, John, Bishop of Buffalo
(Pennsylvania, 1797–1867) On September 4, 1864, Timon visited the infamous Elmira, New York, prison, which reportedly housed ten thousand Confederate prisoners, preached and prayed with them. The next day he ordered reading material for the prisoners, and tried unsuccessfully to get a chaplain for the Irish Catholic Union soldiers guarding them. He did gain permission to have a priest from the area to hear confessions there, however.

Wood, James Frederick, Bishop of Philadelphia
(Pennsylvania, 1813–1883) A convert from Unitarianism and the first archbishop of Philadelphia, Wood visited Fort Delaware in 1864 to give spiritual comfort to his godson, the Confederate General Basil Duke. Wood continued to correspond with Duke, and later had a prayer book and overcoat delivered to him as well. He also visited Satterlee Hospital several times (April 1863, February 1864) to confirm adult converts to Catholicism.

Confederate (Twenty-Seven Chaplains)

Bergrath, Innocent Anthony (Nashville Diocese)
(Prussia, 1836–1881) Ordained in 1860, a pastor in Nashville then Knoxville at the outset of the war, Bergrath's bishop refused to appoint him chaplain formally. He then decided to minister informally, and very faithfully, to Confederate troops throughout eastern Tennessee until 1862, then to hospitals and Union troops who moved into his district from 1864 to 1865.

Bixio, Joseph (Jesuit)
(Italy, 1819–1889) A true character with a nose for trouble, Bixio had been ministering in California but came to Virginia at the outbreak of

the war seeking to serve in some way, becoming a pastor in Staunton, Virginia, in 1861. Unable to return to his parish after early Civil War battles there, he volunteered to be a Confederate chaplain, but also started turning up in Union camps to build his connections. In 1864 he impersonated the ailing Catholic chaplain of the 9th Connecticut (Leo Rizzo de Saracena) and "appropriated" Union supply wagons, which he then drove into the Confederate lines. Another Confederate chaplain paid a months-long price in prison for this (James Sheeran), while Bixio wound up back in California in 1866 with a trunk of useless Confederate money. (Cf. chapter 11.)

BOGLIOLI, CHARLES (Vincentian)
(Italy, 1814–1882) A quiet, selfless Italian immigrant who spent most of his priesthood in Louisiana, Boglioli was stationed in Donaldsonville, Louisiana, during the war years. He followed the Donaldsonville Cannoneers into Virginia and became their informal chaplain for about a year. After the war, Boglioli became known as the "leper priest" for his work among patients with Hansen's disease in New Orleans. He died of the disease, was buried quietly, and his grave remained "lost" for many years.

CHAMBODUT, LOUIS CLAUDE (Galveston Diocese)
(France, 1821–1880) Called by his nun-niece "the first secular priest ordained for Texas," Chambodut was rector at St. Mary's Cathedral in Galveston, and vicar-general of the diocese for twenty-seven years. Described as an ardent Confederate, he was in private communication with Confederate General John B. Magruder before and during the Confederate recapturing of Galveston on January 1, 1863. He then ministered at the military hospital in the Ursuline academy and convent, and is reported to have given heroic care to the wounded of both sides there. The legend exists that he pulled the lanyard of a Confederate cannon during the battle of Galveston.

CLAVREUL, HENRY (Savannah, St. Augustine Dioceses)
(France, 1835–1923) A French-born priest whose career was mostly in Florida, from 1862 on Clavreul was in Savannah, Georgia, where he was

asked by Bishop Verot to minister to area Confederate soldiers and hospitals. When Andersonville Prison was discovered, Clavreul was assigned to assist Peter Whelan. He remained for thirty-six days until his health failed, but returned for twelve more days after recovering at a nearby Macon church. He later worked with Union prisoners in Savannah, and then in the hospitals until the end of the war. Clavreul's detailed diary of the hundreds of men he gave sacraments to is a remarkable document.

CORNETTE, ANDREW (Jesuit)
(France, 1819–1872) A teacher of physics and mathematics at the Jesuit Spring Hill College in Mobile, Alabama, Cornette also ministered to the Confederate troops in the area forts. On June 3, 1865 (the day Lee's army surrendered in Virginia), Cornette and another priest barely escaped a Confederate fort under attack where they had gone to help Catholics make their Easter duty.

HAMILTON, WILLIAM JOHN (Savannah Diocese)
(Ireland, 1832–1883) In May 1864, while pastor in Macon, Georgia, and responsible for all area Catholic missions, Hamilton was the first priest to stumble upon Andersonville Prison. He received a pass from Captain Henry Wirz and stayed several hours, but then returned the following week for three more days "discharging his duties as a priest." After that visit he immediately notified his bishop, who then assigned Peter Whelan to minister there. Later a rector of the cathedral in Mobile, he died in Louisville at age fifty after a long illness.[20]

KIRBY, JOHN F. (Savannah Diocese)
(Ireland, ?–1872) While the pastor of Holy Trinity Church in Augusta, Georgia, native Irishman Kirby went to Andersonville Prison to minister for two weeks, replacing Henry Clavreul, who had been forced to leave due to illness. Kirby had been pastoring in Augusta since 1854, and after his 1872 death in Baltimore, was interred in the crypt beneath the Georgia church where he spent most of his adult ministry.

NACHON, FRANCIS (Jesuit)
(France, 1820–1867) A Jesuit priest stationed at St. Charles College at Grand Coteau, Louisiana, Nachon ministered to troops in the forts

around Mississippi and Louisiana in a reportedly dedicated and zealous priest. In October 1863, Nachon died from the yellow fever epidemic at a church in Washington, Louisiana, the same place where just two weeks later his confrere Anthony de Chaignon also contracted the fever and died.

O'KEEFE, MICHAEL (Baltimore, Richmond Dioceses)
(Ireland, 1828–1906) O'Keefe certainly aspired to be a chaplain, and was named chaplain of Mahone's Virginia Brigade but the position itself was apparently honorific, and he never followed troops into battle. In April 1862, he was assigned to General Albert Blanchard, who was sacked by Lee the next month. Though a pastor in Norfolk throughout the war, known as a dedicated priest, and called an "unreconstructed Confederate" in his January 28, 1907, obituary in the *New York Times*, O'Keefe's actual military record is too vague to categorize him as a formal chaplain.

O'NEILL, JEREMIAH, JR. (Savannah Diocese)
(Canada, 1826–1868) One of three "Rev. Jeremiah O'Neills" in the Savannah Diocese in the Civil War years, "Fr. Jeremiah, Junior" acquired a reputation for ministering to wounded soldiers in northern Georgia, caring for the wounded of both sides. He died in Baltimore at only age forty-two of throat cancer, with his uncle (known as "Fr. Jeremiah, Senior") caring for him.

PLUNKETT, JOSEPH (Richmond Diocese)
(Ireland, 1819–1870) As a Civil War pastor at St. Paul's in Portsmouth, Virginia (across the river from the Norfolk Navy Yard), Plunkett is frequently cited as having been a chaplain for both sides during the war. However, given the lack of formal military records and his ongoing pastorship, his ministry can best be described as occasional.

RYAN, ABRAM (Vincentian)
(Maryland, 1839–1886) The debate over Abram Ryan's actual Civil War chaplaincy has long been discussed, but with the absence of any formal records and only anecdotal evidence of his supposed work from 1863 to 1865, Ryan can only be considered occasional at best. It seems

he did spend some time in the field with Confederate troops, but only in short periods and never in any official way. The myths surrounding Ryan and his work have to a great degree been dispelled by modern scholarship. (Cf. chapter 11.)

SEARS, OSCAR (Richmond Diocese)
(Virginia, 1830–1867) Pastor of St. Francis Xavier in Lynchburg, Virginia, Sears's residence was a convenient stopping place for numerous Confederate chaplains throughout the war. He served informally as chaplain to Lynchburg's thirty hospitals from 1862 to 1865, ministering basically to area troops. In 1865 he was transferred to Martinsburg to rebuild the church there, which had been used as both prison and stable for sixty Union horses during the war.

TEELING, JOHN (Richmond Diocese)
(Ireland, 1823–?) Described in some records as "chaplain CSA" and "a chaplain at Bull Run," a lack of corroborative records leads to the conclusion that Teeling was likely more of a post chaplain in Richmond who ministered to various troops and hospitals there during the war. He has been anecdotally connected to the 1st Virginia's Montgomery Guards, to Wheat's Louisiana Tigers, and then to various hospitals in Richmond from May 1861 to March 1862, then from November 1863 until end of the war.[21]

USANNEZ, JOSEPH (Jesuit)
(Savoy, Italy, 1819–1895) A Jesuit stationed in Louisiana during the Civil War, Usannez ministered in that area, but is also one of several priests who ministered at Andersonville Prison in the summer of 1863. Records say he "suffered many privations and hardships" while working there.[22] Called "Father Hosannah" by one writer unfamiliar with his name, Usannez (like Peter Whelan and William Hamilton) considered the postwar trial and hanging of Henry Wirz an unjust "judicial murder."

Bishop William Elder's "Clerical Foreign Legion"

Bishops John Quinlan (Mobile) and William Elder (Natchez) both had issues with the commissioning process for Confederate chaplains. They (unsuccessfully) sought a more flexible system that would have granted them the flexibility to allow their few priests to freelance rather than have formal appointments. Elder frequently sent a number of his foreign-born priests to various places in his Mississippi diocese to serve the troops and hospitals as needed.

ELIA, BASIL (Natchez Diocese)
(Italy, ?–1863) Though information on him is scant, Elia's Mississippi church had been dispersed by mid-1863, so he requested that Bishop Elder let him work with dying Union soldiers at Young's Point, Louisiana, during Grant's Vicksburg campaign. Elia was there only three weeks when he caught one of the rampant diseases in that swampy place; he died in Memphis on April 2, 1863.

FINUCANE, JOHN L. (Natchez, Erie Diocese)
(Ireland, 1835–?) Ordained in June 1861, he was sent in 1862 and 1863 by Elder to minister to soldiers (Jackson) and hospitals (Brookhaven), and to be a pastor in Port Gibson (September 1863). His health and attitude apparently became issues, and in February 1864 he was given a three-month leave of absence. In a cryptic remark, author Blied comments that around this time, Finucane gave "great scandal in Lebanon, Kentucky, by toasting Jefferson Davis, and . . . almost embroiled two young priests." He eventually found a home in the Erie Diocese (Pennsylvania), working in the oil boomtowns of Venango County, Pennsylvania, where ironically the former Union chaplain Napolean Mignault (17th Wisconsin) also ended up.[23]

GEORGET, HENRY (Natchez Diocese)
(France, 1824–?) A French-born priest who worked in the Natchez Diocese for nearly thirty years, in November 1862 Georget was called from his Biloxi, Mississippi, parish to Natchez (and other cities) to help minister to soldiers there, as a Union invasion was soon expected. A year later, Georget wrote to Bishop Elder that he had gotten too sick to continue in that work, and he returned to Biloxi. He continued ministering in the Natchez diocese into the mid-1880s.

GUILLOU, JULIAN MARY (Natchez Diocese)
(France, 1824–1863) One of the many French priests recruited by the Natchez Diocese, Guillou went to serve the New Orleans–based Washington Artillery fighting at Shiloh, arriving at Corinth on April 12, 1862. He ministered to the wounded and dying at the Tishomingo Hotel until the sick and wounded had been evacuated in early May. Guillou then returned to his parish greatly weakened by his efforts. He died of consumption on February 7, 1863.

HUBER, PHILIP (Natchez Diocese)
(Germany, 1827–1903) Huber became a short-term chaplain for the 10th Tennessee Regiment in late 1862 after being pastor at a struggling Port Gibson parish and having worked with the wounded and dying after Shiloh. Bishop Elder tried to dissuade Huber because of parish needs and personal health issues, and was proved right when Huber returned to Natchez after struggling with winter weather and contracting dysentery. He returned to parish life, putting in forty-five years of distinguished diocesan service before his 1903 death.

PICHERIT, HENRY A. (Natchez Diocese)
(France, 1831–?) After arriving in America in 1854 and failing in his attempt to become a Jesuit, Picherit settled into a long and successful career in the diocese instead. While a pastor in Brookhaven, Mississippi, he ministered to the wounded in Corinth after Shiloh, visited Union camps after 1863, and brought medicine up from New Orleans when needed. Called "the great Confederate Chaplain" in the book *Angels of Mercy* (a bit of an exaggeration), Picherit did become a dean in the diocese and pastor in the diocese's largest parish (St. Paul's in Vicksburg).

Southern Catholic Bishops Known to Have Ministered to Troops

ELDER, WILLIAM HENRY, BISHOP OF NATCHEZ (1857–1880)
(Maryland, 1819–1904) While guiding his diocese through the incredible challenges of war, destruction, and sickness, the unionist turned secessionist Elder was an extremely active and mobile pastor as well. He was at Corinth ministering after Shiloh, frequently visited hospitals

around his diocese, and dispatched his clergy regularly to "put out fires" where he found them. He became archbishop of Cincinnati in 1880, and died there in 1904. (Cf. chapter 10.)[24]

MCGILL, JOHN, BISHOP OF RICHMOND (1850–1872)
(Pennsylvania, 1809–1872) Northern by birth but strongly Southern in his sympathies, McGill blessed battle flags, established a hospital in Richmond for the wounded, visited the Northern soldiers held at Libby Prison, and sent his priests to give the sacraments there as well. Well respected by Confederate leaders such as Robert E. Lee, McGill wrote a book in 1861 specifically for Confederate Catholic soldiers (*The Catholic Devotional for Confederate Soldiers*). Prevented by the Union from traveling during the war, he did so afterward, painfully helping rebuild his diocese (which covered all Virginia) after the horrendous destruction the war caused within its boundaries.

QUINLAN, JOHN, BISHOP OF MOBILE (1859–1883)
(Ireland, 1826–1883) A student of William Elder in the seminary, Quinlan helped minister at Forts Morgan and Gaines on the Gulf of Mexico, blessed battle flags, and helped care for the wounded of both sides around Corinth after the Battle of Shiloh. Though greatly stressed during the war years (and held in custody himself overnight on one occasion), Quinlan's Mobile Diocese did not endure as much destruction and damage as did other Southern dioceses.

VEROT, JEAN AUGUSTINE, BISHOP OF SAVANNAH (1861–1876)
(France, 1819–1876) A combative, independent man, Verot justified slavery in the abstract but condemned many of its concrete features. He traveled great distances in his two-state territory (Georgia and Florida) to give the sacraments to Catholic soldiers (Union and Confederate) and civilians, ministered at Andersonville Prison himself twice for several days in July 1864, and personally supported the priests who worked there.[25]

WHELAN, JAMES, BISHOP OF NASHVILLE (1859–1863) (Dominican)
(Ireland, 1823–1878) This Irish-born Dominican allowed his cathedral to be used for a hospital after the First Battle of Bull Run and ministered

himself in the Nashville area between 1862 and 1863. The tensions of nearly constant occupation were overwhelming for Whelan, who left the diocese in July 1863, resigned in 1864, and returned to a Dominican monastery.

Not Chaplains (Whose Service to Civil War Troops Is Unconfirmed and the Evidence Is Insufficient)

BECKER, THOMAS A. (Richmond)
Becker was ministering in West Virginia when his church was turned into a barracks. Becker later became the first bishop of Wilmington, Delaware (1868–1886), then the bishop of Savannah, Georgia (1886–1899).

CARR, FELIX (Charleston)
Not considered a chaplain by Germain nor myself.

COOK, WILLIAM (Philadelphia)
Not considered a chaplain by Germain nor myself.

CREEDON, MICHAEL (Buffalo)
Not considered a chaplain by Germain nor myself.

DUGGAN, GREGORY (Savannah)
Pastor in Atlanta during the war.

DUMORTIER, LOUIS (Jesuit)
Yet another fascinating Jesuit, but only an itinerant missionary in Kansas from 1855 to 1867.

GIRARDY, TERREOL (Redemptorist)
Not considered a chaplain by Germain nor myself.

HAVILAND, ARTHUR P. (Philadelphia)
Not considered a chaplain by Germain nor myself.

HEIDENKAMP, JOSEPH (Wheeling)
According to one source, Heidenkamp baptized General Micah Jenkins after the battle of Cloyd's Mountain (May 1864).

KILROY, E. B. (Holy Cross)
Kilroy turned down a Naval chaplain commission, but was delegated by Indiana governor Oliver Perry Morton to bring the soldiers' money to their families.

MALOY, PATRICK (Alton)
Reputedly served at the US Hospital in Alton, Illinois.

REILLY, MICHAEL (Baltimore)
Not considered a chaplain by Germain nor myself.

Mistakenly Named as Catholic Chaplains by Germain[26]

BARBER, SAMUEL (Jesuit)
Germain confused him with a Baptist chaplain of the same name in the 47th Virginia.

CUNNINGHAM, JAMES T. (3rd Regiment Mississippi)
He was a Methodist Episcopal minister from Tupelo, Mississippi, married with children.

JORDAN, WILLIAM H. (18th North Carolina)
A Baptist pastor from Anson County, North Carolina, where the first Catholic church was not built until 1946.

MEREDITH, WILLIAM C. (4th Virginia Cavalry)
Meredith was an Episcopal priest at Christ Church in Winchester, Virginia, who married four times with seven children in all.[27]

THE WARTIME MINISTRY
OF CATHOLIC PRIESTS

Several excellent books have been published in the past decades focusing on the work of Civil War chaplains. Some of the ones focusing on the wartime ministry of chaplains both in general and specifically are these: *Soldiers of the Cross* (Kurtz and Endres), *Chaplains of the United States Army* (Honeywell), *Chaplains in Gray* (Pitts), *For Courageous Fighting and Confident Dying* (Armstrong), *Soldiers of the Cross* (Dollar), *The Spirit Divided: Memoirs of Civil War Chaplains—Union* (Maryniak and Brinsfield) and *The Spirit Divided: Memoirs of Civil War Chaplains—Confederate* (Brinsfield), *In God's Presence* (B. Miller), and the collaborative work *Faith in the Fight* (Brinsfield, Davis, Maryniak, and Robertson). There are also plenty of articles available on the history of Civil War chaplaincy as well. However, as mentioned in chapter 2, in all of these, the term "chaplain" itself is consistently not clearly defined nor clarified as to length of service, official status, and so on.

This fact has a ripple effect on our ability to delineate the unique ministries which chaplains from different denominations might have undertaken. All Christian religious denominations have some common foundational beliefs and practices (e.g., belief in a Supreme Being, prayer, Scripture, preaching, music, etc.), but they can differ greatly on specific liturgical practices, rituals for worship, prayer styles and the customary ecclesial practices of each group. All these things can, of course, change *within* denominations occasionally as well, given the flow of the overarching culture, changing societal values, and ecclesiastical policies and polities.

Thus, when reading the writings of Civil War Catholic priests, one certainly sees some general similarity in their work with non-Catholic chaplains. This includes worship services and preaching, hospital visits, funerals, visiting soldiers in camps, giving instructions, temperance work, letter-writing, delivering mail, and assisting soldiers in any variety of ways. As with all chaplains, some Catholic priests had an enormous influence on soldiers outside their own "flock." Some gained renown for their preaching to the men of their regiments. Nearly all had an important leadership role simply by virtue of their status, and were a clear and important moral influence on soldiers and officers. On the battlefield, their ministry could be incredibly powerful and life-changing. (As a general rule, although priests first sought out Catholics on battlefields, there is no record of any Catholic chaplain not attending to the spiritual needs of anyone who needed them.)[1]

Before speaking of the unique work of Catholic priest-chaplains, a brief word is in order about the "demands" of the governments for chaplains appointed for Civil War services. There was a complete lack of official government guidelines on the specific duties of a chaplain. Colonel Thomas Higginson (a Congregational minister himself) wrote that "in a little world . . . where every man's duties and position are absolutely prescribed, the chaplain alone has no definite position and no prescribed duties." Especially in the Confederacy, chaplains were essentially allowed to fashion their own ministries "under the watchful eye of their commanders, fellow officers, and soldiers of the line." But on both sides, after a chaplain had been appointed and mustered into service, the one clear expectation that emerged eventually was holding regular religious services and conducting of public services for deceased members of the regiment. In May 1861, the Union required a quarterly chaplain's report to the regimental commander regarding the moral and religious state of his regiment, but there was no obligation for officers to pass those on to the adjutant general's office, or even act on them. A further change occurred in April 1864 requiring monthly chaplains' reports to be directly submitted to the adjutant general. The Confederacy had no such guidelines.[2]

Catholic priests were set apart from other chaplains in their ministry both by their faith and by their religious practices. To understand the priests' wartime ministry, one must understand the theological and liturgical principles that guided them. The antebellum American Catholic Church had a very hierarchical structure and understanding of authority, with the pope atop the pyramid (Pope Pius IX was in office for thirty-two years from 1846 to 1878, including the years of the Civil War), followed by bishops, priests, and then laity (i.e., non-ordained people). God's revelation to humanity was indeed found in the Word of God (the Bible), but for antebellum Catholic clergy, the role of sacred tradition held equal influence over their ministry, teaching, and practice. The concept of any type of collaboration in ministry with non-Catholics (called "ecumenism" today) would have been rare in an era of denominational bias and prejudice. Finally, the actual practice of Catholicism during the Civil War would have been heavily centered around the rituals of Catholic sacraments and personal devotional prayers (such as the rosary), with preaching being used as a key motivational factor for all believers, especially "back-sliding" Catholics.[3]

For Catholic chaplains between 1861 and 1865, without a doubt, performing the Catholic sacraments was their most regular routine, as well as perhaps the bulk of their ministry. All seven Catholic sacraments require a priest (or bishop) to perform them, and four in particular were absolutely essential parts of any faithful Catholic's regular spiritual life. A Catholic soldier began his spiritual journey with baptism, sustained it with holy communion at weekly Mass, cleansed his life of sin by regular confession, and was prepared for possible death by extreme unction (anointing the sick at the time of pending death). More than members of any other religious denomination in the antebellum era, Catholic soldiers thus required priests for the active and faithful practice of their faith.[4]

In the lengthy diaries, letters, and accounts of Catholic chaplains like William Corby, James Sheeran, Hippolyte Gache, Michael Nash, John Bannon, Peter Tissot, and others, one always notices the amount of time spent in sacramental ministry. Priests even frequently gave the sacraments to people in the towns and areas they passed through on their marches—since the war had greatly disrupted the regular worship life of so many, and a good number of rural Catholics hadn't seen a priest in months or years. Though priests performed a wide variety of ministries to officers and troops during the war, their ministry of the Catholic sacraments remained central. Their lives were indeed ordered around the rituals and public routines of daily Mass, hearing confessions, and anointing the sick.[5]

The words of two wartime chaplains—one Confederate, one Union—illustrate well the impact and importance that sacramental work played in their wartime chaplaincies. First, the irascible and outspoken chaplain of the 14th Louisiana, the Redemptorist priest James Sheeran (whose story is told in chapter 6). He reflects here on one poignant and powerful incident of his sacramental work: "This was one of my most laborious days: it [was] spent from morning till late at night hearing confessions, administering Extreme Unction, baptizing, and in washing and dressing wounds. . . . Late this night we received orders to prepare to march in the morning. I threw myself down for a few hours in the open air but slept little."[6]

The Jesuit Peter Tissot served the 37th New York for more than two years between 1861 and 1863. During the Peninsula Campaign of April 1862, he shared this marvelous vignette in a letter to his Jesuit confreres about his work during that time.

Although it was Sunday, we had no Mass, because our chapel was behind in the wagons; but I preached and said prayers. Heard confessions the whole afternoon and late at night, until 12:30, in a small tent, without fire and on the wet ground. I prepared 102 for Communion, mostly from the 63rd Pennsylvania, 2nd Maine, and 38th and 40th New York. The men had the fear of the Lord, for they did not know how soon they might have to fight. I was obliged to put off hearing the confessions of my own men.[7]

HEARING CONFESSIONS

The Catholic tradition of confession (today called the "sacrament of reconciliation") comes from the words of Jesus in John 20:23: "whose sins you forgive are forgiven them, and whose sins you retain are retained" (NABRE). This was done most often on one's death bed in the early centuries of Christianity, but Irish monks in the early Middle Ages began the practice of regularly confessing one's sins to a priest on some frequent basis. By the time of the Civil War, confession was normative for Catholics before receiving communion or any major sacrament (such as holy communion, confirmation, or marriage).

During the Civil War, hearing confessions was the one aspect of a chaplain's work that took the most time and effort yet could be the most incredibly rewarding and spiritually beneficial. Priests were constantly hearing soldiers' confessions, especially in camps and hospitals, before and after battles, at times doing so for hours on end or going through the entire night. Peter Paul Cooney, the legendary chaplain of the 35th Indiana, once heard confessions for eight hours straight in Kentucky on the eve of an expected battle. Using three rifles with bayonets in the ground, the soldiers erected for him a makeshift hut so he could continue his work despite the elements. While on house arrest in 1862 at the episcopal residence in Richmond, Union chaplain Peter Tissot (37th New York) had the honor of hearing Bishop John McGill's confession. The confession followed an exchange between them in which the bishop hesitatingly gave permission to Tissot to hear Confederate soldiers' confessions, "provided you do not talk against the South."[8]

Thomas Ouellet, the Jesuit chaplain of the 69th New York of the Irish Brigade, gained high praise and a reputation for endurance and disregard of personal danger as he ministered to soldiers in need. "In anticipation of each recurring engagement, it was his custom to . . . prepare by confession and Communion the soldiers under his spiritual command to face the coming danger . . . the good Soldier of the Cross unheeding the bullets that fell would pass through the kneeling ranks and administer a conditional absolution." While visiting a hospital in Mississippi during the 1863 Vicksburg Campaign, Joseph Carrier (6th Missouri Cavalry) heard dozens of confessions, including that of one badly wounded but ecstatic Irishman. "Oh Father, what a happy day for me, I would have given the whole world when I fell wounded to have a priest at my side for a few moments only. Thanks be to God and to you, Father. I am now at peace with my Maker and with myself!"[9]

An anecdote from the Congregational minister Joseph Twichell speaks to the importance of confession at the time of death.

> During the battle of Spotsylvania I found in the hospital a dying man anxious to see a priest. Father O'Hagan was not with us then and I rode two miles before I found Father Corby and urged him to return with me. "But," said he, "there are fifty right here whose souls may be passing. I cannot leave them . . . tell [the man] to confess to you, and tell him I said so and that whatever you say to him or do for him is right." I rode back in haste . . . kneeled upon the grass beside him, listened to what he had to say, offered such comfort and hope as was given to me . . . and commended him into the keeping of our gracious Lord. He seemed to be satisfied and presently the light faded from his eyes and he was gone.[10]

Aside from medical care, there were few things that could provide more comfort to a horribly wounded soldier than confessing one's sins. The French priest residing at Vicksburg during the 1863 Union bombardment, Charles Heuze, was not a formal chaplain, but did his share of ministering to Confederate soldiers in "the terrible scourge of death, sorrow and desolation on all sides" that the Vicksburg siege was. The horrific suffering of one Louisiana soldier named Hebert struck Heuze particularly deeply. "The blood flowed out in waves. The flesh fell off in shreds and all the entrails were laid open. His first words were in Creole: 'My Father, O, my Father, I am dying' . . . He then confessed with all ardor and sincerity possible believing in his approaching death. I gave him absolution and administered Extreme Unction when he cried out 'Father—I die, may God have pity on me! Jesus pardon me!' I then commenced the prayers that follow Extreme Unction—He was no more."[11]

Despite being often portrayed as extraordinary, it was actually quite common during the war for priests to offer a general absolution to an entire mass of troops gathering for battle. The famed William Corby

(88th New York) became legendary for doing this on the second day of Gettysburg for the Irish Brigade, although that was not the first time he had done so. At Antietam, Corby galloped in front of the Irish Brigade as they were rushing into battle, told the men to make an act of contrition, and gave them a hasty absolution. There are dozens of accounts of other priests doing the same thing. Bishop William Elder did it while accompanying area nuns to safety. Paul Gillen performed a hasty general absolution on the evening of the Battle of First Bull Run (July 21, 1861). The Jesuit chaplain of Sickles' Excelsior Brigade, Joseph O'Hagan, offered a general absolution for Catholics (non-Catholics removed their caps out of respect) at Williamsburg on May 5, 1862, during the Peninsula Campaign. One of the Protestant officers there said it was the most moving religious ceremony he had ever witnessed. At Fredericksburg in December 1862, Peter Tissot absolved the Union troops as they crossed the river before their deadly assault. He "was accustomed to take up a position by the roadside and give general absolution to the men, in groups, as they passed by him. The men understood perfectly what he was doing, for he had instructed them."[12]

One of the longest serving Catholic chaplains, Peter Paul Cooney (35th Indiana) would regularly give general absolution before conflicts. At the Battle of Stones River (Murfreesboro) in December 1862, he wrote his brother that "every morning before the battle would commence (for there were five days of fighting), I would come out before the regiment drawn up in line of battle, and after offering a prayer and making an act of contrition, all repeating with me, give absolution to them while kneeling. The General saw us the first morning, and he was so edified with our example that he sent an order to the Protestant chaplains to do the same. Poor fellows, what could they do?" The Dominican priest Constantine Egan was chaplain to the 9th Massachusetts during the Mine Run Campaign of late 1863, and gave a general absolution to his troops and the 159th Pennsylvania as they were readying to assault the Confederate works. He "stood on a stump or a cliff in the woods, publicly invoked the blessing of Almighty God on all the troops . . . he also invoked divine forgiveness of sins for all present about to offer their lives for their country. This scene was most impressive and inspiring, irrespective of creed."[13]

On December 31, 1862, a priest who was chaplain for both sides at different times, forty-year-old Jeremiah Trecy, was serving unofficially with General William Rosecrans's army as the Battle of Stones River broke out. Amidst the shifting battle lines,

> Trecy rode to the front, raised himself in the saddle and with a stentorious voice cried out "Men prepare yourselves! I will give you the general absolution!" It happened that . . . almost all were Catholics. He recited the Confiteor aloud for them, told them to make an Act of Contrition while he pronounced the words of general absolution. In an instant all the hats were off and the soldiers were on their knees. The scene was indeed striking. The ceremony over, the priest dashed through the line to the rear of the batteries where he joined a portion of the staff. The battle raged, wounded men were carried to the rear and the priest was again at his work. . . . He carried with him two canteens one containing whiskey and the other water. During this struggle, as in many others, he was frequently seen with some poor fellow's head on his knees giving him a reviving draught so as to enable him to make his confession, and prepare himself for eternity.

Trecy was later universally praised for his wartime bravery and ministry; dispensing whiskey at times would certainly not have hurt his cause in that regard.[14]

CELEBRATING MASS (EUCHARIST)

Arranging for the regular celebration of Mass for the troops was a major personal and spiritual responsibility for priest-chaplains. The Catholic public prayer called informally "Mass" (from the old Latin dismissal "*Ite, missa est,*" known today more aptly as "Eucharist") is patterned after the Last Supper of Jesus, and immediately became the central gathering ritual for Christians through the centuries. For mid-nineteenth-century Catholics, as today, attending Mass on Sunday was considered an obligation, and missing it could be considered a sin. If troops were in camp on a Sunday, chaplains would try to set up a large chapel tent (if they could obtain one) to celebrate the sacrament, which was all in Latin except for the readings and preaching. But with the many uncertainties of military life (drills, marches, exhaustion, and "worldly distractions") priests more often than not had to celebrate on the fly (especially while marching or not in camp) and create makeshift altars in open-air settings if a tent was not available. William Corby speaks of this in his *Memoirs*.[15]

> The next day was Sunday, and the chaplains did all they could to sanctify the day. I do not remember what the other chaplains provided, but I remember very distinctly the altar constructed under my supervision, for I was determined to say Mass. There were no boards, no boxes, no tables in the entire camp, and the camp was in a dense woods. The soldiers cut some pine branches and fastened them to a tree, as a slight shelter for the future altar. Then they drove four crotched sticks in the ground and out two short pieces from one crotch to the other; they then cut down a tree, split one log in two, and placed the pieces of split lumber, flat side up, lengthwise, to form the table of the altar. This, the rudest of altars, I dressed, as best I could, with altar linens. Two candles were lighted, and Mass was celebrated in the forest of Virginia, after a fashion to rival that of the most destitute Indian missionary that ever put foot on the soil of the Huron Nation.[16]

It was often a challenge for priests on both sides to be able to celebrate Mass in the first place. Like all believers throughout history, Catholic Civil War soldiers could be lackadaisical and perfunctory in their religious practices, poor in church attendance, and easily swayed by other excuses not to attend Mass (though this was less a problem when a potential battle loomed). Chaplains routinely "rousted out" Catholics from their tents to announce Mass or prayer times (e.g., the rosary), with some chaplains not hesitant to use more persuasive motivational measures. In one amusing incident, Thomas Ouellet found many men sitting in their tents about breakfast time with little interest in prayer. Father Ouellet noticed the backsliders, and descending from the hill where the church was located, walked the company streets and kicked the vessels containing the coffee over, spilling their contents, amid the general howls of the hungry soldiers. He then ascended the altar and addressed the assembled veterans as follows: "The good came here this morning to thank God for their deliverance from death, and the rest who remained to satisfy their appetites were fellows that were coffee-coolers and skedaddlers during our retreat." Ever afterward, there was little necessity to call the attention of the men when circumstances permitted the celebration of the Mass.[17]

A further challenge for chaplains was finding the needed materials to celebrate Mass—namely an altar, vestments, chalice, hosts, wine, tent, and so on. Peter Tissot mentions how grateful he was for the simple vestments and wine given to him. "The vestments, red and green, were of silk . . . they were a present from the Manhattanville Convent. One bottle of wine lasted me a full month." The chaplain of the 9th Massachusetts, the Dominican priest Constantine Egan, "was granted 5 days leave of absence 16 January 1864, to visit his home in Washington DC in order to purchase a horse, and many things necessary to the celebration of the Holy Sacrifice of the Mass." In March 1862, as his chaplain's tenure in the Irish Brigade was just beginning, William Corby describes the chaplains' efforts to get basic supplies, then added "I, being the youngest of the chaplains, was started back in advance to secure altar breads, altar wines, etc. for the Peninsular Campaign."[18]

Whenever a priest happened to lose his Mass kit or ran out of supplies, it occasioned great efforts, like a short leave, to pick up new supplies for this key sacramental work. After the Jesuit priests Peter Tissot and Joseph O'Hagan were captured in June 1862 and then released, both took several weeks' leave to replace their lost sacramental materials. In April 1862, James Dillon was given a six-day leave of absence to visit Baltimore Maryland "to obtain sacred oils from the Archbishop, which are absolutely necessary for all the Catholic Chaplains of the Division." After a battle at Santa Rosa, Florida, in October 1861, Michael Nash (6th New York) wrote, "This is the feast of Blessed Alphonsus Rodriquez, but I was deprived of the comfort of offering the Holy Sacrifice as all my effects, vestments, chalice, altar furnishings, were burnt up. I have written to St. Francis Xavier's for a new outfit but it has not arrived yet."[19]

Peter Tissot's diary entry for Sunday, July 28, 1861, indicates how wearying a typical Sunday could be for a chaplain. "Said a first Mass for my regiment and a second one for the Mozart Regiment. Remained with them the whole day; preached at Mass and in the evening; heard confessions the whole afternoon; prepared 75 for Communion, 12 of those for their First Communion." Tissot speaks of the many confessions he heard and Communions he gave apart from Mass, but his entry of November 20, 1861 (while encamped near Alexandria), captures the effect that the Catholic Mass could have on others. "Said an early Mass in my camp and a second one in Col. Lugeans' [sic] camp. The Colonel brought all his men. The 63rd Pa. Regiment, being encamped near, also came. I officiated under a tree. When about to begin I told them that Mass being Catholic worship, those who were not Catholics might withdraw, but none did so. At 2 P.M. Col. Lugeans [sic] gave a grand dinner to the officers of his regiment and to the staff officers of the 61st and 63d Pa. Many speeches were made."[20]

As with all Christians, holy days were especially significant, and James Sheeran (14th Louisiana) wrote very poignantly about Easter Sunday, April 5, 1863.

Today, Easter Sunday, is one which I shall ever remember. . . . The snow had been falling all night and early in the morning it continued to come down so thickly that one could hardly see fifty yards distant. . . . But to my surprise I found a large concourse of boys around my tent. To see so many of our brave soldiers knee-deep in the snow, cheerfully awaiting the offering of the Holy Sacrifice of the Mass, was perhaps one of the most consoling sights of my life, and never did I pray more fervently for my congregation than on this occasion. . . . My sermon this day was necessarily short as I did not wish to detain the poor men in the cold. I announced that I was to leave camp on the following day in order to visit the other portions of Gen. Lee's army and give the Catholic soldiers belonging to it an opportunity of making their Easter Communion.[21]

William Corby's diary mentions Mass frequently, but he is cred-
ited for creating a truly memorable way to celebrate this sacrament—
one he called a "Military Mass." Described at length in several places in
his diary, the celebration for St. Patrick's Day 1863 while encamped at
Falmouth was especially elaborate. Securing the permission of General
Thomas Meagher, he had a special church constructed with area pines,
used silk vestments gifted to him by the officers and men, brought in
the Jesuit Joseph O'Hagan to preach, invited General Joseph Hooker
and his staff to attend (they did) and then celebrated a Mass featuring
cannons firing at the consecration, soldiers wearing full dress uniforms,
and bands playing.

Following the Mass, horse races and sports were held, lunch and
lemonade was served to many, and "it was estimated that fully twenty
thousand participated in, or at least witnessed, the sports of the day."
Corby was justifiably very proud that day, by both the Irish Brigade
and a Catholic faith that could produce such an amazing ceremony at a
time of war and destruction. He later wrote, "Here we have no organ
on the 'tented plain,' nor the shadow of a lady to supply the parts of
alto, or soprano. All is stern manhood wrought up to its highest tension of honor and duty; duty to fellowmen, duty to country, duty to
family and kindred; but, above all, duty to the greatest God seated on
the rock of ages directing the destinies of all nations."[22]

PREPARING SOLDIERS FOR DEATH

Along with confession, the Catholic sacrament of extreme unction was
a vitally important spiritual practice, especially for the badly wounded
on battlefields and in hospitals. This ritual involved an anointing with
blessed oil given to a seriously sick person in grave danger of dying. It
is based on the words of James 5:14: "Is there anyone sick among you?
Let them call the elders of the church to pray over them and anoint
them with oil in the name of the Lord" (NABRE). Although the words
used would have been in the Latin (the language of the Catholic church
until the twentieth century), most soldiers would have immediately
known what the priest was doing, and found great consolation despite

the pain of their medical condition. Ministering either confession or extreme unction (which included the absolution of sins) was a standard routine during and after battles as chaplains moved among the wounded soldiers on the field and in the hospitals.

While mourning the deaths of so many at Fredericksburg in December 1862, William Corby reflected on the great spiritual power that sacraments like confession and extreme unction had during his ministry there. "No help for it now; it was useless to sigh over the past, though many orphans might weep and mothers and wives bewail at home. The great nation groans at the loss of her brave sons in a fratricidal, cruel war. Nevertheless, we must settle down to business once more. We must hold regular services, for the holy sacraments bring consolation to pious, repenting souls, when all earthly comfort fails to do so." The French-born Confederate chaplain Francois Turgis feared that his regiment would expect him to be a good preacher, but his battlefield consolations more than made up for any deficiencies in that area. His file at the New Orleans Archdiocese—despite its undoubtedly hyperbolized recounting—remarks that he gave "pardon and absolution for forty-eight hours during the Battle of Shiloh, when he found himself the only priest amid 20,000 Catholics." On the day after the battle, Turgis was cited for heroism at Shiloh by the Catholic General P. G. T. Beauregard in his order of the day.[23]

An anecdote from the diary of John Bannon (1st Missouri Brigade) illustrates the immense power a chaplain's battlefield sacramental ministry could have. One of the casualties from the battle of Champion Hill (May 16, 1863) was a Rebel artilleryman who was fatally wounded, but not yet dead. As Bannon came to minister to him, he found the man in a foul mood roaring aloud because he found himself next to a wounded Yankee soldier: "Take away this Yankee, boy! I can't lie quiet here with this Yankee by me!" Bannon knew the man, and immediately spoke strongly to him, telling him to attend to his own soul first, as his skull was split open, and he would soon die and meet his Maker. After anointing him, Bannon ministered to the Union soldier next to him, a German who understood no English, but "kissed fervently the crucifix which I held to him, and seemed intensely grateful at meeting with a Catholic Priest."

The next day, Bannon was retreating with the Confederates to Vicksburg when he found the same Rebel artilleryman in a wagon, still alive. He was horribly wounded, but recognized the priest, and cried out to him. Bannon wrote later how surprised but pleased he was to find him, because he had some doubts about the man's spiritual "worthiness," given his bad treatment of the dying Yankee. But the soldier immediately said, "I can't help thinking of that poor Yankee. I behaved like a brute to him. He died last night, but after you left him he never stopped saying his prayers, and he prayed like a good one. He made me think, I can tell you. I'm just sorry for the way I treated him, and if you can give me any more penance for it, do. Now if you'll stop by me, I'd like to make my confession again." He then confessed at the top of his voice, saying, "I have been a bad man. . . . I have given bad example, and I want to do some penance for it." When he had finished, Bannon wrote that "I consoled him, telling him I should give him no penance, for he had done enough. I then gave him the last absolution, and in an hour he was a corpse."[24]

The Dominican priest Joseph Jarboe (2nd Tennessee) was also said to have ministered at Shiloh, and in a later newspaper account of his life remarked that

comrades of Fr. Jarboe were falling on all sides while he was busy administering to the dying. Finding a young soldier suffering from a mortal wound, Fr. Jarboe was preparing to cut away his boots for the anointing of the when a bullet shattered the knife he held in his hand. Before the priest recovered from this shock an exploding shell struck the injured soldier and hurled his body some distance across the field. As it did so, a penknife dropped from one of the soldier's pockets and was put to use by the chaplain. Fr. Jarboe always thought this second knife was sent to replace the one shot from his hand. He kept the knife as a memento of the war and would often show it to his friends.[25]

When the sacrament of baptism is administered, it also forgives sins, hence this sacrament was used frequently on the battlefields when death appeared imminent. After his 9th Massachusetts unit was disbanded in

June 1864, Constantine Egan was commissioned to serve in the Fifth and Ninth Corps until the end of the war. As a fitting sign of own impartiality toward soldiers on both sides, Egan ministered to a fallen Confederate soldier, shot by his own officer, on the final day of the war. We have his own description of the event:

> I alighted from my horse and went over to him to aid him spiritually if he wished, and if not, at least to render him all the temporal aid I could in consequence of his great suffering . . . Examining the wound, I found it was fatal, and from his agony and suffering I concluded that the poor fellow had not long to live; I told him so and entreated him now to fight the last battle for Heaven. I asked him if he had been baptized, he replied in the negative. I told him that baptism was necessary in order to go to heaven, and he seemed willing to be baptized after the instructions I gave him. Then, laying hold of a canteen of water, I baptized him "In the name of the Father, and of the Son, and of the Holy Ghost."[26]

In his letters, Hippolyte Gache (10th Louisiana, Danville Hospital) also spoke of his encounter with a mortally wounded, older Confederate colonel who had also never been baptized despite being raised by Baptist parents. The wounded officer told him, "I am not [Catholic] but my wife and children are. I like their church very much. It is the only one I attend." Gache then remarks that he "assured him that he had the faith and necessary depositions, baptized him, and left him in a state of joy and gratitude to God and appreciation for what I had done. He kept saying over and over: 'Blessed be the Lord. Now I will die in peace.'"[27]

Preparing soldiers who were to be executed was always a profound and pathos-filled event for chaplains who wrote of being involved in the process. Many Catholic chaplains would later recount their ministry at those immensely difficult times—Tissot, Sheeran, and Corby among them. In December 1864, Peter Tissot was summoned by General Benjamin Butler to minister to a soldier to be shot for deserting. The man was described as being "in despair—fearing he would have to die without the Sacraments." Tissot ministered to the soldier, gave the sacraments, and left the man only when he had been buried.

Soon after, another execution took place, but this time there were two Protestants and one Catholic. Tissot remarks that the Protestant minister could not speak the German language of one of the Protestants and so left him. But Tissot "knew enough to be of service and trusts the new convert and the old Catholic were fellow travelers to Heaven. The tranquil passing of the Catholics impressed all who stood by . . . many Catholics of another division . . . gladly took advantage of [Tissot's] presence to make their confessions."[28]

In the night hours before the October 4, 1862, battle of Corinth, the "the fighting chaplain" John Bannon disdained his own sleep and rations to give his men the sacraments of extreme unction and confession. Going from one watch fire to another all night long, the thirty-three-year-old Irishman woke up soldiers, heard their confession, then sent them to summon others. Several hours later, as troops prepared to attack Union fortifications at Corinth, he went along the lines of troops as they stood in ranks anointing them with the oil of extreme unction before they launched their ill-fated attack. As one writer later said, "no men fight more bravely than Catholics who approach the sacraments before battle."[29]

Finally, the only Catholic chaplain who was killed of wounds received during the Civil War died while ministering the Catholic sacraments on the battlefield. At Jonesborough, Georgia, on July 31, 1864, as Confederates were retreating from the field, the Benedictine Emmeran Bliemel (10th Tennessee) went back to the badly wounded Colonel William Grace, and bent over his commanding officer to administer extreme unction. He was struck by a cannonball and died instantly, though his body could not be removed until the next day. Bliemel was the first Catholic American military chaplain to be killed in action. He was only thirty-two years old. (His story will be told in greater detail in chapter 9.)

PREACHING MINISTRY

Generally speaking, Protestant theology and public worship focuses more on the proclamation and preaching of the Word of God (the

Bible), whereas Catholic theology and liturgy is more sacramental and ritual at its core. However, Catholic priests were and are also powerful and effective preachers in their own right. While not all Catholic priest-chaplains were gifted speakers, all of them preached as a routine part of their ministry (whether at Mass, or outside of it at less formal gatherings held generally in afternoons or evenings in camp). There were some priest-chaplains (most notably those from Catholic religious orders well-formed in preaching) who became extremely popular preachers outside their own church membership. Priests serving Confederate troops, especially those who preached well, often found a very warm reception from Protestants, who frequently attended their preaching (outside of Mass). (The heavily Protestant South valued good preaching, even if from Catholic priests.)

The Catholic chaplains who gained great preaching reputations consequently had a powerful influence upon both Catholics and Protestants alike during their wartime ministry. Religious orders such as the Jesuits, Redemptorists, and Dominicans were renowned for their outstanding preaching skills, and priest-chaplains from those orders often stood out in that regard. In letters, journals, and diaries, priests such as James Sheeran, Egidius Smulders (both Redemptorists and Confederate chaplains), Constantine Egan (Dominican Union chaplain), Peter Tissot, and Joseph O'Hagan (Jesuit Union chaplains) are noted as prominent examples of such extraordinary preaching.

Peter Paul Cooney, the Holy Cross chaplain of the 35th Indiana, wrote of one Easter he spent ministering in a unit other than his own, "where he preached every evening and about 1,000 attended each night, and not over 100 were Catholic in the brigade." Despite the words of a fellow Jesuit (Hippolyte Gache) that he was "serious, pious and decidedly humorless," Peter Tissot (37th New York) was a fine speaker and a prolific writer who kept a diary that was posthumously published. His diary reveals that he regularly preached to Catholic troops in very effective ways, which many Protestants appreciated and attended as well. Tissot wrote war letters to his brother in France, some of which were later published. In his letter of April 20, 1863, Tissot describes one context in which he preached, and the impact that it had.

On Sundays he preaches in the open mounted on a box. One of the regiments has four Catholic officers, one of whom is a convert, the son of a minister. The officers of all seven regiments are told that the Chaplain will preach to their men, if they, the officers, will be on hand too. They promise. Wherefore at sunset, getting up, not so decorously as efficaciously, on the top of a cask, while the congregation sit round on the grass, and keeping ever before his fancy scenes in Palestine when the Way, the Truth, the Life instructed the people, he preaches with all the fervor he can put into the sermon. Most of his hearers are Protestant. A deputation of officers waits on him after the preaching to beg him to deliver another sermon next Sunday evening and as often as he can. But the regiment soon disbands and the field whitening unto the harvest must be left unreaped.[30]

In the winter days before the Battle of Fredericksburg, the men of Tissot's 37th New York had become dispirited and discouraged. Their regiment had suffered three recent defeats, their numbers had dropped, and their spirits were low. The chaplain pondered what to do to care for the spiritual morale of the men, and came up with the idea of retreats— three days of talks three times a day, on eight different subjects. The impact on the troops was all he had hoped for: "The men came forth from it reformed and radiant. The start had succeeded beyond his rosiest hopes."[31]

Of course, there were some who were, as Tissot described it, "obdurate of heart," especially one "young blade who sadly needed a refurbishing." Tissot writes that he "made up to him in a most winning way, and fervidly painted the joys of a soul in grace." His efforts bore fruit, as at the end of their talk the young fellow left with "instructions to gather a dozen of his own stripe and lead them to the Chaplain's tent; he himself leading the line or bringing up the rear just as it pleased him." The former "obdurate" must have been a great salesman for "at the end of two hours he handed the priest a list of eighteen names. Their bearers were the elite of evil. Through three days and at that, three times a day, he came punctually on the hour to the Chaplain's tent with his reprobate dozen all present. The Chaplain's best work in the army was done by the retreats."[32]

The native Irishman James Sheeran (14th Louisiana) was a clerical "character" who truly stood out from other priests—not just in having been a married man with three children who became a priest after his wife died, but also by the detailed diary he left behind of his Civil War years. By September 1863, the irascible Irishman had made a strong impact, both in action and words, on the Confederate troops of the Army of Northern Virginia. He remarked that he welcomed large crowds at his Masses (including Protestants), often heard confessions until late at night, and noted the numbers who received Holy Communion were consistently large. On Sunday, September 6, 1863, he described having at his Mass "a very large congregation, so much so that I feared the galleries might break down. I observed a great many Protestant officers and some citizens present."[33]

By April 1864, Sheeran had become good friends with General Richard Ewell and his new wife (and first cousin) Lizinka Campbell Brown. (Ewell had in fact given Sheeran a small tent for his personal use.) Lizinka was strongly Episcopalian in her beliefs, but respected Catholic teaching and loved discussing religion. Having frequently visited their tent and shared food with them, he was asked by Ewell to "have service at his headquarters every other Sunday." But Sheeran replied, "I told him not. There were too many Catholics who needed my services, but I might preach for them occasionally." Just two days before on April 19, 1864, Sheeran had preached a special sermon at 3:30 in the afternoon, and the commanders "had relieved all those who wished to go to 'preaching' from all camp duties. As a result, I had an immense congregation. . . . I addressed the assembled thousands for over an hour and was never more edified with the attention and good conduct of my audience . . . every head was uncovered during the sermon. One of the Mississippians was heard to say 'That fellow is not afraid to talk!'"[34]

Sheeran's fellow Redemptorist, the Belgian-born Egidius Smulders, was chaplain of the 8th Louisiana, and had been Sheeran's pastor and spiritual director before he had become a priest. Smulders had a long, distinguished career as a Redemptorist before and after the war, and was known (as many members of that order are) as an extremely gifted speaker. He was fluent in four languages (French, German, Flemish, and English), and his preaching of "parish missions" across the country (i.e., extraordinary preaching and ministry events in parishes) was the principal heritage he left behind when he died at age seventy-three. One layman witnessed to the power of his preaching when he wrote "he preaches a very important sermon . . . you might have heard a pin fall up the floor, so breathlessly did the congregation listen, and they gave audible signs of their emotion."

Though he wrote little of his work, Smulders was not only chaplain of the 8th Louisiana, he was also an 1864 hospital chaplain in South Carolina, and preacher of wartime missions in Richmond, Lynchburg (1865) and Charleston (1863). He later wrote to his superior that at the Charleston mission, although it lasted three weeks and was very well-attended, the church was constantly in range of a persistent Yankee bombardment. The people showed no fear and attended the mission, but one evening the bombing was so bad that Smulders had the congregation kneel and recite three Hail Marys. Apparently in answer to prayer, the shelling stopped very soon thereafter, because water had gushed onto the island from which the Union was firing, and the shooting was halted. Bad weather then prevented further shelling for the following days, thus allowing the preaching of the mission to remain the dominant sound in the church.

In May 1864, Smulders and Sheeran endeavored to hear the confessions of all Catholics in Lee's army. After the war he wrote about this period of his life, remarking that

> after I got well enough [from dysentery] and before I returned to the Army, I made my retreat of ten days. And these were the most happy days of the campaign. I returned to camp and, as usual, Father Sheeran and myself tried to hear all the Easter confessions of Lee's army. Then commenced the famous campaign in the Wilderness, Spotsylvania Court House, Richmond, and Petersburg. . . . The last three months, I spent mostly along the prisoners of war. I said Mass in the prison, heard as many confessions as I could, prepared daily ten or fifteen for death, and gave a retreat to 700 of them who were paroled and kept in a camp near Salisbury.[35]

PRESENCE ON THE BATTLEFIELD

How priests choose to minister during a battle depended upon their personality and unique style. A common procedure for many chaplains was to be in the hospital where the wounded were coming. In fact, Civil War chaplains were considered part of the medical staff in the structure of the Army. Peter Tissot seems to have viewed the chaplain's role in this way, writing in one place that a chaplain's place was in the hospital instead of at the front. "A chaplain should expose himself as little as possible. If he does expose himself, he may be of service to a few ... but if in doing so he is killed, he will deprive numbers of others of his services after battle." However, the regimental surgeon later stated that Tissot was "often in the thickest of the fight, and on more than one occasion, his life was in imminent danger, for at Fair Oaks his horse was shot under him."[36]

However, other chaplains like John Bannon, Paul Gillen, and Michael Nash clearly made the decision that they needed to be near the front, with their troops. Stories abound in diaries and letters of these three, and many other Catholic chaplains, being on the actual battlefield, during the conflict, ministering to wounded and dying, and even "taking charge" if needed. After the battles, it was routine for many priests to walk or ride the field, ministering to the dead and wounded they found (belonging to both sides), and the needs they found were nearly always overwhelming. Several examples illustrate this courageous but dangerous aspect of the ministry these daring chaplains chose to engage in.

The amazing Paul Gillen of Notre Dame, the oldest Catholic chaplain on either side (age fifty in April 1861), was also one of the longest-serving and most active, tromping all around Union encampments and over battlefields administering the sacraments and spiritual aid wherever he could. Upon his death 1882, one Civil War veteran wrote a letter specifically to mention "his great services in the army." He went on to say that Gillen's "devotion to his men while in the field was remarkable. During the heat of battle, he would frequently expose himself to great danger in order to administer the rites of the Church to the dying man and at last his commanding officer was obliged to order him to the rear as he was constantly in danger from the fire of the enemy. He gained the greatest respect of the men of his regiment both Catholic and Protestant."[37]

In early September 1862, when Jeremiah Trecy arrived at the camp of the Catholic General William Rosecrans, he immediately became busy with "routine" priestly work, saying Mass and hearing confessions of both officers and men. When the battle of Iuka (September 19, 1862) broke out several days later, although it was the first time he "saw the elephant," Trecy quickly distinguished himself by his courageous presence on the battlefield and with the wounded.

> At one time when there was considerable confusion, he rode forward and, in his masterly and powerful voice, commanded a halt, which was obeyed. He then began upbraiding the officers and men for turning their backs to the enemy . . . and stopped a panic at this particular place. [Then] . . . the enemy's artillery made havoc in the demoralized ranks. The priest's attention was now called to the wounded men going in swarms to the rear and on those he remained in incessant attendance until darkness set in, when he repaired to the hospital where he gave his services to such of the wounded as needed them. It was two o'clock the next morning before, tired and weary, he was able to seek some repose.[38]

In seeking that repose, Trecy stumbled upon John Ireland hearing confessions at night for troops in his 5th Minnesota regiment who thought they too might soon be fighting. After eating and getting some sleep, the next morning "the two fathers proceeded to the hospital to look after the wounded. [General Sterling] Price had fled during the night. The wounded were moved into Iuka, and the priests had plenty to do. They were careful to show no favor to Federals or Confederates, but to give their service equally to all."[39]

Roy Honeywell, the author of an excellent, comprehensive overview of American chaplains, mentions that Civil War chaplains were occasionally asked to serve as aides-de-camp or assistant surgeons, sometimes even placed in charge of refugee camps, hospitals, or ambulance trains—all without relinquishing their spiritual duties. Richard Christy (78th Pennsylvania), an American-born priest serving a primarily non-Catholic regiment, was one such example. During the Atlanta Campaign, when the officer of the supply train guard had not appeared, Christy buckled on a sword and took the train through. Such courage and willingness to share the hardships of the troops, despite his rank and vocation, made chaplains like Christy extremely popular figures. At New Hope Church in the Atlanta Campaign on May 27, 1864, he was again conspicuous for his leadership and bravery. One officer wrote of him:

> The enemy was swarming in our front and overlapping us on the left. Father Christy, undeterred by the terrible cross fire, was continually moving along our line, helping the wounded into the woods in our rear; and those men too badly hurt to help themselves, he took up in his arms and bore to a place of safety. About sunset, our ammunition began to fail . . . I called to Father Christy and asked him to hunt up . . . our brigade commander, and make known our situation, and the absolute necessity for an instant supply of ammunition . . . Our chaplain soon returned with the information . . . however [he] had begged ammunition from a regiment in our rear and his pockets and handkerchief were stuffed with the much-needed stuff. The enthusiasm of the soldiers was raised to its utmost, at this brave conduct of their chaplain. . . .[40]

Christy is also an excellent example of the jack-of-all-trades nature of the best chaplains of either side. He was not hesitant to help with whatever job he could assist with during his service. In 1862, with the struggle at Fort Donelson looming, his brigade was suddenly ordered to assist Grant, leaving many sick and wounded behind. As was later related to David Conyngham, "such was the confidence in the energy and ability of Father Christy, that everything was placed in his charge. Not only had he to move the sick, and procure transportation, but he also had to provide for their necessities, acting in the triple capacity of priest, quartermaster, and commissary."[41]

The always expressive Peter Tissot, even though not on the battlefield at Fredericksburg, wrote honestly of his own fears amidst the horrors of that day.

> The Chaplain frankly avows he would have been much more at home were he far away from that carnival of death. When the wounded began to be brought to the field hospital he visited their quarters to prepare them for death. Although the position was sheltered by a ridge, cannon balls would drop as near as a couple of yards, dashing the men with earth. In the precincts of a captured battery his men were lying about in the muck of soil and blood. No fire could be lit, and in the black darkness many confessed to the unseen priest. A short while before midnight he is back again to the hospital after being rudely jarred by falling into three trenches, so dark was the night.[42]

Like all Civil War troops, chaplains were not immune from fear and trepidation at the onset of battle. It appears that some chaplains consciously chose not to go onto the battlefield itself (Hippolyte Gache may have been one example). Just as some soldiers more readily overcame their fears to act with enormous courage in battle, so too with Catholic chaplains. Nearly all ministered long and wearying hours in camp, at hospitals, and with the sick, but it was a far smaller number who demonstrated that extreme courage of being active on a deadly battlefield with their men. Some of the priests who regularly did were Michael Nash, Jeremiah Trecy, Richard Christy, Paul Gillen, James Sheeran, Isadore Turgis, Darius Hubert, Peter Paul Cooney, James Dillon, William O'Higgins, John Ireland, Emmeran Bliemal, John Bannon, Joseph Jarboe, and William Corby. All are recorded as having been in the thick of battles ministering to the dying and wounded, with a few occasionally even assuming a leadership role in absence of superior officers. Those priests who, like the troops they served, risked their lives to be in the middle of the fighting, were never forgotten—and rose to a new level of appreciation among the troops.[43]

THE CURIOUS ROLE OF LIQUOR
IN PRIESTS' MINISTRY

Alcohol and its consumption to excess, as Civil War historians know well, was a perennial issue for troops dealing with the boredom of camp life, being far away from home, and facing the terrors of battle. Intoxication was one of the "standard" sins that all chaplains preached against in camp—the full list being drunkenness, profanity, sexual sins, and Sabbath-breaking (in the South, dueling was added). Intoxication was not in itself a military offense, and indeed in Union armies, a whiskey ration was often given to troops after a long and difficult battle. (William Sherman's division was issued whiskey rations as often as three times daily after Shiloh.) Among Confederate troops, alcoholic consumption was different only in degree. "Of an estimated 64,000 gallons daily output of spirits produced in the South, a fair portion of it eventually reached the armies. . . . The enlisted man seems to have escaped the charge of drunkenness, not through any unusual show of moral strength, but simply because his share of the alcoholic beverages available was 'cinched' by his superiors, the officers, and surgeons."[44]

As nearly all chaplains did, many Catholic priests felt they needed to address this issue specifically, especially those working in predominantly Irish regiments. One priest lamented that payday meant drinking and "a picture of hell I had never seen." Francis McAtee wrote that he "made himself Chief of Police" on paydays, "when King Alcohol oftentimes vanquished Mars, producing a Saturnalia in camp." Joseph Dillon became particularly noted for attempting to "guard" his troops from drunkenness, the "father of all crimes" as he declared. His campaign in the 63rd New York earned it the name "Temperance Regiment," with hundreds of men joining the temperance movement and receiving unique medal coins to help them honor their commitment. Several prominent officers were induced by Dillon to hold offices in this society. Another Notre Dame chaplain, Peter Cooney, regularly sent money from his Irish regiment home on behalf of troops to help them remain temperate and judicious in both camp and battle. He believed more men would take the pledge and would keep their word if he didn't demand too much at one time, so he simply asked them to promise not to drink for only six months or a year.[45]

Catholic priests have no intrinsic problem with having a drink occasionally—indeed, wine with a certain required percentage of alcohol is needed for every Mass they say. Thus when reading the writings of some chaplains—Protestant and Catholic—one discovers that liquor occasionally played an important role in their ministry. It does not surprise any Civil War afficionado that sometimes soldiers needed to be "motivated" in unexpected ways—not only to continue to do their duty in truly difficult times and foreign places, but also to endure horrific pain and suffering during or after battles. Thus, we discover a surprising number of Catholic chaplains who wrote about their experiences of using liquor in various motivational ways with troops.

A few days after Gettysburg, Joseph O'Hagan brought a bottle of wine and clean clothing to Thomas Dooley, a hospitalized former Georgetown student of his. As mentioned above, Jeremiah Trecy carried two canteens with him on battlefields, but he was far from the only chaplain to do so—his southern Catholic compatriot John Bannon also did so regularly. At Pea Ridge (March 7–8, 1862), Bannon moved among his brigade's wounded armed with his oils for anointing, tourniquets, and a bottle of whiskey. The memoirs of General Dabney Maury record that on their retreat from Corinth, Bannon told him, "'General you are tired, take a drop of whiskey.' The good Father never drank a drop himself, but was indefatigable in his care for the wounded and wearied people, and always carried into battle a quart canteen full of good whiskey."[46]

Even the rather "proper" Jesuit, Hippolyte Gache, made this remark in a letter to a Jesuit confrere about how he preserved his health in the difficulties of Civil War ministry. "I am getting along very well here, in spite of all the petty inconveniences of camp life. . . . But do you know how I preserve my precious health? I'll tell you in a low voice. Now don't be scandalized, and whatever you do, don't tell anyone else. I've been taking w-h-i-s-k-e-y. Of course, I don't like it and never will. But certain trustworthy people assure me that it is a sine qua non for the life I lead. Hence reason dictates that I finish off a bottle every ten days." In the immediate days after the Confederate surrender, Gache recovered in the Washington, DC, Jesuit house from his poor health by drinking "undiluted water . . . [thanks to] this appallingly pure beverage . . . I soon found myself feeling chipper and again capable of doing great things."[47]

Two other Notre Dame priests are also notable for their connection to drinking. One was the science professor, Joseph Carrier, who arrived at Vicksburg in the summer of 1863 after a long, wearying, and arduous journey from Indiana. Exhausted from the trip, he went immediately to General William Sherman's tent (whose Catholic wife had instigated the process leading to Carrier's arrival), and in great thirst, before even introducing himself, immediately asked for something to drink. "Porter or wine?" General Sherman asked him. Carrier took the port, and only after drinking a few sips did he proceed to introduce himself formally to the general, who had been expecting him. On the other hand, his more elderly confrere Paul Gillen got in a bit of trouble when a letter about his supposedly excessive drinking was sent to his superior at Notre Dame. Upon investigation, the matter was dropped, and he continued to serve three years as one of the war's most active, effective chaplains. (I will not comment on any possible connection between that allegation of drunkenness and the fact that Gillen was rarely sick or absent from the troops during his three years!)

There is even a rather humorous story about how whiskey may have made a convert. An occasional chaplain himself, Bernard McQuaid (pastor of St. Patrick Cathedral in Newark and later a bishop), told the story of how he made a convert through whiskey at a Fredericksburg hospital in May 1864. A wounded Protestant soldier was enduring a long, sleepless night, and watched Father McQuaid intently as he was giving small doses of liquor to a soldier in critical condition as part of his ministering. Later the Protestant told the priest that if it was his faith that taught him to care for his neighbor in that way, he too wished to become Catholic.[48]

At least one Protestant chaplain is known to have carried liquor as well, the well-known chaplain of the 1st Tennessee, medical doctor, and Episcopalian priest Charles Todd Quintard. After the October 1862 battle at Perryville, he speaks of carrying a canteen filled with whisky "to help the wearied and broken down keep up in the march." However, another Protestant chaplain from the Reformed tradition, which did not condone drinking, had some issues with Catholic clergy "imbibing," as one incident revealed. Congregationalist minister Joseph Twichell had become a friend of his fellow chaplain Joseph O'Hagan in the Excelsior Brigade, but was a little taken aback when he visited O'Hagan's Jesuit community in Georgetown in March 1862. He found the Jesuits enjoying one of their community times, when cigars and alcohol were available for a time while they were socializing. In a later letter about that visit, Twichell referred to the Jesuits' "fleshy indulgences," indicating that he at least did not appreciate the unique Christian teaching of "all things in moderation."[49]

OTHER MINISTRIES AND UNIQUE BENEFITS

As we have seen, the ministries that Catholic priests performed during the war were diverse and wide-ranging. Most were directly connected to camps, battlefields, and hospitals, but others were broader than that, extending even after the war and encompassing many varied activities. Some of the unique and different ministries Catholic chaplains of the Civil War also undertook were as follows:

- Catholic religious sisters needed special patronage, guidance, and chaplaincy as they performed their good works, especially when traveling to new places to minister. A number of priests (Louis Lambert, James Sheeran, Francis Leray, Dominic Manucy, Joseph Jarboe, Hippolyte Gache, Patrick Coyle, Peter McGrane, and James Bruehl, for example) had special relationships with specific orders of nuns, and some were chaplains to convents during the war years. Some accompanied the nuns as they traveled to new places—Charles Croghan did so in the latter part of the war, bringing eight Sisters of Mercy from New York City to their new ministry in Charleston, and also the Jesuit James Bruehl, who in July 1862 accompanied nine Sisters of Mercy from New York to Beaufort, South Carolina. Some priests also recovered from their wounds or sickness in convents, where better and more personal care could be obtained.

- After being captured and released at Vicksburg, John Bannon went to Europe in late 1863 on a special mission for the Confederate government in an attempt to win the Vatican's support and curtail Irish immigrant enlistments for the Union cause in his native Ireland. However, the long-term effects of these campaigns were relatively fruitless, as were the overseas attempts of several other American bishops to influence European nations for their causes (John Hughes of New York, Michael Lynch of Charleston, John Fitzgerald of Boston, Michael Domenec of Pittsburgh, and the Benedictine Boniface Wimmer).[50]

- Even though literacy rates were high for most Civil War soldiers (estimated at 80 percent for Confederates, and 90 percent for Union troops), reading, writing, or mailing letters on behalf of soldiers was still a common practice for chaplains. In *The Union War*, Gary Gallagher notes that one Union regimental chaplain sent out 3,855 letters in a single month.[51] Catholic chaplains were no exception, with a number of chaplains working in a clerical capacity for their troops. Michael Nash described in one of his letters how "men come to me at all hours . . . to read and write letters." Priests were at times trusted with the disposition of a soldier's effects and last letters to loved ones.[52]

- Some chaplains routinely brought soldiers' pay and packages to the express offices. We have already mentioned Peter Cooney in this regard, but Peter Tissot in April 1862 remarked that he "brought the men's money to the express office . . . had about 100 packages. During my two years, I brought thousands of packages to the express. Only one was ever lost . . . the men would hardly trust another besides the Chaplain." Joseph O'Hagan and William Corby kept accurate records of all the deposits they held for soldiers from various regiments.[53]

- Several Catholic priests ministered for a time in Civil War prison camps, including Andersonville, Georgia (Peter Whelan, Anselm Usannez, Henry Clavreul, William Hamilton), Point Lookout, Maryland (Basil Pacciarini), Camp Douglas, Illinois (Patrick J.

Murphy, an occasional chaplain), and Salisbury, North Carolina (Egidius Smulders).

- The Jesuit Bernadin Wiget was the confessor to Mary Surratt (executed as a co-conspirator in planning Lincoln's assassination), a character witness at her trial, and accompanied her to the gallows when she was hung, wearing his white stole. He can be seen standing close to her in the famous picture of that execution.[54]
- The chaplain of the 17th Illinois Cavalry, Edward O'Brien, went on after the war to briefly hold the post of superintendent of refugees for the Cape Girardeau, Missouri, district of the Bureau of Refugees, Freedman, and Abandoned Lands (from June to December 1865).[55]
- The much-beloved Charleston priest, Peter Whelan, ministered to both Henry Wirz (in prison) and Jefferson Davis (at Fort Monroe, Virginia) after the war. As related elsewhere in this book, Whelan, Anselm Usannez, and William Hamilton (Andersonville chaplains) all felt that Henry Wirz's death sentence was unjust, and that he was merely a symbolic scapegoat.
- The southern Jesuit chaplain Darius Hubert boarded the ironclad CSS *Virginia* (*Merrimack*) on March 8, 1862, to minister to some Louisiana soldiers he knew who were serving aboard. He was the only Catholic chaplain formally detailed to serve as a navy chaplain.[56]

In closing, despite the challenges and burdens of their far-reaching and heavily liturgical Civil War ministry, Catholic priest-chaplains did have some unique benefits which came to them simply because of who they were. There was an unspoken bond uniting Catholic clergy and laity in the strongly anti-Catholic milieu of nineteenth-century America, thus various amenities were available to Catholic priests that were not as easily accessible to other chaplains. Catholic priests were a rare sight in many areas of the United States. Because of the great respect priests generally had among the laity, however, they frequently found Catholic homes where they were quickly welcomed, and (depending on the resources of the family) would receive food, drink, clothing, and even a comfortable bed. In return, they would minister to the family or surrounding Catholics as best they could given the march they were on or time they had.

There was a built-in network of Catholic dioceses, bishops, and churches in all but the most remote areas of the country to which chaplains could quickly connect as they passed through. We have already referred to the three Union chaplains (O'Hagan, Tissot, and Scully) who stayed in Richmond churches at Bishop McGill's episcopal residence for several weeks after they were captured during the Peninsula Campaign of 1862. James Sheeran's extensive diary at times reads like a travelogue of different priests and churches he spent time with during his three years of marches with the Army of Northern Virginia. (True to Sheeran's outspoken nature, his diary reveals his unvarnished thoughts about many of them.)

Chaplains who belonged to religious orders, such as the Jesuits and Redemptorists, found immediate accommodation and hospitality at the religious houses they encountered along the way of their travels. The bond of Catholic religious life, and the emphasis on community life present in those residences, meant that traveling priest-chaplains — especially if they were brothers from the same order — would nearly always find a warm welcome, food to eat, and a place to sleep for as long as was needed. The convent of the Daughters of Charity in Emmitsburg, Maryland, demonstrated a unique and striking example of religious hospitality during the war. Aside from the priest-chaplains who found food and a brief respite there, the nuns fed troops passing by before and after the Battle of Gettysburg (July 1–3, 1863), sent eleven sisters to the battlefield to care for the wounded, baptized dying soldiers (including some sixty Confederates), searched the battlefield for living amidst the unburied dead, and continued their care for the wounded long after the battle.[57]

Two post-battle anecdotes capture the enormous impact that the religious care and spiritual concern of both Catholic priests and nuns had on many during the horrible sufferings of the war. An old man traveled to Emmitsburg after the Battle of Gettysburg to find his wounded son. He checked into the Gettysburg Hotel, and upon seeing the Daughters of Charity coming and going from the hotel, caring for wounded soldiers, he asked the hotel's owner, "Good God, can those

Sisters be the persons, whose religion we always run down[?]" The owner replied: "Yes . . . they are the very persons, who are run down by those who know nothing of their charity."[58] The same sentiment was expressed by a clergyman of the Methodist Episcopal Church, who wrote after the war acknowledging the broad scope of work of Catholic chaplains had done. "I truly express the sentiments of thousands of my own faith, when I say that a more unselfish, more devoted, more courageous set of men never served in any army."[59]

PART 2

THE GIANTS OF CATHOLIC CHAPLAINCY

Every morning before the battle would commence
(for there were five days of fighting), I would come out
before the regiment drawn up in line of battle, and after
offering a prayer and making an act of contrition, all repeating
with me, I gave absolution to them while kneeling.

—FATHER PETER PAUL COONEY,
35th Indiana

CHAPTER 4

THE ORIGINAL "FIGHTING IRISH"

Notre Dame's Chaplains

It was the year 1888. The well-known Bishop John Ireland of St. Paul, Minnesota (former chaplain of the 5th Minnesota), was preaching in the pulpit of a new Catholic church in northern Indiana. The pew nearby was occupied by an old priest who was clad in gold vestments, sporting a tremendous white beard and flowing silver locks. His name was Father Edward Sorin, and he was celebrating his fiftieth year of priesthood. Archbishop Ireland was making the most of a rather lengthy and typically Episcopal discourse, but old Father Sorin suddenly perked up when he heard these words:

> It is a lamentable fact that few priests were sent to the front to minister to the soldiers. Father Sorin's community was weak in numbers; the absence of even one stopped important work at home. He sent forward seven to serve as chaplains. . . . Father Sorin appealed to the Sisters of the Holy Cross; and they . . . rushed southward to care for the wounded and soothe the pillows of the dying. Few things in the past half century were done to break down more effectually anti-Catholic prejudice than the sending of [these people] There were other priests, and other Sisters in the war . . . [but none excelled] those of Holy Cross . . . in daring feat and religious fervor. Father Sorin, you saved the honor of the Church.[1]

Just who was Edward Sorin? He was a member of a Catholic religious order called the Congregation of the Holy Cross, which had been founded in 1837 in France by Abbe Basil Moreau. Sorin had been sent to America as a missionary in the early 1840s. In 1842 he opened a little French boarding school in the wilds of Indiana which few thought would amount to anything. But as the head of this little school, he would send eight priests to render spiritual aid to Civil War soldiers (seven became chaplains), and influence over sixty nuns from the Sisters of Holy Cross to serve as nurses. No other Catholic institution in America, and only one other Catholic religious order (the Jesuits, who have no female order associated with them) made such a huge contribution of professional religious people to serve Civil War soldiers.[2]

In 1860, the University of Notre Dame campus in northern Indiana consisted of only 213 students and thirteen priests. In essence, it was basically a French boarding school with a prep school, college, manual labor school, and a seminary. There also was a girl's academy across the street with some two hundred nuns in residence; it had moved there six years previously, and eventually would become St. Mary's College. In mid-1861, as superior at Notre Dame, Father Sorin was convinced (as so many were at the time) that the war would not last long—so he did not assign any priests to help the troops.

However, at the request of the local bishop John Henry Luers, toward the end of June 1861, Sorin sent Paul Gillen to Washington, DC, the headquarters of the Union's Grand Army. While in the Northeast on university business, Gillen had been impressed with the numbers of Catholics joining the Union army, and appealed to Sorin to become a chaplain. About the same time, another Holy Cross priest—James Dillon, also in the East on business—had become acquainted with the officers recruiting for the 63rd New York. He volunteered to be their chaplain, and Sorin approved. The facts that gave rise to the well-known "fighting Irish" nickname of Notre Dame University were about to unfold. Here are the seven Holy Cross priests who served in some capacity during the Civil War: Julian Bourget (Mound City Hospital in Illinois), Joseph Carrier (6th Missouri), William Corby (88th New York, Irish Brigade), Peter Paul Cooney (35th Indiana), James Dillon (63rd and 182nd New York, Irish Brigade), Paul Gillen (170th New

York, Corcoran's Irish Legion), and Zepherin Leveque (New York State Militia). All seven will be discussed in greater detail below.

PAUL GILLEN (170TH NEW YORK) AND JAMES DILLON (63RD AND 182ND NEW YORK)

Paul Gillen (1810–1882) was a "late" vocation, joining the Holy Cross priests and brothers only just before the Civil War broke out. He was a lean, wiry, native-born Irishman, who previously had been a newspaper agent for the *Boston Pilot* (Catholic paper). Though in his fifties at the time, Gillen would be with his soldiers for three years until discharged in July 1865, and was never known to have been incapacitated during the entire war. He became the oldest of all Catholic chaplains of either side to serve as a formal chaplain, and perhaps also one of the most indomitable.

Gillen began ministering to the heavily Catholic Irish Brigade upon his July 1861 arrival in Washington, DC. He followed them to the Manassas battlefield, overtaking the 22nd New York just before the battle began. Although he heard confessions late into the night, his spiritual work was unfinished when the troops were ordered to advance. So, he gave general absolution to all who had not been able to make it to confession. The next day, as many Catholics and others lay dead on that field, the Union army beat a hasty retreat to Washington; Father Gillen was with them.

Gillen's regular chaplain's work then began, although at first he only sought to be a roving chaplain, not wanting a formal officer's commission in the United States Army to "tie him down." To do this work, he rigged up a unique contraption—a horse-drawn buggy carrying all his supplies, which could be converted into a sleeping compartment, eating quarters, or a chapel as needed. With this unique contraption, Gillen drove from one Union regiment to another, administering the sacraments and giving comfort to whatever Catholic soldiers he found. Only after General Ulysses S. Grant issued an 1862 order against civilians and unauthorized vehicles being within the army's lines was Gillen forced to obtain a formal commission as chaplain of the 170th New

York (Corcoran's Irish Legion) in order to could freely continue with his chaplain's work.[3]

The soldiers were always amazed at the "elderly" Gillen's energy and courage, as he frequently exposed himself to danger on the battlefield to administer the sacraments to soldiers. He also walked seemingly unafraid behind enemy lines after battles, a practice that led to at least one amusing incident. Upon returning to Union lines after the battle of Drainsville (December 1861), Gillen was mistaken for a Confederate, and was met by General John Reynolds, who examined his pass and asked if he was not afraid of being captured. Gillen said "not in the least—I have strong forces at my back in cavalry, artillery and infantry." Reynolds said "Go on then," and after Gillen had left, remarked to his staff that Gillen "was the damndest venturesome old clergyman" he had ever seen.[4]

Though Gillen was always held in good standing by soldiers and officers, his reputation was in danger of being tarnished in 1861 when a rumor arose about his excessive drinking and money-gathering for personal purposes. These rumors were put into writing by two bishops (Francis Kenrick of Baltimore, and James Wood of Philadelphia) and sent to Father Sorin at Notre Dame; they were in fact false. Once Kenrick publicly admitted he had been mistaken, Gillen continued with his service and did not leave until after the surrender at Appomattox. He returned to Notre Dame after the war and only died at age seventy-two in October 1882.

Following the First Battle of Bull Run in August 1861, a second Holy Cross priest was formally sent to Washington, where he soon joined the legendary Irish Brigade and worked with the 63rd New York. James Dillon (1833–1870) was a twenty-eight-year-old Irishman who was full of enthusiasm and a ready talker. He was described by William Corby in his *Memoirs* as "young, but of mature mind, and quite eloquent. He was impulsive and ardent, and threw his whole soul into any good work he undertook. . . . he was a young man in the prime of manhood at the time." His ardent nature was in full display at Malvern Hill (July 1, 1862) when most of the officers in his area had been shot and were out of action. There was great confusion among the troops about whom to obey, when one of the men exclaimed, "This is Father Dillon's regiment!" A chorus began yelling in agreement, "Yes, yes! Give us Father Dillon!" Dillon then began shouting orders to the soldiers, rallied the regiment, and led it until relieved by a more fitting officer.[5]

Though he began his chaplaincy work in the 63rd New York (Irish Brigade), around the late fall of 1862, Dillon was transferred to the command of General Michael Corcoran and became a chaplain in his Irish Legion (the 182nd New York specifically), which was located for a time in Suffolk, Virginia. Of the Catholic chaplains on both sides, there may have been no bigger promoter of temperance issues for his predominantly Irish troops than James Dillon. Drunkenness was endemic to army camp life, but Dillon declared it publicly to be "the father of all crimes." Working with Fathers Corby and Ouellet, Dillon established a Temperance Society, which hundreds of men joined on the spot, and which also increased attendance at Mass greatly. Dillon eventually had medals struck for the approximately seven hundred men who joined the society and took the pledge. "It was not intended to promote total abstinence—a near impossibility with Irish fighting men, Father Corby observed—but rather moderation and the elimination of drunkenness."[6]

Unlike his tough elder compatriot Father Gillen, however, Dillon's health was far more delicate, and the toughness of camp life exacerbated his previous lung troubles. Thus in October 1862, less than a year after mustering in, Dillon was forced by disability to resign his chaplain's commission. Though he attempted to rejoin the Union 2nd Corps troops during the Petersburg Campaign, his health would not allow him to do so, and he returned to Notre Dame. Despite that community's efforts to help him (he went to Europe for a year, then California), Dillon died at the early age of thirty-seven in December 1868 due in large part to the lung problems that were heightened during his time as a chaplain.

WILLIAM CORBY
(88TH NEW YORK "IRISH BRIGADE")

When James Dillon reached Washington in August 1861 and joined the Irish Brigade, he quickly realized that he had far more work than he could handle by himself. He wrote back to his superior, Father Edward

Sorin, and requested that another priest be sent. Thus it was that William Corby resigned his professor duties and headed East to serve the Catholic troops of the Union army.

When one hears mention of Catholic Civil War chaplains, the usual name that springs to mind is that of William Corby (1833–1897). This is in no small part due to his marvelous Civil War memoirs and his postwar prominence, but it also did not hurt to have a wartime comrade (General St. Clair Mulholland) actively promoting his cause postwar. Likewise, having a statue of him erected on the Gettysburg battlefield and a painting dedicated to his Civil War work helped enhance and promote Corby's already stellar chaplain career.[7]

On his own merits, Corby was a unique man. As with nearly one-fifth of all Catholic wartime chaplains, he had been born in the United States (Detroit), studied at Notre Dame, and then ordained there in 1860. He had a rare combination of courage, wisdom, and prudence, and was a marvelous writer and speaker. His influence on the officers and men of the 88th New York, and the Irish Brigade in general, was indeed profound and long-lasting. Corby's first battle was on June 1, 1862, at Fair Oaks—a bloody, indecisive battle, in which both sides lost over twelve thousand men combined. Later on the night of the battle, when both sides had retired with their dead and wounded, a weary Corby found an old envelope and scribbled this simple message on the inside: "The battle is over, and we are safe." When Father Sorin finally received the badly battered note, he was so thrilled that he read it to the assembled student body.[8]

The next years would be highly eventful for Father Corby, and most of it is detailed in his excellent biography, *Memoirs of a Chaplain's Life*. The book chronicles not only his actions throughout the war, but that of many of his fellow Catholic chaplains—Paul Gillen, James Dillon, Constantine Egan OP, and many others. Corby spent the next three years with the Irish Brigade in all their worst battles. He was present at Chancellorsville, Antietam, Fredericksburg, and Gettysburg. The losses sustained by the troops in these last two battles severely weakened the Irish Brigade. Corby himself became seriously sick from malaria once, and was at one point the only Catholic priest in the entire Army of Potomac. He frequently ministered to soldiers and officers in a wide variety of ways until late in the night, celebrating regular Masses for the troops, including the special Mass he created with extra pomp and splendor called a "Military Mass."[9]

One anecdote from his famous *Memoirs* illustrates Corby's fine sense of humor. When asked at one time what he did as chaplain, he remarked laconically that Catholic chaplains "spent their time in much the same way as parish priests do—except that we had no old women to bother us, nor pew rent to collect." Another excerpt from his *Memoirs* helps to capture the challenges of his and all Catholic chaplains' ministry. As the Battle of Antietam began on September 1862, Corby describes his frantic actions to prepare his troops for the impending fighting and death.[10]

> I gave rein to my horse, and let him go at full gallop till I reached the front of the Brigade, and, passing along the line, told the men to make an act of contrition. As they were coming toward me on the double-quick, I had time only to wheel my horse for an instant toward them and gave my poor men a hasty absolution, and rode on with General Meagher into the battle. . . . In twenty or thirty minutes after this absolution, 506 of these very men lay on the field, either dead or wounded. . . .
>
> I shall never forget how wicked the whiz of the enemy's bullets seemed as we advanced into that battle. As soon as my men began to fall, I dismounted and began to hear their confessions on the spot. Every instant bullets whizzed past my head . . . the bullets came from the Confederates at very close range.[11]

However, the event for which Corby gained his greatest renown occurred on July 2, 1863, the second day of Gettysburg. As the battle for Cemetery Ridge raged back and forth, at about 4:00 p.m., it became clear the Irish Brigade would be sent forward and certainly face horrible causalities. Corby approached Colonel Patrick Kelly (then in charge) and asked to speak to troops. He mounted a nearby rock, spoke for several minutes, and put on a purple stole (symbolic of priestly authority) over his shoulders. All the soldiers of the Brigade, whether Catholic or not, fell to their knees as they knew Corby was about to pray.

The moment was so poignant and powerful that even the notoriously profane commander of the Second Corps, General Winfield Hancock, removed his hat and bowed his head. Corby blessed the troops and pronounced over them the Latin words of absolution from sin from the Catholic sacrament of confession (called in such circumstances general absolution). The troops then rose and went off into the infamous Wheatfield, where they suffered 198 casualties out of the 530 men making the attack. This powerful scene would be long remembered by Irish Brigade veterans and others. One captain rode up to Corby a week later and told him, "While I have often witnessed ministers making prayers, I never witnessed one so powerful as the one you made that day." To this day, the only Civil War battlefield statue of any chaplain is that of the Catholic priest William Corby on the very rock upon which he stood and prayed at Gettysburg.[12]

After the war was over, the former commander of the 116th Pennsylvania (St. Clair Mulholland) spearheaded an effort to get Corby the Medal of Honor for his wartime courage. The War Department turned this down, which even Corby regretted, not so much for himself but for the patriotic service rendered by thousands of Catholics in the war. Corby would go on to be president of Notre Dame twice after the war, a superior in the Holy Cross order, and the commander of the fraternal GAR (Grand Army of the Republic) Post 569 at Notre Dame—a highly unique post because it was the only one composed of all ordained priests or professed religious. Upon Corby's death in December 1897, his body lay in state for two days and hundreds of mourners accompanied him over snow-covered grounds to his burial site.

JULIAN BOURGET (HOSPITAL),
ZEPHERIN LEVEQUE (HOSPITAL),
AND JOSEPH CARRIER (6TH MISSOURI)

Frs. Gillen, Dillon, and Corby—all Irishmen—went East to serve because of the highly Catholic Irish Brigade and Corcoran Legion. However, the remainder of the Notre Dame religious who contributed to the war stayed near home, serving instead in the West. For the sake of accuracy, we might have entitled this section the "fighting French" — because three of the seven Holy Cross priests who ministered during the war had French roots. They were Joseph Carrier (1833–1904), Julian Bourget (1831–1862), and Zepherin Joseph Leveque (1800–1862). Though both Bourget and Leveque did work briefly as Civil War chaplains, they are considered only occasional chaplains because of the brevity of their service. These two Frenchmen unfortunately became part of the unfortunate Civil War statistic that twice as many soldiers died of sickness than wounds.

Julian Prosper Bourget had been asked by his superior, Father Sorin, to minister to the wounded and dying soldiers at the huge military hospital in Mound City, Illinois, where the majority of Notre Dame's Holy Cross sisters were also serving. He had just come to the United States from the Holy Cross Mother House in France in early 1862, but contracted malaria very soon after arriving at the Mound City hospital complex. He died there in June of 1862 after several months of service. He would certainly not be the first nor the last of Catholic chaplains to live a shortened life because of disease or illness brought about by wartime service.[13]

Zepherin Joseph Leveque was a Canadian Frenchman, a very zealous man, and extremely willing to serve the troops when asked to do so by Father Sorin in 1861. (Sorin had approached Leveque after hearing the rumors of Gillen's supposed intoxication, which proved to be untrue.) Unfortunately, like Bourget, Leveque was also of a sickly disposition. Just a few months after he had arrived in the United States, he too became a wartime casualty, dying in a state of exhaustion in New Jersey in February 1862 after visiting a priest-friend there. Like Gillen, Leveque did not have a formal commission as a military chaplain, but his funeral was attended by members of the 12th New York Militia regiment, an indication of the group he may have ministered to.[14]

The third French priest-chaplain from Notre Dame was Joseph Celestine Carrier (1833–1904). Carrier was a promising young scholar in France who came to the United States in 1855, and shortly thereafter decided to become a priest. His patron was the bishop of St. Paul, Minnesota, who unfortunately died before he could act on Carrier's budding priestly career, so he entered instead the Notre Dame community in 1860 and was ordained the next year. Because of his brilliant intellect he was marked for a scientific career as a faculty member, but his plans were interrupted in the spring of 1863 when Father Sorin received a very distressing letter from a woman he could not easily ignore.

Ellen Ewing Sherman was the wife of General William Sherman, and a very strong Catholic woman. In fact, she had convinced her non-practicing husband in 1862 to allow their children to attend Notre Dame. (Eventually, four of their six children would do so.) Ellen had become quite perturbed over the fact that there were no Catholic chaplains in the Union army around Vicksburg, and that her two Catholic brothers who were there (General Hugh Ewing and Captain Charles Ewing) had no opportunity to attend regular Mass. Thus, she wrote to Sorin asking whether he could send them a priest.[15]

Though his own priestly ranks were greatly depleted, Sorin could not easily say no to a prominent general's wife (especially since they had children studying at Notre Dame), so Joseph Carrier was sent south to Vicksburg in May 1863. He was officially commissioned as chaplain of the 6th Missouri Infantry, but in fact his work extended to the entirety of Grant's army. He arrived just in time to see the forty-seven-day-old siege end, and to send his superior the last issue of the city's newspaper, which had been printed on flowered wallpaper. While in Vicksburg, Carrier not only briefly met the well-known Confederate chaplain John Bannon (1st Missouri CSA), but also briefly visited the sickly chaplain of the 17th Wisconsin, Napolean Mignault, who "was very much enfeebled and suffering badly from chronic dysentery." After the city was taken, Carrier ran into a fellow French priest, the local priest Charles Heuze (1833–1883), a resident at St. Paul's Church, who had lived for fifteen days in his cellar for fear of the Union shelling. Heuze was himself an occasional chaplain to area Confederate troops, and described the horrendous conditions he had faced, remarking that "Sebastapol itself could not have surpassed the horrors of Vicksburg."[16]

Carrier was more bookish than the other Notre Dame chaplains, and seems to have been far more sensitive to the constant presence of sudden death around him. In his book *Notre Dame and the Civil War*, James Schmidt relates a story about Carrier shortly after he arrived at Vicksburg.

In advance of the great "Vicksburg mine" explosion on June 25, 1863, Father Carrier witnessed a Union soldier being killed by a Confederate sniper. Father Carrier was much moved by the terrible sudden . . . death of the soldier and sat at the foot of the tree. Rather than watch the historic detonation, as his fellow officers were doing, Father Carrier fell into a deep and irrepressible reverie, left the scene, went back to camp and threw himself on his cot. To his credit, Father Carrier returned to the lines and ministered to some of the soldiers wounded in the post-explosion charge.[17]

Carrier was only with the army for three months, but his priestly skills were required for two major events that occurred just before he returned to Notre Dame in October 1863. First, he assisted the Sherman family with the sad and untimely death of nine-year-old Willie from fever, ministering to the boy as he died. As related earlier in this book, Carrier also wrote a very important letter to President Lincoln on behalf of Father Sorin and the Holy Cross Order asking for an exemption from the draft for their priests and religious (a conflict all other Catholic religious groups had to deal with as well). Carrier himself went to Washington with that letter, had an interview with Lincoln and Secretary of War Stanton, and won that exemption—thanks to the good support of Generals Sherman and Grant.

Once Carrier was called back to Notre Dame in October 1863, he began his career and placed Notre Dame's science program on a strong foundation. He became curator of the museum there, a longtime professor of chemistry and physics, and later a professor at St. Laurent College near Montreal. There he taught and expertly maintained the St. Laurent museum until his death in 1904.

PETER PAUL COONEY (35TH INDIANA)

The seventh and final Notre Dame chaplain—and arguably the hardest working, most courageous, and perhaps most cantankerous of them all—was Peter Paul Cooney (1822–1905). Cooney was born in County Roscommon, Ireland, came to America when he was five years old, and at age thirty went to study at the University of Notre Dame. Upon graduation, he taught for a time in country schools, then joined the Holy Cross community, and received ordination in 1859. Like other priests of the Holy Cross community, he was preparing to do mission work when the war broke out. He volunteered for service after Governor Morton asked for help with the Indiana troops then being raised, and in October 1861 at age thirty-eight was appointed chaplain to the 35th Indiana. Cooney had one of the longest tenures of any Catholic chaplain in entire Civil War, from October 1861 to July 1865.

Fortunately for us, Cooney immediately began writing letters to his brother in Monroe, Michigan, which describe his work, the regiment's activities, and such personalities as the strongly Catholic William Rosecrans. Described by one writer as "a peppery man," Cooney always signed himself "P. P. Cooney," and was insistent on order and discipline among his Catholic troops.[18] He had no problems speaking out boldly to anyone regardless of their rank. Soldiers and officers alike heard a lecture from him if some correction was needed. However, like all best chaplains, Cooney possessed an enormously generous and courageous spirit, which made him legendary as a Civil War Catholic chaplain.

Cooney was an unusual man and priest in several ways. At the time he became an official chaplain, no distinctive chaplain uniform as prescribed (eventually there was an official, loosely described one). The one Cooney designed for himself instead was certainly unique. He described it as having "quite a military appearance":

> There are gold cords down the side of my pants and on my shoulders . . . black velvet pieces about 4 inches long and 2 inches wide surrounded with gold lace in the shape C-N. The cross in the center is embroidered with gold thread. The C-N, the first and last letter of the word "chaplain," are embroidered with gold also . . . around my hat I wear a gold band with gold tassels. I wear my Roman collar [and] around my waist I wear a blue silk sash with tassels. The whole makes a very appropriate uniform for a priest. The Bishop of Louisville was very well pleased with it.[19]

Thus, as a professed member of a religious order (like the Jesuit chaplains Prachensky and Hubert, who will be discussed in chapter 5), Cooney's vow of poverty did not stop him from "dressing up" his position a bit either! It seems that even his horse had an attitude—Cooney once wrote in a letter to his brother that the horse "carries his head so high that the other day when I was riding him, he struck me with the back of his head in the nose."[20]

Unlike his Eastern religious confreres, Cooney didn't get into any battles until late 1862. Throughout that year, the 35th Indiana was chasing elusive Confederates through Kentucky and Tennessee. As 1863 neared, the regiment (as part of the 3rd Division of Thomas Crittenden's Wing in the Army of the Cumberland) found themselves at Stones River, Tennessee. It was Cooney's first war experience—and he did himself and his community proud. In what was a relative rarity, his commander's official post-battle report had this note: "To Father Cooney, our chaplain, too much praise cannot be given. Indifferent as to himself, he was deeply solicitous for the temporal and spiritual welfare of us all. On the field, he was cool and indifferent to danger, and in the name of the regiment, I thank him for his kindness and laborious attention to the dead and the dying."[21]

Cooney himself described in a letter to his brother what he did at Stones River. "Every morning before the battle (there were 5 days of fighting), I would come out before the regiment drawn up in line of battle, and after offering a prayer and making an act of contrition, all repeating with me, give [general] absolution to them while kneeling. General Rosecrans saw us the first morning, and he was so edified with our example that he sent an order to the Protestant chaplains to do the same. Poor fellows, what could they do?"[22]

Since the most effective Civil War chaplains were the jacks-of-all-trades, Cooney succeeded because he did whatever needed to assist his troops. Certainly that included traditional spiritual work—he built a rustic chapel of evergreen boughs, organized a choir, said Mass daily, heard confessions (one time in Kentucky for eight hours straight before potential battle), and baptized many. But Cooney also went above and beyond the religious norm, as noted by Aidan Germain in his remark that "it was his custom after each payday to return to Indiana with the money of the men of his regiment and distribute it to their families, or deposit it for them, if they were without kin." One time the amount he carried was $24,000.[23]

Like many other chaplains on the battlefield, Cooney was nearly killed numerous times. After the battle of Nashville in 1864, he wrote that "I was standing one time on the battlefield attending a wounded man, and stepped to one side one pace without knowing why, and instantly a cannonball tore up the ground on the spot I occupied but 5 seconds before. Nothing but the protecting hand of God could have saved me." He was later recognized for gallant service at that battle. General William Rosecrans (a devout prewar Catholic convert whom Cooney admired greatly) wrote this about the Irish priest in one of his letters: "The joy of the army, a perfect model of the Christian here. Solely on account of him soldiers consider it an honor to belong to the Army of the Cumberland."[24]

As the long campaigns of 1863 to 1864 in the western theater wore on, Cooney became very weary and deeply fatigued, and consequently expressed a desire to leave the army. The difficult battles he had been through—Chattanooga, Chickamauga, Lookout Mountain, Missionary Ridge, Ringgold, Sherman's March, Franklin, and Nashville—all took an immense toll upon him physically and emotionally. But, when the officers and troops of his regiment learned about his desire to leave the army, there was strong resistance. They franticly petitioned Father Sorin at Notre Dame to intercede and even order Cooney to stay with them. Cooney eventually acquiesced, only leaving the army after nearly four years of continual service in June 1865.

Father Cooney returned to Notre Dame to serve in a variety of ways: as a traveling missionary, the provincial of the order for a time, and a charter member of the Notre Dame GAR (a fraternal order about which more follows below). He died in May 1905, having suffered many health issues in his later life from the exposure and labors of his war years. As the last of Notre Dame's surviving Civil War chaplains, Cooney's funeral was filled with military honors and well-attended by veterans and friends. He is buried in the Notre Dame cemetery, along with the other chaplains and veterans who had later joined the order because of the wartime example of Notre Dame's finest men.

NOTRE DAME'S GRAND ARMY
OF THE REPUBLIC POST 569

The conclusion of the Civil War and the return to religious life led Notre Dame's former chaplains to new pastoral assignments. One might think the war slowly faded from their minds and memories, but in the autumn of 1897, a truly unique event occurred: the former Notre Dame chaplains began on campus their own post of the Grand Army of the Republic, the most active Union veterans' organization in the country. Post Number 569 was the only GAR post composed entirely of ordained priests or professed religious men as members. For men like Corby and Cooney, in the challenging postwar days, the creation of this post was an attempt to stake a claim to both Civil War history and American identity for all Catholics, especially Catholic priests. A newspaper speaking of the event remarked that "in no other country of the world is there to be found a more interesting and unique aggregation of battle-scarred veterans than those forming the very latest post to be added to the Grand Army of the Republic."[25]

The inaugural ceremonies of the new post were held on October 5, 1897. A band played a march before a large and enthusiastic crowd, who watched Peter Paul Cooney being installed as chaplain and William Corby (who died two months later) as the commander of the new post. The speaker that day, General St. Clair Mulholland, couldn't resist a bit of humor as he praised the efforts of the Holy Cross men to keep the memories of the war alive. "On the way to Petersburg I came upon two Irishmen having a chat. One said 'Blarney, I don't know what the divil [*sic*] brought ye here. . . . Why ye came I don't know?' 'Why,' said he, 'I'll tell ye why I came. I am a married man, and came to war to have peace.'" Mulholland then added "Why the members of this post went to war I don't know. They certainly have no such reason as that."[26]

A Notre Dame brother (Aidan O'Reilly CSC) wrote of that event, remarking:

> It is to be regretted that this movement was not begun years ago. Then many of the Brothers, who have since died, would have made the Post twice as large as it is, and would have added many

interesting soldiers into its ranks. Foremost among these would have been Brother Sebastian. He was wounded 7 or 8 times, but until a few years ago sought no pension. Brother Leander one day persuaded him to go to the pension Bureau and make application. He handed in the name of his commanding officer, who [said]: "If old Tom is alive yet above all he deserves a pension. When General Cobb of the Confederates was doing destructive work on our left flank, I ordered Tom (Bro. S) to dismount and rest his piece on my shoulders and aim at General Cobb. This he did, and the General fell. In mounting again Tom received his severest wound."[27]

The priests and brothers of GAR Post 569 kept detailed handwritten notes of their meetings in the years ahead; the minutes were always read, and new eligible veterans were continually added. Many of the new members were priests from other parts of the country who had been chaplains in the war. William Corby's December 1897 funeral was an occasion of great mourning, with the minutes of the Post recording that "we feel the loss so severely that we hardly have courage to pen our feelings." Similar feelings were recorded many times in the years ahead as slowly all the Notre Dame Civil War veterans went to their eternal rewards. As James Schmidt records in *Notre Dame and the Civil War*, "Notre Dame's GAR Post 569 continued to meet and conduct their business, but in time the campfires became less frequent and the minutes less copious, until they consisted of little more than annual ledgers of the very few members still living."[28]

THE HOLY CROSS NUNS

Time and the focus of this book does not permit a fuller development of the topic, but we cannot talk about Notre Dame in the Civil War without mentioning the incredible work done by the Catholic nuns of the Holy Cross community, the sister order of the Holy Cross priests. Founded by Father Basil Moreau (who also founded the men's order) in 1841 in France, the Holy Cross nuns came to Indiana in 1855 to begin St. Mary's Academy in South Bend. By 1860, there were some two hundred nuns teaching there or serving immigrants nearby. The sisters were led by their strong and gifted Irish superior, Mother Angela Gillespie (1824–1887).

Some sixty-three nuns in all were sent to serve as nurses in ten hospitals during the Civil War: in the western theater (including Mound City, Memphis, Cairo, Paducah), in Washington, DC, and even aboard the *Red Rover*, America's first floating hospital. Thus, these Catholic nuns became the first female nurses ever to work aboard a US Navy Hospital Ship. And not to be outdone by William Corby, the Holy Cross nuns also have a monument to their Civil War work. The "Nuns of the Battlefield" monument in Washington, DC, has twelve life-size figures representing all the women's religious orders who served as nurses in the Civil War.[29]

There are dozens of glowing references about the impact the nuns had, but let us just cite one:

> Without doubt, many of the soldiers who were brought to the hospitals laid eyes, for the first time, on women garbed in the habit of a religious. Some were simply curious, others hostile. But there is not a single instance recorded by the Sisters . . . where that hostility persisted. When it came time to die, hundreds of non-Catholic soldiers whispered that they, too, wished to die as Catholics. After the grace of God, nothing but the evident goodness of the Sisters could account for such a change. So salutary was their influence that, from a mere natural point of view, General Sherman demanded that Sisters be placed in charge of all military hospitals.[30]

THE NOTRE DAME INFLUENCE

The impact of the Notre Dame chaplains and nuns in the Civil War was truly unique, perhaps arguably more than any other Catholic order or group (though Jesuit historians might disagree). Over one hundred priests, nuns, or students from Notre Dame served in some capacity as chaplains, nurses, or soldiers during the war. Enrollment at Notre Dame actually increased during the Civil War—including the enrollment of over forty students from Confederate states.

Most of the children of General William Sherman eventually attended Notre Dame, and one student, Orville Chamberlain (74th Indiana), won the Medal of Honor for bravery at Chickamauga. At least ten former soldiers joined the Holy Cross order in the postwar years because of the influence of Notre Dame religious. In 1941, Notre Dame President J. Hugh O'Donnell CSC spoke of this impact and Notre Dame's commitment to serve in the later American wars, saying that "the peaks of Notre Dame are shrouded in war."[31]

CHAPTER 5

"GOD'S MARINES"

Jesuit Chaplains

The men of the Society of Jesus (commonly known as the Jesuits) are legends in the Western Christian world. Their influence has been immense: they've founded hundreds of schools of higher learning (dozens in the United States), developed enormous intellectual prowess, and engaged in worldwide missionary work (in the Americas, Africa, China, and Japan, to name but a few). No less than twenty-one of the Jesuits' American members are connected to Civil War chaplaincy as either official or unofficial chaplains—a number unmatched by any other Catholic religious order or diocese. (This does not include countless other Jesuits who ministered to the troops in other informal capacities during the Civil War.) Despite recent declines in numbers, the Jesuits remain even today the largest Catholic male religious order in the world.

Yet few if any groups in Christian history have generated as much outside suspicion and hatred as the Jesuits. Their work has spawned responses in the form of books with titles like *The Enemy Unmasked* and *The Suppressed Truth of the Lincoln Assassination* (the Jesuits and the Pope were behind it!). No less than US President John Adams wrote to Thomas Jefferson: "I do not like their appearance . . . If ever there was a body of men who merited eternal damnation on earth and in hell, it is this Society of [Ignatius de] Loyola."[1] It did not help that, despite having powerful friends in the decades after its founding, the Society also had wealthy and powerful enemies. Due to political pressure from some of these enemies in several prominent Catholic countries, the Jesuits were suppressed by the Pope for a time (1773–1814). Yet wherever the Jesuits have gone, their influence has been deeply felt.

The Jesuits came into existence in sixteenth-century Europe (1534) when a wounded Spanish soldier named Ignatius of Loyola (1491–1556) had a post-battle conversion experience. Over several decades he began to draw together men willing to follow his unique vision of Catholic fidelity. Three characteristics, the marks of Ignatius's own faith and beliefs, came to characterize the Jesuit ethos throughout the world even to this day.

First, Jesuits were strong defenders of the Catholic Church and the Pope. This was a conscious goal of Ignatius in the volatile, anti-Catholic, post-Reformation world of his time that dealt immense theological criticism and resulted in many defections from the first century, one church of Jesus Christ. Second, they were men who were very well-trained intellectually. Ordination for Jesuits usually did not come until they were thirty-three years of age in order that the candidate might be thoroughly educated and pastorally experienced. To this very day, Jesuits are renowned as educators, and on the eve of the Civil War in 1861, there were no fewer than twelve Jesuit colleges already established in the United States.[2]

Third, and finally, Jesuits possessed enormous missionary zeal and were willing to take the Christian message anywhere in the world. Indeed, it was members of the Jesuit order who evangelized many of Europe's peasants after the Reformation, as well as assisting in bringing the gospel and the Catholic Church to such countries as Brazil, India, China, Japan, Mexico, and the Americas. Throughout the centuries, Jesuits have frequently worked underground in countries whose rulers persecuted Christians, and many of them suffered martyrdom.[3]

The new order grew phenomenally fast after its formal approval in 1540. Membership in the Society went from 3,500 in the first twenty-five years to 11,300 after merely fifty years. For a Catholic Church trying to respond (not always well) to unprecedented attacks from the "upstart" Protestant denominations, the Jesuits quickly became the front-line Catholic shock troops. They quickly gained a reputation as tough, smart, and courageous spiritual warriors who fought against the intellectual attacks of Protestants and would go into any foreign place where a vibrant Catholic presence and education was called for.

When the United States was founded in the late eighteenth century, it was considered by the Vatican to be a missionary territory in need of priests and churches. But the Jesuits had already been there for over one hundred years! The first French missionaries had arrived in the early 1600s, and a steady stream of Jesuits followed. Known as the "Black Robes," much of their early work was with the Native Americans (especially the Hurons), but they also established twenty-three missions between 1687 and 1704 in modern-day Arizona and north Mexico, and built seminaries in Canada. The first Catholic bishop elected in the United States—John Carroll (elected by local clergy, in a rarity)—was a Jesuit. As mentioned earlier in this book, several of the first Catholic clergy to be approved as chaplains for American troops were Jesuits.[4]

Therefore, it was no surprise that Jesuits were in the front ranks of Catholic chaplains in the Civil War. Within one month of the Battle of Fort Sumter, the superior of the Jesuits in America had written to Archbishop John Hughes (New York) to tell him that "their Society would be prepared to furnish . . . for North and South, as many as ten chaplains, speaking all the civilized languages of Europe or America." Although Hughes did not respond to that letter, the Jesuits did serve on both sides of the conflict, with one even attempting to "play" both sides at the same time (Joseph Bixio, whose story is told in chapter 11). Of the 126 Catholic chaplains (official or situational) enumerated in this book, eleven Jesuit priests can be considered formal chaplains. Four were Confederate chaplains and seven were Union, but ten other Jesuits also served occasionally. In all, at least twenty-one Jesuits are recorded as being involved with ministry to Civil War troops in some way. This is far and away the highest number from any Catholic religious order who served as chaplains.[5]

Typical of the Society's international makeup, the Civil War Jesuit chaplains were of mixed nationalities—Irish, French, Italian, Spanish, German, and French Canadians among them. Some had come to the United States when the Jesuits were suppressed after 1773 (they were restored by Pope Pius VII in 1814), with many arriving after the 1848 cultural revolutions, especially those in Italy and Germany. All were highly educated, most were multilingual, and nearly all were European by birth. Five were or would become college presidents (Joseph O'Hagan, Peter Tissot, Bernardin Wiget, Joseph O'Callaghan, and Anthony de Chaignon); several wrote profusely during the war (Peter Tissot, Michael Nash, and Hippolyte Gache). A Jesuit accompanied the controversial Mary Surratt to the gallows (Bernardin Wiget); another ministered on the *Merrimack* during the famous naval battle at Hampton Roads (March 8–9, 1862) and later offered a prayer at the funeral of Jefferson Davis (Darius Hubert). A Jesuit was at nearly every major Civil War battle in the East, and members of the order frequently "faced" each other on the battlefield, likely without ever knowing it.[6]

CIVIL WAR JESUIT CHAPLAINS LIST

I will briefly list all of the twenty-one Jesuits known to have ministered during the war, but for purposes of length, I cannot cover in depth all these informal or occasional chaplains, and unfortunately have to abbreviate some of the full-time chaplains' stories. The Jesuits who will be spoken of at greater length elsewhere in this book will be noted after their names.

Union

Thirteen Jesuits are recorded as serving in some capacity.

> Robert Brady (informal hospital chaplain at various hospitals in Washington, DC)
> James Bruehl (hospital chaplain, Beaufort and New Orleans; see chapter 8)
> Francis McAtee (31st New York)
> Michael Nash (6th New York)
> Joseph O'Callaghan (69th New York Militia)
> Joseph O'Hagan (73rd New York)
> Bernard O'Reilly (69th New York Militia)

Thomas Ouellet (69th New York, and hospital chaplain at
New Bern)
Aloysius Roccofort (informal chaplain at various hospitals in
Washington, DC)
Peter Tissot (37th New York "Irish Rifles")
Charles Truyens (12th Kentucky)
Basil Pacciarini (prison camp chaplain in Point Lookout, Maryland)
Bernardin F. Wiget (US Hospital, Washington, DC; see chapter 8)

Confederate

Eight Jesuits are recorded as serving in some capacity.

Joseph Bixio (informal ministry; see chapter 11)
Andrew Cornette (forts in Mobile, Alabama, area)
Anthony de Chaignon (18th Louisiana)
Hippolyte Gache (10th Louisiana)
Darius Hubert (1st Louisiana)
Francis Nachon (Confederate soldiers in Washington,
Louisiana, area)
Joseph Prachensky (3rd Alabama)
Anselm Usannez (Andersonville prison chaplain)

JOSEPH O'HAGAN (73RD NEW YORK)

During the Civil War, chaplains were usually selected by the vote of
regimental officers. Around late September 1861, a group of tough New
York City soldiers—the 73rd New York Fire Zuoaves—held an election for the type of chaplain they wanted. The results of this election
led to Joseph O'Hagan (1826–1878) becoming one of the first and certainly the youngest of the Jesuit chaplains. (Though a priest, he had not
yet finished his formal Jesuit formation.) O'Hagan was a native-born
Irishman, and became one of the longest serving and hardest working
of all Union chaplains. His wartime relationship with fellow regimental chaplain Joseph Twichell (a Congregational minister, and later a

good friend of Mark Twain) is a moving example of the comraderies beyond denominational differences that developed occasionally during America's deadliest war. However, O'Hagan's introduction to these tough New York firemen of the 73rd New York was rather a personal shock. At the time of his October 1861 election, O'Hagan wrote this of his first impressions of his "flock":

> Such a collection of men, I think, was never before united in one body. . . . Most of them were the scum of New York society, reeking with vice and spreading a moral malaria around them. Some of them had been serving terms of penal servitude at the outbreak of the war, but were released on condition of enlisting in the army . . . about half the regiment (perhaps two thirds) called themselves Catholics, but all the Catholicity they had was the faith infused into their souls by baptism. The majority of these so-called Catholics were the [abandoned] children of Irish parents . . . cast upon the streets of New York [as] pests to society. Fighting was their normal condition, and when they could not meet the common enemy, they "kept their hand in it" by daily skirmishes among themselves. . . .
>
> I returned to the tent assigned me, & never in my whole life, in sickness or health, have I suffered so much as I did on that day in half an hour. What an apostolic priest I was, ready to cry like a homesick girl, because I had not found every rough soldier a cultivated gentleman & a perfect Christian![7]

But, like many other clergy who went through the same experience, O'Hagan later had a change of heart about these tough men. About six months later, he wrote that "the men, being removed from the city and not having the facilities for dissipation at hand, settled down into comparatively decent fellows. I had a neat chapel built and I prepared quite a large number of fellows for their first Confession and Communion. They had become attentive to their religious duties, and I had as much to do in the 10 regiments of the division as I could well look to. My work, though hard, became a labor of love."[8]

Although personally asked by Lincoln himself to become a hospital chaplain in a September 1862 memo, O'Hagan was instead commissioned for the approximately 1,300 Catholics in the 73rd New York, and was a very active, involved, and well-liked chaplain there. He was with his troops through most early battles of the eastern theater, such as the Peninsula Campaign, Second Battle of Bull Run (Manassas), Fredericksburg, and Chancellorsville. O'Hagan and his fellow Union Jesuit chaplain Peter Tissot (37th New York) were captured in the White Oak Swamp on June 30, 1862, during the Peninsula Campaign, when they stayed behind to look after Union wounded. The two of them, along with Thomas Scully, who was also captured, were held for three weeks in Richmond before being paroled.

O'Hagan was forced to resign his position in September 1863 when his superior ordered him back to his college in Frederick, Maryland, to finish his Jesuit formation and take his final vows. But still feeling dedicated to his men, one year later O'Hagan reenlisted with the 73rd New York, and finished out the war with Union troops as they marched triumphantly into Richmond. He went on to thirteen more years of priestly ministry after the Civil War, including becoming president of Holy Cross College in Worcester, Massachusetts. Unfortunately, he died while at sea in December 1878 on his way to California to try and recover his health.

THOMAS OUELLET (69TH NEW YORK), MICHAEL NASH (6TH NEW YORK ZOUAVES), AND FRANCIS MCATEE (31ST NEW YORK)

Another Jesuit chaplain serving in the Army of the Potomac—specifically the 69th New York Irish Brigade—was Thomas Ouellet (aka Willett, 1820–1894). Ouellet was French-Canadian, a short, nimble man known for his great energy, and also his frank, outspoken attitude. No less than the legendary Irish Brigade chaplain William Corby in his famous *Memoirs* called him a "martinet." Ouellet was certainly not afraid to confront anyone—officer or enlisted man—whom he found dishonoring the Catholic faith. On one occasion, for example, he found Catholic soldiers eating breakfast when they should have been at Mass, and he kicked over their coffee pot and forcibly led them to where

Mass was being held. He acquired a reputation for frequently publicly confronting Union officers about their profanity as well.[9]

Ouellet was also known as a very brave and effective chaplain to the troops. He distinguished himself especially at Malvern Hill on July 1, 1862, when he was seen constantly moving up and down the battle lines, even using a lantern at nighttime, to comfort the wounded and dying. All the while, he was exposed to Confederate fire. His pattern was to ask each man he met if he was a Catholic, and if he wished to receive the sacrament of confession (i.e., forgiveness). One soldier he met replied, "No, but I would like to die in the faith of any man who has the courage to come and see me in such a place as this."[10]

Ouellet was one of three priests who were full-time chaplains in the famous Irish Brigade—the other two being Notre Dame's Holy Cross priests, James Dillon (63rd New York) and William Corby (88th New York). In reading Corby's *Memoirs*, one frequently finds Ouellet mentioned as being one of Corby's most regular companions. In the winter of 1862–1863, when death and disease had reduced the 69th New York to a handful of men, Ouellet resigned his position, which was met with great regrets but good wishes from both his regiment and the division. Ouellet then departed for North Carolina, where he served as an official chaplain in the Union hospital at New Bern. He later rejoined a reorganized 69th New York in 1864 in response to the personal request of the new colonel, and served until the end of the war.

After the war, Ouellet worked in parishes in New York and Canada, and in 1879 he began a fourteen-year ministry to Native Americans in the West. Poor health brought him back to Montreal in 1893, and he died there the following year at age seventy-five.

Another chaplain from the Jesuit Georgetown community was Francis McAtee (1826–1904). In fact, both he and Joseph O'Hagan left that Jesuit school together in July 1861 to join the Union army as chaplains. Their superior had assigned these two faculty members to this task with the Union army, and just like his confrere O'Hagan, McAtee too served in a New York regiment—the 31st New York. However, unlike O'Hagan and other Jesuits, much of McAtee's wartime and postwar ministry remains relatively unknown. Germain mentions that he was at the battles of Fredericksburg, Antietam, and Chancellorsville, and that he was with the 31st New York from October 1861 to June 1863.

McAtee did write a brief account of his wartime service later in his life in the Jesuit *Woodstock Letters*, commenting that he "was sent to the army of the Potomac to attend the spiritual needs of a regiment for two weeks, but the time lengthened into two years." When he arrived at his regiment and met the Colonel, he writes that he wondered to himself, "How must a spiritual campaign begin? Neither my own experience nor the sage counsel of other clergymen with whom I had previously associated, had taught me a method of procedure." He immediately made an inspection tour of his troops, and finding himself well-received, he scheduled a Mass for the next morning; "many listened to my invitation and were present daily."[11]

Described later as a gentle and friendly man, even "the ideal priest" according to some soldiers, McAtee also ministered to about thirty Catholics in Captain George Hogg's company of the 2nd New York Heavy Artillery. Hogg commented on his presence in an 1862 newspaper article, remarking that McAtee would add to the Catholics of the 2nd New York Artillery soldiers "from other companies, until he often marched those 60 men down to the camp of the 31st, where stood the little chapel of the Jesuit priest." McAtee also had a supportive patron of sorts in General John Newton (VI Corps, Army of Potomac), for whom he said daily Mass.[12]

In a humorous vein, McAtee described one specific predicament he got in when his regiment was sent away, but he had no transportation to follow them.

How will I proceed? I must become a Cavalryman, I must have a charger to attack the spiritual foe, not only in the front, but I must make raids on the rear and flank. Alas! No one offered me even a mule! Keep away says one. I will not expose my horse to be captured, killed or stolen, says another . . . I made a raid upon a livery stable. Give me the best horse in your equine establishment, says I. Show me the liveliest trotter you own. I'll deposit the greenbacks . . . I paid his salary to the owner, thirty-one dollars.[13]

McAtee wound up with a horse he named Major, who "barely had ten pounds of meat to compress his bones together." But apparently, his hard-won prize served him well, as he wrote later that "everyone admired and no one dared challenge Major." Following the end of his service in 1863, he became pastor in St. Thomas Manor, Maryland, where half of his three thousand parish members were Black, and a fire had destroyed the church and residence the year before. He ministered next in Philadelphia, celebrated his golden jubilee of priesthood in 1895, and died in March 1904 at the ripe old age of seventy-nine.

Michael Nash (1825–1895) was another native Irishman—a witty, eloquent man who arrived in America with his father in 1825 and helped begin Fordham College in 1846. In June 1861, at age thirty-six, he volunteered and enrolled in New York City to serve two years as a military chaplain. Nash served a very colorful group of Federal soldiers known as the 6th New York Zouaves, under the even more colorful Colonel Billy Wilson. Wilson was himself only a nominal Catholic and not well educated in the faith, but he was very pleased to have his own Catholic chaplain. Much like O'Hagan's 73rd New York, these 6th New York Zouaves were nearly all raised in Catholic homes yet were without much in the way of religious formation. They were a ragtag, motley group, poorly disciplined, and famous for their devilment, drinking, and mischief.

On June 15, 1861, the 6th New York set sail for Fort Pickens, Florida, and Santa Rosa Island, a forty-five-mile-long spit of sand off Rebel-held Pensacola in the Gulf of Mexico. (Coincidentally, another Jesuit chaplain, Hippolyte Gache, had been a Confederate chaplain there across the bay in Pensacola just a month before. It is unknown whether the two Jesuits met.) It was the only Union stronghold in the area, and it was the job of the 6th New York to reinforce it and keep it from General Braxton Bragg's Confederates. Fortunately for later historians, Nash wrote eleven long letters while he served in Florida, leaving a brief but intense portrait of his two years of military service. He had a full and lively ministry, taking part in some fifty-two battles (mostly small engagements by Civil War standards).[14]

Thanks to his eleven letters recorded from wartime and some postwar commentaries on his work, a number of fascinating incidents about his service have been preserved. On one occasion, his own altar boy was shot while Nash was saying Mass. He and his regiment were once attacked as they slept, and had to flee for their lives, "the bullets whistling by my ears like mosquitoes." Several other incidents are worth relating in detail.

> As the months went by, Nash [would] walk miles every day from camp to camp visiting the sick and making himself available to Catholics and Protestants alike. The zealous Capt. Wilson told him in a moment of irrational enthusiasm that he was so inspired by Nash's devotion that he [wanted] to use his sword to make Catholicism the one true religion. Indeed, [Wilson actually] forced Protestant officers from the fort who attended Mass to kneel down like himself.[15]

When would-be Protestant chaplains showed up and argued for equal access to the troops, Wilson would stand them on a barrel and challenge them to preach. One of them, certainly not knowing his audience well, delivered a long tirade against Papists. The feisty 6th New York troops listened silently, then ran him out of camp.

Once, after surviving a failed attack against their position, Nash followed the Union troops in their pursuit of the fleeing Confederates and attempted to aid all the wounded and dying he passed. A mortally wounded Protestant corporal who had attended Nash's first island Mass called out to him for baptism. His canteen empty, Nash ran to the Gulf of Mexico, soaked his handkerchief, and dashed back to squeeze the saving waters of the sacrament onto the soldier's forehead. "'Father, do not leave me,' he pleaded. Nash replied, 'There are at this moment many others stretched on the sand . . . as near death as you are.' 'That is true,' the soldier said, 'but they are Catholics; they know how to die.'" The soldier's last wish was for Nash to find his family and help them overcome their prejudice against the church. Six years later, as Nash says in a footnote to his published letters, the boy's brother heard how he died and entered the Catholic Church himself.[16]

Florida's scorching heat and sun were quite tough for Nash. While some priests said Mass at dawn (like Peter Tissot), Nash found that the best time for the troops he served was a Sunday noon Mass. This time was convenient from a camp perspective, but it wasn't beneficial for Nash's health. When the time came for his first Sunday Mass, the sailors organized a choir, the altar, and everything else. However, the Catholic Eucharistic fast of that time required a priest to abstain from food and water from midnight until his morning Mass. As Nash had not eaten well, nor slept the night before, and with the hot tropical sun beating down on the assembly, the priest soon became weak and too exhausted to preach: "his lungs had no power."[17]

Nash finished that Mass and many others, though, and went on to serve without furlough until his regiment was mustered out in June 1863, despite personal health problems that always challenged him. After recuperating during the rest of the summer of 1863, he returned to Jesuit ministry as the prefect at Fordham. He went on to serve in the Jesuit novitiate and missionary band, and then pastored for thirty years in upstate New York. In 1894 he celebrated his golden jubilee as a Jesuit, and died at the age of seventy in Troy, New York, on September 6, 1895. Upon his death, New York Archbishop Michael Corrigan spoke and remarked that Nash "was an exact religious, much loved by the poor wherever he went and (he) never spared himself in laboring for them."[18]

PETER TISSOT (37TH NEW YORK) AND BERNARD O'REILLY (69TH NEW YORK MILITIA)

Like all Catholic chaplains, Jesuit chaplains had one unique aspect of their ministry—administering the Catholic sacraments. Two other Jesuit chaplains illustrate this sacramental aspect of Catholic ministry very well. Peter Tissot (1823–1875) was a native Frenchman who had come to the United States at the age of twenty-three for political reasons. He later taught at Fordham College (New York), and in May 1861 was commissioned as chaplain in the 37th New York Volunteers (also known as the Irish Rifles, part of General Thomas Corcoran's Irish Legion). He ministered for two years as a chaplain, and as his diary indicates, was a hard-working priest, as well as a very courageous man. (He had three horses shot out from underneath him.)

Perhaps because he tended to be somewhat pious, serious, and humorless, Tissot's pastoral style appears to have been more distant and formal than other Catholic chaplains. Early in the war, he was criticized at least once for not being near the front with his troops. Later in the war, however, he was described as being "always in the front lines to hear confessions and administer the Blessed Sacrament to the wounded." The French Jesuit was a good letter-writer and kept a Civil War diary (from June 1861 to June 1862), providing a valuable source of information about both the Jesuits and the broader Catholic faith of that time.[19]

As previously mentioned, Tissot (along with O'Hagan and Scully) was captured during the 1862 Peninsula Campaign and was held in Richmond at the residence of the Catholic Bishop John McGill. Their stay must have been highly interesting; Tissot remarks in his diary that there were no fewer than eleven Catholic priests staying with McGill at that time. Three were the Union chaplains Tissot, Scully, and O'Hagan, but also there were three Confederate chaplains (Hippolyte Gache, Darius Hubert, and either James Sheeran or Egidius Smulders), as well as other religious (possibly Jesuits and a Redemptorist). One cannot help but chuckle today at Tissot's undoubtedly understated comment that there "were many lively disagreements among some . . . and food was scanty and poor!"[20]

Tissot also remarked that Bishop McGill was "very kind, but very strong in his Southern convictions." This was proven when Tissot asked the bishop for "faculties" to hear confessions in his diocese (that is, formal permission to do so). McGill granted it—but only for Northern soldiers. Tissot writes, "This did not satisfy me . . . why should I not hear their confessions too?" Bishop McGill then responded, "Well you may, provided you do not talk against the South." McGill then gave Tissot the honor of hearing his own confession, and Tissot mentions in closing that "before leaving I offered him some money, which he refused to take."[21]

Upon his return to service, he participated in the battles of Fredericksburg and Chancellorsville but began having medical problems, experiencing what he described as "chronic sub-acute gastritis." Throughout 1862 and 1863, his health issues continued, resulting in his being incapacitated for twenty days by jaundice and stomach problems ("chronic derangements of stomach, liver and bowels"). All this eventually led to his June 22, 1863, resignation from chaplaincy because of health concerns. He then became busy with a variety of successful postwar ministries—holding several offices in the Jesuit order, writing frequently, and giving missions and retreats around the country. But even after the war, his health problems persisted. Tissot was forced to resign as vice president of then Fordham University after less than a year because of his poor health. A variety of infirmities continued to plague him until they finally developed into a triple cancer, of which he died in 1875 at age 52.[22]

The Jesuit Bernard O'Reilly (1820–1907) was yet another native Irishman who served with New York troops, although he is classified only as an occasional chaplain. O'Reilly served for three months as a chaplain with the original 69th New York Regiment State Militia, the militia troops who were disbanded after they fought at Bull Run, and later reformed as part of the Irish Brigade. He succeeded Thomas Mooney (1824–1877), who had been removed in July 1861 by Archbishop John Hughes because of his "baptism" of a cannon. Records about O'Reilly's service are scant (Germain does not count him as a chaplain), though there are several unverified references to him departing for New York City in July 1861 with soldiers' pay for distribution to their families.

Originally, O'Reilly was ordained as a diocesan priest in Quebec in 1843, but later he joined the Jesuits and was attached to St. John's College (now Fordham University) at the outset of the war. He left the Society of Jesus at some time after the war was concluded, becoming a prominent member of the Archdiocese of New York. He was a well-known writer of numerous articles and several prominent books, including a life of Pope Leo XIII. After traveling extensively in Europe, he lived for a long time in Rome, became a monsignor, and died in April 1907 in New York City.

For the sake of completeness, one other Jesuit—Joseph O'Callaghan (1824–1869)—has been called by some sources a chaplain of the 69th New York National Guard as well. Born in the United States, O'Callaghan was a seminarian in Boston "loaned" to the Jesuits by Bishop Joseph Fenwick (himself a Jesuit) who then decided to join the Society.

He was the president of Loyola College in Baltimore from 1860 to 1863, then was stationed in Frederick, Maryland, with some unofficial sources listing him as mustering in June 23, 1863, for a thirty-day chaplaincy, and mustering out on July 27, 1863. Because the official records are nonexistent in this regard, however, we can only classify him as an occasional chaplain. O'Callaghan died suddenly on January 21, 1869, on a trip back from Rome representing his Jesuit Province, when a storm wave swept over his ship killing him and two others.[23]

BASIL PACCIARINI (PORT LOOKOUT) AND ANSELM USANNEZ (ANDERSONVILLE PRISON)

Since the Society of Jesus is a religious order known for ministry in unexpected places, it should not be a surprise that the Jesuit presence was felt even in Civil War prisoner-of-war camps. Two of the twenty-one Jesuits connected to the war had a brief ministry in the prison camps, which were generally regarded as hellholes, no matter which side or what location (though some became truly infamous). Within the St. Inigoes, Maryland, parish boundaries of Basil Pacciarini (1817–1884) was the largest Confederate prisoner-of-war camp in the North, Point Lookout, near where the Potomac River meets Chesapeake Bay. This former resort was converted into a military hospital once the war began, and after the July 1863 Battle of Gettysburg, a prisoner-of-war camp was established at the site. Officially called Camp Hoffman, the 40-acre prison at first held only 1,700 Confederates, but swelled in size to twenty thousand by June 1865, well more than the stockade's designed capacity. By the end of the war, more than fifty thousand prisoners had passed through Point Lookout's gates, making it the largest prisoner of war facility in the North.[24]

Pacciarini was an Italian who joined the Jesuits at age eighteen, came to America in 1846, and was ordained in 1848. In 1864, he requested to be appointed as chaplain at Point Lookout while maintaining his residence as pastor of St. Inigoes. He went to Point Lookout two or three days a week, or more frequently when required. There apparently never was any formal government response to his request, though the request from the Provost Marshall to Edwin Stanton does exist. Thus Pacciarini is considered an occasional chaplain since his main ministry continued to be his parish community, which consisted of both African Americans and whites. There are no known written public records of his Civil War prison work. His health began to weaken in 1874, and he was sent to Fordham in New York to be a local chaplain in that area. In 1884, he celebrated his golden jubilee as a Jesuit, but died in October of that same year.

While Pacciarini ministered to Confederate prisoners, a fellow Italian Jesuit, Anselm Usannez (1819–1895), ministered to Northern prisoners. Pacciarini had been born in the Umbria area of central Italy; Usannez was a native of Aime, Savoy, and he arrived in the United States soon after his 1848 ordination. The Italian Jesuits had just been expelled from Sardinia in the 1848 uprisings, and Usannez and several other Jesuits were sent to the Jesuit Southern Mission (Louisiana and Alabama), while others (the devious Joseph Bixio among them) went to other American missions. In 1858 Usannez became minister of Spring Hill College in Mobile, Alabama, then rector of St. Charles College at Grand Coteau, Louisiana, from 1859–1861 (where Anthony de Chaignon, later chaplain of the 18th Louisiana, also resided).[25]

From 1863 to 1864, Usannez was back in Mobile working as a missionary and spiritual director, when he was suddenly transferred to Georgia, perhaps due to a clash with his Jesuit superior. It was from there that, for about two weeks in September 1864, he ministered at the infamous Andersonville prison camp to the over thirty thousand Union prisoners. Usannez was one of only a handful of priests ministering at Andersonville. Peter Whelan (of Savannah, Georgia) is the best known, though the local bishop Augustine Verot and two other priests, John Kirby and Henry Clavreul, briefly assisted there as well.[26]

Like Basil Pacciarini, Anselm Usannez is considered an occasional chaplain because of his very limited Civil War service, but his connection to the infamous Andersonville is notable. The immense challenge that all the priests who ministered there had can be seen in what Peter Whelan went through during his four months in the 26-acre hellhole (see chapter 11). The fact that the camp commander, Captain Henry Wirz, was a Catholic himself and supported priests coming to the camp despite its atrocious conditions (he was subsequently tried and hung), reminds one of the poignant nuances that faith always brings to history. As for Usannez himself, he was described by his Jesuit family as "an effective speaker . . . a learned and accurate theologian. He was extremely prudent, and never gave a decision in difficult matters without first spending some time in careful reflection. As a confessor, he was a universal favorite, and [people] praised his fatherly kindness and tender compassion." Usannez's final days were spent peacefully in the Jesuit house in Grand Coteau, Louisiana, where he suffered from dementia for several years before his March 1895 death.[27]

HIPPOLYTE GACHE (10TH LOUISIANA), CHARLES TRUYENS (OCCASIONAL), AND FRANCIS NACHON (OCCASIONAL)

Like all wartime chaplains, the Jesuit priests endured enormous personal challenges in their work. Aside from the uncertainties and challenges of being in camp or on the march, several were captured at some time of the war (Tissot and O'Hagan in October 1862, and Nash briefly in Florida in 1861). Most knowledgeable Civil War readers know that twice as many soldiers were killed by sickness as bullets; the Jesuits were no exception to being plagued by serious health problems. At least three Jesuits particularly struggled with serious health issues because of their wartime experiences.

Peter Tissot's health issues were already mentioned, but Louis-Hippolyte Gache (1817–1907) was a second priest on whom the war took its toll. Gache was a native Frenchman who left Europe in 1847 with five Jesuit companions because of political conditions, and was serving in Alabama at the Jesuit Spring Hill College when war broke out. He was subsequently sent to New Orleans specifically to be a Confederate chaplain, and in May 1861 he briefly became chaplain to Confederate troops in Pensacola, Florida, across the harbor from the Union-held Fort Pickens (which the Confederates unsuccessfully attacked in the months ahead).

In July 1861 Gache was assigned to the 10th Louisiana Volunteers, who were called "Lee's Foreign Legion" because of the seventeen countries they represented. In addition, 70 percent of the soldiers were Catholic. Although Gache was with 10th Louisiana in Florida for a short time, and then in the Seven Days Campaign of mid-1862, it appears he may have had little further direct ministry experience with active troops or in actual battles after that. Most of his subsequent ministry took place in Civil War hospitals and churches in Danville, Lynchburg, and then Richmond.

Fortunately for historians, Gache did write seventeen Civil War letters in French to confreres at Spring Hill College near Mobile, so we have a good sense of who this man was. Although his English was quite poor ("all but unintelligible," according to the editor of his letters, Joseph Durkin), Gache was an urbane man, with a sharp tongue, caustic temperament, and ultraorthodox Catholic beliefs. In part because his sister was a Carmelite nun, Gache was personally devoted to the Daughters of Charity and served as their chaplain in Lynchburg and elsewhere. He wore his traditional black Jesuit habit in camp: a long black robe, cincture with rosary beads attached, and biretta squarely on his head. Gache developed friendships with several influential people during the war, including the Ewell family (General Richard Ewell and his sisters Elizabeth and Rebecca), Varina Davis, and the Catholic Semmes family from Maryland and Louisiana (Admiral Raphael Semmes and Confederate senator Thomas Semmes).[28]

Gache's tenure from July 19, 1861 to April 14, 1865 ranks him among the longest continually serving Jesuit chaplains. He ministered in Florida, with the 10th Louisiana, then in hospitals at Danville and Lynchburg (where it is said that he baptized one hundred persons), before accompanying ten Sisters of Charity to Stuart Hospital in Richmond in February 1865. By that time, the exertions of his work had taken their toll. In a later letter he reflects that during his chaplain's tenure in Richmond, his "health was far from excellent; during the five preceding months I had always been more or less sick, since the hospital diet and my stomach were engaged in a war of their own." But perhaps just in time, he received a blessing. As the victorious Union troops entered Richmond in the first days of April 1865, Gache located a familiar face marching with General Edward Ord's army—his Jesuit confrere Joseph O'Hagan (73rd New York).[29] The two warmly greeted each other, and after O'Hagan arranged with Ord for Gache's surrender and parole, the two returned to their Jesuit community at Georgetown on Easter Sunday 1865, where he writes, "there we were very warmly received." In Georgetown, Gache spent much time recuperating at the houses of some "dear rebel ladies" (including the Ewell family), and then returned to ministry, having a long and successful academic postwar career at Grand Coteau, then at Loyola, Georgetown, and Fordham. The caustic, conservative Frenchman died in October 1907 near Montreal, Canada. In a bit of irony that he would likely have appreciated, the ultra-French Gache was buried in a Jesuit cemetery in upstate New York that is adjacent to what is now a culinary school specializing in French gourmet cooking.[30]

The third Jesuit upon whom the Civil War experience took its medical toll was occasional chaplain Charles Truyens (1813–1867), a Belgian immigrant who was ordained in 1846 and part of the Jesuit Mission in the Midwest. At age forty-eight, Truyens was one of the oldest of all Jesuit chaplains. He spent many prewar years on missions to the indigenous peoples in Kansas, and eventually was named pastor in Bardstown, Kentucky. Truyens served as the chaplain of the 12th Kentucky Infantry in January 1862 and was even at the battle of Mill Springs (January 18, 1862), but he left the chaplain's position a mere six weeks later.

It appears the Civil War was a fairly miserable experience for the older Truyens. Though he kept no diary and wrote only a few letters, he would later report that not only did he lose his health during those six weeks, but the weather was absolutely horrible, he had to sleep on the ground, and there was a strong anti-Catholic bias among some of the Union troops. In a January 11, 1862, letter, he wrote that "I have already suffered very much from hunger, and can hardly recollect myself. . . . I try to make my meditations and examens, but I hope God will be satisfied with my endeavors . . . unfortunately there are no other Catholic chaplains here. When I will be able to say Mass, I do not know."[31]

Although Truyens's ministry was short-lived, it appears to have been quite effective, and it drew the positive attention of those who saw him. One commentator wrote:

He attracted the notice of both officers and soldiers by his attention to the wounded and dying on the battle-field, where he spent the entire night, hurrying hither and thither, as directed by the cries and groans of the suffering, to serve and comfort them in their wretched condition. In after years he often spoke feelingly of a non-Catholic officer who had sought him for several hours of the night in order to guide him to a wounded soldier of the Southern army who had begged piteously to see a priest. [He arrived] in time to see the wounded and forlorn man die in peace, after having received the sacraments of penance and extreme unction.[32]

This short but physically stressful chaplaincy weakened Truyens, and upon his return to the Jesuits, he was unable to function as pastor for several months due to stress. Though he did eventually return to pastoring his Bardstown parish, Truyens died an early death, just two years after the war, in December 1867 at St. Louis University.

Francis Nachon (1820–1867) was another of the many Frenchmen who comprised the majority of Jesuits working in the Mission in the South. Joining the Society in 1841, he worked out of the Jesuit New Orleans community, and was described as a devoted and zealous man. He is considered only an occasional Civil War chaplain, though, since his ministry was sporadic and limited to Confederate soldiers in forts along the Mississippi and in Washington, Louisiana. He became a victim of the yellow fever epidemic of 1867, dying on October 1, 1867, two weeks before de Chaignon (discussed below) at the very same church in Washington, Louisiana, where they were both helping. He is buried in the Jesuit cemetery at Grand Coteau, Louisiana.

DARIUS HUBERT (1ST LOUISIANA),
JOSEPH PRACHENSKY (3RD ALABAMA),
ANTHONY DE CHAIGNON (18TH LOUISIANA),
AND ANDREW CORNETTE (OCCASIONAL)

We finish out our list of Confederate Jesuit chaplains by introducing Darius Hubert (1823–1893), yet another native Frenchman assigned to the American South by his Jesuit superiors in 1847. After serving for several years as pastor in Baton Rouge, he was personally asked by Colonel Albert Blanchard (later made a brigadier general) to be chaplain of the 1st Louisiana Infantry as it was being formed in New Orleans. Hubert was close to Blanchard, who in 1865 wrote to try and convince the priest to come to his latest assignment, and "bring books." During the war, he was well known to Lee, Jackson, and even Jefferson Davis, and after the war was frequently called on to "recount and celebrate the dignity of those who had fought and died in the Lost Cause."[33]

Hubert and his Jesuit compatriot Hippolyte Gache (10th Louisiana) went on to accompany their respective Louisiana units through several shared engagements in the early war years. However in contrast to Gache (whose English was poor and who was relatively incompatible with Protestants), Hubert wrote and spoke comfortably (even elegantly) in English, and worked well with Protestants as well as Catholics; he was in fact revered by both.

One other characteristic of Hubert set him apart from Gache even more: his chaplain's attire during the war. In stark contrast to the consummately traditional Gache, who always wore his black religious habit in camp, Hubert chose a more "extravagant" military attire, described caustically in one of Gache's letters. "Imagine a young dandy: his hair was elegant, his beard was splendid; gold-braid was festooned upon his blue kepi, and embroidered upon the sleeves of his high-collared frock coat; the golden buttons of his waistcoat were emblazoned with the Louisiana pelican; his gold-filleted trousers fell neatly into a pair of comely boots. This dazzling sight was none other than Father Hubert himself. Can you blame me for scarcely recognizing him?" Both Jesuits had taken a vow of poverty, but it didn't stop Hubert from dressing for his "worldly" position to the fullest.[34]

Hubert gained great respect as an extremely hardworking, model chaplain of the Army of Northern Virginia. He was well-known to Robert E. Lee (who is reported to have "never met him without a respectful bow"), "Stonewall" Jackson, and Jefferson Davis (for whom he offered a public prayer at his 1889 funeral). In March 1862, Hubert ministered on board the Confederate Merrimack (aka Virginia) during the famous two-day battle of Hampton Roads (April 8–9, 1862). A number of the soldiers on board had been recruited from his regiment, and despite initial resistance from Confederate Admiral Franklin Buchanan, Hubert's persistence paid off, and he eventually was permitted on board. Hubert was slightly wounded in the arm at Gettysburg, and in the spring of 1864 had to take a medical furlough from field service because of recurrent health issues. He finished the war as a chaplain formally assigned to Catholic soldiers in all the Richmond hospitals. Informally, he visited the sickbeds of soldiers regardless of their faith, as well as civilians in the beleaguered city.[35]

Though severely exhausted and plagued by poor health, Hubert remained in Richmond for several months after the surrender. At Bishop McGill's request, and with fellow Jesuit Joseph O'Hagan on the altar, he gave the Easter homily at St. Peter's Cathedral there on April 16, 1865, less than two weeks after the city fell and two days after Abraham Lincoln's assassination. Hubert then lived and ministered in New Orleans, continuing to work for his adopted, defeated "country," and speaking at many Confederate veterans' reunions. During the yellow fever epidemic of 1876, he went to Savannah, Georgia, to care for the sick, one of many such errands of mercy he undertook. However in 1891 he was stricken with paralysis. At the suggestion of physicians, he was moved to Macon, Georgia, for his health, and he died there at the Jesuit novitiate, St. Stanislaus College, on June 14, 1893. Hubert was buried, perhaps quite appropriately, in the area near where the Confederate trenches had been dug during the war around Macon (though in 1920 his remains were moved to the Jesuit cemetery at Spring Hill College in Mobile, Alabama).[36]

Joseph Prachensky (1822–1890) was a native German who, like so many other Jesuits, came to America from revolutionary Europe. He was stationed in the Jesuit Southern Mission, in Mobile, Alabama, where he joined the newly organized 3rd Alabama on the Peninsula in September 1861. Prachensky was apparently a very strong-willed and independent man. Like Hubert, during his brief five-month career as a chaplain, he took great pride in wearing a Confederate officer's uniform—although not that of a captain (the generally accepted chaplain's rank), but a major. (This partially German author does wonder, however, whether Prachensky's native temperament had something to do with that.) In addition, Prachensky also grew a mustache and chin whiskers to supplement his chaplain's attire. Again, one can easily imagine the sardonic comments that drew from his traditional Jesuit confrere Hippolyte Gache.[37]

Prachensky's chaplaincy ended under strange circumstances. He resigned his chaplaincy in a letter dated February 3, 1862, citing therein "duties in the ministry calling me to the South West frontier," but instead turned up in a Jesuit-run church in Troy, New York. Germain cites as his reason that the regiment was being transferred and he did not want to accompany them; whereas a Jesuit historian remarks simply "apparently he changed his mind about the merits of the Confederate cause."[38] Whatever his reasons, shortly thereafter Prachensky went to Fordham, where he remained until the 1868 opening of the Ward's Island Insane Asylum in New York. There he built a church and a residence; he lived apart from Jesuit community life for two decades and devoted himself heroically to the residents in those the asylums and hospitals. In 1889 Prachensky returned to Fordham in time to celebrate his golden jubilee as a Jesuit, and died there in July 1890.[39]

The final Jesuit who served as an official Confederate chaplain was the Frenchman Anthony de Chaignon (1806–1867). In the pattern of most foreign-born Jesuits of the time, de Chaignon and sixteen other Jesuits arrived in New Orleans on May 1848, after the Society's expulsion from France. He ministered in a variety of ways before the war, including being president of the Jesuit-run St. Charles College in Grand Coteau, Louisiana, alongside Anselm Usannez in 1861. De Chaignon was stationed at the Jesuit's Baton Rouge parish when his chaplain's commission to the 18th Louisiana was issued him on February 2, 1862, though it seems he was involved with the troops before that; he also appears on the October 1861 muster rolls of the same regiment. His formal chaplaincy appears to have been of short duration (only six or seven months), and Germain remarks that almost nothing is known of him aside from the basic fact of his chaplaincy, although he is mentioned in several places in a Jesuit journal as being at Shiloh and then Corinth (April 1862).[40]

One reference says that de Chaignon was one of only four priests ministering to the wounded at Corinth, Mississippi, after Shiloh (although details are scarce), while another remarks he was "wounded while with the Army in Tennessee." A letter of April 8, 1862 (the day after the Battle of Shiloh), from Francis Pont (13th Louisiana) to Bishop John-Marie Odin of New Orleans refers to de Chaignon as "at the hospital, almost recovered." Later in April 1862, he returned at least briefly to the Jesuit house at Grand Coteau, Louisiana, where a record of the time remarks he "had assisted at the battle of Shiloh and earned from the soldiers the reputation of 'the coolest man in the army.'" Military records then show de Chaignon returned to the 18th Louisiana and was present at muster rolls in July and August 1862, with his last wartime reference being that he was "absent for 10 days leave of absence since 23 Aug, 1862."[41]

The oldest of all Jesuit chaplains who served in the war, de Chaignon survived and returned to his Jesuit community to minister in and around southern Louisiana, but unfortunately died at the young age of forty-four in October 1867. In the summer of that year, a deadly yellow fever epidemic hit Louisiana's Gulf Coast hard and killed thousands of people. While assisting the parish priest in Washington, Louisiana, de Chaignon and a fellow Jesuit, Francis Nachon, both succumbed to the fever.[42]

The final Jesuit in the Civil War annals of this prestigious order is Andrew Cornette (1819–1872), who was born in Fleury, Cote d'Or, France. Cornette was a truly gifted scholar—a member of the Académie des Sciences in Paris, he taught in several Central American states before the Jesuits were expelled from Columbia in 1857, and then made his way to Spring Hill College (Mobile, Alabama), where he resided for the remainder of his priesthood. Cornette wrote scientific articles for the *Mobile Times*, composed manuscripts on historical and scientific studies, and taught physics, chemistry, and mathematics at the college. Because he only ministered informally to Confederate troops in the forts around Mobile (Forts Morgan, Gaines, and Powell, and the Spanish Fort), he is considered an occasional chaplain. However, the story that came to be told about his so-called escape at the very end of the war is a most fitting way to conclude this chapter.

On Saturday, April 7, 1865, together with Confederate chaplain Isidore Turgis, Cornette went to the Spanish Fort near Mobile to prepare the Catholic soldiers there for their Easter Communion (i.e., Turgis and Cornette were most likely hearing confessions). The Union monitors were bombarding the fort day and night at the time, and they arrived in the entrenchments at midnight under the fire of bullets and cannonballs. The next day, which was Easter Sunday, the bombardment increased and the commanding general (Randall L. Gibson) decided to evacuate in the evening. As one Spring Hill student and future priest Henry Semple described it, the two priests escaped in the dark by boat at literally the last second before the Union entered, after "a shell from the monitor was planted near the two, and exploding under the earth, buried both in the sand. They got their heads out of their graves with the aid of the spades in the soldiers' hands."[43]

The Jesuits were then, and are today still, a robust religious family—a tight-knit spiritual community. In the end, the brotherhood these "sons of Ignatius" shared was a far stronger bond than any gray or blue uniform they wore during the Civil War. As to their impact on others, perhaps the words of an anonymous Englishman who served with the Confederates early in the war best captures their core charism. This officer had little use for chaplains in general, but of the Jesuit priests he had met, he grudgingly had to admit his unqualified admiration.

The Jesuits were perfect soldiers in their demeanor. . . . [the Jesuit chaplain] "was ever at the head of a column in the advance, ever last in retreat; and in the battlefield, a black cassock, in a bending posture, would always betray the posture of a disciple of Loyola, ministering to the wounded or dying. No hospital could be found wherein was not a pale-faced, meek, and untiring man of this order. Soldierly in their education and bearing, (Jesuits) are ready for anything—to preach, prescribe for the sick, or offer a wise suggestion on military or social affairs."[44]

CHAPTER 6

OTHER RELIGIOUS
WHO SERVED
AS CHAPLAINS

Although the Holy Cross priests of Notre Dame and the Jesuits dominated the numbers of religious who served as chaplains, many priests from other religious orders achieved equal wartime recognition (and sometimes greater). In this chapter we will introduce a number of other priest-chaplains, all members of religious orders, who were well recognized at the time and later for the prominent spiritual roles they played as chaplains during the Civil War.[1]

THE REDEMPTORISTS: SHEERAN AND SMULDERS

The order known as the Redemptorists (formally called the Congregation of the Most Holy Redeemer) was founded in 1732 by the Italian St. Alphonsus Liguori to work for the poor and most abandoned in the Naples area. Known for its emphasis on preaching, the order sent priests to America in 1832. On the eve of the Civil War, the Redemptorists had established strong foundations in New Orleans, St. Louis, Maryland, and Washington. It was from their New Orleans church, where they were ministering to several different language groups, that two of the war's most prominent chaplains emerged—James Sheeran and Egidius Smulders. Both men served in Louisiana regiments in the famed Army of Northern Virginia, and were distinguished by the longevity of their service (nearly four years for each) and the influence that they had on soldiers and on the Catholic Church in general.

James Sheeran (14th Louisiana)

Truly a captivating character, James Sheeran (1819–1881) was born in Ireland, immigrated to Canada at age twelve, then to New York at age fourteen (where he may have studied law for a time), and in 1841 married a devout Catholic woman named Margaret, whose last name has been lost to history. He and his wife moved to Pennsylvania for five years, then to Monroe, Michigan. The couple eventually had three children (two boys and a girl), about whom relatively little is known, though one boy died as a baby. Sheeran taught and then directed a school for a number of years, was involved briefly in the heated debate over Catholic schools, and (in an interesting historical twist) had some significant spiritual encounters with Egidius Smulders, who was then the superior of the Redemptorists in Monroe, Michigan, from 1845 to 1847. These encounters had a great influence on Sheeran's own faith and the vocation he subsequently chose to pursue.[2]

After his wife died unexpectedly in 1849, Sheeran sent his remaining son and daughter to boarding schools and headed east to pursue studies and training to become a Redemptorist priest. He entered the Redemptorist novitiate in 1855, was ordained in September 1858, and was sent in 1859 to St. Alphonsus Church in New Orleans for his first assignment, where he was reunited with his spiritual director, Egidius Smulders. After Louisiana seceded in January 1861, the New Orleans bishop (Jean-Marie Odin) asked the Redemptorists for chaplains, and six men responded; the superior chose Sheeran and Smulders for that work. Sheeran went to Pennsylvania briefly in February 1861, likely for the funeral of his daughter, Isabella, who had joined a convent but died there. He then returned to New Orleans. In August he joined Valery Sulakowski's 1st Polish Brigade as their chaplain, which was soon renamed the 14th Louisiana. That regiment fought in the East throughout the war, took part in nearly all the major engagements of Lee's Army of Northern Virginia, and surrendered at Appomattox with just two officers and twenty-five men remaining. Except for a four-month furlough from October 1863 to January 1864, Sheeran was a fixture among his Louisiana troops in camp, on the march, and on the battlefield until October 1864.[3]

What makes Sheeran so significant as a Civil War chaplain is what he left behind: a two-volume, leather-bound, 1,600-page diary of his Civil War service. Only one other such published Civil War journal written by a Catholic chaplain exists: William Corby's well-known *Memoirs* from the Union side. (As highlighted elsewhere, the wartime letters of chaplains such as Peter Paul Cooney, Michael Nash, Louis-Hippolyte Gache, and Peter Tissot are also insightful historical resources.) The opening page of Sheeran's journal remarks that the record was "meant for my Redemptorist confreres" and "if something should happen to me, it should be burned." Thankfully the diary was not, and it was recently published in unabridged form, revealing not as much a spiritual account of the war as a journal with "an eloquence and depth of feeling not often found in this [diary] genre." Reflecting many personal anecdotes, detailed accounts of battles, and his own deep dedication to the chaplain's task throughout the war, the reader discovers an outspoken, argumentative priest and feisty Irish Confederate. Never shy about expressing his biases or opinions about politics or the Catholic Church, at times Sheeran is often prone to "bouts of hyperbole and bloviating" (as his most recent editor Patrick Hayes comments).[4]

However, Sheeran's diary offers an incredibly insightful and accessible wartime eyewitness account—thus anecdotes from his service are scattered throughout this book. A few examples here will suffice to capture the picture of war he left behind. On April 2, 1864, Sheeran traveled to Orange Hanover Junction, Virginia, to minister to Maryland Confederate troops there. Though the hospitality was warm, the accommodations proved problematic. "It rained and snowed all night; and in the morning the earth was a sea of half-melted snow. My quarters were not weather proof . . . during the night the canvas yielded to the weight of the elements, rendering our church not a bay, nor a lake, but an indescribable body of fresh water . . . I celebrated Mass, and gave Communion to many. I suffered much from cold, [but] being so busily engaged hearing confessions, I neglected my fire until it went out. I went to bed this night about 11, cold and fatigued but very much consoled after my day's labor."[5]

On February 7, 1864, Sheeran described in great detail an encounter he and his brigade had with Union troops they had just discovered crossing the Rapidan River at Morton's Ford.

> In about ten minutes officers were in their saddles, your humble servant along them, and the men under arms. . . . Within three miles of Morton's Ford, the low and frequent reports of artillery were heard; soon too, the sound of distant musketry struck our ears. The work of death had already commenced. . . . Our boys commenced a "double-quick" regardless of the mud and darkness for it was now quite late and constant rain was still falling. I remained some four hundred yards behind our boys in line of battle, with the ambulances, expecting soon to have to perform the sad duty of binding up their bleeding wounds. But thank God we were agreeably disappointed . . . Gen. Gordon with his brigade of brave Georgians, charged the enemy's right and drove them in confusion to the banks of the Rapidan, which they re-crossed during the darkness of the night . . . At about 8 o'clock all was quiet again.[6]

On November 4, 1863, Sheeran describes a testy encounter with a German "infidel" (Protestant) Confederate who "had a high idea of his own knowledge and a correspondingly low one of the intelligence of those around him . . . He hated the Pope and endeavored to show the Confederate officers that the Pope was the enemy of human progress." Sheeran bided his time listening, but then resolved "to shut him up . . . 'Now, sir, let me ask you a few questions, if you please. . . .'" He then wrote two pages in the journal to describe how he took the man to task for misinformation, avoiding answers to *his* questions, and for ignorance of the situation in Italy with Giuseppe Garibaldi and the Pope. Although he remarked there that "it is painful, sir, to be compelled to expose a man's ignorance, particularly in company," nevertheless Sheeran was not shy about doing so, concluding that "the fellow felt the blows and evidently withered under them. He would insult me, but saw the Confederate officers present would not permit him, so he tried to make an apology by saying he didn't know I was a Catholic priest."[7]

Sheeran's denouement occurred in October 1864, while he was ministering to troops of both sides for about two weeks after the battle of Cedar Creek (which featured the famous charge of General Philip Sheridan, rallying Union troops to victory). Sheeran requested permission to reenter Confederate lines after his concluding his two-week ministry to the wounded, but due to events he was unaware of until months later, he was instead detained by Union authorities, then imprisoned for two months in two vermin-filled Baltimore prisons. As will be described in chapter 11, Sheeran did not discover until much later that the credentials of Union chaplain Leo Rizza (9th Connecticut) had been stolen and fraudulently used by the Jesuit Joseph Bixio to get wagonloads of supplies and then take them into Confederate lines. Sheeran had simply been at the wrong place at the wrong time, and incurred the ill-placed wrath of General Sheridan, who simply arrested the first Catholic Confederate chaplain he found.

For five weeks, Sheeran endured horrible prison conditions that greatly weakened his health; even there he did not lose his boldness. He describes his first night with hardened prisoners at Baltimore's notorious Fort McHenry prison. "We had barely laid our weary bodies down . . . than the inmates of this institution . . . had a quarrel [with such] obscenity, vulgarity & profanity as I had never heard before. . . . Then names surpassing anything to be found in any vocabulary were applied to each other. One would burst out with a verse or phrase of an obscene or vulgar song. Then one grunted like a hog, others barked like a dog, another quacked like a duck. Needless to say I slept none, for who could sleep." The next morning the irascible Irish priest confronted one of the loud men, found out he had been brought up Catholic, and had the man gather his companions. Sheeran gave them all a "severe lecture," saying he didn't mind some harmless recreation like playing cards, but all lights had to be out by 9:00 pm, and there was to be no swearing.

After that motivational speech, Sheeran had no more trouble with them, but still suffered from a lack of sleep, the rodent "greyback companions" active every night, and his own decreasing health. Finally, on

December 5, 1864, after a public letter-writing campaign that involved the leading Catholic paper (*The Freeman's Journal*), the Redemptorists, and even Secretary of War Edwin Stanton, General Sheridan released the priest. But then Sheeran twice refused to take the oath of loyalty, finally agreeing to sign one saying he would give no military information to the enemy. He subsequently had two personal meetings with Sheridan in which he lambasted the general for the "ungentlemanly, barbarous way he had been treated." He received in the end only a half-hearted apology from the nominally Catholic officer. After several more arduous misadventures while traveling back into the south, Sheeran finally arrived at an infirmary in Richmond, Virginia, where he passed the last days of the war. After the surrender of Lee at Appomattox, Sheeran had recovered enough to make his way back to New Orleans to his old Redemptorist house.[8]

Sheeran's unique path through life continued in unexpected ways after the war. The man described succinctly as "passionate, educated but prone to snobbishness and stubbornness" and who had become a Redemptorist when his wife died, left the order around 1870. The Southern patriot of 1861 actually went north in 1871 to the Newark Diocese, where he became a pastor in Morristown, New Jersey, for a decade! There he proved to be a bundle of energy, building a new church, establishing a school and cemetery, working with a rural, growing Irish parish, and even managing to return to Ireland to see the land of his birth. His fiery temperament had not changed—a number of irritated members eventually complained to his bishop about Sheeran's "stern demeanor and strict manner," and twice the Newark bishop Michael Corrigan had to come to "pour oil on the troubled waters" of his Morristown parish.[9]

In a truly ironic end to his fascinating life, a Union general (Joseph Revere) who had faced Sheeran at Chancellorsville and was now a member of his parish, became a friend and was buried close to him in the parish cemetery. And when Sheeran's new church building was dedicated in 1873, none other than newly elected President Ulysses S. Grant attended the dedication. Sheeran's health had long suffered from his Civil War hardships, and on Sunday, April 3, 1881, the dedicated, irascible priest died, joining "the great majority in the Great Beyond" (in the words of legendary Civil War historian Ed Bearss). His funeral homily was preached by former Civil War chaplain Monsignor George Doane of the Morristown Diocese.

Egidius Smulders (8th Louisiana)

As outspoken and feisty as James Sheeran was, his compatriot—the veteran Belgian Redemptorist priest Egidius Smulders (1815–1900)—was the polar opposite. A very gifted man, Smulders spoke four languages (French, German, Flemish, and English) and was described as having a "cool and calm judgement, prudence, an unalterable kindness, [and] a Christ-tolerance of human frailty." Ordained in September 1843, Smulders worked first in Belgium for eighteen months before volunteering to come to America, then labored literally across the United States for a half century. Becoming one of the most prominent members of the Redemptorists in the late nineteenth century, Smulders held multiple roles there (missionary preacher, superior, pastor, novice-master), founded churches in several states, and was considered "first among equals" in a religious order known for its extraordinary preachers, particularly those who worked in formats known as parish missions.[10]

In the antebellum years, Smulders was assigned to churches in Michigan, Maryland, and New York while preaching missions in the East and Midwest. In December 1860, following his mission preaching in New Orleans, Smulders was appointed temporary rector there because of nationalistic squabbles that had arisen in the community. As mentioned above, when a full-time superior was appointed, and Bishop Odin requested help, Smulders and Sheeran were selected to become chaplains to the Confederate troops then being raised in and around the Crescent City. Smulders was assigned to the 8th Louisiana, with nine hundred men mostly from the Louisiana parishes around New Orleans who were mustered in on June 19, 1861. The Belgian priest served with them for more than three years, then spent the last months of the war in the hospitals and among the prisoners of war, continuing the latter ministry from July to October 1865 on the Petersburg staff of General Zebulon York.

Smulders had several serious illnesses during his years of service, including typhoid fever and dysentery, but always recovered enough to return to his highly effective work. Since the 8th and 14th Louisiana regiments were in the same brigade for the greater part of the war, Smulders frequently worked with James Sheeran, sharing confession work, Masses, meals, and their mutual troubles and joys. (The Jesuit Darius Hubert of the 1st Louisiana is also mentioned regularly in Sheeran's journal.) The meetings between the two Redemptorist priests were frequent and often poignant, as many anecdotes from Sheeran's journal convey.

> November 10, 1862: I found Fr. S. sleeping in an ambulance. We gave [him] quite a surprise. . . . During my short stay, I found that he was nearly barefooted as well as myself. The soles of our boots were bad and the uppers worse. My stay with the Fr. was necessarily short, as I had to return to the house of Mr. Reardon about four miles distant.

> August 22, 1863: This afternoon I received a visit from Father Smulders and in company with him visited the old mansion of President Madison [at Montpelier in Orange, Virginia]. The old study room of the President is one of the greatest curiosities of the house. It now being dark we could see but little of the gardens, groves or cemetery, so we resolved to visit it again on some more convenient occasion.

> May 15, 1864 [at Spotsylvania]: "This was another military Sunday. Neither Father Smulders nor myself had vestments; they being with our staff wagons some three miles distant. Both of us could not leave the hospital, not knowing what moment more wounded would be brought in; we agreed the Father should go to the wagon yard and say Mass and I should remain in the hospitals. It rained all the afternoon."

> June 18 and 21, 1864 [at Lynchburg]: "I met Father Smulders who succeeded in getting aboard the cars yesterday with Gordon's Brigade. . . . I said mass at 10 a.m. and Father Smulders preached.

We visited the College Hospital and took dinner there . . . [June 21] About 10 a.m. we started after the army. Father Smulders' horse was in rather bad traveling condition. Suffering much from the effects of short rations, bad care and worse riding; the Father being very hard on horse flesh. We had not gone more than two miles when Father's horse very unceremoniously refused to go further, or in other words, broke down. What was the Father to do? I left him to decide for himself. He resolved to return to the army before Richmond; and I, bidding him a good-bye, continued my journey."[11]

These two very different priests were certainly a strong support for each other in the difficult war years, but it seems their contrasting personality styles also opened some doors that might have remained closed to the more pious Smulders. In April 1864, as the Confederates prepared to move toward what would become the Battle of the Wilderness, the two priests identified the need for a general pass to go anywhere needed within Confederate lines to minister to Catholics scattered throughout the Army of Northern Virginia. In classic fashion, Sheeran's journal relates what happened. Smulders and Sheeran went directly to General Robert E. Lee's tent. They were at first refused entry, but upon Sheeran's insistence, were soon allowed in by the Adjutant.

Sheeran describes Lee as at first "distant" to the two priests, saying he did not know them and that they should have gotten permission from their brigade commanders before coming. Sheeran explained that it was to avoid exactly this trouble that they had come, and that they sought no personal favors but simply to be more efficient in their pastoral ministry. Lee then said, "You are like other officers and should not expect privileges which they do not have." Whereas the humble Smulders might have acquiesced at those words, the inimitable Sheeran would not be denied. The journal relates Sheeran's version of the subsequent events:

I now became a little warm at the unexpected refusal. "Gen., you say you do not know me. I have been with you in all your campaigns. I have been present at every battle fought by your army. I have never been absent from my duty. There are few officers in your army who do not know me, and I am surprised, Gen., that you do not. I protest against being placed on a level with military officers. I am a Catholic Priest and as such I am even *your* superior, Gen.!"

The Big General and the Little Priest were now standing and sternly viewing each other. For a few moments there was a silence. The Gen. at last addressed me thus: "Pardon me, sir! it is just now that I recognized you. Had I known you when you first came in, you should have had no trouble. I now remember you well. Now tell me what you want, and I will do anything I can for you."

Apparently taken aback by Sheeran's bluntness, the legendary Confederate leader then wrote out in his own hand a pass which lasted Smulders and Sheeran until the end of the war. In a humorous follow-up anecdote from two months later at a Division Military Review, Lee recognized Sheeran as he passed by. "Lee did not allow me to escape his notice and extended his hand in a most cordial and friendly manner. This mark of respect and friendship attracted universal attention, for I was the only one of all the Chaplains he seemed to notice."[12]

As a gifted speaker, Smulders often preached outside troop settings, mentioning in a letter to his superior a well-attended mission he gave in Charleston in 1863 lasting three weeks. At the time, the church was in the range of Yankee artillery, though the people showed no fear and still attended the mission. One evening the bombing was so bad that Smulders had the congregation kneel and recite three Hail Marys, at which the shelling stopped soon thereafter, because (providentially for the Confederates) water had gushed on the island from which the guns were placed, thus halting shooting for several days.

Smulders wrote little of his Civil War experiences, but in a September 1865 letter from Fort Jennings, he briefly summed up his wartime ministry.

When I arrived at Camp Pickens on the 7th of September [1861], I commenced my career as chaplain, placing myself and our Catholics under the protection of our dear Mother. . . . We had a large portion of the time, to sleep under the blue heavens on a horse blanket spread on the ground, another blanket to cover, and the saddle for a pillow. Our food was generally sufficient to keep soul and body together; we had no time to think of luxuries. Three times I was seriously sick. The first [was] chronic diarrhea. . . . My second illness was typhoid fever. . . . The last spell of sickness was in January 1864. It was dysentery. I was taken care of by the good Sisters of Charity at the infirmary at Richmond. . . .

On the battlefield we often had much more work with the enemy's wounded, for they did not care to carry off the badly wounded of their army. When there was no battle, we had our Mass and sermon every Sunday; and in camp, every day Mass, AM and Rosary PM which was well attended. Not only did our Catholics attend, but also a large number of Protestants attended divine services. In all the divisions of the army, we always met the greatest politeness and respect from the officers and men; and generally the colonel or major would give up his tent to us for confessions and holy Mass. Even the Protestant chaplains treated us with the utmost deference, although we would never associate with them, nor adopt their uniform.[13]

As mentioned above, when the war concluded, Smulders went on to thirty-five more years of very influential priestly work as a Redemptorist priest. He founded a church in Detroit (Holy Redeemer), was the superior of a community, traveled the country preaching retreats and missions, became a member of order's leadership team, and celebrated his Golden Jubilee in September 1893. This immensely gifted Belgian priest died in April 1900 in St. Louis at age eighty-four, having been a priest for fifty-six years.[14]

THE DOMINICANS:
JARBOE, EGAN, MCGRATH, ORENGO, AND NEALIS

The Order of Preachers, known as the Dominicans, is one of the oldest and most recognized Catholic religious orders. They were approved by the Pope in 1216, and begun in France by St. Dominic de Guzman (1170–1221) to combat heresy and preach the gospel. Over time, the order became known for its intellectual tradition, producing many leading theologians and philosophers (e.g., Meister Eckhart, Thomas Aquinas, and Albert the Great). Though individual Dominicans came to America as early as the sixteenth century, the order was not formally established in the United States until the early nineteenth century, with its first foundation (St. Rose Priory) beginning in 1806 near Springfield, Kentucky. (Parts of the original structure remain to this day, and the priory is still used as a church.) The college formed there several years later boasts among its distinguished alumni the young Jefferson Davis—who, along with his wife, in later years remained quite favorable to Catholics, even going so far as to employ only Catholic nurses for their children.[15]

The first province of the Dominicans, St. Joseph Province, was founded not in the East but in the Kentucky frontier at St. Rose Priory, because John Carroll (1735–1815), America's first Catholic bishop, wished the order to minister to the flood of westward-moving Catholics who were begging for priests. Five Dominican chaplains went forth from their Kentucky base, for varying lengths of time, to render their services as chaplains during the Civil War. Two of the five, John Nealis and Luigi Orengo, were only occasional chaplains who served their respective parish areas; Matthew McGrath was a recognized hospital chaplain during the war, and Constantine Egan and Joseph Jarboe were regimental chaplains.

Joseph Thomas Jarboe

Joseph Thomas Jarboe (1806–1887) was a descendent of English Catholics from Maryland who come in 1787 to Lebanon, Kentucky, in a mass Catholic migration. One of six children, he studied at the Dominicans' St. Rose school and showed exceptional educational aptitude there even as a youth. He was ordained in June 1830 by Bishop Edward Fenwick, also a Dominican. Jarboe's health at the time was so poor that he was physically supported by another priest to receive ordination, yet he went on to outlive most of his contemporaries and serve fifty-seven years in the ministry. He served first in positions at St. Rose Priory and performed heroic work during an 1833 cholera epidemic near Springfield,

Kentucky. He helped convert a Puritan Yankee named Henry Vincent Browne, who later became a prominent priest in the Nashville Diocese (and a chaplain as well). During the late 1840s he was head of the Dominican college in Sinsinawa, Wisconsin, and in 1859 even had his name submitted to Rome to become a bishop (it appears his partial deafness prevented that from occurring, though).[16]

When the war broke out in 1861, Jarboe was a pastor at Zanesville, Ohio. His superiors asked him to minister to a Confederate regiment forming in Memphis, Tennessee: the 2nd Tennessee Infantry (Walker). Also called the Irish Regiment, the 541 volunteers went first to Fort Pillow, then fought at Belmont (November 7, 1861), and suffered heavy casualties at Shiloh (April 6–7, 1862) before being consolidated and merged into Smith's 5th Confederate Infantry. Although Jarboe was given permission by his order to be a chaplain, and is listed in the general Confederate records as being a chaplain for that unit on July 1, 1861, there is no official Confederate record of any formal appointment to the position. It appears he served as chaplain from about May 1861 to April 1862; he is mentioned in Dominican archival records as distinguishing himself in his care for the wounded and as being at the Battle of Shiloh.[17]

At Shiloh, it appears he was heavily involved in ministry, as indicated by the event spoken of earlier in chapter 3 where a bullet shattered the knife Jarboe was using to cut away a soldier's boot for anointing. An equally curious event occurred when he was captured by Union soldiers after the Battle of Shiloh had concluded. Conflicting accounts exist about what happened, but the common element is that Jarboe was ministering to wounded soldiers, which apparently put him in the Federal lines. The most accurate and reliable retelling of what happened next includes him being captured, accused of being a spy, and being brought to face General William "Bull" Nelson. Nelson was about to shoot the priest when Jarboe was providentially recognized by the Provost Marshall, John G. Key, and set free. (Jarboe himself would write later in the Catholic *Daily Freeman* that he simply escaped and headed north. Nelson was shot and killed by General Jefferson C. Davis on September 29, 1862, after a heated argument in a Louisville, Kentucky hotel.)[18]

Whatever the exact truth of the matter, Jarboe survived the encounter, spent some time recovering with friends, and then left the chaplaincy to return to more traditional Catholic parish ministry. From the end of the war in 1865 to 1884, he continued his labors throughout Tennessee, serving in several different capacities. He ministered at an orphanage, was chaplain to a Nashville community of nuns, and served as vicar general of the Nashville Diocese from 1869 to 1884. At that time, his age, general deafness, and various infirmities of aging caused him to retire, and he returned to the Dominican house at Somerset, Ohio, where he died on March 27, 1887. He is remembered in the annals of the Nashville Diocese as among the first and greatest of missionaries in Ohio, Kentucky, and Tennessee.[19]

Matthew Francis McGrath (Union Hospital Chaplain)

Matthew Francis McGrath (1833–1870) was born in Tipperary, Ireland, in 1833 to a successful hardware merchant who decided to educate him for the priesthood in Ireland. But the chance visit of a Dominican priest in 1850 led the young McGrath to America and into the Dominican Order instead, where he took his vows in 1853 and was ordained in June 1856. He first ministered in Kentucky by teaching and giving missions, until he was transferred to the order's Washington, DC, priory and St. Dominic church in 1858. In the nation's capital, McGrath became one of the city's great preachers, and it is said he won many converts to the Catholic Church because of his zeal and eloquence. However, as the Civil War began, McGrath also became concerned about the gradually increasing numbers of wounded Union soldiers coming into the city's hospitals as the war's casualties increased; as a result, he expressed an interest in serving as chaplain.

On May 20, 1862, Congress formally approved President Lincoln's request from six months earlier to authorize "a chaplain for each permanent hospital, whose pay . . . shall be the same as that of regimental chaplains in the volunteer force." On June 13, 1862, McGrath was one of several Catholic priests to be appointed as the Union's first hospital chaplains, thus receiving a presidential appointment to the United States Hospital at Georgetown (also known as Seminary Hospital).

His work and that of all Catholic hospital chaplains will be covered more in detail in chapter 8; for now, suffice it to say that McGrath continued in that position formally until resigning on October 1, 1863.[20]

McGrath resigned because in that year, his order gave him permission to visit family in Ireland, and upon his return, he ministered briefly in Ontario, Canada, before being sent back to St. Rose Priory in Kentucky where he again engaged in very successful parish and missionary work. After a brief attempt in 1869 to seek to leave the order due to the "arbitrary ways and peculiarities" of a new superior, McGrath retracted his petition and was on the verge of returning to the Dominicans when he died unexpectedly in December 1870. The order allowed him to be buried in their community cemetery at St. Rose Priory.[21]

Constantine Louis Egan (9th Massachusetts)

Another chaplain mentioned frequently in William Corby's wartime *Memoirs* is Constantine Louis Egan (1828–1899, 9th Massachusetts). Well educated in his native country of Ireland, after immigrating to the United States, he taught school in various places in Kentucky, then briefly considered life as a Trappist monk at Gethsemane Abbey before finally joining the Dominicans, professing vows there in June 1855 and being ordained in September 1860. For two years, Egan taught at the college in Sinsinawa, Wisconsin, which the Dominicans operated, then was moved to St. Dominic's Church in Washington, DC, in late summer 1863.

On August 25, 1863, a messenger from the War Department arrived at the church asking for a priest to minister to five men (two of them Catholic) who were about to be executed. Egan went to them, spending some time there hearing their confessions and saying Mass. When this ended, the Colonel Patrick Guiney of the 9th Massachusetts invited Egan to his regiment to minister, and following that, he was asked to continue his spiritual work for General Charles Griffin's troops (1st Division Commander in the 5th Corps). Working with soldiers in both the Union's 5th and 9th Corps, Egan remarked that "he liked camp life better than the easier, but desultory life of a friar," and agreed to remain as a formal chaplain if so appointed. After obtaining permission from his superior, he joined the 9th Massachusetts in time for the late fall 1863 battles of the regiment (Bristoe Station, Rappahannock Station, and the Mine Run Campaign). As mentioned previously, at that time he gave a dramatic, general absolution of sins to the amassed Union troops, even though the proposed attack never occurred.[22]

Egan was a popular and effective chaplain in a variety of positions, and because of Corby's *Memoirs* (and the recently published Conyngham manuscript), we have a good history of his war years. Beginning in mid-1863, the native Irishman ministered to the 9th Massachusetts. When their term of service expired in June 1864, Egan became chaplain to the 5th Corps as a member on the staff of General Charles Griffin, and a hospital chaplain at City Point. In early 1864, his pastoral work was especially wide-ranging and expansive. He worked first among army regulars in the 14th US Infantry, then went into several brigades in the 5th Corps, "giving missions through the whole corps." Next, he pitched his tent near the 1st Corps to meet their spiritual needs, living next to several cavalry brigades (Custer, Merritt) and "meeting a large number of Catholics, especially among the New York regiments." Finally, he returned to his own regiment in March 1864, and when they marched a month later to Brandy Station, he ministered to 6th Corps troops before rejoining the 5th Corps and the 9th Massachusetts for their bloody battles at the Wilderness and Spotsylvania in May 1864.[23]

During the final Union push to Appomattox, Egan stopped to baptize a badly wounded Confederate soldier, who continued to utter very fervent prayers long after the priest's ministry was done. Egan remained with the suffering soldier until he was finally forced to leave the man in order to follow after the rapidly moving Union troops. When he caught up to the troops, he found out that the Confederates had just surrendered, and the officers on both sides were mingling freely. Following some final ministry work in late April 1865 of appealing for a delay in the execution of a Union soldier (in which he succeeded), Egan returned to headquarters, and on July 15, 1865, he mustered out with an honorable discharge.

Egan went on to be prior of the Dominican house (St. Louis Bertrand's) in Louisville twice (building a new priory in the process), was chaplain to a convent of nuns (the Sisters of St. Mary's of the Springs in

Columbus, Ohio), and pastored churches in Ohio and Minnesota. He died at his Louisville church in July 1899, and was buried in the Dominican cemetery at St. Rose. His epitaph was well expressed by one soldier: "A true priest, chaplain, and noble-hearted Christian gentleman, greatly beloved by all the regiment and highly respected throughout the Fifth Corps and the Army . . . wherever his priestly duties called him in the army, there he was to be found: in the camps, hospitals and on the battlefield. . . . His presence and priestly service was, indeed, a blessing."[24]

James Aloysius (Luigi) Orengo (Occasional)

The two final Dominicans known to have assisted with ministering to Civil War soldiers are both considered occasional chaplains due to their lack of formal assignment and irregularity of their Civil War ministry. Yet both are fascinating characters in their own right. James Aloysius (Luigi) Orengo was born in Italy in 1820, and joined the Dominican Order in Rome at the young age of sixteen, apparently to avoid military conscription in the Piedmontese army. After receiving his habit and being ordained in 1843, he was sent to America the next year with several other members of the order and assigned to St. Rose Priory in Kentucky. For the next twenty-five years, Orengo is described as "traveling Tennessee from end to end . . . on his faithful steed . . . occasionally spending the night in the forest," while doing missionary activity to the scattered Catholic communities spread throughout middle Tennessee.[25]

Orengo is a classic example of the itinerant missionary work that many priests (particularly those in religious orders) undertook in the late nineteenth century. These missionaries rarely stayed in one place very long, were constantly on the move gathering widespread Catholics together ministering to them, and established Catholic parishes—they truly were foundational figures in the formation of the strong Catholic presence in many parts of the United States. Orengo himself journeyed tirelessly through central Tennessee, founding at least twelve churches, clearing debt from many others, and in the process securing his name's spot on several historical state monuments markers. His work was such that it was said of him that "he went everywhere, knew everybody, and everybody seemed to know him."[26]

Orengo is mentioned as having met and ministered to many Civil War soldiers who passed through war-torn Tennessee, especially in the Nashville area. But the people and places of his specific labors are without note or recognition, as his work did not allow him to remain in one place to ever become a formal chaplain or to establish an uninterrupted chaplain's ministry. One history of the Dominicans captured his itinerant work well: "Often he had narrow escapes from the soldiers, whether of the north or the south, while in the pursuance of his duties, Nature gave him the happy combination of the simplicity of a dove and the cunning of a serpent. And many are the tales still told of how he used it to save himself and his horse on such occasions."[27]

Around 1873, Orengo finally set aside his travelling ministries, and returned to live at the St. Rose Priory house, but several years later Orengo was encouraged by his superior to return to his native Italy to live out his last years. He did so, eventually dying in March 1909 at age eighty-nine, having been a Dominican for seventy-two of those years and a priest for sixty-five.

John Thomas Nealis (Occasional)

The story of John Thomas Nealis (1832–1864) is that of equal pastoral zeal, but sadly with a much shorter life than his confrere James Orengo. Born in New York City in either 1831 or 1832, Nealis professed his vows as a Dominican in 1852 and was ordained to the priesthood by Cincinnati Bishop John Purcell in August 1856 along with Michael McGrath. In 1859 he was sent to Memphis (St. Peter's Church), then in either late 1861 or early 1862 to Chattanooga as a pastor of Saints Peter and Paul. In late 1863 he was living and working out of Nashville. In all three of these cities, he was thrust into the heart of Tennessee's painful Civil War tensions, as both the Union and Confederacy struggled for mastery throughout the state. (Nashville was captured by Union forces in February 1862, Memphis in June 1862, and Chattanooga in September 1863.) Though known to be a splendid horseman "who knew no fear," and once called a Confederate chaplain by the Catholic *Freeman's Journal*, Nealis was never a formal chaplain, and ministered only occasionally to Civil War troops of both sides as they crossed through his parish boundaries (mainly Chattanooga and Nashville).[28]

It was in Chattanooga that Tennessee's torn wartime loyalties impacted Nealis in a most unfortunate way. Sometime around the middle of 1862, the priest was accosted by "ruffians," who beat and then shot him. Specifics about the attack are vague, but in an 1888 War Claims Committee report, Nealis was said to have been "so enthusiastically and outspokenly loyal that he was shot through the body by a rebel bushwhacker," thus implying some perceived pro-Union sympathies might have been involved. Soon thereafter, priest-chaplain Jeremiah Trecy (14th Union Corps) passed through Chattanooga, and found Nealis's church ransacked. He searched for him and found the priest "on a sick bed suffering from a dangerous wound received at the hands of two miscreants while in the discharge of his duty amongst his countrymen in the coal mines on the Raccoon Mountains." Placing a guard on the church, Trecy was rewarded by capturing seven men "about to renew their work of spoliation," and "two of them were found to be Irish Protestants."[29]

Nealis recovered and was able to resume ministry (he even accompanied Bishop James Whelan on several area confirmations), but his health was permanently affected by the attack. Nealis unfortunately became subject to intermittent fainting spells, and on March 19, 1864, sometime during the early morning hours, he fainted and fell to his death from an upper window of the Nashville cathedral where he was residing. He was interred first in the Nashville cathedral itself, and then Nealis was later moved to the St. Rose Priory Cemetery in Kentucky, where his Province mourned his untimely passing; great things had been expected of him.

THE FRANCISCANS: RIZZO AND GOMBITELLI

The final Catholic religious order that sent official chaplains to the war were the Franciscans (formally the Order of Friars Minor, one of several Franciscan communities worldwide). Founded by the legendary St. Francis of Assisi in 1209, and originally known for their austere poverty, they arrived in the Caribbean with Columbus in 1492, and in the next centuries established missions in Florida, California, and numerous southern states. In the mid-1850s the order was invited into the newly established Buffalo Diocese in western New York, and in 1858 volunteers from several Italian Franciscan provinces established both a friary (i.e., a residence for the monks) and St. Bonaventure College in Allegany, New York. Two Italian Franciscan priests from the friary connected to that college served as Civil War chaplains—Giacomo "James" Titta de Gombitelli and Leoneda "Leo" Rizzo de Saracena.

Leoneda "Leo" Rizzo de Saracena (9th Connecticut)

Leoneda "Leo" Rizzo de Saracena (1833–1897) was born in Calabria, Italy, professed vows as a Franciscan in January 1850, was ordained a priest in September 1856, and came to the United States four years later. Known as a man of "scholarly interests . . . who spoke English with an Irish brogue," Rizzo served very briefly in Pennsylvania, then became a pastor at St. Mary's Church in New Haven, Connecticut, beginning what would become a long and cherished connection with the Hartford Diocese. In April 1864, the heavily Irish 9th Connecticut Volunteers returned to their 1861 recruiting base in New Haven on furlough from three years in Louisiana minus their previous chaplain Daniel Mullen, who had resigned in August 1862 due to typhoid fever and diarrhea. "Father Leo" was a friend of Mullen and enlisted as the new chaplain, being commissioned on July 24, 1864, just days before the regiment boarded a steamer that was intended for Louisiana, but (after orders were changed) disembarked instead at Bermuda Hundred, Virginia, on the James River.[30]

In Virginia, the 9th Connecticut had three engagements with Confederate troops: in the Petersburg Campaign at Deep Bottom (July 27–29, 1864), in Sheridan's Shenandoah Valley Campaign at Third Winchester (Opequon, September 19, 1864), and at Fisher's Hill (September 22, 1864). Despite being described by one officer at the time as "fine-looking and robust," it seems the scholarly Rizzo was ill-suited for the rugged life of a foot soldier (he never was able to obtain a horse). He did march with the troops, shared their hardships, and was well appreciated by the troops for his spiritual work. But though he was formally listed as being with the regiment for three months and these battles, Rizzo was hospitalized in Harpers Ferry on August 23, 1864, likely with typhoid fever and possibly an injury of some sort (though that is unclear). While he may have recovered enough to rejoin his regiment briefly after that, we do know that by late September he again became confined to his bed in Harpers Ferry "near to death at one point." At this time his chaplain's credentials were stolen by a Jesuit priest-chaplain, Joseph Bixio, who used them to misrepresent himself as Rizzo and obtain wagon loads of Union supplies, which he then drove into Confederate lines in Staunton. (As mentioned above, James Sheeran subsequently paid the price for Bixio's chicanery.)

Rizzo eventually found out about this deception, and after an irate General Philip Sheridan cleared the innocent Italian of any fault in the incident, the ailing priest was honorably discharged from his chaplain's position on October 26, 1864. He returned to Connecticut where he became a pastor (St. Joseph's in Winsted, Connecticut), superior and provincial in his order, and then president of St. Bonaventure College from 1877 to 1880 before returning to his beloved Winsted parish. With his fiery temperament, yet humble and kind disposition, Rizzo became known as "the lion of Winsted." He was beloved in his community and a reputed confessor to four bishops of the Hartford Diocese. He met Pope Leo XIII on an 1891 visit to his Italian homeland, and died in his Winsted parish in November 1897. A later biography described his funeral and the tremendous impact this well-known Franciscan had on people: "Upon his death in 1897 all public business was suspended and the Governor of Connecticut was an honorary pallbearer. All city officials were present as well as two military officials. Four bishops, more than two hundred priests and fourteen hundred others crowded into the church for the Mass, while an estimated four thousand remained outside. This was a fitting tribute to the unrelenting energy and dedication of a zealous man of God."[31]

Giacomo "James" Titta da Gombitelli
(13th Pennsylvania, 117th Pennsylvania)

Giacomo "James" Titta da Gombitelli (1831–1877) was born in the small central Italian village of Gombitelli, professed his vows as a Franciscan while still in Italy, and was ordained a priest there in 1854. Described as "ruddy-faced, fair haired and often mistaken for an Irishman," he arrived in the United States in December 1859, and immediately joined the Franciscan community at St. Bonaventure in Allegany, New York, serving as vice president in that inaugural year of the college. He was soon assigned to the new St. Patrick Church in Buffalo as part of the first group of Franciscans to pastor the parish there, which had been established by Bishop John Timon in the heavily Irish industrial district of Buffalo (also known as the "Hydraulics" district).[32]

Exactly how Titta became a priest-chaplain is unclear, as are the historical accounts of his work. In his first years in America, Titta ministered in western New York and Pennsylvania, and it is possible his connection to Pennsylvania soldiers came from there, but ultimately his motivations are unknown. Military records show that on December 23, 1862, he was enrolled as chaplain to the 13th Pennsylvania Cavalry (first designated as the 117th Pennsylvania Volunteers) in Baltimore, and that he served until June 7, 1863, when he tendered his resignation (honorably accepted). The Italian priest would likely have joined his regiment at Point of Rocks, Maryland, as they guarded the Potomac River line in late 1862, and remained with them through subsequent small engagements at Woodstock, Virginia (February 26, 1863), Strasburg in the Valley (April 22, 1863), and Piedmont Station (May 1, 1863).[33]

Upon resigning his commission five months later in June 1863, Titta interestingly stated that "most of the members of my Regt. are a different denomination than my own." In scanning regimental lists, one does not find many Irish names (presumably Catholics), which may be evidence for his comment, but the relatively detached status of his regiment might have also contributed. In this regard, Titta's situation is not unlike other Catholic chaplains whose service began with high hopes of providing spiritual services for Catholic soldiers, but was cut short for various reasons. Titta may have resigned in part due to the lack of Catholic soldiers in his regiment. In the case of priest-chaplain Gustavus Miettinger (2nd New York), one can point to the lack of German Catholics as a deterring factor. Other priest-chaplains faced their own breaking points: John Ireland was called back home, Louis Lambert's regiment struggled with internal issues, and George Doane lasted only three months in the New Jersey Militia Regiment.[34]

Once he resigned, Titta then returned to his Franciscan friary in Allegany, from where he and another priest were sent to Meadville, Pennsylvania, in 1864 to attempt to start another Franciscan college. Their intentions were announced in the local paper (*Crawford Democrat*, August 8, 1865), which stated that "a Catholic College will be opened in this place about the 1st of September." If it ever was opened, the school was apparently not a success; both men left Meadville in December 1865 and returned to their Allegany home community.

Titta ministered in western New York for several more years, then was sent to the new Italian parish in New York City given to the Franciscans, St. Anthony of Padua. There he was named provincial of all the Franciscans in the United States, and served in that position for about six years. When his term ended, Titta remained at St. Anthony's again as pastor, and it was there that he died in March 1877 at the young age of forty-five. At his death, Titta was highly esteemed by the people to whom he had ministered, which by then embraced not only Italians but English-speaking Catholics. He was buried in the Franciscan cemetery at St. Bonaventure College.

THE VINCENTIANS: RYAN, BOGLIOLI, BURKE, SMITH, AND BURLANDO

To close out this chapter, we turn briefly to one other religious order that had Civil War chaplains connected to them in some manner, though the service of each of them is perhaps best considered occasional. The Vincentians (also known as the Lazarists) were founded in Paris by St. Vincent de Paul in 1625 with the purpose of evangelizing the poor and educating men for priesthood. Arriving in the United States in 1815 and

1816, they settled in the St. Louis area, but rapidly spread out, starting mission churches and conducting seminaries in numerous states. Only two priests from the Vincentians are mentioned publicly as ministering in more than a merely casual way as chaplains, and both are somewhat remarkable, for very different reasons.[35]

The famed "poet-priest of the Confederacy," Abram Ryan (1838–1886), was a member of the Vincentian order—entering their seminary twice due to vocational "issues" that arose after his first stay (1851). This inauspicious beginning to his religious and priestly career was an early indication of the troubles he would later have in life. Following Ryan's 1860 ordination at the tender age of twenty-two (priests are rarely ordained that young), he left the Vincentian order, being dispensed of his vows two years later in September 1862. Abram Ryan's captivating life as a Civil War figure will be covered more in detail in chapter 11.

Another Vincentian priest with a Civil War chaplaincy connection—albeit vague—was Charles Boglioli (1814–1882), who left his native Italy in 1840 to be ordained in America in March 1841. After teaching for several years, he spent the next sixteen years as a missionary pastor in Louisiana, in the Donaldsonville and Bayou Lafourche areas. When the Civil War broke out, it seems Boglioli may have accompanied the Donaldsonville Cannoneers to Virginia as their chaplain for "more than a year." Unfortunately, little or no formal documentation exists to collaborate this claim, which was made in several articles and his extensive obituary notice from July 1882.[36]

Boglioli is described as a large, powerfully built, strong man "whom no danger could intimidate." His Civil War service may be unconfirmed, but his remarkable postwar ministry to New Orleans lepers was truly heroic. Beginning after the Civil War and continuing through the yellow fever epidemic of 1878, Boglioli worked with patients who had leprosy at Charity Hospital until he contracted the disease himself. He was an inspiration to countless people and continued to say Mass when only his thumb and forefinger remained intact as a result of the disease. Boglioli was described as "the Father Damien of Louisiana . . . our saintly Brother" and "a good friend of the poor." He died on July 23, 1882.[37]

Two additional Vincentian priests worked with sick and wounded troops in the areas in which they were living. In Missouri in 1861, the order had already begun working with Union soldiers stationed around their Cape Girardeau college, regularly saying Mass and hearing confessions for them. In their St. Louis parish of St. Vincent de Paul, the Irish immigrant Thomas Burke (1808–1877) developed a personal ministry to hospitalized soldiers there. His provincial, Stephen Ryan, described him as "a great man in the city, wearing a long grey beard, and being known in all the Hospitals especially with the military men. He does much good among them baptizing many, distributing books and instructing in our holy faith." Following the war, Burke was an efficient procurator of several Vincentian houses in Missouri, and his October 1877 death left the order there in some consternation for a time.[38]

With the burgeoning immigrant population of America, building new churches was a common nineteenth-century occurrence. One such priest who did this at least twice (in Brooklyn and Chicago) was Edward M. Smith (1835–1896). He immigrated to the United States from Ireland, studied at the Vincentian house in Perryville, Missouri, and was ordained on July 23, 1860. He was soon named pastor at the Vincentian parish of St. Joseph's in Emmittsburg, Maryland, and was there at the time of the Battle of Antietam in September 1862. The Sisters of Charity there (whose roots also went back to St. Vincent de Paul, through Mother Elizabeth Seton) answered an urgent request to help with the wounded of the battle. Along with Father Smith, they gathered a large quantity of clothing, provisions, remedies, food, and money for the wounded. Edward Smith then accompanied two of the sisters to nearby Boonsboro, reaching the town by twilight and setting out for the battlefield the next day. He ministered to soldiers, prepared several for their death, and was about to perform burial rites for one just as General George McClellan rode up to greet them. After speaking with the priest, McClellan joined the procession to the cemetery and remained with them until the interment. The nuns and Smith remained for six days to serve amid seven Boonesboro hospitals that were housing wounded soldiers, until most of the injured men had been removed from the area. Smith celebrated two Masses at the home where he had been staying, and then he and the nuns returned to Emmitsburg. He went on to pastoral ministry in New Orleans, Brooklyn, and Chicago, where he died on September 24, 1896.[39]

As was common with many female orders of the day, the Daughters of Charity of Emmitsburg were technically subject to male directors. In their case, this person during the Civil War was the provincial of the Vincentian order, Francis J. Burlando (1811–1873). As their formal chaplain, he accompanied them on much of their "mission" work during the war years, and specifically ministered with them at a number of hospitals after battles. Two days after Gettysburg, Burlando and twelve nuns left for that battlefield "taking refreshments, bandages, sponges, and clothing, with the intention of doing all that was possible for the suffering soldiers and then returning home the next evening." They went to the town of Gettysburg, and were shown to a temporary hospital in St. Francis Xavier Church, where they quickly used up their supplies. While there, Burlando "visited as well he could the various military hospitals where the Sisters were stationed. [My] care would not extend beyond the line of hostilities." Burlando and two nuns then returned to Emmitsburg to bring additional nurses to relieve the first group. Ten days later at the Port Lookout hospital in Maryland, he was "constantly engaged among the soldiers, instructing, baptizing and hearing confessions. On Sunday mornings he said the first Mass at the encampment, and the second in the little chapel."[40]

The words of a letter Burlando wrote written five days after the battle poignantly describe the post-battle ministry of nurse-nuns, doctors, and clergy, while also capturing the depth of anguish and sorrow that war always brings.

> Provisions have been sent by the government, the poor wounded succored, and inhabitants have given assistance to thousands of suffering and dying. Eleven sisters are now employed in this town transformed into a hospital. We shall send some Sisters and necessities tomorrow if possible. While I write to you, the sound of cannonading re-echoes from the Southwest, where another engagement takes place. My God, when will you give peace to our unhappy country?[41]

As chaplain of the Daughters of Charity's Emmitsburg community, Burlando faithfully guided, supported, and ministered with them throughout the war, and is mentioned fondly throughout the wartime hospital accounts of these nuns. Barton's classic, *Angels of the Battlefield*, remarks of Burlando's wartime care that "by his constant vigilance, consummate prudence . . . and continual prayers, he had the consolation of seeing the whole community free from all reproach and danger." On February 16, 1873, Burlando died in Emmitsburg, where he spent the majority of his ministry years.[42]

CHAPTER 7

PROMINENT DIOCESAN CHAPLAINS

All wartime Catholic Civil War chaplains belonged either to a religious order (as those discussed in the previous three chapters) or to a geographic diocese in the American Catholic Church (a district governed by a bishop). During the war, religious orders based out of universities or community houses provided the most reliable source of chaplains for the armies (nine of the fifteen full-time chaplains were religious). As Will Kurtz accurately states, "Not beholden to parish duty or the commands of hesitant bishops as were secular [diocesan] priests, the religious orders proved crucial in supplying men to units such as the Irish Brigade." However, priests from specific dioceses did actually comprise the majority of wartime chaplains on our list of Catholic priests who served. Sixty-six percent of the verifiable Catholic chaplains identified in this book came from individual local dioceses and with the support of their bishops. These diocesan priests, serving under bishops in specific geographic dioceses, certainly faced their own distinct challenges.[1]

At the war's outset, one issue was that politicians and military leaders often took greater initiative to find priest-chaplains than regional Catholic bishops themselves did. For example, it was Indiana's governor (Oliver Morton) who first reached out to Notre Dame about supplying chaplains, as did Minnesota's governor (Alexander Ramsey) to priests of his area. Lincoln himself requested priests for hospitals from Archbishop John Hughes (New York), who then forwarded the request to a lukewarm Archbishop Francis Kenrick (Baltimore), who finally did recommend two priests. Likewise, diocesan priests needed the direct support of their bishop to become chaplains, and when they did so, most often they did not have the benefit of a local support network, such as religious order priests did, to fall back on in times of troubles. They were also more susceptible to being recalled to their diocese due to local needs and issues in their church there (e.g., John Ireland).

Catholic wartime bishops tended to put the pressing needs of their flocks at home ahead of caring for the troops in the field. Due to general priest shortages, massive immigration (especially in urban areas) of new parishioners, and the pastoral care (mainly the sacraments) required by the Catholic faith, most bishops of the mid-nineteenth century were so stretched they could not spare priests to serve troops outside their diocese. A final factor was that some priests were simply considered "unqualified" for service, and others were not able to handle the arduous tasks chaplaincy required. For all of these reasons, diocesan priests did not serve as chaplains for as long as religious order priests did. In reality there was never any overarching common plan for ministering to Catholic Civil War soldiers by the American Catholic hierarchy.[2]

Nevertheless, there were a number of diocesan priests who did become long-term, outstanding chaplains for both the Union and Confederacy during the Civil War. In this chapter we will introduce a number of these priests who made a significant impact by their wartime chaplaincy.

UNION DIOCESAN CHAPLAINS

Joseph "Napoleon" Mignault (17th Wisconsin)

The Canadian Joseph Edward "Napoleon" Mignault (1826–1895) provides a good transition into this chapter, as he was at different times a member of both a religious congregation and a diocese. Born near

Quebec, he studied for seminary in that diocese, but had to return home when his health failed. He then studied law, but after a severe accident brought him close to death, in gratitude he vowed his services to the Church. Resuming his seminary studies, he joined the Missionary Oblates of Mary Immaculate (OMI)—a French order begun in the early eighteenth century with a strong missionary outreach—professing his vows in November 1849, then being ordained just one month later by Quebec Bishop Joseph-Bruno Guigues (also a member of the order). Mignault was immediately appointed director of studies at the new College of Bytown (now the University of Ottawa), and then superior of his religious order in 1851 at the youthful age of twenty-five.

While the good bishop undoubtedly had the best of intentions in mind, and great confidence in this new priest, it appears that this rush of spiritual advancements may have been simply too much for Mignault. He ended up leaving his congregation shortly after he was named superior (his illnesses were likely also an issue), then journeying to Massachusetts to minister to Franco-Americans (French-Canadian immigrants) in the New England area for about six years. This ministry to French-speaking people in America comprised the bulk of Mignault's forty-four-year priestly career, which he spent "wandering" through four separate dioceses in all. He was in the New England area for about a decade, then moved on to northern Wisconsin from 1857 to 1864, working with the French-speaking who had been attracted by the fur trade and lumber industry there, and ended his career in the Erie Diocese (Pennsylvania).[3]

Described in one place as a "good-natured and genial man, who could adapt to his environments, and lend a hand whenever necessary," Mignault ministered in an open and broad-based way.[4] Notwithstanding his primary focus on the French-speaking populace, he reached out to any ethnic group that had large numbers of Catholics. This would have included the Irish. During Mignault's Wisconsin sojourn, it was this connection to the Irish that seemingly helped awaken his interest in serving as a chaplain during the Civil War. In his book *Catholics and the Civil War*, Benjamin Blied comments on Mignault's actions just prior to enrolling as a Civil War chaplain:

As early as 18 November 1861, Mignault showed his interest in the Irish by giving a lecture in Cole's Hall, Watertown, on "Irishmen at Home and in America." . . . After emphasizing the evils of British rule abroad, he exhorted his hearers to do their duty as the Germans, French and Norwegians were doing—to support the constitution against the traitors who were trying to dismember a republic that had brought to all nothing but blessings, prosperity and honor. A few weeks after delivering that fiery speech, to be exact, on 11 December 1861, he was commissioned for the 17th WI, and he remained in the army until 9 Feb 1864.[5]

The seventeenth Wisconsin Infantry was organized at Camp Randall (in Madison), went into service in March 1862, moved to Pittsburg Landing, Tennessee, in April, was part of the battle of Corinth, and then the Vicksburg and Atlanta Campaigns. Though it was at times known as the "Irish Brigade/Regiment," the overall ethnicity of the seventeenth Wisconsin is debated. There was an entire French company in it, together with Native Americans and other ethnic groups, along with the Irish. Mignault was the first of two Catholic chaplains for the regiment (the Austrian Francis Fusseder followed him in July 1864; cf. chapter 11), and served until the Battle of Vicksburg (summer 1863). As he wrote no journal or letters that we are aware of, details of his service in the seventeenth Wisconsin are scarce. We do know that local Wisconsin records later indicate that Mignault had once been captured by Confederate guerrillas, but upon learning of the nature of his work, they treated him courteously and let him go. In a December 22, 1862, general order, the French cleric was thanked "for his proffered services" by an aide-de-camp of General Ulysses S. Grant's staff, Colonel George Ihrie.[6]

We also know that the approximately eighteen months of Mignault's actual service took a physical toll upon the French Canadian, whose health had been frail in the past. General Grant's troubles with disease and sickness in the swamps and bayous of Louisiana before crossing the Mississippi River are well known, and it seems Mignault likewise fell victim to these maladies (cf. chapter 12 for more about the priests who died in those swamps). In June 1863, Holy Cross priest

Joseph Carrier (6th Missouri), then serving in Vicksburg, encountered the ailing Mignault, an event recounted in the Irish Catholic journalist David Conyngham's postwar manuscript.

> In the afternoon [June 21, 1863] he paid a visit to Father Mignault who he heard was worse and on the eve of leaving the army. He found him very weak, prostrated by fever and dysentery and preparing to leave for Montreal in a day or two. Not knowing when he would have another chance to see a priest, Father Carrier availed himself of Father Mignault's presence and made a confession after which they bid each other goodbye.[7]

Mignault was honorably discharged for physical disability on February 9, 1864 (though he had long since left the army), returning to Canada to recover from his serious wartime ailments. But the native Canadian had more stamina than expected—he lived another three decades, moving into the Erie Diocese of northwestern Pennsylvania as a pastor in Titusville (the birthplace of America's oil industry) from 1864 to 1871. He returned to Canada in 1889 to retire, but then made a trip to Europe, visited numerous countries, spent three months in Rome, and had the honor of two audiences with Pope Leo XIII. Mignault died in his native Saint-Hyacinthe, Quebec, in December 1895.

William T. O'Higgins (10th Ohio)

William O'Higgins (1829–1874) is the first of two influential, albeit somewhat "quarrelsome" priests whose bishops were likely happy to have them out of their dioceses for Civil War service. Perhaps best described as a priest with some "authority issues," O'Higgins served under four different bishops in his priestly career, frequently having run-ins with religious peers and superiors. Born in Ireland, he had studied at the well-known Maynooth Seminary in County Kildare, where his uncle and patron, Bishop William O'Higgins (1793–1853, bishop of Ardagh and Clonmacnoise) had taught. When the bishop died in 1853, William lost his protector and sponsor, but due to the desperate need for priests, he was not without work. Bishop John Hynes of British Guinea (now

the Republic of Guinea-Bissau) immediately recruited him for missionary work in his West Indies diocese, and in fact rushed him through
three major Catholic holy orders in three days in August 1853 to do so
(a rare event in Catholic clerical training).[8]

After four years of very difficult ministry in the West Indies, O'Higgins emigrated to America in 1857, offering his priestly services to
Cincinnati Bishop John Purcell (1800–1883), who accepted him. However, at one of his first assignments in the United States (St. Patrick's
Church in Columbus), O'Higgins immediately butted heads with the
pastor of that parish, Richard Gilmour. Thinking he was about to be expelled from the diocese, and not wanting to lose Purcell's favor, O'Higgins volunteered to be a Civil War chaplain instead, which the strongly
pro-Union Purcell immediately approved. On June 3, 1861, O'Higgins
mustered in with the heavily Irish 10th Ohio, under the command of
William Haines Lytle, a veteran of the Mexican-American War. His ministry began immediately. In October 1861, he gave twenty-one soldiers
their first communion before they even left Camp Denison, Ohio, for
service in what would soon (in 1863) become West Virginia.[9]

Whatever O'Higgins's personal issues may have been, his wartime
service and commitment were truly commendable. The Irish priest
ministered for four straight years in the 10th Ohio, one of only six diocesan priests to serve full-time as a chaplain. He faithfully performed
the usual Catholic duties that would have been expected—celebrating
Mass daily (when possible), hearing confessions, giving the sacrament
of extreme unction, and so on. But, as there were many non-Catholics
in the 10th, much of his work assumed a more ecumenical approach.
O'Higgins would frequently offer prayers for military functions like
dress parades and reception of regimental colors; he ministered to
homesick soldiers whatever their background, and comforted the regiment's sick and injured.

His bravery in battle was frequently noted, as at Carnifex Ferry
(September 10, 1861): "He was constantly with his men. He courageously crawled between lines amidst enemy fire to bring water from a
spring to help soothe the parched throats of the wounded Tenth Ohio-
ans." In one amusing incident, O'Higgins went on a patrol during General Henry Heth's invasion of northern Kentucky in September 1862.

While wandering away from his troops, he was fired upon by the Confederates, and attempted to retreat to Union lines but was fired upon by them as well. The priest was then seized, dragged into camp, and denounced as a "long haired rebel spy" by Union pickets who did not recognize him. When his identity became known, there was "general amusement" and "inextinguishable laughter" from his soldiers, who named it the "O'Higgins charge"![10]

As one of the longest serving wartime Civil War Catholic chaplains, O'Higgins was well-known and respected for his work by the troops and officers. On one occasion when the priest reentered camp following a battle, a war correspondent wrote that "every man turned out to greet him—he is unquestionably one of the most popular officers in the army. He always has a kind word for everybody, and feels as much at home in the soldier's tent as in the General's marquee." But no matter popular he was with the troops, O'Higgins's relations with his fellow Catholics chaplains appears to have been less cordial. Several of his 1863 letters detail numerous petty complaints about Jeremiah Trecy (who seems to have had General Rosecrans's ear), allegations of "worldly transactions" by "the Dutchman" Joseph Stephans, and references to Peter Cooney acting in "a low way." His oblique references to "those scallywags of priests roaming about seeking some poor devils hard earnings" seem to indicate that O'Higgins must have been a challenging man to live or minister with.[11]

Following the unfortunate death of General William Lytle (September 1863), and having some medical issues of his own in mid-1863, O'Higgins was mustered out in June 1864 with a small remnant of the 10th Ohio—"its ranks thinned and banners blood-stained and torn."[12] His postwar career was marked by a return to the Cincinnati Diocese for four years, followed by a rather surprising move to the formerly Confederate city of Little Rock, Arkansas. He lived at St. Andrew Cathedral there for two years, and likely ministered to soldiers stationed there at the US Arsenal.[13]

Again, for unknown reasons, O'Higgins departed from Arkansas for the Cleveland Diocese, where he taught philosophy for one term in the seminary, until a new bishop was appointed—unfortunately, the same Cincinnati priest with whom he had a run-in in 1860 (Richard

Gilmour, who was bishop of Cleveland from 1872 to 1891). O'Higgins found the installation unacceptable, and in light of his ongoing medical issues, he returned to his Irish homeland in 1871 to live near family and try to recover his health. There, this often petty, peripatetic but multi-faceted Irish chaplain met his Maker in November 1874, where his longest continued tenure of priestly service—Civil War chaplaincy—was undoubtedly rewarded greatly.

Thomas M. Brady (15th Michigan)

The second "quarrelsome" diocesan priest serving full-time as a Union chaplain was Thomas M. Brady, who ministered to the 15th Michigan from January 1862 to August 1865. Born in County Fermanagh, Ireland, in 1824, he had come to America to study, then met Bishop Joseph Timon of the Buffalo Diocese, who ordained him in 1854. For the next six years, Brady ministered in upstate New York at several parishes, where he became acquainted with a community of Irish nuns (the Brigidine Sisters) who were teaching in the area. In May 1860, Brady and several of these nuns transferred to the Detroit Diocese; Brady served at St. Andrew's Cathedral in Grand Rapids from July 1860 to January 1862. But in Michigan, Brady's over-controlling attitude toward these nuns and a legal confrontation with the diocese over a church he built led to troubles. He lost a lawsuit he had filed against the diocese in that regard.[14]

Although described as zealous and enthusiastic in his New York ministry, in Michigan Brady alienated both the superior of the Brigidine nuns (Mother Angela McKey) and the Belgian bishop of Detroit (Peter Paul Lefevere). It was therefore certainly a relief for all parties involved that in January 1862 Brady volunteered to be a Union chaplain and was released by Bishop Lefevere to do so. (Conyngham's manuscript remarks that Brady was asked by the regiment to become their chaplain.) In March 1862, he was mustered into the 17th Michigan, the "Mulligan Regiment," a group raised in Detroit, Monroe, and Grand Rapids under Colonel John M. Oliver. They were immediately marched south to Pittsburgh Landing, just in time to be part of the Battle of Shiloh (April 6–7, 1862).[15]

Brady was with the 15th Michigan at Shiloh, Corinth, Vicksburg, and Chickamauga, but likely did not go through the entire Vicksburg Campaign, and certainly was not with the regiment during the Atlanta Campaign, because he was ministering at a Chattanooga hospital. As with O'Higgins and the 10th Ohio, whatever transpired between Brady and his religious superiors, his Civil War service to the troops appears to have been outstanding and dedicated. His early ministry with the soldiers was described in Conyngham's manuscript. "He labored night and day, both in the camp and hospitals, hearing confessions, nursing & consoling the sick and wounded, and cheering the last moments of the departing with the rites of his holy Church." Several humorous anecdotes about Brady do survive from various places he ministered at during the war.[16]

Several times it seems his Catholic credentials were insufficient to overcome Southern prejudice against Yankees. While in Memphis, "he met with considerable annoyance, even from members of his own Church whose devotion to the Confederate cause blinded them to the Christian duties of a Catholic chaplain. These extremists assailed him as a Yankee priest and a supporter of the Yankee invasion. The good Father bore all this with humility." In late 1863, when the regiment was briefly detached to the Army of the Cumberland, his arrival in Huntsville, Alabama, was not warmly received. Despite not having seen a priest for some time, Brady's offer of ministry "was coldly received, particularly by the ladies, who seemed far more bitter against the Northerners than the men in the field. One Irish lady refused to shake hands . . . and commenced a virulent abuse of the Yanks. . . . Madame was a very bitter rebel, and did not attend Mass, because it was celebrated by a Northern priest."[17]

In Chattanooga an amusing yet poignant situation occurred when Brady entered the hospital one morning. After giving his usual greeting of "God bless all here," one distrustful soldier responded, "If he does, I rather guess you'll come in for a fair share; for I never saw a preacher who had not the best furnished table, and come in for more than his fair share of all the good things." A nearby sergeant retorted, "Shut up! Shure he is a priest and no preacher!" Brady then engaged the cynical invalid, and discovered he belonged to no denomination and had never been baptized. Despite further comments from the sergeant, Brady "talked for some time with the other on religious subjects, and so great an impression had his solemn advice had upon him and others, that after a few days, they asked to be received into the Church, to the no small delight of the Pennsylvania sergeant who took upon himself the full credit."[18]

Brady rejoined his regiment in front of Atlanta briefly, which greatly pleased him as he "had a paternal affection for his own boys," but was again called back to the hospitals at Chattanooga. Then in late 1864, when the Confederates (under General John Bell Hood) threatened the city, more Union troops were concentrated there, which only added to Brady's already overloaded priestly work. Conyngham's journal relates that "indeed, so overpowering and laborious were his duties, night and day, that his health gave way, and he began to break down rapidly." After Hood was ultimately defeated at Nashville (December 15–16, 1864), Brady recovered enough to accompany Union troops to Wilmington, North Carolina, and even rejoin his old regiment at Raleigh. He marched with them from North Carolina to Washington, DC, and there had the great satisfaction of being part of the Grand Review of the Armies before President Andrew Johnson (May 23–24, 1865).

Returning south, the 15th Michigan mustered out in Little Rock, Arkansas, in August 1865 and returned home to Detroit on September 1, but Brady's postwar days in Michigan were few. His health had been failing for quite a while, and he was sustained in his final weeks only by seeing his old regiment and being united with them again. Within days of the regiment returning to Michigan, Brady's medical conditions took a turn for the worse, and he was hospitalized at St. Mary's Hospital in Detroit. He died there about a week later, on September 10, 1865. "Thus had the good priest fought the good fight, and worked untiringly in the vineyard of God . . . 'well done, good and faithful servant.'"[19]

Richard Christy (78th Pennsylvania)

Another diocesan priest who served full-time as a Union chaplain (October 1861–November 1864) was Richard Callixtus Christy (1829–1878). Of the fifteen full-time chaplains on both sides, only he and

William Corby were born in the United States, with Christy coming from the all-Catholic community of Loretto, Pennsylvania. His pastor had been Father Demetrius Gallitzin, known as the "apostle of the Alleghenies" for his pioneering ministry in the area. Christy followed in his footsteps, becoming the first priest of the new Pittsburgh Diocese in August 1854 when he was ordained. He then pastored several parishes in western Pennsylvania, making a very favorable impression, as one parish history relates. Christy was "of above medium height, being rather heavy. He had a very sociable disposition and was an eloquent preacher. . . . Father Christy won the hearts of his parishioners. . . . [and] in today's vernacular, was a 'mover and shaker.'"[20]

Upon Lincoln's 1861 call for volunteers, young men from Butler County (where Christy was ministering) responded, being described in the regimental history of the 78th Pennsylvania as mostly "farmers, students, mechanics and laborers, with an average age of not more than twenty-one years." The history then records that "Rev. Richard C. Christy, a priest of the Roman Catholic Church, was commissioned as chaplain, September 10, 1861. A very large majority of the Regiment were Protestants, and the selection of the Rev. Mr. Christy was seriously objected to by many; nevertheless. Chaplain Christy succeeded in securing the love and confidence of the soldiers and officers of the regiment without regard to denominational distinction. He had a kind and generous heart, and entered into the fullest sympathy with the men with whom he was associated." With only about fifty Catholics in the entire regiment, Christy's selection was unique among all Catholic chaplains, but one for which he proved his worth in many ways.[21]

Part of Negley's Brigade of the Army of the Ohio (later the Army of the Cumberland), Christy and the 78th Pennsylvania fought a few smaller engagements and several notable ones, Stones River, Chickamauga, Lookout Mountain, and Missionary Ridge. Along the way, many anecdotes of both courage and poignancy about the priest were gathered by Conyngham through his correspondence with Captain Charles Gillespie of the regiment. While in Alabama, Christy was attempting to rejoin his troops when he tipped over his dugout canoe, nearly drowning before he was finally able to touch bottom. On another occasion, he was sitting beneath a tree next to a river when a rebel sharpshooter across the water spotted him, and planted a minié ball just inches above his head. At Tullahoma, his horse walked into a nest of yellow jackets, leaping and lunging, yet Christy sat calm and cool throughout, resisting all efforts to be unhorsed, to the cheers of nearby soldiers.

Because of the few Catholics in his regiment, his reputation was truly won by bravery and courage on the battlefield. In the winter cold of the Battle of Stones River, with supply trains far in the rear, Christy trudged to the wagons, returning with blankets and overcoats for the freezing soldiers, then moved back and forth across the battlefield attending to wounded, carrying some away to hospitals. At Chickamauga, he was out at the front attending wounded men, and became separated from the regiment between the two lines, enduring the dangerous fire of both sides for a time. At the battle of Missionary Ridge, with the 78th Pennsylvania assigned to Fort Negley with no fighting, Christy instead joined the 14th Corps as they charged up the mountain slope and over it, and ministered to both Union and Confederate soldiers as he found them.

Christy did suffer from illnesses during the war, which necessitated several leaves for him; this may have led to the charge of him being absent without leave while the regiment was encamped on Lookout Mountain in late 1863. Perhaps through a misunderstanding, his pay was withheld for several months, which greatly inconvenienced the priest. But the troops of the 78th Pennsylvania chipped in at that time and raised a good sum of money, which kept Christy going until his pay was restored by the Quartermaster.

Returning to the campaign in spring 1864, Christy was with General Sherman's Army in the Atlanta Campaign, and was again conspicuous for his duty and bravery. At New Hope Church (May 25–26, 1864), with the regiment desperately short of ammunition, "Christy begged some ammunition from a regiment in our rear and his pocket and handkerchief were stuffed" as he went "along the line eking out his cartridges to those who needed them the most." Later in the campaign, after Atlanta had been taken, Christy found troops drawn up into front of headquarters who had been ordered to protect a departing train, but lacked a commissioned officer to take command. He buckled on his sword and marched them off efficiently, riding the train with them to their destination and bringing the troops back. Asked later what he would have done if attacked, the feisty priest responded, "Why I would have told the boys to pitch in!"[22]

As much as any other Civil War chaplain, Christy epitomized the words of William Corby, who later wrote in his *Memoirs*, "In the war-time army, courage is the currency with which men's hearts are purchased." In November 1864, the 78th Pennsylvania was mustered out at Kittanning, Pennsylvania, and Christy returned to his Pittsburgh Diocese, serving with great distinction at the Church of the Holy Name in Edensburg until just before his death in October 1878. He truly earned the fine words written later of him in a Butler County history. "Wherever the battle raged the hottest, there would [Christy] be found ministering to the wounded and the dying, speaking words of comfort and consolation, and encouraging all by word and example. Because of his courage and devotion, Father Christy became known throughout the Army of the Cumberland as the 'Fighting Chaplain.'"[23]

John Ireland (5th Minnesota)

Although his Civil War service spanned only nine months, the life and fifty-seven-year priestly career of John Ireland was arguably the most illustrious of all Civil War chaplains. Born in September 1838 in Ireland, he immigrated with family to America in 1848, settling after a year in a place he would never leave, St. Paul, Minnesota. The first bishop of that diocese, Bishop Joseph Cretin, chose Ireland to study for the priesthood, so he studied in France and was ordained in December 1861 in St. Paul. In June 1862, the young newly ordained priest was appointed by Minnesota governor Alexander Ramsey to serve the many Catholics in the 5th Minnesota (comprising one third of the regiment).[24]

Following months of endless marches, in September and October 1862, the 5th Minnesota and their young chaplain were engaged at Iuka and then Corinth. Although Ireland apparently never wore the blue Federal uniform, and at least once went unrecognized by those unfamiliar with him, Ireland quickly showed himself to be courageous, hardworking, and willing to assist however he could. At Corinth, on October 4, 1862, when the regiment was helping stop a Confederate breakthrough and ran short of ammunition, Ireland ran down the line dispensing ammunition he had obtained for the troops. Then when the fighting ceased, he tirelessly tended the wounded and gave the last rites to those whose wounds were beyond human help.

Always willing to hear confessions (once for an entire night) or minister to anyone who needed his help, Ireland worked long hours and went out of his way to provide spiritual assistance. He once visited with one convalescing soldier who would not believe he was a priest, saying, "There are always jokers ready to make fun and play tricks." Ireland responded, "I don't blame you. I respect you: I cannot prove my priesthood . . . but I swear I am a priest." So the two sat down under a tree, the soldier made a half-hour-long deep and heartfelt confession, and remarked in tears afterward, "Oh I know you are a priest and that I am forgiven! Thanks be to God!"[25]

The troops were very fond of the young priest and built him a portable altar from saplings. His direct, blunt, and brief sermons were also popular with the men, and he never talked down to people. Ireland was noted for his sunny disposition, quick wit, courage, and also for his ability as an enthusiastic chess player who was willing to take on all comers in the evenings in camp.

Although one article claims that ill health forced his resignation from the army in March 1863, Ireland himself wrote at the time that he had been "called back" because he was needed in his St. Paul Diocese; his replacement there had taken sick. Whatever the case, in 1892 Ireland said, "My years of chaplaincy were the happiest and most fruitful years of my ministry." John Ireland went on to become a postwar pastor in St. Paul (1867–1875), his bishop's representative to Vatican One (making many contacts helpful to him in subsequent years), a coadjutor bishop of the diocese in 1875, and then bishop of St. Paul in 1884. At his September 1918 funeral, besides the congregation, eight archbishops, thirty bishops, and seven hundred priests were in attendance. Ireland's illustrious postwar career and achievements will be discussed further in chapter 12.[26]

CONFEDERATE DIOCESAN CHAPLAINS

John Bannon (1st Missouri)

The first of three Confederate Catholic diocesan chaplains we will speak in greater detail about is a captivating priest who has merited at least two books and numerous articles (and several previous mentions in this book)—John Bannon (1829–1913) of the 1st Missouri Brigade (Confederate). Born in Ireland, he (like William O'Higgins) studied at famed Royal College of St. Patrick at Maynooth (the national seminary of Ireland). Bannon was ordained a priest in June 1853 during the time of the Irish Potato Famine, when many were immigrating out of the country. Bannon decided to respond to the request of Archbishop Peter Kenrick of St. Louis, Missouri, for priests to serve his poor and burgeoning Irish population; he left for America shortly after his ordination. Described as a "handsome man, over six feet in height, of great personal magnetism, conversing eloquently and with originality and great wit," Bannon soon became recognized as one of the leading religious and civic figures in St. Louis. In 1858, he was assigned to St. John the Apostle Church on the then west side of the city, and supervised the building of a new church there. He had a special prominence in the city's Irish community, many of whom joined him when he went to war.[27]

As the Civil War loomed, St. Louis was a deeply divided city, which led to Archbishop Kenrick adopting a policy of neutrality toward the war and the politics around it. But his popular young priest John Bannon was not so shy, joining the Southern-committed Washington Blues militia as a chaplain in November 1860. One online history of St. Louis during the Civil War describes how the young priest then became a formal Confederate chaplain.

> After the firing on Fort Sumter . . . Bannon remained close to Captain Kelly's troops at Camp Jackson on the western edge of the city. After the surrender of Camp Jackson its troops, including Bannon, became prisoners of the Federal forces until released on May 11, 1861. Bannon returned to St. John's where he remained until December 15, 1861. At the time of his departure Bannon was targeted

for arrest by Federal authorities due to the views which he had expressed from the pulpit.

On the night of the 15th, Bannon snuck out of the back door in disguise and a false beard, while Federal officials entered the front door. He then continued his clandestine journey across Missouri to Springfield where he became a member of the "Patriot Army of Missouri," under the command of General Sterling Price. He then commenced his service as a chaplain, initially voluntary, to the First Missouri Confederate Brigade.[28]

Although Bannon was only formally appointed a Confederate chaplain on February 12, 1863 (postdated to January 1862), he was with the 1st Missouri Confederate Brigade until the unit surrendered at Vicksburg in July 1863. The six-foot, four-inch Irish priest quickly became a fixture not only in his brigade (in which Bannon estimated there were fifteen thousand Catholics), but to the larger Confederate army. At the three-day battle of Pea Ridge (March 6–7, 1862), Bannon disobeyed orders for the chaplains to remain in the rear, instead joining the soldiers on the firing line, giving human assistance to the wounded, and offering divine assistance (the last rites) to those beyond human aid. Bannon ministered as well to any Protestant soldier who wished, baptizing some if they so desired. He is also said to have also routinely joined artillery crews (especially the Catholic Henry Guibor's Missouri Battery) to assist them after some of the crews were wounded or killed by Union fire. To distinguish himself among the troops, Bannon devised a white armband with a cross on it, not unlike those which medics would wear in later wars.[29]

Quickly gaining a reputation for utter fearlessness and courage (and for carrying whiskey onto battlefields), Bannon thought that chaplains who remained out of harm's way became "frequently objects of derision, always disappearing on the eve of an action, when they would stay behind in some farm house till all was quiet." Echoing William Corby's sentiments about the courage required to be a chaplain, he felt that a priest's place was with the soldiers, and he was quite willing to risk his life to do so. Following the battle of Pea Ridge, Bannon wrote in his journal: "I am doing God's work, and He has no use for cowards or skulkers. A Catholic priest must do his duty and never consider the time or place. If I am killed, I am not afraid to meet my fate. I am in God's keeping. His holy will be done."[30]

Bannon was present at many critical western theater battles—Pea Ridge, Iuka, Corinth, Grand Gulf, Port Gibson, Champion Hill, and the siege of Vicksburg. Like with many chaplains, nights before a battle were always busy for the priest. As later recorded, he "would go up to a watch-fire, and waking one of the men, called him aside, hear his confession, and send him to summon another. The whole night would be spent thus in going from campfire to campfire. The men were always willing to come, generally too glad of the opportunity; some would even be watching for me." While the troops went into battle, Father Bannon routinely gave them general absolution. "When the time came for advancing, I made a sign for them all to kneel, and gave them absolution (and) I then went to the second line, or the reserve, till it was their turn also to advance."[31]

During the siege of Vicksburg (May 18–July 4, 1863), when the Irish priest was not in the trenches with the troops, or riding the lines, he was in the hospital helping the wounded. The regular Union bombardments made life in Vicksburg precarious for all, and Bannon had many close calls, including when an artillery shell whizzed by his head during a Mass he was celebrating, and another landed between him and two doctors at a hospital. Many of Bannon's Vicksburg exploits are related in his later writings, including his high praise for the Sisters of Mercy (who had a school there, and served as nurses) and the Daughters of Charity. Both orders of nuns had volunteered as nurses, and their nursing skill, lack of fear, and kindness in caring for the wounded in the area hospital and makeshift infirmaries reputedly led to many conversions and transformed attitudes toward Catholics.[32]

Bannon's courage and excellent reputation reached its apogee at Vicksburg, and it was with great sadness that he witnessed the garrison's surrender on July 4 at 10:00 a.m. "Went out to see our men stack arms— General Grant entered [Vicksburg] at 10 ½ o'clock—Yankee troops & officers scattered thru town." The surrender marked the end of Bannon's formal chaplain's career, but not his usefulness to the Confederacy. After traveling to Richmond and happening to attend Mass at the cathedral, he met Stephen Mallory there (the Catholic Confederate Secretary of the Navy), who brought him to Jefferson Davis. The priest was asked to go to Ireland to explain the causes of the Confederacy to the people, and to help prevent them from migrating to America to fight for the Union. Bannon ultimately broadened this mission to include a stop in Rome, in hopes that he could help convince Pope Pius IX to recognize the Confederacy.[33]

On October 3, 1863, Bannon's ship successfully ran the blockade; and while at sea, he met a Confederate sailor (John Bannister Tabb) who was so taken by the charismatic, war-weary priest that he later converted and became a priest himself. Though diligent in his work in both Ireland (writing circular letters to journals and priests) and Rome, and successful in some small ways, Bannon's work overseas had minimal effect on Irish immigration or on Vatican policies. (The same is true of Charleston Bishop Patrick Lynch, who also made overtures on behalf of the Confederacy internationally.) Despite Bannon making a good impression on the pope, by 1864 it was clear that official recognition by the Vatican was simply not going to happen. Unwilling to return to the United States after the Confederacy's defeat in 1865, Bannon decided to become a Jesuit and entered their novitiate in Dublin, Ireland, on January 9, 1865. Though only formally professed in 1876, he went on to a long and illustrious Jesuit "second career" as a well-known preacher traveling throughout Ireland. He died just one month after his sixtieth jubilee of priesthood, on July 14, 1913.[34]

Isidore-Francois Turgis (30th Louisiana)

The French-born Isidore-Francois Turgis (1813–1859) was the second full-time diocesan priest turned chaplain serving Confederate troops, working with soldiers of the 30th Louisiana. Despite being described as not a physically strong man, Turgis was ordained in France in 1846, then joined the French Corps of Chaplains in 1857, serving French troops in the Second Italian War of Independence (1859–1861). According to some sources, he then served with the French army in Cochin, China (Vietnam), though this author has not verified that connection. In 1860 the adventuresome French priest decided he was called to minister in New Orleans, which had many French-speakers within the city confines and outlying parishes.[35]

Later in this book (chapter 10), we will discuss the unique role that French immigrant priests played, and the challenges they faced, in staffing priest-poor southern dioceses. Isidore Turgis certainly fell into that category. He is said to have come to the United States in August 1860 out of a desire to serve Black Catholics in Louisiana. Like other French priests, he arrived without a clear notion of what awaited him in terms of weather, language difficulties, and the American political and religious climate. New Orleans's Archbishop Jean-Marie Odin (also French-born) appointed him to the mixed-race congregation at the St. Louis Cathedral, where both clergymen soon took an interest in the formation of the Orleans Guard (Bataille des Guardes d'Orleans)—a regiment composed of many affluent white Creoles from New Orleans. In March 1862, when these 411 Guardsmen began mustering for fighting around Shiloh, Tennessee, Turgis was appointed by Odin to be their chaplain.[36]

Not officially named a chaplain by the Confederacy until June 1863, Turgis's initial concern centered around his language skills; he is reputed to have said, "God give me strength for I am not a good preacher."[37] But letters from troops in his Sumpter Regiment (which later became the 30th Louisiana Infantry), and from Turgis himself, attest to his courage, kindness, and faith. Just days after the April 1862 Battle of Shiloh, he wrote to Archbishop Odin about that deadly fight, remarking that there were "about 18 to 20 thousand Catholics, all speaking or understanding French," but he was the only priest. He "gave absolution for 18 hours without stopping, but cannot [stop] weeping continually in thinking about those thousands of Catholics who asked for him and whom it was impossible to see. The pastor of the cathedral had told him there would be 6 or 7 priests and that he would be unneeded, but without him the elite of their Creole population would have been exposed to being lost for eternity."[38]

Some sources speak of Turgis having some narrow escapes during that battle, in which his valiant behavior did not go without notice. Lieutenant Colonel S. W. Ferguson, an aide-de-camp to General Beauregard, had command of a brigade at Shiloh, one of whose regiments was the Orleans Guard in which Father Turgis was chaplain. In his report to Beauregard, Ferguson commended the priest's courage, stating "and of Father I. Turgis, who, in the performance of his holy offices, freely exposed himself to the balls of the enemy." But in his own letter to Odin, the priest humbly downplayed his own role, remarking "the Orleans Guard are so favorable to [me] that they exaggerate everything, regarding as self-sacrifice that which is only the accomplishment of a duty."[39]

Following the siege of Port Hudson (May 2–July 9, 1863), Turgis marched away with the defeated and exchanged troops of his brigade where, on July 20, his kindness was again noted by one soldier. "Francois Turgis walked most of the way, giving his horse to exhausted privates. With Napoleon III's armies, he had never experienced a retreat. We camped that night in a dreary wilderness-looking place on the banks of the Strong River [Mississippi]." Further specific information on the French priest's subsequent wartime ministry is scarce, though it seems he continued as chaplain until 1864 with the reorganized 30th Louisiana through their affiliation with the Army of Tennessee in the Atlanta Campaign and Hood's Tennessee operations. When he wasn't tending to his soldier flock, Turgis also ministered to Catholics wherever he was at the time, as his regularly reported his activities to Archbishop Odin of New Orleans.[40]

Turgis returned greatly weakened to New Orleans after the war. At the request of surviving Confederate soldiers (including General P. G. T. Beauregard), in February 1866 Turgis established a chapel specifically for Catholic veterans (the Mortuary Chapel on Rampart Street). Due to his poor health and inability to become a full-time pastor, this building became his retirement residence, and he lived in a room behind the worship space. But his ministry continued—Turgis became director of a hospital for invalid soldiers, founded an asylum for soldiers' widows and orphans, administered sacraments, and provided guidance and fellowship to veterans struggling after the Confederate defeat. One veteran wrote of these gatherings that "evening after evening found no less than fifteen or twenty of the old soldiers gathered in his room at the presbytery just back of the chapel. They represented every creed; they loved him and delighted to recount with him the days that so bitterly tried their hearts and souls."[41]

Already in poor condition, the diminutive French priest was further weakened by the 1867 yellow fever epidemic, and died from stomach cancer and fatigue on March 3, 1868. His funeral "was one of the largest ever reported in the city" one Catholic paper reported, with "the wealthiest and the poorest, the most distinguished and the most unknown, all contributing to pay the last tribute of their veneration to his memory."[42] With Confederate veterans carrying his coffin, Turgis was buried in St. Louis Cemetery Number 3 under an epitaph reading "Pere Turgis, Armee du Tennessee, C.S.A., 1861–1864."[43]

Thomas O'Reilly (Post and Hospital Chaplain)

A final diocesan priest deserving mention in this chapter was only formally named a chaplain for a short time late in the war (February–April 1864), although he served informally for far longer. Thomas O'Reilly (1831–1872) remains to this day a legend in Atlanta for his actions during the war—notably his near single-handed preservation of several important buildings from burning by General William Sherman's Union troops. Born in Ireland in 1831, O'Reilly was ordained in 1857 and that same year sailed to the United States to serve in the Savannah Diocese (Bishop John Barry). He survived yellow fever soon after his arrival, and O'Reilly then served in several Georgia churches before becoming pastor of Immaculate Conception Church in Atlanta in 1861. When the Civil War arrived, he is said to have ministered to both Union and Confederate who were wounded at Chickamauga (September 1863) and elsewhere, but his primary reputation comes from his work in Atlanta.[44]

In 1861, Atlanta became not only a Confederate manufacturing and supply depot but also a medical center with at least ten hospitals where thousands of wounded were treated. Those hospitals, and others in the area, became the focus of much of O'Reilly's ministry, and he is said to have turned his own church into a hospital where all soldiers, Confederate, or later Union, were treated the same. On September 2, 1864, after the battle of Jonesboro, Atlanta fell to the Union army when the Confederate General John Bell Hood evacuated the city. As Sherman's Union troops occupied the city, a mutual spirit of charity and concern for the wounded seems to have prevailed among the Catholic priest-chaplains. According to his parish's history, O'Reilly assisted the Union Catholic chaplains Thomas Brady (15th Michigan), Richard Christy (78th Pennsylvania), and Peter Cooney (35th Indiana) in the Federal field hospitals around Atlanta.[45]

Later that fall of 1864, Sherman planned his total war march to the sea at Savannah and ordered Atlanta to be burned. Upon hearing this, O'Reilly sent word to Sherman that burning homes and churches was beyond the normal boundaries of warfare, but his pleas were ignored. The Irish priest had become known to many Union soldiers through the Masses he offered during the siege and occupation. In a desperate attempt, O'Reilly sent word to General Henry Slocum (a Corps commander whom Sherman had made Atlanta city commandant) that if they persisted in the plan to burn down the Catholic church, the Irish who were still in the city were ready to defend it, and Sherman could also face massive desertions among the Catholics in his own Union army. O'Reilly's intercessions helped motivate a change in Sherman's orders, and saved not only his church from a fiery fate, but four others too (St. Philip's Episcopal Church, Trinity Methodist, Second Baptist, and Central Presbyterian), as well as the courthouse and city hall, which were physically close to O'Reilly's own Immaculate Conception Church. A memorial plaque erected by the Atlanta Historical Society in October 1945 stands today in front of Immaculate Conception Church to commemorate O'Reilly's heroic November 1864 actions.[46]

As the Federal army moved out on its infamous march to the sea, only a fraction of burned Atlanta still stood, with merely five hundred or so people still in the city. All the churches that had been spared became places of refuge to temporarily house the homeless returnees. O'Reilly's own Immaculate Conception Church had been badly damaged by shells, and the parishioners decided to build a new structure, laying the cornerstone in September 1869, although it was not completed and dedicated until 1873. Sadly, O'Reilly himself did not live to see the project completed. The troubles of the war years led to his health failing by 1871, and he went to a Virginia sanitarium, dying at the age of forty-one in September 1872. His remains were subsequently brought back to the city for the largest funeral ever held up to that time in Atlanta.

O'Reilly was buried in a vault beneath the brand-new church. As time passed, his grave gradually became forgotten until a 1982 fire in the church led to the roof collapsing and breaking through the cathedral floor. Father O'Reilly's long-forgotten crypt was rediscovered (along with that of his successor, Francis Cleary), resurrecting the story of this "hero" of Atlanta. Today a small adjacent room contains museum-style glass cases with artifacts of the Church's history and the story of the amazing priest who preserved Atlanta's spiritual heritage from the fires of the Civil War.[47]

OTHER DIOCESAN CIVIL WAR CHAPLAINS

Other diocesan chaplains besides those whose lives are detailed in this book served in part-time ways during the Civil War. Though perhaps not as prominent in their service as others discussed in this chapter (or in what we know about them), they do deserve to be acknowledged briefly:

- Edward P. Corcoran (61st Ohio) (1832–1866). An Ohio native, Corcoran was pastor in Hamilton, Ohio, and had just finished building a church there when the war began. He resigned his parish and volunteered as chaplain on the 61st Ohio, and was with them in several small engagements in Virginia before being present at the Second Battle of Bull Run (August 2, 1862). In the fall of 1862, when the 61st was defending Washington, Corcoran was sent to Ohio on business but was captured by the Confederates while returning. During his short imprisonment, his health was compromised by contracting tuberculosis, and he never quite recovered his strength. His resignation was accepted in January 1863, but he died in Cincinnati shortly after the war.[48]
- George Herbert Doane (New Jersey Militia) (1830–1905). A fascinating man who was both an Episcopal convert to Catholicism and a medical school graduate, Doane was appointed by the governor as chaplain to the New Jersey Militia during their three-month service from May to July 1861. He accompanied them to Northern

Virginia, and was reported by some to have been under fire at the Battle of First Bull Run (July 21, 1861). Doane had a distinguished career both before and after the war in his home diocese of Newark, including being vicar general of the diocese and acting bishop for a year (1880–1881). He preached at James Sheeran's April 1881 funeral.[49]

- Charles Louis Lemagie (Carrollton, Louisiana, post; 2nd Louisiana Cavalry) (1811 or 1812–?). Another itinerant priest whose behavior at times (described as "foolish talk and strange manner") was questioned by some church leaders, by the time of the war he was in the New Orleans Diocese, in a town called Carrolton. He served faithfully as a post chaplain for the Union army there for several years, but was also assigned to the 2nd Louisiana Cavalry for about a year until its consolidation. Lemagie served in five different dioceses in all, likely because of his French heritage and language, ending his career in the newly formed Green Bay Diocese.[50]

- John McCosker (55th Pennsylvania) (1830–1862). Born in Ireland, McCosker was ordained at the age of twenty-three in 1853, and served in Middletown, Pennsylvania, until the war broke out. In response to the governor's request to Bishop James Wood for chaplains, McCosker and fellow priest Michael Martin (discussed in chapter 9) volunteered to serve. He was appointed to the 55th Pennsylvania, mustered in December 1862, and served with them in South Carolina. Unfortunately, his service lasted only six months, as he died suddenly while on a leave of absence to procure materials for celebrating Mass.[51]

- Thomas Quinn (Rhode Island Militia, Artillery) (1829–1871). Born in Canada and ordained in 1851, Quinn worked in the Hartford Diocese and volunteered as chaplain, serving in three regiments. He was briefly associate chaplain of the ninety-day 1st Rhode Island Militia (with Reverend Augustus Woodbury), then the 3rd Rhode Island (which had many Irish Catholics), and finally was appointed to the 1st Rhode Island Light Artillery in November 1861. Quinn served another short tenure there but resigned two months later, perhaps due to orders from his bishop or to regulations about supernumerary troops for light artillery. He returned to Connecticut to minister and died in August 1871.[52]

- [Confederate] Patrick F. Coyle (Pensacola, Florida, post) (dates unknown). Coyle was born in Ireland, entered America in 1848, and served as pastor in Pensacola in 1861. Facts about him are scant, but parish records there indicate Coyle was then commissioned as a Confederate chaplain, but the South abandoned the city in May 1862 and the church was destroyed soon after. He is then on record as ministering at a Confederate hospital in Corinth in April 1862, was vicar general of the Mobile Diocese, and later pastor of the largest church there (believed to be St. Vincent de Paul, though clear wartime records are scant). Postwar, he apparently transferred into Nashville, but after 1869 no references to him have been located.[53]

- [Confederate] Patrick Ryan (Charleston, post) (1824–1887). Born in Ireland, Ryan came to America with his family, studied for priesthood in Rome, was ordained in 1853, then taught and ministered in various North Carolina parishes. At the time of the war, he was stationed in Charleston and was apparently regularly ministering in the camps and hospitals there when Bishop Patrick Lynch requested a formal commission for him as post chaplain, which was granted on April 13, 1864. After the war, Ryan transferred to the Baltimore Diocese, ministering there until his death in 1887.

PART 3

DIFFICULT SITUATIONS AND UNIQUE MEN

If I were to have any preacher,
it would be that old man Trecy.
He is the damndest sensible one among them.

— Anonymous Union deserter about to be executed

CHAPTER 8

CATHOLIC HOSPITAL CHAPLAINS

The hospital chaplains of the Civil War are the direct ancestors of the present-day Veterans Administration chaplains, and as such deserve special mention, even aside from acknowledging the critical wartime role they played. In an oblique way, hospital chaplaincy in America's military came into existence when the job of post chaplain was established in 1838. Prior to the Civil War, there were no general hospitals; rather, each military post had a hospital to care for its personnel. Some posts had large hospitals attached (like Fort Leavenworth, Kansas, with forty beds), and the post chaplain received extra spiritual duties from that. But it was with the formation of large general hospitals in 1861 and 1862 that "a new field for the chaplain's temporal and spiritual administration was created, and as a result a new type of military chaplain—the hospital chaplain."[1]

Never before in American history had large military hospitals sprung up overnight as occurred early in the Civil War. Except for some small log-cabin hospitals during the War of 1812, the US Army had no practice building hospitals. In the Mexican-American War, churches and convents had been considered good enough to house the wounded. The Union and Confederacy were unprepared for both the scope of the war and the medical and spiritual needs accompanying it.

In July and August 1861, Congress enacted bills that provided for regimental chaplains in the Union armies, but that legislation did not provide for chaplains to serve in army hospitals, an omission glaringly apparent after the First Battle of Bull Run. As the number of sick and wounded mounted, it seemed wise to also have chaplains in military hospitals to minister to the wounded. Some local clergy had already begun volunteering without any commission; the United States Christian Commission even had a provision that their delegates might be sent "to act as volunteer chaplains in such hospitals as have not had chaplains appointed for them by the government."[2]

Although President Lincoln was informed of this early lack of hospital chaplains and sympathized with the need, he felt he had no legal authority to appoint them in the absence of specific statutes. Thus in October 1861 he wrote letters to prominent clergy seeking the names of worthy men he could appoint personally. Lincoln stated the need at hand, promising that "I will recommend that Congress make compensation therefore, at the same rate as chaplains in the army are compensated" (a statute finally enacted on May 20, 1862). Among those chaplains who received letters from Lincoln were two Catholic priests who had already offered their services to Washington's military hospitals—Francis M. McGrath (US Hospital, Georgetown) and Francis E. Boyle (Stone Hospital, Washington). These two, and other later hospital chaplains were then appointed by the president; their assignments were made through the surgeon general of the army.[3]

In their 2007 book on Union chaplains, Brinsfield and Maryniak summarize the situation in the North during the remainder of the war. "From 1862 to the end of 1864, President Lincoln appointed many chaplains personally to US Army hospitals. Eventually more than two hundred Union chaplains served in hospital ministries. These did not include the regimental chaplains who were assigned temporary hospital duty while on campaign . . . Hospital chaplains made regular reports to the chief surgeon each week or month as required. Many of their reports reveal innovative ministries to entertain and educate their patients as well as to offer pastoral support." Once established, the position of hospital chaplain became an attractive one, drawing many applications which far exceeded the positions available. Regimental chaplains with experience received preference (it was seen as a promotion by many), with few civilian clergy receiving direct commissions.[4]

Yet just as with regimental chaplains, the general shortage of faithful, regular hospital chaplains, both North and South, would always be a factor. Herman Norton's classic history of chaplains sums up the situation in the North succinctly. "No more than 175 were in service at a given time; the peak was reached near the end of the war, when there were 173 on duty. The ideal goal of a military minister at each hospital was never reached; when Grant accepted Lee's surrender, 20 of the 192 general hospitals were without a resident chaplain." Of course, nearly all regimental chaplains on both sides visited hospitals regularly—certainly at least field hospitals where their troops were, if not always the larger general hospitals where ultimately many of the wounded were sent.[5]

In the Confederacy, there was confusion at the outset regarding not only the establishment of hospitals, but also setting up efficient operations and guidelines for the personnel therein. The hospital chaplain position was subject to the same lack of clear direction and definition. No special need for them was recognized in Richmond early in the war, such as Lincoln had personally done in October 1861. It was only when casualties mounted, and hospitals quickly filled, that the need for spiritual sustenance as well as medical assistance was recognized. Dr. William Carrington, the inspector of hospitals for the Confederacy, wrote in November 1862 and said, "At no time is there greater need of these ministers, or do they produce greater impression and effect for good than in our Hospitals, both among the sick, wounded and convalescent. I would respectfully suggest that additional chaplains be ordered or appointed to report for Hospital Service in this department."[6]

The Southern initiative to obtain hospital chaplains came primarily not from the government in Richmond, but the hospitals themselves and from individual ministers who saw the need and were subsequently assigned. Richmond's massive Chimborazo Hospital, for example, simply hired chaplains to provide for patients' spiritual needs, to "take a sufficient interest in the spiritual welfare of the soldiers and furnish him with the necessary books, etc. to secure his attention and interest." Officially recognized Confederate hospital chaplains were scarce, with lists like that found in *Faith in the Fight* recounting only one hundred hospital chaplains of the 1,308 total southern chaplains (a mere 7 percent). The work of Richmond post and hospital chaplain Charles McCabe was described as "onerous . . . his labors at various hospitals are sufficient to tax the physical as well as the moral energies of the strongest man."[7]

The uniquely Catholic practice of the sacraments flavored everything Catholic priest-chaplains did during the Civil War. While all hospital chaplains visited the beds and wards to pray with soldiers and lead services, Catholic priests had the additional primary ministry commitment of administering the sacraments of extreme unction (called today the anointing of the sick), confession (reconciliation), and baptism. The physicality of these Catholic rites (using oil on the body for anointing, water for baptism, bread and wine in communion, and physically touching the body) would have been a special and tangible comfort for wounded Catholic soldiers, adding a level of spiritual and personal support unique to men often derided as "papists" in a biased society.[8]

Extensive commentary on the role of Catholic nuns in hospitals is beyond the scope of this book, and their work is well-documented elsewhere (cf. below), but once again must be mentioned here and throughout this book. The presence of these dedicated spiritual women (well more than six hundred, one-fifth of all the sisters in the United States) amid the horrors of Civil War hospitals, with their spiritual training and gentle nursing skills, was a true balm in Gilead (Jeremiah 46:11) and soothed countless soldiers. Their work changed many hearts and led to numerous religious conversions.

In a curious bit of history in this regard, in May 1861 when Confederate officials contacted the Daughters of Charity (at New Orleans's Charity Hospital) for Catholic nuns to nurse the sick and wounded at Richmond and Norfolk, the priest-director of their province, Francis Burlando, would only agree if a Catholic chaplain was in attendance. During the war years, Catholic nuns were generally accompanied by a priest when they traveled, and always worked in close conjunction with them; the sisters regularly frequented the sacraments (especially the Mass) and routinely referred priests to the patients who needed their ministry. This close interplay between the Catholic priest-chaplains and nuns was especially poignant and powerful, and resulted in several humorous conversion stories.[9]

Because of the close bond they had developed with them, many wounded preferred the sisters to the clergy. At the Alton, Illinois, prison where the Daughters of Charity ministered, one sick man asked for baptism, but when approached by a priest, he cried out, "No, I want Sister to baptize me!" In a very unusual gesture for that time, the priest told the nun to go ahead and baptize the man, while he witnessed it standing alongside.

Although not a hospital chaplain, John Bannon (1st Missouri CSA) was told by one nun that one of her patients was willing to convert, so he went to see the man. The exchange between Bannon and the feisty soldier led to the man saying, "I tell you what it is, mister, it's no use of you talking to me. I belong to the Sisters' religion and that's enough." Bannon responded "Exactly, and so do I. I am a Priest of their religion, and I have come to see what I can do for you." He then proceeded to give the man some basic instructions, but met with resistance, "Oh, come now, you don't expect me to believe that!" "Yes," Bannon said, "that is what the Catholic Church teaches, and we are bound to believe it." Still not satisfied, the Confederate soldier called the nun over and asked her "Sister, this man tells me so and so. Is that true?" "Oh yes," the nun said smiling, "quite true!" "Very well," he turned back to the priest, "all right. I believe it. Go ahead, Mister, what's next?" Bannon's closing comment on this encounter is classic: "In the end I baptized him, but it might best be said perhaps to be rather '*in fidem sodorum*' rather than '*in fidem ecclesia*' [in the faith of the nuns rather than the faith of the church]."[10]

WASHINGTON, DC, HOSPITAL CHAPLAINS: FRANCIS BOYLE, MATTHEW MCGRATH, PATRICK MCCARTHY, AND BERNADIN WIGET SJ

In *Doctors in Blue*, George Adams writes that "circumstances made Washington the principal hospital center. Its geographical situation was in its favor . . . and the proximity of the Surgeon General made for better hospital administration." There were sixteen medical departments in the Union, but the top two in bed capacity were Washington and

Philadelphia. As journalist Noah Brooks observed in 1864, "all Washington [is] a great hospital for the wounded," with approximately fifty-six hospitals in the city at one time or the other, sixteen of them being general hospitals with a capacity of thirty-thousand beds in all. Four Catholic priests operated as chaplains in the Washington-area hospitals—two at the same Georgetown hospital, with one unique Jesuit priest (Wiget) actually turning his church property temporarily into a Union hospital.[11]

Francis Edward Boyle was born in Maryland in 1827 and ordained in November 1851 for the Baltimore Diocese. He was known to be an eloquent scholar and philanthropist, and was part of a prominent Irish family that included other priests and one relative who was interim secretary of the navy under President Andrew Jackson. When the war broke out, he was pastor of St. Peter's on Capitol Hill in Washington, DC, but he volunteered to help care for Catholic troops in the city's military hospitals. Because of this commitment, on June 13, 1862, he was one of the seven chaplains personally appointed by President Lincoln to be one of the Union's initial hospital chaplains.

Boyle was assigned to Stone United States Hospital in the District of Columbia, one of the city's general hospitals. The site was also called Warren or Park Hospital (in March 1862), then Frederick Prison Hospital (in February 1863) as caregivers there treated Union prisoners from the various guard houses in the city. Stone Hospital was especially dedicated to treating sick and wounded deserters, who when recovered were then sent back to their regiments. Located on 13th Street north of the Capitol buildings, the hospital began formally caring for patients on March 28, 1862, and closed on July 7, 1865; its remaining patients were sent to Stanton General Hospital in Washington. Boyle lived in the city while he worked at Stone, and remained there throughout the war, only being formally mustered out on July 26, 1865.[12]

In May 1865, he was one of five priests called to testify in the trial of the Catholic Mary Surratt, who was owner of the boarding house in which John Wilkes Booth and others met. Boyle testified that he had met Surratt eight or nine years before and believed her reputation to be that of "an estimable lady," but did not know her attitudes regarding loyalty to the Union. When his chaplain's career was concluded, the

Irish priest resumed his pastoral career at St. Peter's on Capitol Hill, before becoming in 1878 pastor of the prominent St. Matthew the Apostle Church in Washington (often described as "the church of diplomats"). There he built a Catholic school for his growing congregation, but unfortunately died on March 13, 1882, at only fifty-five years of age while undergoing surgery to remove bladder stones. He left behind six siblings. Forty priests attended his funeral Mass, and Boyle was buried among his fellow priests at Mt. Olivet Cemetery in Washington.

Matthew Francis McGrath (1833–1870) has been mentioned already in chapter 6 as a member of the Catholic religious order called the Dominicans (Order of Preachers). While residing at the Dominican priory in Washington, McGrath had already been volunteering to serve wounded troops in the District of Columbia area in 1862, which then merited his receipt of a June 1862 letter from President Lincoln about formal hospital chaplaincy. Upon being accepted three days later, he was assigned by the surgeon general to Seminary Hospital in Georgetown (also called Officers Hospital or Union Hospital).

General hospitals were so named because as soon as a seriously wounded soldier could be evacuated from a field hospital, they were sent to hospitals such as these whose admissions were not limited to men of a specific military unit or post. The war's first hospitals were more the result of immediate improvisation than planning (jails, hotels, warehouses, churches, etc.), and the work of soon-to-be Surgeon General W. A. Hammond in 1862 highlighted the need for these dedicated hospital buildings. By war's end, there were 204 Union general hospitals with 136,894 beds. During the war, some 1,057,523 soldiers received care in Union military hospitals, and perhaps a similar number in Confederate hospitals.[13]

Like many buildings quickly pressed into service when casualties began mounting, Seminary/Officers/Union General Hospital had formerly been the Miss English Seminary for Young Ladies, a school for young women at the rear of the Union Hotel. But after the opening conflicts of the Civil War, the school was confiscated and turned into a general hospital for officers; it opened on June 30, 1861, and closed on June 14, 1865. In another bit of trivia, Walt Whitman, Louisa May Alcott, and John Burroughs, all then unknown writers, were on the staff of this hospital during the war years. McGrath ministered there as chaplain until he resigned on October 1, 1863, and died in December 1870.[14]

Like Francis Boyle, Patrick Francis McCarthy also was a priest residing in the District of Columbia, in what was then the Baltimore Diocese (now the Archdiocese of Washington). McCarthy was born in Ireland in October 1833, studied at two seminaries in Baltimore, and was ordained on June 30, 1860. Few specific details are known about his career either as a pastor or a military hospital chaplain other than reports of the quiet, faithful performance of whatever priestly work he was involved with. McCarthy was approved as a hospital chaplain in October 1863 when his predecessor (Matthew McGrath) resigned, and was assigned to Georgetown's Seminary Hospital, with its 121 beds (one of Washington's smaller military hospitals that focused on caring for wounded officers). Though few if any anecdotes of his service are recorded, the unique element of what he left behind for later generations are the interesting monthly reports of his hospital chaplaincy, which were required by the surgeon general as of April 9, 1864, dutifully sent to the adjutant general, and are now accessible online.[15]

While short on specific details (numbers of soldiers ministered to, types of cases, etc.), McCarthy penned well-written reports of his daily routines in descriptive ways. On July 31, 1864, he wrote that

the moral standing of the Catholic soldiers is most gratifying. In my daily visits from hospital to hospital, and from ward to ward, I find them always awaiting my arrival with anxiety. And it has often been observed that the influence exerted by my ministry has had the happiest effect on their convalescence. Of those who die from the effects of their wounds I have not met one who refused the rites or Consolations of religion. On many occasions they have impromptu expressed their resignation to the will of that Providence which required the sacrifice of their life in their Country and Cause now that they were strengthened with the aids of their Holy Religion. It was pleasing also to find that they were well satisfied with the care and attention bestowed upon them.[16]

In his final 1865 monthly reports, he captures the impact of the war's final days on his own spiritual work in his three hospitals.

The moral condition of the Catholic soldiers . . . has been satisfactory. They have been of those who were wounded in the taking of Richmond. Their wounds are and have been of a serious nature. Consequently, many of them have been called to a better world, strengthened, and consoled in their last moments by [the] holy rites of Religion . . . It is true now that the numbers are comparatively few to what they have been, but whether sick or convalescing, they are always docile, respectful and appreciative of the rites and consolations of Religion. They listen thoughtfully to the admonitions given, and the fruits are evident at least while they are in the Hospital . . . I have attended on all who needed my services day and night.[17]

McCarthy's report reflects the tremendous fluctuation that occurred in military hospitals from 1863 on, due to patients being redistributed to more specialized medical hospitals, and a multitude of new hospital pavilions being erected. Washington's military hospitals had to always be ready to be inundated with the wounded, but also prepared to have them be evacuated to other centers as soon as possible. McCarthy's own chaplaincy reflected this reality well, for by the time his own military service ended in the fall of 1865, he had been assigned to three other larger general hospitals in Washington where he made regular rounds: Armory Square (one thousand beds, visited frequently by President Lincoln), Campbell (nine hundred beds), and Judiciary Square (five hundred and ten beds).

In August 1866, following his leaving the hospital chaplaincy, McCarthy returned to being an assistant pastor in Washington, but soon was named pastor of the new Immaculate Conception Church in the same city. He immediately requested that the Sisters of Charity open a school there, and a few years later built a separate school for girls, while the boys school remained in the church basement. In 1870 he built a new church, paid off the debt he had incurred, and left a legacy of

$15,000 for provide a free school for boys. He died at age forty-nine on November 5, 1882, and like Francis Boyle, is buried at Mt. Olivet Cemetery in Washington, DC.

PETER MCGRANE
(SATTERLEE HOSPITAL, PHILADELPHIA)

Peter McGrane (1815–1891) was born in Ireland (most likely Dublin) in June 1815, just five years ahead of his younger brother Matthew, who also became a priest in the United States. Details from his early life are few, but in 1847 he entered the Pittsburgh novitiate of the Redemptorists, professed vows, and then was ordained a priest in April 1849 as a member of that order. After successfully ministering in New Orleans and the surrounding area for about a decade, in early 1861 McGrane formally left the Redemptorists, moved in with his priest-brother in Holmesburg, Pennsylvania, for a time, then requested (and received) admission into the Philadelphia Diocese (Bishop James Wood).

Just before the war, "P. P. McGrane" (his preferred name per many accounts) was assigned to St. Patrick's Church in Philadelphia as an assistant pastor, and resided there throughout the three years of his hospital chaplaincy. On October 9, 1862, he was formally commissioned into the hospital chaplains of the US Volunteers, and then recommissioned in April 1863 after his enlistment expired the previous month. McGrane is mentioned frequently in various diaries and accounts of the time, such as having ministered to troops after the First Battle of Bull Run, preaching on St. Patrick's Day 1864, and being the spiritual director for the local Catholic seminary. One local Philadelphia newspaper article remarked that he "endeared himself to the Catholic community by his eloquence and untiring exertions for their spiritual welfare." Another source reported that "Protestants were also attracted by the short but beautiful exhortations of Fr. McGrane, who said Mass for us three times in each week."[18]

Philadelphia was the only Union hospital center to rival Washington, and by 1865 would have twenty-seven hospitals with twenty-seven thousand beds. It was said that wounded soldiers preferred to be sent there, "for the food was good, the inhabitants generous, and the Quaker doctors kindly and efficient." The hospital at which McGrane ministered was initially called West Philadelphia Hospital when established on May 25, 1862, but was renamed Satterlee General Hospital after a prominent Army medical officer, General Richard Satterlee. Satterlee General Hospital was the largest Union hospital of the war, with 4,500 beds spread over twenty-one wards and 16 acres. It eventually included a barber shop, carpenter shop, clothing store, dispensary, three kitchens, laundry, library, post office, reading room, and a printing office that printed Satterlee's newspaper, *The Hospital Register.* Over the course of its existence before its closure on August 3, 1865, Satterlee treated some fifty thousand sick and wounded people, losing only 260—a notable accomplishment considering the sanitary conditions and medical techniques of the day.[19]

To augment the work of his professional physicians, Satterlee's commanding officer, Dr. Isaac Hayes, asked the Catholic Daughters of Charity to nurse the sick and wounded there beginning on May 25, 1862. The sisters lived in an adjacent convent under the leadership of Mother Mary Gonzaga Grace, and every day changed bed sheets, emptied chamber pots, dressed festering wounds, and offered emotional solace to lonely men who were in agony, far from home and loved ones. The doctors there (and at other hospitals) enjoyed working with Catholic nuns because of their disciplined work ethic, lack of complaining, and adherence to orders that were given them. Their original chapel was so small that some nuns had to exit the room so others could enter to receive Holy Communion. It was soon expanded to seat four hundred worshippers, with soldiers often arriving several hours before Mass to find a seat. Several wounded soldiers contributed to outfit the chapel, purchasing a set of stations of the cross and taking pains to decorate it for feasts and special occasions.[20]

Peter McGrane not only cared for the spiritual needs of the soldiers but also assisted the nuns stationed at the hospital. Every day, he traveled from St. Patrick's Church to Satterlee to say Mass, hear confessions, instruct, baptize, and frequently arrange for burial. His Archbishop James Wood also visited Satterlee several times to celebrate special sacraments, including an April 1863 ceremony where he confirmed thirty-one soldiers, and a February 1864 Confirmation of forty-four, including one soldier unable to leave his bed. McGrane's hospital work formally concluded on July 26, 1865, when he was honorably mustered out of service, just one week before Satterlee itself officially closed.[21]

In March 1868, when a new diocese in Wilmington, Delaware, was formed, both Peter and his priest-brother Matthew McGrane left Philadelphia and transferred into it. The two priests lived and worked together for two years at St. Peter's Church in Wilmington, where Peter continued to be a popular speaker in the area. His life then becomes a bit unclear, being marked by several moves without accurate documentation. It appears he moved to Kentucky in 1871 and then joined the cloistered Trappist monastery (Gethsemane) near Louisville in 1881, although he apparently never took formal vows, as no such records exist. His death in 1891 is attested to in several places, with one record noting he was buried at Gethsemane's Trappist cemetery. Thus, in the end, despite more than twenty years of stable, dedicated priestly service, it seems the Irish priest's final years were marked by a "searching" for something spiritual that had eluded him.[22]

JESUIT HOSPITAL CHAPLAINS:
BERNARDIN WIGET (WASHINGTON) AND
JAMES BRUEHL (BEAUFORT–NEW ORLEANS)

As mentioned in chapter 5, the Jesuits were by far the most numerous single group of Catholic chaplains, with priests ministering in regiments, brigades, prisons, and hospitals as well. The two members of this order who were official Civil War hospital chaplains were James Bruehl (Beaufort and New Orleans) and Bernardin Wiget (Washington, DC). James Bruehl (1811–1865) was Hungarian by birth, joining the Austrian Province of the Jesuits and being ordained in 1846, then spending most of his priesthood as a missionary in various parts of the world. Likely in response to the Europe's 1848 revolutions (which led many Jesuits to flee), from about 1847 to 1852 he worked in north Africa as a chaplain with the French army in their colonial wars in Algeria. Following that, Bruehl spent the rest of the 1850s in the United

States, stationed first in Westphalia, Missouri, then teaching at St. Charles College in Grand Coteau, Louisiana.

In the early 1860s he was transferred to the Jesuit residence at Fordham in New York City, becoming temporarily part of their Maryland Province. In June 1862, when the Sisters of Mercy in New York City accepted an invitation from General Ambrose Burnside (through Bishop John Hughes and Secretary of War Edwin Stanton) to take charge of a military hospital in North Carolina, Bruehl went with the nuns as their chaplain. With his background as both a Jesuit missionary and a French army chaplain, he was an obvious selection. One Mercy nun wrote a description of him at that time, later published in George Barton's *Angels of the Battlefield.* "The Rev. Father Bruhl [*sic*] was a native of Hungary, sixty years of age. He had a long, flowing grey beard, and while he was not possessed of an adequate knowledge of English, he was equipped with a valuable experience of hospital work incident to warfare. This was derived from long and laborious service in the French army during the war which resulted in the taking of Algiers."[23]

The group boarded the *Catawba* on July 15 and arrived four days later at Hammond General Hospital in Beaufort, North Carolina, as indicated by the July 21, 1862, report of General John G. Foster (commander of the North Carolina Department).

> At the request of Major-General Burnside, nine Sisters of Mercy have arrived from New York, to take charge of the hospital at Beaufort, and under their kind and educated care I hope for a rapid improvement in the health of the patients. The Rev. Mr. Bruehl, their priest, accompanied them, and, in consideration of the worthiness of this gentleman and of the large number of Catholics in the New York regiment attached to my command, I most earnestly recommend that he be appointed chaplain of the United States hospital at Beaufort, N. C.[24]

Foster's report led to a letter from Assistant Secretary of War Christopher Wolcott to Lincoln's private secretary John Nicolay and resulted in Bruehl receiving his formal appointment on July 28, 1862. He served at Beaufort until March 4, 1863, when his term as chaplain expired, and when the nuns' work was not as needed due to declining numbers of sick. However, the party's initial impressions of the Beaufort hospital were certainly memorable, if not favorable. They arrived to find debris, filth, and blood throughout the area, the hospital itself, and their own quarters. "The place contained no furniture except a few miserable bedsteads, and was in a most desolate condition. There was only one broom and very few utensils. The broom . . . was seldom available. Along the shore were wrecks of pianos, tables, chairs, glass, etc. There were no candles or lamps, and everyone was compelled to retire before night."[25]

As usual, this was a situation the nuns quickly remedied, and the very next day, order was restored and the building was transformed by their cleanliness and professionalism. The sudden appearance of nuns and a priest, though, was quite a shock to soldiers and residents who had never seen Catholics before. Initially met by great skepticism, even the hospital steward later said that he remained awake on stakeout in case the nuns tried to "poison the patients or do some other terrible thing, they being confessed emissaries of the Pope." "Great heavens!" one patient shrieked to his nun-nurse, "Are you a man or a woman? But your hand is a woman's hand; its touch is soft, and your voice is gentle. What are you?" The Sister gently responded, "Only a poor servant of the Great Master, come from afar to serve you." As always, their compassionate work changed hearts and lives. One dying patient, who likely had never known any religion, said, "Sister, tell me what to answer when the priest comes to baptize me." When Bruehl was summoned to his bedside and inquired about the soldier's faith, the man simply responded, "what the sisters believe, that is what I believe."[26]

When his appointment in Beaufort expired in May 1862, Bruehl applied for and was reappointed to hospital chaplaincy in New Orleans. The Hungarian Jesuit served for barely a month in that position, however, and was honorably discharged on May 20, 1863, with health issues most likely playing a role in that decision. He then returned to Europe and was stationed at the Jesuit novitiate in Trnava (in modern-day Slovakia); it was there that he died on March 17, 1865.

The life of Bernardin Wiget (1821–1883) resembled Bruehl's in many ways, but digressed because of Wiget's many later civil and political activities. He will be spoken of again in chapter 12 with regard to these actions, but an overview will be given here. Born in Switzerland to very respectable and pious parents, Wiget studied and joined the Jesuits there until the 1847 Swiss civil war occurred. When the Swiss Protestant armies overwhelmed the Catholic forces, a small group of Jesuits including Wiget feared for their lives and fled the country in disguise. Along with many other Jesuits of the time, Wiget was ordered by his Jesuit superior to go to the United States, where he studied and learned English at Georgetown in 1848 and 1849. Ordained in 1851, Wiget then had a number of different assignments and wound up at St. Ignatius Church at Chapel Point, Maryland, in 1854 and 1855, one of the oldest Catholic churches in the United States. There he established a college preparatory school for boys close to his Jesuit residence, whose most notable students were the two sons of Mary Surratt, Isaac and John. A long history with the quite poor Surratt family began there, which included Wiget presenting the 1854 first communion to Mary's daughter Anna.

In 1856, he was sent to Boston, where he immediately formed an impressive youth group (also called "sodality") for boys and was deeply embroiled in the contentious March 1859 Eliot School controversy. From 1860 to 1868, Wiget was stationed in Washington, DC, as the rector at Gonzaga College and pastor of St. Aloysius Church. In September 1862, the government demanded that his church be taken over to be used as a hospital, but Wiget made a counter-proposal: he would build a hospital on their property so the sacred space of his church would not be "profaned." This was done so quickly that St. Aloysius General Hospital (Washington Post Hospital) was open and running on October 7, 1862, though it closed a year later and patients were transferred to other area hospitals. Wiget himself became an official chaplain there at the time the hospital opened, and served until his honorable discharge in November 1865.[27]

With the closure of St. Aloysius Hospital, Wiget followed his patients to Stanton and Harewood Hospitals in Washington, though he also ministered at Douglas, Eckington, and Finley Hospitals as well. His monthly reports, though terse, give a good account of Catholic chaplains' routines. "I give Divine Service every Sunday at Stanton Hospital, and daily at Douglas Hospital. I visit these two Hospitals daily, and the surrounding Hospitals Finley, Eckington and Harewood according to necessity. The visits to these last three Hospitals were not very frequent this month [April 1864]." In his January 1865 report, he added a few other details about his work.

> I visit these hospitals [Finley, Eckington, Stanton] constantly either by myself or through one of the Rev. gentlemen under my care. The rest of the Hospitals I visit in the same way occasionally and according to necessity. Being the only Catholic Hospital Chaplain in the city speaking the German language, I am often called to the service of the German Catholic believers in the surrounding Hospitals. The moral condition of the Stanton Hospital is excellent.[28]

Wiget was mentioned frequently as "becoming a familiar sight astride his horse, Jackson, visiting the troops in their camps and around the city." He also became the confessor to Mary Surratt, a character witness at her trial, and accompanied her to the gallows, wearing his white stole and remaining with her when she was hung. The question of Mary Surratt's actual complicity in the assassination of Lincoln remains a debated point, but undoubtedly Wiget would have agreed with many others who felt that she "suffered on the scaffold for the crimes of others."[29]

His war service completed in November 1865, Wiget resumed his fulltime work at Gonzaga and St. Aloysius, then oversaw the construction of Washington's second German church, St. Joseph's (on Capitol Hill), which opened in 1868. Wiget served there as pastor until 1873, but in 1868 his superiors briefly sent him back to his native Switzerland to recruit his health, which had become exhausted by his labors during and after the Civil War. Upon his return, he was again sent to St. Thomas Manor (St. Ignatius Church) in Charles County, Maryland — the scene of his first American assignment. From 1878 to 1883 he was again pastor there, but "infirmities brought on by untiring labor made him aged before his time," and in January 1883 Wiget died at St. Thomas Manor. He must have gone to his Maker pleased, however, because the federal government had finally agreed (only in 1869) to return to the Jesuits the hospital property that he had worked so hard to build for the Union.[30]

OTHER UNION HOSPITAL CHAPLAINS

The following priests also served as official hospital chaplains, but their lives and work have been more thoroughly described in previous chapters of this book. Thus, we will not repeat their stories, but will just briefly mention their names and places of hospital ministry:

- Constantine Egan OP, hospital of 5th and 9th Corps (see chapter 6)
- Thomas Ouellet SJ, hospital in New Bern, North Carolina, in which the Sisters of Mercy served (see chapter 5)
- Edward McGlynn, US hospital in New York, New York, in which the Sisters of Charity of New York served (see chapter 12)
- Joseph Stephan, US Hospital in Nashville, Tennessee, in which the Sisters of Charity of Cincinnati served (see chapter 12)
- John Vahey, US Hospital in Alton, Illinois, in which the Daughters of Charity served (see chapter 12)

CONFEDERATE HOSPITAL CHAPLAINS

The "butcher's bill" of Civil War casualties led to hospitals quickly springing up to attempt to meet the overwhelming medical needs. By 1865, on both sides "there were about 400 general hospitals with about 400,000 beds. There were two million admissions to these hospitals with an overall mortality of 8%."[31] In the Confederacy, there were eventually 153 principal hospitals, though many other buildings (barns, churches, private homes, warehouses, schools, courthouses etc.) were converted and used as temporary hospitals during the war years. In the major cities closest to the fighting, Chattanooga had fifty hospitals, Lynchburg had twenty-five general hospitals, and the state of Georgia alone had general hospitals in thirty-nine cities. Of course, Richmond was by far the largest hospital center, with massive Chimborazo Hospital (the largest Civil War hospital on either side) boasting 77,889 wartime admissions, and Winder Hospital close behind with its 76,213 patients.[32]

According to Confederate records, eight Catholic priests in all served officially as chaplains in hospitals, with five also being considered post chaplains for troops at those same locations. (As mentioned, it can be argued that all hospital chaplains were in essence post chaplains since they served at the same location.) Three other priests were never officially named hospital chaplains, but served informally for significant periods while still connected to their regiments. Seven of these eleven have already been described in greater detail elsewhere in this book, so their stories will not be repeated here. I will simply summarize their hospital work.

- Hippolyte Gache SJ was never formally named a hospital chaplain, but he served at the Danville Hospital in the late summer of 1862, at Lynchburg's hospitals from 1863 to1865 (where he is reported to have baptized one hundred persons), and was transferred with the Sisters of Charity to serve in Richmond's hospitals in 1865. Officially assigned to the 10th Louisiana, Gache was not with them much, if at all; they were greatly reduced in numbers during the final three years of the war.[33]
- Darius Hubert SJ (chaplain of the 1st Louisiana) ministered in the hospitals of Richmond and Manchester (then a suburb of Richmond) while recovering from a Gettysburg wound in spring 1864. He was not attached to any medical facility, and reported directly to the medical director of all Richmond hospitals, Dr. William Carrington. See chapter 5 for more of Gache and Hubert's stories.
- Francis Leray served as a post and hospital chaplain in Oxford, Mississippi, likely also in Shelby Springs and Jackson. The Sisters of Mercy from New York ministered in all of these hospitals.
- John Mouton served as a post and hospital chaplain along the Mobile–Ohio Railroad in eastern Mississippi.
- Francis Pont served in hospitals in Mississippi. For more on Leray, Mouton, and Pont, see chapter 10.
- Thomas O'Reilly served in hospitals in Atlanta; see chapter 7 for further detail.
- Egidius Smulders CSsR, always remaining chaplain of the 8th Louisiana, served with the Sisters of Charity at their Manassas hospital in late 1862, and attended the wounded at Petersburg hospitals for three months in 1864. The last three months of the war he was assigned to special duty among the paroled prisoners in Salisbury, North Carolina. More of Smulders's story is told in chapter 6.

MONTGOMERY WHITE SULPHUR SPRINGS: LAURENCE O'CONNELL AND CHARLES CROGHAN

Before the war, Montgomery County (Virginia) was an idyllic holiday destination, thanks to several hot springs resorts in the area. One of the largest was the Montgomery White Sulphur Springs farm, which was in the spring of 1861 transformed into a Confederate general hospital under Chief Surgeon J. Lewis Woodville. At its peak, the hospital accommodated seven hundred sick and wounded Confederate soldiers, although space was so limited at times that soldiers had to sleep in the bowling alley. Among the employees there were enslaved persons, Catholic nuns (the Sisters of Mercy), and two successive Catholic chaplains, Laurence O'Connell (1826–1891) and Charles Croghan (1822–1880).[34]

Laurence Patrick O'Connell, born in County Cork, Ireland, in September 1826, was one of three priest-brothers who served in the Charleston Diocese (South Carolina). After immigrating and studying at Fordham, he was ordained in March 1850 and sent to St. Joseph Church in Columbia as assistant to his older brother, Jeremiah J. O'Connell (1821–1894), who was pastor. The two priests (known as L. J. O'Connell and J. P. O'Connell) lived in Columbia, ministering to the people there and to the smaller outlying mission churches in the area. They were joined eventually by their younger brother, Joseph J. O'Connell, and the three lived in Columbia together for nearly twenty-five years, throughout "the disastrous period of the Civil War" (as Joseph later phrased it). In his 1879 history of Catholicism in the area, his brother Jeremiah described Laurence as "a solid and able public speaker, a sincere, grave man, and an efficient priest . . . [who] filled the office [of Vicar General] with commendable meekness and efficiency."[35]

In April 1861, when the Sisters of Mercy (under their superior Sister DeSalles Brennan) went to take charge of the new Confederate hospital in White Sulphur Springs, it was with the stipulation that the priest with them should become an army chaplain. Thus, on November 16, 1861, Laurence was appointed by Bishop Patrick Lynch (Charleston) as chaplain of the Confederate post and general hospital there. (At the time, this was in Virginia, although in June 1863, it became part of the new state of West Virginia.) O'Connell faithfully fulfilled his assignment for almost two years, from November 1861 until April 1863, but by then his health had badly broken down. Though details here are scant, a letter from Bishop Lynch of April 18, 1863, remarked that "two winters in the mountains have pretty well broken him down and he has had to come home and does not feel at all able to stand it any longer. I understand he would not venture to travel home except in company with a physician. Anyhow he wishes not to go back, and to seek a transfer."[36]

Though details may be scant on his Civil War hospital chaplaincy, what is fascinating about O'Connell's life is his presence at the pillaging and burning of Columbia, South Carolina, by Union troops on February 17, 1865. All three O'Connell priest-brothers lived there at the time, although Laurence appears to have faced the worst of it, for as his brother wrote later, he "lay sick in the house, after his long services in Virginia hospitals, was dragged out into the night air, and held as prisoner under guard until morning."[37] Jeremiah O'Connell wrote later that this event was utterly shattering for Columbia residents, stating unequivocally that "it was only when in possession of the United States army that the fire originated, and that Columbia was destroyed. How far that commander is to be inculpated, I leave the world to judge." Already clogged with refugees from Sherman's March to the Sea, two-thirds of Columbia and all public buildings were destroyed before the Union army left three days later.[38]

In an article he wrote for the Catholic newspaper about the event, Laurence himself mentions that St. Mary's College (founded there in 1852 by his brother) was

> robbed, pillaged and then given to flames . . . the property of four priests, who were its professors and lived there, was also consumed . . . [I myself] was made prisoner, and though pleading to save the holy oils etc., [my] prayer was rejected. A sacrilegious squad drank their whiskey from the sacred chalice. The sacred vestments and consecrated vessels . . . were profaned and stolen . . . Of the college itself, and the property which it contained, nothing was saved but the massed ruins . . . the clergymen saved nothing beyond the garments which they had upon their persons.[39]

After his hospital chaplaincy, Laurence O'Connell freely served the sick and wounded of both armies, which likely contributed to his health issues during the burning of Columbia. Following that event, he continued to serve the far-flung Catholics of the Charleston Diocese (both North and South Carolina at the time). In March 1868, North Carolina was taken from the Charleston Diocese (becoming what is termed a "vicariate apostolic") and Laurence became its new vicar general, performing that job and pastoring St. Peter's Church in Charlotte until 1882. As will be shown in chapter 10, there were immense challenges beginning a new diocese with very scattered churches and believers, especially in the south and west. In 1872, there were only eight priests on missions, and ten churches and chapels, in all of North Carolina. But Laurence labored there faithfully, ending his career as a hospital chaplain once again in the late 1880s at St. Vincent's Hospital in Norfolk, Virginia. It was there that he died "of inflammatory rheumatism contracted during the war" on April 18, 1891.[40]

In April 1863, another native Irishman replaced O'Connell at the Montgomery White Sulphur Springs Hospital, Charles Joseph Croghan (1822–1880). He was born in Galway, Ireland, immigrated to America in April 1841, and after his seminary studies was ordained in July 1847, also for the Charleston Diocese (South Carolina). He ministered for three years on Sullivan Island, as well as briefly teaching in an area college, before being sent to New Bern (North Carolina), which was then considered "mission territory" in his diocese. In a parish whose territory literally covered one-third of the state, his was a much-traveled, stressful life, as described later by Jeremiah O'Connell. "During that time, his life was Arabic; he had no fixed abode, and through poverty was unable to pay for his board . . . [but] wherever he went he was hospitably entertained." Croghan would have stayed in the homes of Catholics in the "mission territories" he was visiting at the time.[41]

In 1863 he was sent back to Charleston to pastor the German congregation of St. Peter's, but also visited Catholic missions in the surrounding country and Confederate soldiers in their camps along the line of the Savannah River. In the spring of 1863, after O'Connell left the White Sulphur Springs Hospital due to his own sickness, Croghan was sent by Bishop Patrick Lynch to replace him. He remained there working with the Sisters of Mercy until Lee's surrender in April 1865, when "there were over three hundred sick and wounded" still there, "sixty of which were Federal soldiers, and not more than two days rations" for them all. The nuns managed to procure food, and they remained there six more weeks until all the wounded had either recovered or passed away. Intending to return to Charleston, Croghan accompanied the nuns to Lynchburg, but unable to return to their home, he raised monies to enable them all to go to New York City.[42]

In July 1865, Croghan became pastor at St. Joseph Church in Charleston (known as the church of the Irish), following Leon Fillion, the vicar general of the diocese, who had just died of typhoid fever. Croghan rebuilt the church (almost in ruins from the shelling of Union artillery on Morris Island), paid off the debt, and remained there ministering to his flock until his death in June 1880. Croghan's lifelong reputation for wisdom and assiduous work did not go unnoticed. When Bishop Lynch was asked in 1864 by the Confederate government to go to Rome on their behalf, it was Croghan he consulted, who expressed his strong support for the endeavor. His final epitaph was best expressed in 1879 by fellow Charleston priest and writer Jeremiah O'Connell, who said "Croghan . . . is full of life, activity and good nature, his labors are as assiduous as in early days . . . He is a polished writer, a scholar of general information, and one of the most learned divines in moral theology in the United States. He is a man without blemish, and a remarkable priest, without reproach."[43]

THE MINORCAN COUSINS:
ANTHONY PELLICER AND DOMINIC MANUCY

The Florida city of St. Augustine is known as "the nation's oldest city," and among its oldest nineteenth-century residents was a community of immigrants from Minorca (a small island off the coast of Spain). They were a tight-knit community who had initially come to the city in 1777, fleeing from horrendous working conditions at the nearby indigo plantation in New Smyrna. A strong and vibrant community of tradesmen, they were also heavily Catholic, and in 1823 and 1824 two boys were born there whose lives would be forever intertwined: Anthony Pellicer and Dominic Manucy. Born within a year of each, they were raised and studied together, were ordained and later consecrated bishops together, and both served in the Civil War post and hospitals of Montgomery, Alabama.[44]

Anthony Dominic Pellicer (1824–1880) was descended from the leader of the Minorcans of New Smyrna who had originally revolted against the tyranny of the cruel plantation owner there. Because his mother died during childbirth, he was raised by his cousins Pedro and Maria Manucy, who were Dominic's parents. Both grew up in St. Augustine's Minorcan Quarter, where Pellicer was known as "Neco." Both Anthony and Dominic attended an area academy. In 1837 the two boys went away to the Jesuit college at Spring Hill, Alabama, where upon completion of thirteen years of studies, they were ordained together on August 15, 1850, for service in the Mobile Diocese.[45]

The two priests parted ways at that point, at least in terms of ministry. Manucy went to Mobile, while Pellicer was sent to St. Peter's Church in Montgomery, where he was pastor for eleven years and built a new brick church to replace the original 1833 wooden structure. He went to Mexico City to raise funds for his new church, and was very successful in doing so, but unfortunately on returning, his stagecoach was attacked by bandits and he lost everything. Undaunted, Pellicer then traveled to Cuba, where he successfully again raised the funds needed for his Spanish-style church building. As was required for ministry among the widely scattered Catholic community of the South, Pellicer regularly visited many other small communities in the surrounding area, beginning at least one other church and organizing another congregation in Selma.

After Abraham Lincoln's election in November 1860, secession fever struck the state quickly, and on January 11, 1861, Alabama voted to secede from the Union. In February 1861 delegates from other seceded states met in Montgomery to form the new Confederate nation. A month later Jefferson Davis took the oath of office there, in the first capitol of the Confederacy (which moved to Richmond several months later). When early dreams of a short-lived war proved to be wrong, Montgomery became a destination for wounded and sick soldiers.

Situated away from main battlefields, with good rail and river connections, the city was ideal for Confederate hospitals; six general hospitals operated there during the war. Established in buildings used previously for other purposes, none of these were large hospitals, with the overall capacity of all six being only 1,350 beds. One visitor from Richmond's massive Chimborazo Hospital would remark later in the war that they "did not compare with those I had left in Virginia, either in arrangement, cleanliness or attendance."[46]

When Montgomery's wartime hospitals opened in 1862, it was natural for Pellicer to begin visiting them, since there were only forty-five thousand people in the whole county (including 23,700 enslaved persons), and Catholics were but a small minority. He started working at the hospitals in the fall of 1862, though his formal government appointment was dated November 3, 1862 (and had been curiously delivered first to Stephen Mallory, who likely assisted Pellicer in obtaining the commission). Pellicer worked at St. Mary's General Hospital "under the charge of the Sisters," described as being "Sisters of Mercy" in one newspaper clipping. A patient calling himself *Cives Miles* (Latin for "citizen soldier") raved about the sisters' work at St. Mary's, saying "it would be unpardonable if I omitted to mention our common obligations to the 'Sisters of Mercy' for their untiring attentions to the sick, and above all for the warm sympathy and cheerful kindness with which they minister to the suffering."[47]

As with many hospital chaplains, little is recorded of Pellicer's daily work at this particular post, though it would have certainly included care for the members of his own parish, regular celebration of the sacraments in hospitals, and the general spiritual care of both sisters and patients in all six area hospitals. The one description we have of his two years of work was highly complimentary, remarking that Pellicer "was unremitting in his attention to the sick and wounded. His zeal and devotedness struck those who were strangers to the faith, and as many as three hundred sought his guidance." Late in 1864, Pellicer was recalled by his bishop to the cathedral church in Mobile, and thus had to resign his chaplaincy. In his December 2, 1864, resignation letter, he recommended his cousin as the replacement for him in the Montgomery hospital, and this was accepted by Secretary of War James Seddon.

Pellicer's career after the war reflected the high esteem in which he was held. He had already been mentioned in 1860 for the vacant Savannah Diocese bishop's seat; he became vicar general of the Mobile Diocese and rector at the cathedral there in 1867. When the new diocese of San Antonio, Texas, was established in 1874, Pellicer was named its first bishop, and consecrated (along with his cousin) on December 8. He immediately visited the entire diocese on horseback or by wagon, often sleeping on the open prairie. Acquiring an intimate knowledge of each church (and learning conversational "Tex-Mex" along the way), he labored mightily to grow the diocese, usually donating his own salary and free time to help area "unfortunates." Sadly, his work was so unceasing and challenging that health issues soon arose that complicated his diabetes. His death on April 14, 1880, was partly due to exhaustion. He is buried under the floor of San Fernando Cathedral in San Antonio.

The early years of Dominic Manucy (1823–1885) are very similar to those of Pellicer, so only the details which make his story unique will be covered here. After his 1850 ordination, Manucy spent twenty-four years ministering at churches in Mobile. Then, as mentioned above, in late 1864 he succeeded his cousin in Montgomery in two regards: as both chaplain at the post of St. Mary's Hospital and as pastor of St. Peter's Church there. Pellicer's letter of recommendation had stated that "Father Manucy is to be stationed at Montgomery in my place, as he will have to attend to the Sisters in charge of the Hospitals here, and ought by rights be appointed Chaplain of St. Mary's Hospital under the charge of the Sisters. Please do all you can for his appointment." His commission was formally given by Secretary of War James Seddon in January 1865. When Manucy's relatively short hospital chaplaincy ended, the Minorcan priest remained for ten years in Montgomery as rector of St. Peter's Church there.[48]

In 1874, the large Galveston Diocese was divided into the new San Antonio Diocese and the Vicariate Apostolic of Brownsville Texas. Manucy was selected for this episcopal post of Brownsville in September 1874, where resident Catholics were few and very poor. His task was daunting—to organize, fund, and evangelize this new Catholic "territory," composed of many *rancheros* with no fixed home but living nomadic lives following sheep and herds (which they seldom owned). After being consecrated with his cousin in December 1874, Manucy was constantly on the move in a lifestyle almost as difficult as that of the *rancheros* themselves. Due to troubles with the Masonic Order in Brownsville and because of the already strong presence of Catholics under the Oblate Fathers there, Manucy ended up setting up his diocesan residence in Corpus Christi, which eventually became a new diocese in 1912.

In January 1884, Manucy was shocked to be notified by the Vatican that he had also been named Bishop of Mobile without being allowed to give up his onerous Brownsville responsibilities. He was installed on March 30, 1884, but served as bishop there for less than a year. Debt, diocesan issues, and personal illness combined; the challenges of handling both places were simply too much for him. He resigned as bishop of Mobile on September 27, 1884, intending to return to Brownsville, but he died in Mobile on February 7, 1885. Manucy is entombed in the crypt of the Cathedral Basilica of the Immaculate Conception in Mobile, Alabama. The two Minorcan chaplains, bishops, and cousins are undoubtedly together again now, as they were so often in this world.

CHAPTER 9

CHAPLAINS FOR THE IRISH

The largest ethnic group served by Catholic chaplains were the Irish. Immigrants from Ireland comprised the most visibly Catholic group in America, supplied a majority of priests and religious for the "mission field" that America was, and controlled much of the ecclesiastical structure by the 1860s and beyond (in 1861, 33 percent of Catholic bishops were Irish, followed by American-born bishops at 29 percent). The mid-1840s potato blight in Ireland, and the subsequent famine that followed, led to an unparalleled and massive immigration to the United States in the decades just prior to the Civil War. Between 1845 and 1855, approximately 1.5 million Catholics from Ireland resettled in America, far more than the three hundred thousand or so that went each to Canada, Great Britain, or Australia. The great majority of these immigrants wound up in the northern United States, especially in urban areas such as Boston, Philadelphia, and New York. In 1860, there were actually more Irish-born living in New York City than lived in Dublin, Cork, or Belfast. It is estimated that only about eighty-four thousand Irish lived in the Confederate states, the majority being in the New Orleans (the nation's most Catholic city, with eighteen Catholic churches) and Nashville areas.[1]

The Irish were a minority in both the North and South, comprising only 12.1 percent of the Northern states' and 5.4 percent in the

Confederate states' populations in 1860.[2] More than any other ethnic group, they were defined by their Catholicism. In the United States, they faced intense prejudice and hatred because of their faith in addition to their ethnic status and position in society. Within years of their increased arrival in the country, nativist sentiment against Irish immigrants sprung up. Groups such as the Native American Party of the 1840s and the Know Nothings of the 1850s arose, marked by rhetoric like this from an 1855 *Chicago Tribune* article: "The great majority of the members of the Roman Catholic Church are Irishmen . . . Who does not know that the most depraved, debased, worthless and irredeemable drunkards and sots which curse the community, are Irish Catholics? Who does not know that five-eighths of cases brought up every day before the Mayor for drunkenness and consequent crime, are Irish Catholics?"[3]

For the Irish population, Catholicism was an anchor in an unfriendly United States. Though poor, the immigrants quickly established parishes, which "provided an island of safety and comfort in an alien land, while easing their transition into American life . . . [and] also served as a vehicle for preserving the culture they brought from the old country." Partly because of the central role of the Catholic sacraments, the Irish tended to rely more heavily on the clergy for direct leadership than other ethnic groups did. This may also have been because of the role priests played in the old country, where they served as "guardians of Irish culture in the face of British imperialism, as well as in directly ministerial roles. The stereotype of the Irish pastor ruling his parish with an iron hand had more than a little truth supporting it."[4]

When the Civil War broke out, recruiting ethnic units was a way for the Union in particular to help win the Irish to their cause—an important issue since most of these immigrants tended to be more sympathetic to the Southern struggle for independence, given their own people's struggles against Great Britain. An additional large inducement for the Irish to fight—for both North and the South—was the guarantee of a Catholic priest-chaplain. Starting with the first all-Irish regiments recruited (63rd New York from Staten Island, and the 69th and 88th New York from the Bronx), Catholic priests were and would remain a conspicuous presence among Irish troops throughout the war.

There were about 200,000 Catholics in the Union army, of which the Irish were about 145,000 to 150,000—making up about 11 percent of the total troops (with Germans making up about 12 percent). It is estimated that 25,000 to 40,000 Irish fought for the Confederacy, although ethnic determinations there are far harder to clarify. As historian Phillip Tucker remarked, "Irish Confederates were in general longer-term residents of America than the Irish in the North . . . [they] had more successfully assimilated into mainstream southern life and society." Reflecting ethnic heritage in the names of Confederate regiments was also not as important for South armies. In all, it is estimated that slightly over 200,000 Irish fought on both sides—150,000 Union, 30,000 Confederate, 23,000 Union Navy, with some 12,000 troops stationed in California.[5]

Some of the most distinctive Civil War regiments, companies, and flags were those of the Irish. Nearly every regiment had some version of the generic yet striking Irish flag—an emerald green background, the sun shining behind it, a golden harp in the center (the national symbol of Ireland), shamrocks below, with the battle cry "Clear the way" in old Gaelic at the bottom (*Faugh-a-ballagh*).

In the North, in September 1861, Thomas Francis Meagher (perhaps the most prominent political hero of all Irish Americans) formed the famous Irish Brigade, building it upon three New York regiments. Then in July 1862, with Abraham Lincoln's support, Michael Corcoran (former colonel of 69th New York State Militia) formed the Irish Legion, also called Corcoran's Brigade. Both of these groups would suffer enormous wartime casualties. The Irish Brigade fought in every major battle of the eastern theater, and followed only the 1st Vermont and the Iron Brigade in numbers of combatants dead. The Irish Legion suffered terribly during the 1864 Overland Campaign, especially at the battles of Spotsylvania (May 8–21, 1864) and then Cold Harbor (May 31–June 12, 1864), where they had the highest casualty rates of any engaged that day.[6]

The South had no distinctively Irish units of comparable size, but did have one regiment-sized unit of mostly Irish extraction, the 10th Tennessee, often called the Bloody Tenth. It was formed by Colonel Randall McGavock from the counties around Nashville, Tennessee, with seven companies of Irishmen from Nashville itself and three other companies coming largely from Irish enclaves in middle Tennessee towns. New Orleans was the Confederacy's largest, and the nation's most Catholic city (45.9 percent of the city was Catholic). Given its historical Spanish and French immigration patterns, it is no surprise that more Catholics lived in Louisiana than anywhere else in the South (27.9 percent of the state was Catholic), with the majority of them (about 25, 000) residing in New Orleans. In the immediate prewar period a significant proportion of that Catholic population was Irish. Louisiana not only had more Irish Confederate troops, but also more Catholic chaplains than any other state in the Confederacy. In all, there were Irish companies in at least nine Louisiana brigades, and nine Catholic chaplains who served those troops officially.[7]

Since many of the chaplains who served Irish troops in both the Union and Confederate armies have been spoken of previously, their stories will not be repeated here, but their names and wartime connections will briefly be mentioned. More time will be spent outlining the stories of those Catholic priests not described elsewhere in this book so that their unique lives and Civil War ministry may be captured for posterity.

IRISH CATHOLIC UNION CHAPLAINS

The majority of Catholic chaplains, especially the full-time ones, were assigned to units with a high percentage of Catholics, and many of these would have been heavily Irish units. In the Union army, there were eighteen chaplains who served what might be called "distinctively Irish units," although some forty-five priests of Irish birth or descent contributed their services as chaplains during the war—by far the most significant ethnic group among Catholic chaplains (over 60 percent of all Union chaplains). We will discuss these chaplains in order of the history, size, and prominence of the military unit in which they served.[8]

69th New York State Militia

On April 15, 1861, President Lincoln issued a proclamation calling up state militias to respond to the attack on Fort Sumter. The Irish patriot commander of the 69th New York State Militia, Michael Corcoran, was spared a court martial because of his ability to influence and raise volunteers from the motherland (he had refused to parade the militia before the visiting Prince of Wales). When his heavily Irish 69th New York State Militia left for Washington on April 23, Thomas L. Mooney (1824–1877) sailed with them, having mustered in as their first chaplain three days previously. Born in Manchester, England, ordained in 1853, Mooney was the pastor of St. Brigid's Church in New York. How he became associated with the 69th is not clear, but some believe he was the spiritual advisor of one of the companies, which was made up of ship workers who lived in his parish. While the ship carrying the militia was at sea, Mooney said Mass on deck when the weather permitted, and in early June 1861 his spiritual work was in fact captured in a well-known Matthew Brady photo of him posing outside a tent while saying a Mass.

While the 69th labored to build Fort Corcoran (named after the colonel of the regiment) as part of the outer defenses of Washington, DC, Mooney continued to care for their spiritual needs and tried to keep them out of trouble. But on June 13, 1861, Mooney himself got into trouble while the regiment was helping place a rifled cannon in Fort Corcoran. The priest was called upon that day to bless the newly placed cannon, but instead he baptized the cannon, comparing a baby's cries following the pouring of the baptism waters with the cannon's "first utterances . . . of this promising boy [who] will speak for the first time, in loud, clear accents . . . and hunt traitors from this fort."[9]

Mooney's actions and words upset some Catholic leaders, prompted criticism in the Baltimore Catholic paper, and motivated Bishop Francis Kenrick of Baltimore to write to Mooney's superior, Bishop John Hughes of New York, to have him recalled. Hughes wrote a letter to Mooney on July 3, 1861, remarking how disappointed he was in Mooney's "inauguration of a ceremony unknown to the Church . . . which was sufficiently bad, but your remarks are infinitely worse." Hughes (nicknamed "Dagger John" both for his aggressive personality and his custom of preceding his signature with the cross) ordered Mooney to return to his parish within three days of receiving his letter. In fact, it was a curious irony that Hughes removed Mooney for his actions, when Richmond Bishop John McGill himself blessed the pikes of the local Montgomery Guards (1st Virginia), and Mobile's Bishop John Quinlan blessed the flags of their local Emerald Guards (8th Alabama).[10]

Mooney complied with his bishop, though, and did indeed return to St. Brigid's Church, where he spent twenty-five very successful years there as pastor. He continued to follow the fortunes of the 69th New York State Militia through the First Battle of Bull Run (July 21, 1861), its mustering out in early August 1861, and the subsequent transition of many of its soldiers into the 69th New York Infantry of Meagher's Irish Brigade. He was a close friend of Michael Corcoran in his July 1862 formation of the Irish Legion, and remained a friend of Northern Irish troops until his tragic death after being thrown from a carriage on September 13, 1877.

Union Irish Brigade (69th, 63rd, and 88th New York; 28th Massachusetts; 116th Pennsylvania)

After its formation was authorized in September 1861, the Irish Brigade rapidly became the focal hub of Catholicism in the Army of the Potomac, and arguably in the entire Union Army. Its five regiments had eight chaplains in all through the war years, several of whom have already been discussed previously. The first three mentioned below and discussed previously were members of religious orders (Corby, Dillon, and Ouellet), and formed the steady spiritual backbone for this predominantly Catholic brigade throughout the war, as their combined length of service reveals. The other five priests, all members of specific dioceses in the country, also served with great honor and renown, and went on to great postwar success.

- William Corby (1833–1897), from Notre Dame, Indiana, is easily the most famous Catholic chaplain of the entire war. He served from October 1861 to September 1864 in the 88th New York, through the entirety of the Irish Brigade's most difficult engagements. Corby's *Memoirs* is the preeminent primary source detailing the experiences of Civil War Catholic chaplains, along with the diary of Confederate chaplain James Sheeran. Both of these well-written accounts make for fascinating reading and insight into the oft-ignored world of chaplains.

- James Dillon (1833–1868), preceded Corby in serving the Irish Brigade. In fact, his letter to Father Edward Sorin is what resulted in Corby being sent. Dillon worked with the 63rd New York from October 1861 to October 1862. He was a regular companion of Corby throughout that time, and is mentioned throughout the *Memoirs*. Dillon also ministered as chaplain for the 69th New York until August 1864. Unfortunately, in Corby's own words, Dillon "contracted in that army the disease that carried him to an early grave in 1868."[11]

- The Jesuit priest Thomas Ouellet (1819–1894) served the 69th New York twice between November 1861 and the end of the war in June 1865, in between which he served in a Union hospital in New Bern, North Carolina. He too is frequently mentioned in Corby's *Memoirs*, where he is given special praise for his work and bravery, as well as for the deep respect and love that the troops had for him.

- The 116th Pennsylvania joined the Irish Brigade in August 1862, and with them came their chaplain, Edward McKee (1826–1891), a native of Ireland and priest of the Philadelphia Diocese. He served only a little over three months and received an honorable discharge on December 1862, suffering from either a wound received or sickness contracted at Fredericksburg (December 11–15, 1862). Germain cites the surgeon's report, which certified McKee's disability and incapacity to perform his duties. McKee receives a humorous mention in Corby's *Memoirs* from the tough experience he had riding his new horse when he first joined the regiment. After enthusiastically riding forty-four miles on a new saddle on a new horse, the brand-new chaplain "kept to his bed for three weeks, while the horse rested and he grew fat, and he arose an older and wiser, if not a sounder man." McKee returned to his diocese and served in one church, St. Laurence in Catasauqua, Pennsylvania, for twenty-five years, until health issues forced him into chaplaincy at a convent, where he died in December 1891.[12]

- Michael F. Martin (1818–1884) was also from the Philadelphia Diocese, mustered in with the 69th Pennsylvania in October 1861, and was honorably discharged for disability in June 1862. A surgeon of the 116th described Martin as a kind and gentle man, and author Germain mentions that Martin was "with his regiment at Yorktown, Fair Oaks and Garnett's House, Virginia (June 18, 1862)." He is only briefly mentioned in Corby's *Memoirs*, with the most detailed description being the last time Corby mentions him: Martin was "much older than the rest of us, in fact too old for such life . . . he was forced to resign and return home." After his return to Philadelphia, Martin served as chancellor of the diocese for a time, pastored at five different parishes, and died in February 1884 at his parish in Schuylkill, Pennsylvania.[13]

- Bernard J. McCollum (?–1879) was the second chaplain of the 116th Pennsylvania, mustering in with them in November 1864, and serving during the Richmond-Petersburg Campaign that ended at Appomattox. He was honorably discharged at Petersburg in June 1865, with the general mustering out of the entire regiment. McCollum was a pastor in both the Philadelphia and then Scranton Dioceses. Unfortunately, beyond this, there is a dearth of accurate information about McCollum, either of his birth or later life ministry. We do know that he died in Rome on March 22, 1879.[14]

- The 28th Massachusetts was the second primarily Irish infantry regiment recruited in that state (the 9th Massachusetts was the first). It went on active duty early in 1862, joining the Irish Brigade in August 1862, and receiving a special flag (made by Tiffany) presented by Thomas Meagher himself. Reputedly, their chaplain was Nicholas J. O'Brien (1818–1876), but his term of office and actual service is dubious. Though on record as mustering in near Boston on January 11, 1862, Germain describes the confusion: "There are no War Department records on him, but the Adjutant General's Office of Massachusetts indicates he was enrolled as chaplain of the 28th MA on 7 Jan 1862 but never joined his regiment. A discharge was issued 5 May 1862." Hence, though listed in state records as a chaplain, and likely working with them in some capacity temporarily, for the purposes of this book, he is not considered truly an "official" chaplain.

The records of the 28th Massachusetts also indicate the anomalous situation surrounding him. The regiment sailed to Hilton Head Island on February 14, 1862, but a veteran's record for "Nicholas O'Brien" curiously shows him sailing *back* to Boston on February 22, 1862. If this is the same chaplain, it would seem he barely arrived before turning around and going back to Boston! Nevertheless, subsequent records show that O'Brien did go on to a very prominent ministry as preacher, pastor, professor, and newspaper founder in the Boston Diocese. He died in April 1876, and was buried in a vault in the floor of St. Augustine Chapel in Boston.[15]

- Lawrence Stephen McMahon (1835–1895) had been a priest in Boston for three years when the request for another chaplain for the 28th Massachusetts reached his bishop in June 1862 (the previous chaplain, Nicholas O'Brien, had been discharged the month before). The story of McMahon's volunteering was told in a 1911 article from a Boston College in-house magazine.

> Bishop Fitzpatrick received an urgent call from the men of his diocese who were doing duty in South Carolina—they were dying in heaps and they wanted the consolations of religion. The administrator of the diocese, in the absence of the Bishop, read the letter at the table. The scene of conflict was beyond his jurisdiction and he could not order any one to the front. Father McMahon was the youngest man at table. He modestly waited till the administrator had ended his appeal, and as no one else volunteered, he placed himself in the hands of his superior. This was on Friday night. On Saturday he received his commission from the Governor. He preached in the Cathedral on Sunday, and on Sunday night was off to New York. Within a week he had landed at Hilton Head, South Carolina.
>
> The battle of James Island was at hand. The night before the engagement he spent hearing the confessions of the men; nor did he finish his labors till the drum beat called the soldiers to action. He went forward with the rest. After the battle he was the only Catholic chaplain in the command, and his ministrations were given to all without exception.[16]

The newspaper account goes on to mention that McMahon was subsequently at the Battles of Second Bull Run (August 29–30, 1862), Antietam (September 17, 1862), and Fredericksburg (December 11–15, 1862). In May 1863, his health badly weakened ("disability incurred in the line of duty," according to Germain), he went to a Washington, DC, hospital and then to Boston to recover, but returned to his troops to conclude the War and march in the Grand Review. In 1879, after fourteen postwar years as Pastor, he was named the fifth bishop of Hartford, Connecticut, where, in his years there, he completed the cathedral, and established forty-eight parishes and sixteen Catholic schools. He died in August 1893, and is buried in the Bishop's Plot of St. Benedict's Cemetery in Bloomfield, Connecticut.[17]

Before leaving the discussion about the Irish Brigade, a mention needs to be made of General St. Clair Mulholland (1839–1910). First a colonel in the Irish Brigade's 116th Pennsylvania, Mulholland received wartime brevets of brigadier general and major general, earning a Medal of Honor for his actions at Chancellorsville. After the Civil War, it was he who became the major proponent for William Corby receiving the Medal of Honor (which never happened). But in the 1890s, Mulholland began a movement to have a statue of Corby erected at Gettysburg, which took decades of dedicated advocacy and fundraising to become a reality, and only occurred, sadly enough, shortly after Mulholland's death. The statue of William Corby, atop the same rock he stood upon on the second day of Gettysburg, was dedicated on October 29, 1910. It is the only statue of a Civil War chaplain on a battlefield to this day.

The Corcoran Legion (69th [182nd New York], 155th, 164th, and 170th New York)

There were two Catholic chaplains associated with Michael Corcoran's Irish Legion (also known as Corcoran's Brigade). James Dillon SJ had already served the 63rd New York of the Irish Brigade for a year, and he then become connected with Corcoran's 69th New York (later reconstituted as the 182nd New York). Health issues forced Dillon's resignation in August 1864, and led to his early death in 1868. The second chaplain is another Notre Dame priest already discussed, Paul Gillen

CSC (1810–1882). Dr. John Dwyer, a surgeon from the Irish Legion, later wrote this about the service of the unique Father Gillen, who is described as one of the oldest, heartiest, and longest serving chaplains of the entire war.

> After Fr. Dillon left the Legion, Father Paul had all the duty devotions on himself, and this duty he religiously and faithfully performed . . . I don't remember that he even had one days leave of absence. Father Paul served faithful and laboriously all thru the war and was mustered out with the regiment . . . [at the] battle of the Deserted House near Suffolk which commenced in the dark of the morning on Jan 30, 1863 . . . he gave conditional absolution to an immense mass of kneeling soldiers who were counseled by him to his act on the battlefield . . . I have known many instances of his kindness of heart, and he was the medium of corresponding with the families of many of the soldiers, cheering them with the advice and friendship.[18]

Chicago's Irish Troops
(23rd Illinois and 90th Illinois Irish Legion)

Chicago raised two regiments from among its rapidly growing Irish population. The 23rd Illinois was known as the Irish Brigade of Illinois, and was recruited by James Mulligan, resulting in 1,200 volunteers in just a week in April 1861. The brigade was poorly trained, however, and surrendered to Sterling Price after a lively defense at Lexington, Missouri (September 13–20, 1861), but was eventually reformed by Mulligan. It then served guard duty at Camp Douglas, and went on to fight at the Second Battle of Kernstown (July 24, 1864), where Mulligan was mortally wounded, and died two days later.

- The pastor of Immaculate Conception (Chicago), Thaddeus J. Butler (1833–1897), was on the first list of officers for the 23rd Illinois and became their chaplain as of June 18, 1861. His actual ministry to the troops during that time may have been minimal, though, given his very active role in the diocese. He was Bishop

Thomas Duggan's secretary, on the bishop's council, taught at the seminary, and was pastor of a rapidly growing Chicago church. Still, his formal resignation ("on account of disability incident to the service") was only dated March 1, 1863, with Colonel James Mulligan, the commander and organizer of the 23rd Illinois, stating at the time that he felt sensibly "the loss of his presence and superior example."

The native Irishman Butler had a brother who was also a priest in Chicago, and after his return from the war he went on to serve as pastor at four other churches in the Chicago Diocese. After the great Chicago Fire of 1871, Butler worked to rebuild his church, making several trips outside the diocese attempting to raise funds. In June 1897, he was named bishop-elect of Concordia (Kansas Diocese), but died in Rome on July 16, 1897, just two days before his consecration. A later article on him said that Thaddeus Butler "was considered one of the most prominent figures in the history of the Chicago Archdiocese."[19]

The second Chicago Irish regiment was the 90th Illinois, also known as the Irish Legion or Second Irish. Mustered into service in September 1862, its early history was in the western theater and was relatively quiet. Their baptism by fire came at Missionary Ridge in November 1863; thereafter, the regiment served the remainder of the war as part of Sherman's Army in the Georgia campaign and March to the Sea.[20]

• The chaplain of the 90th Illinois was Thomas Kelly (1828–1864), founder of St. James Church on Chicago's southside, who mustered in with the so-called Irish Legion in September 1862. As Kelly was setting off, his "former parishioners from Bridgeport and Carville IL presented Chaplain Thomas Kelly 'with a sum sufficient to purchase a splendid horse saddle & bridle.'" In December 1862, the 90th Illinois fought against Earl Van Dorn at Holly Springs, Mississippi, and did well. Patrick Sloan of Company C of the 90th later wrote of that battle that "Father Kelly gave us his blessing and we recited an act of Contrition just before the enemy fired on us and when we were in the line of battle each and every company separately."

Kelly's time with the troops was brief (less than a year), but was not without spiritual impact. One Catholic soldier wrote this as he returned to camp on a Sunday evening in December 1862: "The night was a beautiful one, the moon in all the loveliness of her refulgent light shone bright. The merry twinkling stars seemed conscious of the fact that it was Sunday. After tattoo, the men assembled at Father Kelly's tent, as they do every night, and said the rosary with simple piety but seemed a solemn ceremony, beneath inspiration of such a night." A letter printed in the *Chicago Post* added this: "Father Kelly has the rosary every evening, and the spiritual wants of the 'Legion' on the Sabbath are impressive and ready to the minute, rain or shine."

Kelly resigned in July 1863 "due to sickness. My health being so bad that I am unable to discharge my proper duties." Colonel Timothy O'Meara of the 90th Illinois wrote on August 5, 1863, that "Father Kelly poor man has been and is at present very sick. He has just resigned and it has been accepted. He is at present with me waiting and trying to gain sufficient strength before he starts for Chicago. We raised $400 for him which will be a great service to him when he goes back. He never had as much money at one time in his life and the only thing that puzzles him now is to know what he is going to do with it." Kelly returned to Chicago, but died less than a year later, at age 35 on May 3, 1864, from the fever he contracted in Yazoo City, Mississippi.[21]

37th New York Infantry

The 37th New York Volunteer Infantry, known as the Irish Rifles, was organized in June 1861 in New York City, out of what was originally the 75th New York Militia. They served in the Army of the Potomac for two years until mustering out in 1863, with their heaviest losses coming in the Chancellorsville campaign (April 30–May 6, 1863).

The French-born Peter Tissot SJ (1823–1875) was appointed chaplain of the 37th New York by his superior after another Jesuit was unable to fulfill that role. As described in chapter 5, Tissot was a pious man

and a prolific writer who kept a minute diary of his war experiences.
It was there in which he described his June 30, 1862, capture at the
end of the Seven Days Campaign (with fellow priest-chaplains Joseph
O'Hagan and Thomas Scully). On house arrest in Richmond for three
weeks, Tissot then returned to chaplaincy, but chronic stomach and
bowel issues led to his mustering out on June 22, 1863.

9th Connecticut Volunteers

Partly recruited by the Catholic Irish nationalist Colonel Thomas Cahill,
the 9th Connecticut Volunteers was established as an Irish regiment in
September 1861. Its volunteers (many who joined after expired three-
month enlistments) came from seventy-one different Connecticut towns
and cities, and became part of Butler's Army of the Gulf, taking part in
battles at Pass Christian, New Orleans, Vicksburg, and Baton Rouge.
Chosen to lead the Federal army into New Orleans, upon entering the
city they played all the Irish airs they could recall to try to win over local
Irish natives, and succeeded in enlisting two hundred eventually.[22]

- The native Irishman and Connecticut pastor, Daniel Mullen
  (1837–1878), enlisted in the 9th Connecticut in November 1861 as
  their first chaplain, and became greatly esteemed by the regiment.
  He was described as patriotic and cultured, a scholar with a tenacious memory, and a man sincerely dedicated to his troops. Union
  soldiers later recalled that while the 9th was at Baton Rouge in
  June 1862, Mullen distributed copies of *The Soldier's Manual*, or
  prayer book, to officers and men. The work contained very helpful
  spiritual instructions and prayers for his soldiers.

  Mullen was with the 9th in Louisiana when they were put to
  work on the Union's ill-fated canal digging project, attempting to
  bypass Vicksburg. But like the above-mentioned Thomas Kelly,
  as heatstroke, malaria, and dysentery spread throughout the command, Mullen himself became a victim, coming down with typhoid fever and diarrhea. He was declared unfit for further duty,
  with "a distant and very uncertain prospect for recovery," and was
  honorably discharged for disability on August 26, 1862. Mullen

then returned to pastoring in Connecticut for sixteen more years in the Hartford Diocese, before dying unexpectedly in March 1878 after leaving his parish several months earlier due to nervous exhaustion.

His obituary in the *Irish American Weekly* described Mullen as "a ripe scholar [who] possessed a most tenacious memory, grasping firmly whatever he read or heard. With all his talents and acquirements, however, he was simple and earnest as a child, and enjoyed the love of all with whom he came into contact . . ."[23]

- Mullen was succeeded as chaplain of the 9th Connecticut by Leo (Rizzo) de Saracena (1833–1897), an Italian Franciscan from western New York (cf. chapter 6), who was with the regiment for three months (July–October 1864), although sickness and fever greatly limited his work. Arriving at the James River in July 1864, Rizzo was part of General Philip Sheridan's Valley Campaign, being present at the battles of Deep Bottom, 3rd Winchester (Opequon), and Fisher's Hill. As described previously, it was during a time of hospitalization in September 1864 that Rizzo's chaplain's credentials were stolen and impersonated by the Jesuit priest Joseph Bixio, resulting in James Sheeran of the 14th Louisiana being imprisoned for Bixio's actions.

Rizzo was honorably discharged on October 24, 1864, and sent to Connecticut where he became a pastor, superior, and provincial in his order, then the president of St. Bonaventure College from 1877 to 1880. He died in his Winsted, Connecticut, parish in November 1897.[24]

9th Massachusetts Infantry

The 28th Massachusetts was already mentioned above as part of the Irish Brigade, but the first Irish regiment recruited out of Boston was the 9th Massachusetts Volunteers, also known as The Fighting Ninth. It was formed by the native Irishman Thomas Cass in Boston in June 1861; Cass recruited mostly from an Irish-American militia that he had previously commanded. Although the regiment rendered great service and took heavy losses at places like Malvern Hill and the Wilderness, they also gained a reputation in some places for their lack of discipline and excessive consumption of alcohol.[25]

The first chaplain of the heavily Irish 9th was a colorful, Italian-educated Boston Irishman Thomas Scully (1833–1902). Scully mustered in with the troops in June 1861, and was with them from April 1861 to October 1862, actively participating in the Peninsula Campaign, Second Bull Run and Antietam with his regiment. He was a very popular and proactive spiritual figure, frequently challenging soldiers around the many moral issues that arose in Civil War camps. On one occasion, Scully slit open a tent where a card game was going on, and as the soldiers involved quickly scattered, he confiscated all their money laying around.

He could be fearless if called for, as his actions showed on another occasion when he was bringing $22,000 in regimental pay to the mail. The road he had to travel was a dangerous one, and Scully soon observed he had three thuggish men following him who eventually surrounded him. The priest quickly realized their intent, pulled out a revolver, and cocked it. He calmly said, "My men, I am going ahead; if one of you attempts to follow or molest me, I'll drive a bullet through his head." Shocked and unprepared for a priest to react in such a manner, the men left him alone. As one commentator later said, "he never shirked a duty, and knew his men had unbounded faith in him."[26]

Scully was twice taken prisoner after battles. At Gaines' Mill (June 27, 1862), the first battle of his regiment (where 552 officers and men were killed or wounded), Scully remained by his wounded after the fighting and was captured, although he escaped his captors during the night. Two days later, at Malvern Hill, Scully was again taken prisoner (along with Joseph O'Hagan and Peter Tissot) and brought to Richmond. Apparently, he was stricken with malarial fever at the time, and was cared for at the Richmond, Virginia, parish of John Teeling (a Confederate occasional chaplain who will be discussed below). He returned to the north on July 19, 1862, with O'Hagan and Tissot, but asked and received an honorable discharge for health reasons in October 1862.

Scully's postwar career will be covered in full in chapter 12, but was marked by pastoring several Massachusetts churches and being an outspoken supporter of Catholic higher education, particularly during the acrimonious Massachusetts 1899 debates aimed at outlawing paro-chial schools. He was described as a liberal "healthy hornet" who feared no one (except possibly the pope) and took on all opponents of Catholic schools. He became a well-known figure in Massachusetts, pastoring at St. Mary's Church in Cambridge for thirty-five years, and dying in September 1902.[27]

Spoken of in chapter 6, the Dominican priest Constantine Louis Egan (1828–1899) became the second chaplain of the 9th Massachusetts after ministering to a condemned man in Washington, DC. Asked to be their chaplain by the commander of the regiment, Colonel Patrick Guiney, Egan served as a very effective chaplain in a variety of positions during the War. The native Irishman ministered to the regiment after Scully resigned, then when their term of service expired in June 1864, he went on the staff of General Charles Griffin and ministered in the 5th and 9th Corps as chaplain from September 1863 to July 1865. His Civil War ministry was multifaceted—Egan offered general absolution for the troops during the Mine Run Campaign of late 1863, preached mis-sions throughout the 5th and 9th Corps, and assisted surgeons in caring for wounded troops from both sides, especially as he accompanied Grant's army to Appomattox in the last days of the war.[28]

10th Ohio Infantry

The final predominantly Irish American Union regiment was the 10th Ohio, also known as the Montgomery Guards and, after their 1861 and 1862 battles, the Bloody Tenth. Recruited primarily from southwest Ohio, only six of the companies were actually Irish; the other four were a mix of German and other American-born men. But the battle flag of the 10th Ohio did include the Maid of Erin harp and usual Gaelic in-scription, and the Irish predominated in regimental leadership. Their commander, Colonel William Haines Lytle (1826–1863), was a Mexi-can-American War veteran and not a Catholic himself, but sensitive to the regiment's religious character.[29]

The chaplain of the 10th Ohio was the native Irishman William O'Higgins (1829–1874). Described already in chapter 7, O'Higgins was chaplain for four years in this regiment, and his work was exemplary and widespread. He performed the usual Catholic duties expected of a priest, and also reached out to the regiment's many non-Catholics in addition to offering prayers for military functions like dress parades and reception of regimental colors. Brave and well-respected by his troops, O'Higgins mustered out in June 1864 with the remnant of the 10th Ohio because he suffered from health issues.[30]

IRISH CATHOLIC CONFEDERATE CHAPLAINS

As mentioned earlier, it is estimated that between 25,000 to 40,000 native Irish fought for the Confederacy. There was only one heavily Irish regiment (10th Tennessee), and as touched on previously, honoring specific ethnic heritage in regimental names was not as important for the Confederacy as for the Union, though many Irish companies did take distinctively Irish names. Irish Confederates were scattered throughout the South's more regionally raised regiments, and were organized in company-sized units and in several battalions. There were some forty-five distinctively Confederate Irish companies, with names like Shamrock Guards (St. Louis), Emerald Guards (Mobile), Irish Jasper Greens (Savannah), and the Emmett Guards and Montgomery Guards (New Orleans). All were highly regarded for their fighting abilities, with Confederate General Richard Taylor being one outspoken in his praise about the New Orleans Irish under his charge (the 6th Louisiana). "They were steady as clocks and as chirpy as crickets," he later recalled, the regiment being "composed of Irishmen, stout, hardy fellows, turbulent in camp and requiring a strong hand, but responding to kindness and justice, and ready to follow their officers to the death."[31]

In all, the Confederacy had at least twelve Catholic priests known to have served these predominantly Irish troops as chaplains during the Civil War. Six of those priests are considered official and full-time (Bannon, Gache, Hubert, Sheeran, Smulders, and Turgis), with the other six also designated as official but with slightly shorter terms of service. (Julian Guillou briefly served Irish troops, but was never officially designated as chaplain in any records.) Finally, of the twenty-five full-time priests serving the Confederacy, nearly half served predominantly Irish troops from the two states which had the largest percentage of Catholics—Louisiana (with a 27.9 percent Catholic share of all church accommodations) and Tennessee.[32]

Tennessee's Confederate Catholic Chaplains

In contrast to the North having several brigade-sized units of mostly Irish nationality, the South had only one regiment of largely Irish extraction, the Nashville-based 10th Tennessee. As mentioned above, this regiment was informally known as the Bloody Tenth, and was formed by Randall McGavock from the area around Nashville, Tennessee. Seven of its ten companies were Irishmen from Nashville; the other three were grouped from Irish enclaves in middle Tennessee.

The first of the two official chaplains the 10th Tennessee had was a unique priest named Henry V. Browne (1816–1870), a member of the Nashville Diocese (which encompassed the entire state of Tennessee). Browne had been born in upstate New York and converted from being Presbyterian to Catholic in 1839 through the efforts of a Dominican priest Joseph Jarboe (later a Confederate chaplain). By the outbreak of the Civil War, Browne had already founded a church in Chattanooga, and was then living at the cathedral in Nashville, where he had gained great respect in the diocese, serving on Bishop James Whelan's Bishop's Council.

Though like many other chaplains, Browne's ministry to troops had begun before the war, he was officially appointed a chaplain by General Albert Sidney Johnson on November 26, 1861. Browne served the 10th Tennessee and other Confederate Catholics while they were stationed at Fort Henry, also ministering at Fort Donelson. His name was on the muster rolls of the 10th Tennessee at Fort Henry in early September 1861, of which one author opined that "the muster roll looked like a clan map of Ireland . . . they were all young." Browne is mentioned as celebrating Christmas Mass in 1861 and on the first weekend of February 1862, "asking for the Lord's favor in the coming battle and a return to peace. Nearly all the lads of the Irish regiment, of all denominations, attended that Fort Henry Mass on the Tennessee River." He is also mentioned as intervening between two quarreling brothers named Fitzgerald on February 9, 1862, and ministering to wounded 10th Tennessee soldiers at Fort Donelson on February 13, 1862.[33]

But around the time that Fort Henry fell into Union hands (February 6, 1862), Browne left on furlough and never returned to the regiment, though he would only be formally dropped from the rolls in February 1864. It would seem that pressing affairs inside the Nashville Diocese drew him away from his chaplain's duties. There were less than fifteen priests in the diocese at the time, and the Dominican bishop James Whelan was not a popular man in Nashville, especially with his mostly pro-Confederate priests, due to his pro-Union sympathies and friendship with Union general William Rosecrans. Whelan would resign in frustration in July 1863 and eventually returned to life as a Dominican. Upon his return from chaplain's duties, in 1862 Browne became chancellor of the diocese, and later vicar-general and acting bishop, in effect holding the diocese together until a new bishop was named. In April 1870, he died and was buried in Nashville.[34]

In October 1862, General Williams Rosecrans moved his army into Nashville, and before long began to have issues with another priest in that city, Emmeran Bliemel (1831–1864). Bliemel was born in Bavaria, immigrated to America at age nineteen, and joined the newly formed (1846) Benedictine Abbey in Latrobe, Pennsylvania. He professed vows there and then was ordained in 1856. Bliemel served various Pennsylvania parishes for four years before going to Nashville in 1860 when Bishop James Whelan issued a call for priests. Receiving his superior's permission to live outside the Benedictine community, Bliemel began pastoring at a small German church in Nashville (Assumption Church), many of whose members joined the 10th Tennessee when it formed. His first run-in with Rosecrans concerned smuggling medicine for sick Confederates (he was arrested for that but released under a stern warning), but later he was also falsely accused of publishing anti-Union articles in the Catholic *Freeman's Journal*.

On more than one occasion Bliemel asked Bishop Whelan to permit him to serve as a chaplain, but the bishop could not spare him. When the 10th Tennessee was reorganized in October 1863 following its surrender at Fort Donelson, and subsequent exchange at Vicksburg, Bliemel was even elected as their chaplain, though he was still unable to join them. After the Battle of Chickamauga (September 1863), he again repeated his request, and with Henry Brown's recommendation, Bliemel was finally allowed to become an official chaplain. Setting off on horseback and avoiding Union patrols, he finally found the 10th Tennessee at Dalton, Georgia, where they were recuperating from their recent losses. On November 1, 1863, Bliemel presented his letter to his formal superior, Bishop Augustin Verot (Savannah), was given permission to minister, and began his work.

Bliemel quickly became deeply loved and respected by the troops. He often sat around the campfire entertaining the soldiers with jokes, stories, and homilies. Little is known of his quiet ministry in the spring and early summer of 1864 as the Confederates slowly fell back from Rocky Face Ridge, Ringgold Gap, and the other early Atlanta Campaign battles. But the reports that exist all agree that in camp and on the field Bliemel was the same with everyone, no matter what their religion or regiment. In battle he always moved forward with the troops, remaining just to the rear, where his services to the wounded would be most needed. There he would accompany the litter bearers, and was the first on his knees in prayer over the seriously injured. then it was back to the battlefield to help any others who might have been struck down.[35]

As he ministered in the 1864 Atlanta Campaign to the soldiers of the 10th Tennessee, Bliemel also developed an attachment to another group of men, the 4th Kentucky of the famed Orphan Brigade (both were in Bates Division, of Hardee's Corps). By late August 1864, Federal troops under General William Sherman had sealed three of the four railroad exits out of Atlanta. With only one line left (the Macon and Western to the south), Sherman decided to attack at Jonesboro, that last link. On August 31, 1864, as the battle of Jonesboro began, Union cavalry struck Hardee's troops, and under intense Union artillery fire, some 1,500 Confederates were wounded or died, many of whom were from the 10th Tennessee.

Bliemel was active as usual in going to the aid of the wounded with the litter bearers, but just as he was making a trip forward to assist, an order to retreat was given, and he was caught in the heavy Union fire which followed the retreating Confederates. The commander of the 10th Tennessee, Colonel William Grace, was fatally wounded in that fire. Bliemel helped the wounded Grace to the rear, and after the colonel was placed on the ground, the thirty-three-year-old priest knelt to hear his confession. While pronouncing the words of absolution, though, Bliemel was struck in the head by the explosion of an artillery shell, which decapitated him; and he fell dead on top of Colonel Grace. Because of the intense fire which continued, it was only later that evening that his body could be retrieved. Since the troops were leaving the next day, his Catholic troops "hastily but tenderly buried both the priest and his colonel near a clump of trees."[36]

Bliemel's body would in the years ahead be reinterred twice more, and his burial place actually lost for a time, before his remains eventually ended up in Tuscumbia, Alabama, where a Benedictine priest and friend saw to his final Christian burial. Emmeran Bliemel thus became the second American Catholic priest to be killed in combat, and the only Catholic priest to be killed during battle in the Civil War.[37]

The third priest-chaplain who served Tennessee Confederates was the Dominican priest Joseph Jarboe (1806–1887), the same priest responsible for Henry Brown's conversion to Catholicism fifteen years earlier. Jarboe served from May 1861 to April 1862 with the 2nd Tennessee, a Memphis regiment whose 750 Irish solders were often called the Memphis Riflemen. Although little was recorded of his chaplaincy, Jarboe's bravery at Shiloh (Pittsburg Landing) was noted, as was his being captured by Union pickets while attempting to retrieve Confederate wounded. As described in chapter 6, Jarboe was saved from near death by an officer who recognized the Dominican priest. Jarboe was not only freed, but given a permit to continue his work of mercy wherever he might go.

LOUISIANA'S CONFEDERATE
CATHOLIC CHAPLAINS

New Orleans was easily the largest city in the Confederacy, and had the largest number of Catholics as well—more Irish lived in New Orleans (some thirty thousand) and Louisiana in general than anywhere else in the South, with 45.9 percent of the city being Catholic. It makes sense then that Louisiana had more Irish Confederate troops, and more Catholic chaplains serving them than any other Confederate state. Some enlisted out of economic necessity, others because they saw the parallel between the Confederacy's struggle for independence and their native Ireland's fight against British occupiers. But still others were "dragooned into the army from the saloons, jails and alleys" from cities like New Orleans, which certainly contributed to higher rates of criminal behavior and desertion among non-citizens in the Louisiana regiments.[38]

In all, there were Irish companies in at least nine different Louisiana brigades, and correspondingly nine Catholic chaplains that served those troops in some capacity (all official except for Julian Guillou). Curiously, six of the nine priest-chaplains mentioned below were born or educated in France. However, as noted earlier in the book, there were a large number of French priests serving in the Catholics dioceses of the south and west, most notably in Mississippi and also in Louisiana. Here are the chaplains who served the Catholics of these heavily Irish Louisiana Confederate companies and regiments.[39]

1st Louisiana Infantry (Nelligan's)

There were two 1st Louisiana regiments in the Confederate army, and both had Catholic chaplains. Darius Hubert (1823–1893) was a French-born Jesuit priest who served with the 1st Louisiana Infantry under James Nelligan (their final commander) in the eastern theater. This regiment was organized in New Orleans in May 1861 under the devout Catholic Colonel (later Brigadier General) Albert Blanchard, and contained two Irish companies (D and E), the Montgomery and Emmett Guards. The regiment went east into the Army of Northern Virginia, becoming part of the 2nd Louisiana Brigade (1st, 2nd, 10th, and 15th Louisiana Regiments) in July 1862. Hubert was asked to be chaplain by Blanchard himself, received his appointment a month after the regiment was organized, and remained with the 1st Louisiana until 1864, when severe health issues led him to a hospital chaplain's position in Richmond, and subsequent parole when the war ended. See chapter 5 for more details.[40]

1st Louisiana Regulars (Strawbridge's)

The German-born and French-educated Anthony Carius (1821–1893) served with the "other" 1st Louisiana—a regiment that originated as the 1st Louisiana Militia Infantry and entered Confederate service in February 1861. Most of its officers and men were from New Orleans and surrounding areas. It first served at Pensacola before moving to Tennessee and eventually coming under the command of James Strawbridge, and serving in the western theater in the Army of Tennessee, and fighting in such battles as Shiloh, Murfreesboro, Nashville, Mobile, and the Atlanta Campaign.

What little is known of the life of Anthony Carius is captivating, but sadly lacking in details regarding his Civil War years. Carius and Bliemel, though, are both mentioned in the March 1864 diary entry of Bishop Augustin Verot (Savannah), in Dalton, Georgia, on the eve of Sherman's Atlanta Campaign. Of his own ministry at that place, Verot wrote that "where the Army of the Tennessee was encamped under Gen Johnson, I found there many Catholics and two Catholic chaplains, Father Anthony Carius and Fr. Emmeran Bliemel. I spent 2 weeks there hearing confessions, preaching and administering confirmation."[41]

Carius had a much-traveled ministry career in at least four dioceses (ironically dying in none of them), and claimed to have been both a Mexican-American War and postwar United States chaplain (though these assertions are not confirmed). Due to the great need of priests in the mid-nineteenth century, he was always taken in by dioceses, whatever his personal "issues" may have been, and appears to have been well-liked by the people he served. The following insightful comment was made by a parish in Paolo, Kansas, he served at briefly: "A stranger to the way of polite society, of rough and ready manner, as well as careless of dress or appearance, he was possessed of a large and generous heart, was a deep thinker and had very high intellectual attainments, for which his average acquaintance gave him no credit. He was lighthearted and happy, the soul of wit and humor, cared nothing for appearances, and was lavish in his charity."[42]

In the twenty-five years after the war, Carius went on to minister at several Kansas parishes in two dioceses, the Leavenworth (later Kansas City) Diocese, and in the Concordia (later Salina) Diocese. He ended his life as a chaplain at an Ursuline convent in St. Louis, where he died and was buried in September 1893.[43]

3rd Louisiana Infantry

The 3rd Louisiana Regiment had as its chaplain the French priest Pierre Felix Dicharry (1827–1887). This regiment was assembled from six Louisiana parishes, mostly in the northern part of the state. After fighting at Wilson's Creek and Elkhorn Tavern, it was moved to the Mississippi Department, where it took part in the battles of Iuka and Corinth. It was later assigned to Hebert's Division, captured at Vicksburg, then reformed and disbanded in early 1865.

Dicharry was a native Frenchman who grew up during Napoleon's reign, and was thus familiar with war. At the time the Confederate states seceded in 1861, Dicharry was ministering in the diocese and city of Natchitoches, Louisiana. There in the spring of 1861, from the courthouse steps, he gave an impassioned speech supporting the Southern cause, and volunteered personally to be chaplain of the 3rd Louisiana, which was then forming. His bishop (Auguste Martin, another Frenchman) later reluctantly gave him permission to follow the troops, and the two of them heard confessions, blessed flags, and gave soldiers Catholic medals and scapulars in an emotional farewell to the troops.[44]

A fascinating aspect of Catholic priests' ministry is seen in an event which Dicharry was intimately involved.

Chaplains often wrote families about the tragic circumstances of their sons' death. For example, Father Pierre Dicharry . . . brought back to his parishioners in Natchitoches the personal effects of their deceased sons. One example was a picture of the priest, which had an inscription that read "Father Dicharry, who was

with Placide Bossier when he was killed in battle. Phanon Prud-
homme cut a lock of Placide's hair and gave it to Father with his
prayer book to take home." This simple act often became one of
the contributions of the chaplain's service to the Confederacy. It
was a chaplain's duty to give the family of the fallen soldier reas-
surance and words that gave their loss some meaning.[45]

Dicharry served as chaplain from May 1861 to August 1862, when
he resigned. He had been captured by Union troops (perhaps at Elk
Horn Tavern on March 7, 1862), then imprisoned under very poor circumstances (in a "cold, cramped, feces and vermin-filled environment,"
according to one source), which weakened him and may have helped
influence his early retirement. It seems though that the pressing personnel shortages and workload in his diocese may also have played a
role. Germain notes this, citing a comment by Dicharry that "the Right
Reverend Bishop called me back, and needed my services at that place."
He went on to serve prominently in the Natchitoches Diocese as a
chaplain and vicar general, and was buried in the cathedral there after
his death in July 1887.[46]

4th Louisiana Infantry

The 4th Louisiana also had connections to New Orleans, since it was at
least partially composed of affluent Creoles from New Orleans and
Acadians from Iberville, as well as several other Louisiana parishes. It
served first on the Gulf Coast before moving onto Tennessee where it
fought at Shiloh, then later at Vicksburg and Port Hudson, before ultimately becoming part of the Army of Tennessee. Their chaplain, Isidore
Francis Turgis (1813–1859), was yet another French-born priest serving
under a French bishop (Jean-Marie Odin) of the New Orleans Diocese.
  Turgis had led an adventurous life in France even before beginning
his Civil War career. Ordained in 1846, despite some physical frailty,
he was appointed to the Corps of Chaplains in 1857, then was a French
chaplain in the Second Italian War for Independence (1859–1861), and
was even in Vietnam for a time. In 1860, he came to the St. Louis Cathedral in New Orleans and intended to work with Black Catholics,

but instead became popular immediately with the Creole population there. He was asked to become chaplain of "more than four hundred Orleans Guardsmen mustering in preparation for a battle that would take place near Shiloh, TN. Turgis obeyed the archbishop and never fulfilled his original intention to serve as a missionary to people of African descent."[47]

Always a frail man who felt nervous about his preaching due to his poor language skills, nevertheless Turgis ministered admirably, and became deeply beloved among the troops. Several accounts exist about his dedication and bravery, but one will have to suffice here. A Frenchman present at the Battle of Shiloh wrote this about Turgis's actions during and after that battle:

> Moving about the wounded at the [Corinth MS] hospital . . . [was] a frail, coarsely-clad man in a black cassock. His name was Father Isidore-Francois Turgis. There were almost twenty thousand Catholics at Shiloh. Turgis gave absolution for over eighteen hours nonstop during the battle. He was with the men of his battalion during the fighting, administering last rites and helping the wounded; he narrowly escaped death while aiding a mortally wounded Yankee officer. He was bearing the wounded Yankee off the field when a grape shot passed through the man's body and killed him in the priest's arms. The little French priest spent the first week after the battle at Corinth ministering to men of the 4th, 13th, 17th, 18th and 24th LA.[48]

Aside from a reference to him at Vicksburg in 1863, Turgis's activities after April 1862 are vague. Formal Confederate records on him do not exist, and author Aidan Germain does not include him in his list of formal chaplains. But after Turgis's Orleans Guard Battalion militia unit had disbanded in June 1862, some of the former members joined Company F of the 30th Louisiana, and Turgis apparently began serving that unit. He followed the Louisiana troops of the 30th through Vicksburg, Baton Rouge, the Atlanta Campaign, and the final battles at Nashville and Spanish Fort, only returning to his diocese in 1865. He found his frail health much exacerbated by the war, and he became pastor at a Confederate veterans' chapel in New Orleans in 1866. Sadly, the 1867 yellow fever epidemic further weakened him. He died in March 1868, being buried with great affection in New Orleans's famed St. Louis Cemetery No. 3.[49]

18th Louisiana Infantry

The 18th Louisiana Infantry Regiment was mustered into service in October 1861 at Camp Moore, Louisiana, and fought at Shiloh, and the Louisiana Campaigns of Bayou Lafourche (1862), Bayou Teche (1863), and the Red River (1864). The regiment was organized and led through the war from Shiloh to his death at Mansfield by General Alfred Mouton—a charismatic military leader and graduate of the Jesuit-run St. Charles College in Grand Coteau, Louisiana. From the very beginning of the 18th Louisiana's history, their chaplain was the Jesuit priest Anthony de Chaignon (1823?–1867), who had been president of the same St. Charles College that Mouton had attended. (De Chaignon's story has been told in chapter 5.)

A native Frenchman, de Chaignon arrived in New Orleans in May 1848, ministered in a variety of ways before the war, and was formally commissioned to the 18th Louisiana in March 1862. His chaplaincy only lasted about six or seven months formally, but he was at the Battle of Shiloh, according to one Jesuit journal, and apparently was wounded in some way which required a very brief hospitalization.[50] He was then at Corinth caring for wounded Confederates, along with other priests mentioned above (Francis Pont, Isadore Turgis, and a non-chaplain named Francois Bertaud). As mentioned earlier, de Chaignon died in October 1867 in a yellow fever epidemic that swept through the Louisiana Gulf Coast.[51]

Wheat's "Louisiana Tigers"

The colorful "Louisiana Tigers" were raised in the New Orleans area as part of Major Roberdeau Wheat's 1st Special Battalion, Louisiana Infantry. A substantial part of this group were natives from Ireland from the city's wharves and docks, and had previous military experience of some kind. Some at first wore distinctive Zouave-type uniforms, though eventually this was dropped. The priest mentioned as ministering to them in some capacity is John Teeling (1823–?), a native of Ireland. Teeling was ordained in America in the early 1850s, and had chosen to remain with the Richmond Diocese in 1850 when his seminary in Wheeling (then still in Virginia) became an independent diocese.[52]

However, Teeling's actual connections with the Louisiana Tigers are tenuous and nuanced. His name does not appear in any official military rosters, nor in Germain's list as an official chaplain. There are vague references to him as "Chaplain, CSA" in the Officers roster; and a May 1861 note does indicate that he was formally commissioned by General Robert E. Lee. Aside from a ministry connection in some capacity to the Louisiana Tigers, Teeling is mentioned anecdotally as ministering to Richmond's Montgomery Guard (Company C of the 1st Virginia Infantry), where some of the men of his St. Patrick's Church (Richmond) were members. When Teeling was supposedly relieved of duty in March 1863, he was assigned to duty in Richmond's hospitals, serving and being compensated for that role until the end of the Civil War.

Thus, it seems that Teeling should at best be considered an occasional Confederate chaplain, more of a post chaplain in the Richmond area, serving Catholics in Lee's army in an official but unassigned capacity. A native of Ireland, Teeling was part of the Richmond Diocese under Bishop John McGill and served as the wartime pastor of St. Patrick's Church there, from where many Catholics in the Montgomery Guards had come. Though his official chaplain's record may be scant, if nothing else Teeling was certainly outspoken about the Rebel cause. A newspaper item of the time said that "Rev. John Teeling, D. D., officiating Priest at St. Peter's Catholic Cathedral, preached an able discourse yesterday in which allusion was made to the present condition of affairs, and which was listened to with deep attention. . . . The usual prayer for 'the President and people of the United States' was omitted. . . . Mr. T. exhorted his hearers to stand firm in the assertion of their rights against their oppressors."[53]

As mentioned already, in June 1862 Tissot was one of three captured Union chaplains (O'Hagan and Scully were the others) who were detained for about three weeks in Richmond with Bishop McGill,

Teeling (who was pastor there), and several other Confederate chaplains. When released later, one of the three Union chaplains and former captives remarked that Teeling was indeed a "rabid secessionist," and that both he and McGill had very strong opinions about the Confederacy. McGill only wanted Tissot to hear confessions of *Union* soldiers. Teeling later became vicar general of the Richmond Diocese in the years immediately after the war.

Chaplains for the Irish

To conclude this chapter, a brief mention must be made of the three other priests who served Louisiana troops as chaplains during the Civil War, though their stories are summarized elsewhere in this book. Julian Guillou was a short-term chaplain for the famed New Orleans Washington Artillery after Shiloh. The colorful James Sheeran served the 14th Louisiana, a predominantly Irish multinational group, who became known as the Louisiana Wildcats for their raucous drinking and fighting. (The Wildcats were heavily involved in many battles of the Army of Northern Virginia.) And finally, Egidius Smulders ministered in the 8th Louisiana, a primarily New Orleans–based regiment of 845 men, of whom 70 percent were Catholics, according to Smulders. The 8th Louisiana also fought in the Army of Northern Virginia, with Sheeran and Smulders ministering together on many occasions.

Whether they fought for the Union or the Confederacy, Catholicism was truly the anchor for nearly all Irishmen in an unfriendly United States. More ethnically and religiously self-conscious than any other ethnic group in the country, those of Irish descent relied upon Catholic clergy for faith, leadership, inspiration, and courage. In the forge of nationalism that many believe the Civil War was, the dozens of priest-chaplains who served Irish soldiers not only provided courageous wartime leadership, but also helped prepare them and the country for the new day of full acceptance that would dawn in postwar America.

Chaplain Thomas Quinn, 1st Rhode Island Light Artillery. (Between 1860 and 1870.) Photograph, Civil War photographs, 1861–1865, Library of Congress, Prints and Photographs Division. https://www.loc.gov/item/2018668620/.

Photographic portrait of Father Paul Gillen. Francis P. Clark Collection photographs, GFCL-017-048-Gillen, University of Notre Dame Archives, Notre Dame, Indiana.

Photographic portrait of Father Peter Paul Cooney. GMCK-01-03-01, University of Notre Dame Archives, Notre Dame, Indiana.

Photographic portrait of Father Joseph Carrier. GSHR-04-22-01R, University of Notre Dame Archives, Notre Dame, Indiana.

Photographic portrait of Father James Dillon. GFCL-016-028-Dillon, University of Notre Dame Archives, Notre Dame, Indiana.

Photographic portrait of Father William Corby. Francis P. Clark collection photographs, GSBA-01-01-p002-07, University of Notre Dame Archives, Notre Dame, Indiana.

Father Francis Fusseder, 1/th Wisconsin. Courtesy of Dodge County Historical Society, Beaver Dam, Wisconsin.

Father Darius Hubert SJ, 1st Louisiana. Courtesy of Jesuit Archives and Research Center (JARC), St. Louis, Missouri.

Father Charles Truyens SJ, 12th Kentucky. Courtesy of Jesuit Archives and Research Center (JARC), St. Louis, Missouri.

Father Joseph Bixio SJ.
Courtesy of Jesuit Archives
and Research Center (JARC),
St. Louis, Missouri.

Father Michael Nash SJ,
6th New York.
Courtesy of Booth Family
Center for Special Collections,
Georgetown University Library,
Washington, DC.

Father Bernardin Wiget SJ,
hospital chaplain in
Washington, DC.
Courtesy of Georgetown
University Archives,
Washington, DC.

Father Joseph O'Hagan SJ,
73rd New York. Courtesy
of Georgetown University
Archives, Washington, DC.

Father Egidius Smulders CSsR, 8th Louisiana. Courtesy of Redemptorist Archives, Philadelphia, Pennsylvania.

Father James Sheeran CSsR, 14th Louisiana. Courtesy of Redemptorist Archives, Philadelphia, Pennsylvania.

Father Jeremiah Trecy, chaplain for the Union and the Confederacy. Courtesy of the Ron Coddington Collection, Arlington, Virginia.

Father Francis Boyle, chaplain at Stone Hospital, Washington, DC. (Between 1860–1863.) Brady's National Photographic Portrait Galleries. Photograph, Library of Congress. https://www.loc.gov/item/2012646216/.

Father Edward Corcoran, 61st Ohio. Courtesy of the Archives of Archdiocese of Cincinnati, John and Mary Corcoran Family Collection (per Father David Endres).

Father William O'Higgins, 10th Ohio. Courtesy of the Archives of Arch-diocese of Cincinnati, John and Mary Corcoran Family Collection (per Father David Endres).

Father Thomas Scully, 9th Massachusetts. "Chaplain T. Scully, 9th Massachusetts Infantry." (Between 1860 and 1870.) Photograph, Library of Congress. https://www.loc.gov/item/2018667632/.

Father Thomas Mooney, 69th New York Militia. "Rev. Father Mooney." (Between 1855 and 1865.) Photograph, Library of Congress. https://www.loc.gov/item/2017896821/.

Lithograph honoring Father Peter P. Cooney CSC and his work in the 35th Indiana. "Army of the Cumberland, 1861–1865, Atlanta campaign. Divine Service by Rev. P. P. Cooney, C.S.C. Chaplain Gen. of Ind. Troops in the Field." Milwaukee, Wisconsin, Oleograph Co. (About 1877.) Library of Congress. https://www.loc.gov/item/90715232/.

Chaplains of the 9th Corps, with Father William Corby in front. "Petersburg, Va. Chaplains of the 9th Corps." Civil War Photographs, 1861–1865, Library of Congress, Prints and Photographs Division. https://www.loc.gov/item/2018666689/.

Officers of the Irish Brigade, Harrison's Landing, Virginia, 1862. Back row, left to right: Father Patrick Dillon CSC, and unidentified man. Front row, left to right: unidentified man, Father James Dillon CSC, and Father William Corby CSC. Alexander Gardner, photographer. "Harrison's Landing, Va. Group of the Irish Brigade." Civil War Photographs, 1861–1865, Library of Congress, Prints and Photographs Division. https://www.loc.gov/item/2018666201/.

Father Thomas Scully with the 9th Massachusetts, Washington, DC, 1861. "Ninth Massachusetts Infantry Camp near Washington, D.C." (Photographed 1861; printed between 1880 and 1889.) Photograph, Library of Congress. https://www.loc.gov/item/2013647867/.

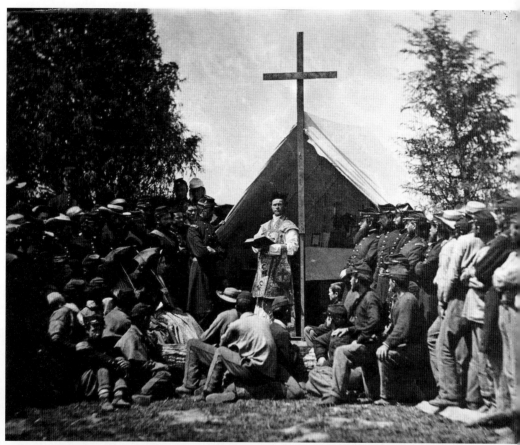

Father Thomas Mooney and the 69th New York Militia at Camp Corcoran, Virginia. "The 69th N.Y.S.V. at Camp Corcoran, Va. Rev'd. Father Mooney celebrating morning service." Arlington, Virginia, 1861. Brady's National Photographic Portrait Galleries. From photographic negative, Library of Congress. https://www.loc.gov/item/2021630075/.

CHAPTER 10

CHAPLAINS
IN THE WEST

Mississippi and New Mexico

A long-running Civil War complaint has been that the battles around the western theater of the war typically receive less attention than those of the eastern theater. Though this has much to do with the proximity of action to Eastern capitals and major population centers, some historians do consider the West the war's most important theater. The battles for control of Mississippi and the vital Mississippi River (the Vicksburg Campaign), the struggles for Louisiana and Texas (the Red River Campaign), the more than one hundred thirty battles in lands west of the Mississippi—all these tend to take a back seat to the major campaigns of the eastern theater. But this same level of diminished wartime priority for American West could have applied equally to the Catholic Church as well. Once a person traveled past New Orleans—the Confederacy's largest city by far, with 168,000 people to Richmond's 40,500—Catholics were rare, churches were few, and priests nearly impossible to find.

In New Orleans, Catholic culture and faith was common and ordinary—as the number of Catholic Louisiana Civil War regiments attested (cf. chapter 9). But outside Louisiana, the story of Catholicism can be described in the apt words of Randall Miller: "no priests, no churches, no money."[1] Two dioceses in what was referred to in the Civil War as the "western theater" are excellent examples of how faith and Catholic communities survived in the toughest of places, and even sent chaplains to minister in this forgotten theater. These two dioceses are Natchez, Mississippi, under Bishop William Henry Elder, and Santa Fe, New Mexico, under Bishop Jean-Baptiste Lamy. As we will see, perhaps because they were both so far off the beaten trail and the priest shortage so great, these two dioceses contained several of the more interesting characters among all Catholic Civil War chaplains.

BISHOP WILLIAM HENRY ELDER
AND THE "FRENCH CONNECTION"

For twenty-three years (1857–1880), the Natchez Diocese was led by one of the hardest working, most pastoral clergyman in the country, William Henry Elder (1819–1904). Elder was born into a family who had been among the first Catholic immigrants to Maryland. He was one of ten children (seven boys, three girls) in a close, faith-filled family. Drawn to the priesthood in his teen years, he was ordained in 1846 in Rome after studying there, then became a professor at Mount Saint Mary's, the same Emmitsburg, Maryland, seminary at which he had studied. Elder was known even then for his care to the area's marginalized, as exemplified by the close relationship he developed, and many resources he provided, for an elderly Black hermit in the area.[2]

The Natchez Diocese was founded in 1837, and comprised the entire state of Mississippi (and continued to until the twentieth century). When Elder was named its third bishop in 1857, he found a diocese that was truly "mission territory" with only ten thousand Catholics, eleven churches, twenty-eight mission stations, and only twelve priests in his entire diocese (along with two religious priests assisting them). Thus, Elder quickly resorted to the same practice that other Southern bishops did (e.g., Jean-Baptiste Lamy of Santa Fe, Antoine Blanc and Jean-Marie Odin of New Orleans)—he turned to seminaries in Europe, and particularly France, to fill his need for priests. Indeed, this chapter might have been aptly called "the French connection" due to the large numbers of foreign-born French priests who eventually came to serve in both the Natchez and Santa Fe Dioceses.

These French-born clergy (and occasionally non-ordained seminarians) were recruited for missionary work in priest-poor southern and western dioceses of America by bishops like Elder and Lamy (or their representatives) who made trips to their European seminaries. Thus, long before the Civil War, French priests who had felt the negative impact of the French Revolution or were following an inner call to serve God in a special way, came to live and work in dioceses like Natchez and Santa Fe. It was not an easy transition for many of them. Any romanticized spiritual notions withered quickly as they discovered the vastness of the territories they were serving, the forbidding climate, the loneliness of missing family and friends, and the challenging language barrier. Likewise, many immigrant priests struggled to adapt the idealized, traditional ideas of church and priesthood taught in France to the uniquely stubborn, independent, and mostly non-Catholic American culture they were thrown into.

But though they had their struggles, they were a great blessing as well. Aside from adding able-bodied clergy to struggling dioceses, these clerical immigrants brought highly developed European and traditional Catholic thought to a relatively young United States church. They thus solidified it theologically and anchored it pastorally by their presence and dedication. As we will see, a number struggled with health issues and language problems, and some moved on elsewhere, but the greater number of these immigrant priests in the south and west (mostly French) were indeed hard-working, faithful pastors. Neither Elder nor Lamy could have accomplished what they did without them.[3]

The clerical "French connection" emerged in April 1862, when the bloody Battle of Shiloh shocked a nation into the reality of a long and bloody Civil War. Elder's Natchez Diocese priests had been drawn into the secessionist fray when local militia groups began forming and members of their churches joined in significant numbers. Some of the bishop's priests began their chaplaincy work in this way (Pont, Boheme, and Mouton, most notably), but it was the aftermath of the Battle of Shiloh (April 6–7, 1862), with its post-battle "butcher's bill" of sick and wounded, that drew the Mississippi priests into action. While it seems only one Natchez Diocese priest was actually at the battle (Francis Pont, pastor in Jackson), it was when the battle ended and the Confederates withdrew to Corinth, Mississippi, that priests gathered from all corners of the state to assist.

Corinth came under siege from Federal forces from April 29 to May 30, when the Confederates decided they could not hold the important railroad crossing there and moved out. But conditions while they were there were horrible, especially for the sick and wounded. The available water was not good, dysentery and disease flourished, and the sick list only grew as the days went on. But Elder's Catholic priests shone brightly in their care and concern for the wounded. He had asked for all the spiritual help he could get; many of his Natchez Diocese priests gathered to minister at the nine makeshift hospitals that grew up after Shiloh. According to one source, Elder himself and Bishop John Quinlan (Mobile, Alabama) were themselves there, as well as nine priests, and two orders of Catholic nuns.[4]

Bishop William Elder was an active spiritual leader, an "occasional" Civil War chaplain himself, constantly on the road to all corners of his diocese, and frequently ministering to troops stationed or hospitalized in Mississippi. He kept a simple but fascinating diary of his pastoral work from October 1862 to March 1865, and it reveals much about the priests of his diocese, and his own frequent trips to Vicksburg, Port Gibson, Jackson, and other places where help was needed or troops required Mass or the sacraments. Elder was confined on house arrest in July to August 1864 for resisting Union regulations about including President Lincoln in prayers during Mass. (After appeals to Stanton and Lincoln himself, he was freed.)[5]

Both Elder and Bishop John Quinlan (Mobile) had issues with the Confederate chaplain commissioning process. They sought (unsuccessfully) a more flexible system that would allow for their few priests to freelance rather than have formal appointments. With the few priests each had, they sought more control over the ministry that their far-reaching dioceses demanded, especially as particular needs arose (e.g., sickness and damage to churches). Thus, both were reluctant to allow priests to leave the diocese as full-time official chaplains, but Elder in particular frequently sent some of his foreign-born priests to various places in his Mississippi diocese to serve the troops and hospitals as needed.

FRANCIS XAVIER LERAY (POST CHAPLAIN)

The first of the three Natchez Diocese chaplains recognized by the Confederate government was Francis Xavier Leray (1825–1887). Born in the Brittany region of France as one of thirteen children, he came to the United States around 1845, entered the Sulpician St. Mary's Seminary in Baltimore, joined the Natchez Diocese under Bishop John Chanche, and was ordained in 1852. He first ministered on horseback to the widely scattered Catholics of the diocese, then served bravely through two yellow fever outbreaks (1853 and 1855), barely surviving being stricken himself with the fever. From 1857 to 1877 he was pastor at St. Paul's Church in Vicksburg, and it was from there that his well-traveled chaplain's life began.

Leray received an official commission as post chaplain for the hospital at Oxford, Mississippi, on November 26, 1862; there is evidence he had ministered as chaplain prior to that. The hospital at Oxford (on the then empty campus of the University of Mississippi) had been set up after Fort Donelson in February 1862, but grew immensely after the Battle of Shiloh (April 1862). Leray likely began working there shortly after the wounded began arriving. A letter of April 24, 1863, requesting a leave of absence from the Confederate hospital in Jackson, Mississippi, indicates another area hospital he cared for, and a May 19, 1864, letter from the Confederate hospital at Shelby Springs, Alabama, reveals yet a third area of his chaplain's ministry.

His ministry at these three widely scattered hospitals can be explained by the progress of the war in Mississippi. The Oxford hospital in northern Mississippi had grown larger after Shiloh (and it became a Union hospital after Grant's forces arrived in December 1862). Jackson also quickly became a Confederate hospital for soldiers from various places, but the city was captured by the Union on May 14, 1863. The Shelby Springs Hotel became a Confederate hospital in 1863 after Vicksburg was threatened, with some accounts saying that Leray and the Sisters of Mercy personally brought many wounded and sick Confederates with them on the train when they came to staff the transplanted hospital.[6]

In his frequent wartime journeys through the northern part of Mississippi, Leray was taken prisoner by Union forces several times, but was always released when he was identified as a priest. He was present at the Battle of Raymond (May 12, 1863) and, according to Bishop Elder's diary, reportedly "galloped across the battlefield to tend to the fallen and dying." Although formally the pastor of St. Paul's Church in Vicksburg, Leray was not there during its 1863 siege and eventual capture, but he did return in 1865 to rebuild the war-ravaged building. Just two years later, he had to deal with a cholera outbreak that struck Vicksburg, and just as he had in the 1850s, Leray showed great courage in actively ministering to residents afflicted by the ravages of a pandemic.[7]

In 1877 he was selected to be the new bishop of Natchitoches and consecrated on April 23; two years later he was summoned to New Orleans to be coadjutor bishop there while still keeping his Natchitoches responsibilities. Placed in charge of the New Orleans Diocese's $600,000 wartime debt, Leray eventually managed to reduce it in half. Upon the death of Bishop Napoleon Perche in 1883, Leray was named the bishop of New Orleans (covering the whole state of Louisiana). He doubled the number of Catholic schools in New Orleans, demonstrating his strong advocacy of Catholic education in the contentious postwar public school controversies (cf. chapter 12). After a long bout with sickness, Leray died in the French village in which he was born on September 23, 1887.[8]

JOHN BAPTISTE MOUTON
(POST AND HOSPITAL CHAPLAIN)

John Baptiste Mouton (1831–1878) was a gifted Frenchman who studied and was ordained in France before entering the Natchez Diocese in 1859. Upon arrival, his English was so poor that he did little more than say Masses for the Sisters of St. Joseph in Sulphur Springs while he "learned" English, although his language skills always remained weak.

A gifted architect, in his nearly thirty years in the diocese, Mouton designed and built numerous church buildings in several Mississippi towns, including Vicksburg (St. Francis Convent) and Columbus (Annunciation Church), both of which remain historical state landmarks to this day. He also apparently had a droll sense of humor, as witnessed by one lady who insisted on him kissing her baby, to which the priest responded, "No, go away! I kiss no one but the bishop and my horse!" Once at Corinth a lawyer wanted to talk with him, but Mouton had no time to stop. "But, I want to join the church," the lawyer said. Mouton responded, "Well, we have so much bad stock on hand that we can't take any more in!"[9]

In 1861 he was sent to the eastern part of the state to see if a priest could be supported there, visiting several small communities to contact and connect the area's isolated Catholics. On April 5, 1862, he received a telegraph from Elder to assist with the large number of troops gathered at Corinth. Elder also requested a formal chaplain's commission for Mouton, which was received on November 24, 1862. After ministering at Corinth with the other priests who had assembled there, Mouton continued to serve the churches under his care, but also tended sick and wounded soldiers in military hospitals and camps along the Mobile–Ohio Railroad (which ran north to south on the eastern side of Mississippi).

A priest contemporary of that time, Father Louis Vally, described Mouton's wartime pastoral work by saying that "during the war he was a chaplain though not of any particular regiment. He went here and there as a chaplain and like the soldiers was dressed in gray." Vally also mentioned an incident where Mouton was being chased by Federal soldiers who were shooting at him. The priest was saved by the swiftness of his horse, "Jim," who soon carried him out of the range of their guns.[10]

After the war, Mouton went on to pastor churches at Corinth, Columbia, and Sulphur Springs, traveling regularly in missionary fashion about the state to reach out to the far-flung Catholics. He was called by some the pioneer of the faith in northeast Mississippi because of his many trips to that specific area. While pastor at Columbia (having designed the landmark church there), he was described as "one of the most popular and highly appreciated pastors. . . . He was affable and courteous and much beloved by all religious denominations and the public generally." Bishop Elder himself said of the French priest, "There have been more converts in proportion to the Catholic population in your mission, I believe, than in any other part of the diocese."[11]

In 1877, Mouton became pastor in Yazoo City and began his characteristic church rebuilding process, but in the summer of 1878, yellow fever again ravaged Mississippi. The clergy of the Natchez Diocese were hit extremely hard; six of Elder's priests died in this one epidemic, and Mouton unfortunately was one. He had courageously asked Elder not to transfer him out of the fever-infested city and succumbed there on October 22, 1878.

FRANCIS PONT (10TH MISSISSIPPI AND HOSPITAL CHAPLAIN)

The third of the official Confederate chaplains in the west was Francis Pont (1831–1867), yet another native Frenchman recruited for the Natchez Diocese. Ordained by the French bishop of New Orleans, Antoine Blanc, in 1859, he was first sent to minister at St. Peter's Church in Jackson. In April 1861, Pont became involved with wartime ministry when the members of his congregation began enlisting in the 10th Mississippi, which was being formed in the Jackson area. He then approached Bishop Elder about following those troops to Pensacola, Florida. Although not enthusiastic about the idea, Elder allowed him to do so, as long as he did not accept a formal commission.

But on May 11, 1861, through either duplicity or misunderstanding, Pont received a formal chaplain's appointment to General Braxton Bragg's army in Jackson (not to any specific regiment, however). Elder apparently acquiesced, but when Pont requested to remain with the army permanently, Elder became upset, and told the young priest what he thought. "You speak of looking on the camp as your home—and say that you told me before leaving there that Jackson was not your home any longer. You are under some strange mistake in that respect. I never once thought of depriving the Diocese permanently of a Missionary. . . . If you have any other views now, I am happy to correct them at once."[12]

Despite this rather severe chastening from his bishop, it would appear that the two worked out the issue somehow, because Pont did in fact spend time with Bragg's troops after they left Mississippi for Florida. The next references to him are found in official military records from Pensacola, Florida: a July 3, 1861, request for a ten-day leave of absence, and a December 1861 request for pay increase. Pont was reimbursed by the Confederate government in March 1862 for travel expenses incurred while taking himself and Sisters of Charity from Warrenton, Florida, to Mobile, Alabama.[13]

By April 1862, Pont was back in Mississippi, and was with Confederate troops at the Battle of Shiloh, where apparently he was slightly wounded. The day afterward, he wrote to Bishop Odin (New Orleans) describing the battle and its casualties, as well as other priests who were there. The University of Notre Dame online archives has a summary of the letter's contents: "For booty, he [Pont] took a military overcoat, a sword, and the envelope he addresses to (Odin). To give an idea of the carnage, the 1st Louisiana [Regulars] Reg(imen)t, which entered the battlefield with about 750 men, has no more than 50 fit for service today. Almost all their officers were killed or wounded. . . . [Pont] was scratched by a bullet which struck his heel and another struck the sole of his boot."[14]

Pont tended to the wounded at Corinth in the weeks following the battle, eventually escorting some of them back to Vicksburg. After a yearlong leave of absence in France for family business, he returned to the Natchez Diocese in May 1863, where he became a very active pastor of St. Paul's Church at Pass Christian on the Gulf Coast. He expanded that church and built two others in nearby towns, improved an area house as a rectory, and built a two-story school (the upstairs of which became his residence, since the nuns took over the rectory as their home). Sadly, Pont's expansion of the parish cemetery was a prophetic omen, although he could not have known that he himself would be laid to rest there. Pont's cemetery shrine notes his death on September 27, 1867, at the tender age of thirty-six, as yet another casualty of a Mississippi yellow fever epidemic.[15]

RECOGNIZED SERVICE BUT
NO OFFICIAL CONFEDERATE RECORD

There were at least two priests in the Natchez Diocese who are known to have ministered as chaplains during the war but did not receive any formal recognition from the Confederate government. For the sake of brevity, I will summarize the lives and chaplaincy of these two, then mention other Natchez priests who ministered occasionally (but without true regularity) to Civil War troops, either at the specific request of Bishop Elder or as needs arose in their own communities.

Ghislain Boheme (1803–1862), was a Belgian who had been recruited for ministry in the United States by Bishop Edward Fenwick, and Boheme was ordained in 1833 at Bardstown, Kentucky. He was a much-traveled priest who worked first in the Indian missions of Ohio, then moved into the Detroit Diocese (ministering to French Canadians around Lake Ontario and then in Grand Rapids, Michigan), and finally settled in Mississippi in 1842. His eighteen years there were spent in the small town of Paulding, where he founded St. Paul Church. Around April 1862, Boheme was asked by Elder to chaplain the 13th Mississippi (commanded by William Barksdale). The Jasper Greys of that regiment had been formed by Irish Catholics from Paulding itself, and it included twenty men from Boheme's own church—some of whom had been his altar boys.[16]

Though he was fifty-nine years old at the time of the request, Boheme accepted, and joined the 13th Mississippi as part of the Army of Northern Virginia. However, the rigors of travel and life in the field during the 1862 Peninsula Campaign were too much for him, as they were for many of the regiment's soldiers, who were greatly affected by sickness. Boheme died of a massive stroke on June 27, 1862, amid the fighting of that campaign.

Julian Guillou (1824–1863) was another of the many French priests recruited by the Natchez Diocese. Guillou was ordained in 1850 and served in several diocesan churches through the 1850s (Yazoo City, Sulphur Springs). He was among the other Natchez priests who helped with the wounded and dying at Corinth after Shiloh, but he then continued serving as chaplain at several makeshift area hospitals and also served briefly as chaplain with the New Orleans–based Washington Artillery.

Although Guillou had survived a bout with the yellow fever in 1853 in Yazoo City, he could not recover from the consumption that came upon him in early 1863. Bishop Elder's diary speaks frequently of the priest's discomfort, weakened condition, and his eventual death on February 7, 1863. The bishop deeply mourned the loss of this French priest, writing in his diary that "Father Guillou's death is a calamity for the diocese. I can truly say he was the best missionary in the diocese . . . I feel as if his death was a judgment on myself."[17]

Information on the Italian priest Basil Elia (?–1863) is scant, but we know he was pastor at St. Joseph's Church in Holly Springs, Mississippi, from the late 1850s until 1862, when General Ulysses S. Grant's Union troops took over the area in December 1862. In reaction to Earl Van Dorn's December 18, 1862, raid on their Holly Springs depot, enraged Union soldiers occupied Holly Springs, ransacked many houses, and desecrated the Catholic church. With his congregation now dispersed, Elia went to Memphis, and in mid-1863 requested that Elder allow him to work with dying Union soldiers at Young's Point, Louisiana (during Grant's Vicksburg Campaign). Elder's own diary describes the subsequent events which led to Elia's death by one of the many rampant diseases in that swampy place on April 2, 1863.

Rev. Basil Elia . . . whom I most esteemed and loved . . . lost his life a year ago from having volunteered with my approval, to go to the assistance of the dying soldiers of the United States Army, opposite Vicksburg, who had no religious chaplain at the time to give them the consolations of religion which he valued vastly more than their lives. His own congregation had been dispersed by the events of the war, and when I wrote to him to come into another portion of the diocese, he asked me to allow him to go rather to those soldiers, because they had more need of his labors. After three weeks of fatigue and exposure he contracted the prevailing sickness and died at Memphis, April 2nd, 1863.[18]

John L. Finucane (1835–?) was newly ordained as the Civil War began, and this Irish immigrant was sent in 1862 and 1863 by Elder to minister to soldiers in Jackson, as well as to serve in hospitals in Brookhaven. Finucane's health also became an issue, and in 1864 he was allowed to leave the Natchez Diocese. Finucane then joined the Erie Diocese (Pennsylvania), working in the oil boom towns of Venango County, Pennsylvania, where ironically the former Union chaplain Napolean Mignault (17th Wisconsin) also finished his career.

Henry Victor Georget (1824–?) was born in Blancafort, France, came to the Natchez Diocese around 1857, and—despite his poor skills in English—worked there for nearly thirty years. In November 1862 he was called by Elder from his Biloxi parish to Natchez to help minister to soldiers in that area, as a Union "invasion" was soon expected. Georget returned to Biloxi a year later, writing to Bishop Elder that he had gotten too sick to continue in that work. He continued ministering in the diocese at Pass Christian and Chatawa into the mid-1880s.

Philip Huber (1827–1903) was a German immigrant who entered the diocese in 1832. Huber became pastor at a struggling Port Gibson parish, and worked with the wounded and dying after Shiloh. In late 1862, he became a short-term chaplain for the 10th Tennessee Regiment, a position Elder tried to dissuade him from because of parish and personal health issues. The bishop was proved right when Huber returned to Natchez after struggling with winter weather and getting dysentery while with the troops. He then returned to parish life, putting in forty-five years of distinguished diocesan service before his 1903 death.

After arriving in America in 1854 and failing in his attempt to become a Jesuit, Henry A. Picherit, (1831–?) settled into a long and successful career in the diocese. While a pastor in Brookhaven, he ministered to the wounded in Corinth after Shiloh, visited Union camps after 1863, and brought medicine up from New Orleans when needed. He was called "the great Confederate Chaplain" in Sister Mary Paulinus Oakes's *Angels of Mercy* (a bit of an exaggeration), but he did become a dean in the diocese and pastor in the diocese's largest parish (St. Paul's in Vicksburg).

The following priests also worked with the wounded at Corinth after the Battle of Shiloh, although they were not from the Natchez

Diocese: Isidore Turgis and Francois Bertrand (Frenchmen from the New Orleans Diocese) and Anthony de Chaignon SJ (the French chaplain of the 18th Louisiana at the time of Shiloh).

In conclusion, the unionist turned secessionist Bishop William Elder was a truly amazing role model—not only for his chaplaincy and priestly ministry during the war, but also his episcopal leadership in the war-ravaged Natchez Diocese. Six of the ten above-mentioned priests either died or left the diocese during the Civil War years, with six of his diocesan priests in all dying in the fatal 1878 yellow fever epidemic. Yet the bishop not only guided his diocese through these challenges of war, destruction, and sickness, but remained always an extremely active and mobile pastor. He would go on to become the archbishop of Cincinnati in 1880, serving until his death at age eighty-five in 1904.

NEW MEXICO TERRITORY
AND THE SANTA FE DIOCESE

The New Mexico Territory that became the home of new bishop Jean-Baptiste Lamy (1814–1888) in 1851 had been Mexico's poorest and most isolated diocese. Just five years after the Mexican-American War had given the United States this area, Lamy was appointed to a land marked by ancient cultures, strong folk religion, and distinctive social and political structures. In theory, the Catholic Church was already strong there, but practically speaking its churches were autonomous—Mexican bishops rarely visited them, secular clergy were rare, and religious authority was in the hands of local clergy, the wealthy laity, and the most powerful landed families. Lamy's first decade in New Mexico would be spent removing these independently minded clergy, bringing in clergy he could work with, and providing resources for his spiritually and materially impoverished diocese.[19]

Lamy had arrived in the United States twelve years earlier with his friend Father Joseph Machebreuf, and had ministered in Ohio and Kentucky before being named bishop. Both priests had come from the strongly Catholic Auvergne region of France, and studied at the doctrinally rigorous Sulpician seminary at Clermont-Ferrand. It was to this

"French connection" that Lamy immediately turned for help, which he received in the form of bringing into the Santa Fe Diocese twenty-one French priests by 1864. In the next seventy years, 120 French priests in all would serve in New Mexico, comprising the majority of clergy in the territory. As the Civil War began in 1861, the Santa Fe Diocese had twenty-four churches, ninety-three scattered chapels and stations, with only twenty-nine priests to serve the seventy-five thousand Mexican Catholics and eighty-five thousand indigenous tribes. Stretched as he was, Lamy still authorized two of his priests to serve Civil War troops in the territory, and a third priest decided on his own to serve.[20]

As far as its Civil War history goes, compared to the bloodshed and army sizes elsewhere, the 1862 Confederate "invasion" of the New Mexico Territory was a fairly minor drama. The Confederacy wanted access to the Santa Fe Trail and possibly to the gold that California was already known for—and of course, the Union resisted their efforts. In all, there were only seven thousand troops involved in the conflict (four thousand Union and three thousand Confederate), and only 280 soldiers died. Most of the Union troops were poor, illiterate Spanish-speaking men who had little knowledge of United States military training (but they did have the Catholic Christopher "Kit" Carson as their second in command). In summary, the Confederates won tactical victories but were forced to limp back to their Texas base empty-handed—defeated as much by the harsh southwest environment and determined people as by the Union troops.[21]

DAMASO TALADRID AND JOSEPH FIALON

Three priests from the Santa Fe Diocese served the Union in the short-lived Civil War history of the New Mexico Territory (two will be discussed in this section and the third in the following section). Again, as with Bishop Elder and Natchez, that was no small accomplishment, given the shortage of priests and the huge diocesan territory Bishop Lamy was responsible for (one of the largest in the country at that time). The first priest who served was Damaso Taladrid (1819?–1869?), a native of Madrid, Spain, whom Lamy had recruited and brought back with him in 1854 while he was at the Vatican working out the details of his new Santa Fe, New Mexico, episcopacy.

Taladrid was a colorful character with a fascinating personal history. He had studied for the priesthood in France, had served as an officer in the Spanish military (according to one account), and been a missionary in Africa, all before meeting up with Lamy in Rome in 1854, and beginning his American career.[22] He arrived in New Mexico with Bishop Lamy (and several other recruits) in 1854, and was assigned to a parish in Taos, New Mexico. He was sent to replace a quarrelsome "holdover" from the previous bishop (a priest named Antonio Martinez), whose Mexican liberation ideals and resistance to instituting tithing (a practice not done in Mexico) got him in trouble with Lamy. However, as Taladrid was not of Mexican background, but Spanish, he was not a good fit to be pastor in the troubled Taos parish, and thus he was transferred to Mora, New Mexico. During these early assignments in the diocese, Taladrid met two prominent men who would influence his chaplain's career—Ceran St. Vrain and Christopher "Kit" Carson, both apparently members of his parish.[23]

When the 1st New Mexico Infantry was formed in July 1861, Taladrid was influenced by Vrain and Carson to become chaplain of this predominantly Hispanic and untrained regiment. At Valverde (February 20–21, 1862), he distinguished himself by his courageous ministry to soldiers while under fire. One author wrote that "he was very brave, and as a military man, did not know fear . . . he walked among the dead and wounded, helping them and absolving them of their sins without fear of the bullets." Carson himself liked Taladrid, feeling that he was a good influence of discipline and instruction for the troops. "I consider him eminently qualified for his position in this regiment . . . has always shown himself willing and capable to perform his own peculiar duties . . . he still does exert a great influence for the good discipline and instruction of the regiment—I do not think another person in the Territory can be found who would do as well."[24]

Unfortunately, after Carson had moved on elsewhere, the charismatic Taladrid ran into trouble in May 1863 with the District Commander Major Joseph Smith, who accused him of "being a bad role model," as well as drinking and playing the popular Mexican card-game *monte* with soldiers. Smith wrote, "I am satisfied that the chaplain was not aware he was committing any offense either Civil or Military for it is their custom to bet and play at Monte.... He is a Mexican [*sic*] and says that this is the custom of the Country and that he was not aware that he was committing any Military offense.... I could do nothing else but to put him under arrest and submit the matter to headquarters." The charges were soon dropped because of Taladrid's great popularity and his ignorance of army regulations, but the Spaniard's pride had been offended. He wrote a long letter to the Adjutant General at Santa Fe (Captain Benjamin Cutler) refusing to take the abstinence pledge they had requested, remarking that he might play *monte* occasionally, but had never been drunk, and was as patriotic as anyone in military.[25]

The end result of all this is somewhat unclear, but Taladrid did take part in several subsequent battles (Warm Springs on June 16, Rio Hondo on July 18, and Conchus Springs on July 22, 1863) before submitting his letter of resignation: "My age and bodily infirmities are such that I cannot bear the many exposures." From letters quoted in Germain's *Catholic Military and Naval Chaplains*, though, it appears that his resignation may have been influenced by the new mission that the 1st New Mexico (and Carson) had set out upon, one that neither Taladrid nor Bishop Lamy supported—namely that of "Carson's plan of extermination of the Navajo Indians." Whatever the circumstances, this was not mentioned in Taladrid's resignation letter, which was accepted August 17, 1863. He went on to serve as pastor in Las Cruces, New Mexico, until mid-1869, when records of him disappear.[26]

Joseph Fialon (1834–1910) was born in Auvergne, France (Bishop Lamy's home region), and was one of the many Frenchmen from that area that the bishop brought to the Santa Fe Diocese during his episcopacy. Fialon arrived in 1856, having been recruited by Lamy's vicar general, Father Joseph Machebeuf, who returned with him and four others during a trip to France. After being ordained in New Mexico in 1857, Fialon was sent to Bernadillo to reestablish a church that had been destroyed by a flood about twenty years before. The small and quaint church he designed and built there (Sanctuario de San Lorenzo) was eventually listed on the National Register of Historic Places. He labored there for nearly five years building the church and caring for four other outlying mission stations (one of which was for the area's Native American tribes).

In October 1862, Congress authorized the construction of Fort Sumner in the Pecos River Valley, for the ostensible purpose of offering protection to nearby settlers from the Apache, Mescalero, Kiowa, and Comanche tribes in that area. The Bosque Redondo reservation was nearby, and over nine thousand Navajo and Mescalero Apaches were forced to live there because of accusations that they had been raiding settlements nearby. In June 1863, Fort Sumner's commander General James Carleton wrote Bishop Lamy, enclosing an order from the Secretary of War declaring Fort Sumner a chaplain post and requesting a "clergyman of energy, and all of those qualities of patience, good temper, assiduity, and interest in the subject so necessary in one who is wanted to teach the Indian children now at Fort Sumner, not only the rudiments of an education, but the principles and truths of Christianity." That same month, Lamy responded back to this request by recommending Joseph Fialon, who "is now in France but will be back in August."[27]

Fialon was commissioned in October 1863, and served officially as a post chaplain until being mustered out in May 1864. His time of wartime service was decidedly dissimilar to any other chaplain north or south, as it dealt mainly with local Indians, troops at Fort Sumner, and occasional raids upon troublesome area Indians. Little is recorded of his work except for an isolated 1863 event, where "the gallant chaplain" was singled out by General Carleton for his role as part of a force of both cavalry and Indians allies that engaged an aggressive Navajo raiding party near Fort Sumner. "He and two others, at the head of thirty Mescalero Apache Indians from the reservation (who one year ago were our mortal enemies), did most of the work, as they were fortunate in being the first to encounter the Navajos." Fort Sumner was only in existence for six years, and after Fialon's post chaplaincy ended, in the next thirty years before his 1910 death, he served parishes and outlying mission stations around Sapello and Paraje, New Mexico, then superintended the construction work for the new Santa Fe cathedral.[28]

"PADRE POLACO":
A CHAPLAIN, BUT A PRIEST?

Among the list of truly colorful and inimitable Catholic Civil War chaplains, Lamy's third wartime chaplain, Alexander Grzelachowski (1824–1896), has to rank very high. Although he is considered an official Catholic chaplain (albeit for only about four months), the more relevant question is whether he was even technically an active priest at the time. The story of this unique man began in Gracina, Poland, where he was born to affluent parents; his father was an 1812 military officer, and thus could be considered Polish nobility. After studying at a French seminary, Grzelachowski was ordained and motivated to immigrate to America after visits from Lamy in 1848 and Bishop Louis Rappe (Cleveland) in 1849. After immigrating in 1850, Grzelachowski went to Ohio, where he ministered as the first resident pastor of French Creek (now St. Mary's) in Avon, Ohio. It was there that he first made his application for citizenship, eventually granted in October 1855 in New Mexico. In 1851, however, he decided to serve in the Southwest under Bishop Lamy and journeyed there with him via New Orleans and Galveston on a wagon train escorted by cavalry.

In the Santa Fe Diocese, the amiable Grzelachowski proved to be a natural linguist, mastering Spanish quickly, and becoming known as "Padre Polaco" while serving in several New Mexico villages, including Las Vegas, for a time. After ministering to communities of area Indians for several years, in November 1857 he moved to Our Lady of Sorrows in Manzano, which proved to be his last formal priestly assignment because (as one biographer says) around then "he had begun to lean towards a secular life." By 1859, Grzelachowski had "relinquished his parish assignment and moved to Las Vegas . . . bought a tract of land and entered the business world." Yet curiously, in 1860, he still told the Federal census taker that "he was 36 years old, a Roman Catholic clergyman."[29]

He may also at one time have been an unofficial chaplain at Fort Union in northeastern New Mexico, as some credit him with doing a baptism there, although accurate records do not exist. But when the Civil War broke out, Grzelachowski volunteered to be a chaplain for the Second New Mexico Volunteers when it was organized in July 1861. He received an appointment but apparently was never mustered into service, instead simply attaching himself to the command and functioning as a clergyman. He may have been at Valverde (February 20–21, 1862) when the Confederates of General Henry Sibley defeated the Union forces of Colonel Edward Canby, but again evidence is unclear here. But it was at Glorieta Pass (March 26–28, 1862) that the Polish priest made his biggest Civil War–related contribution.[30]

As the Confederate force moved to attack Union troops near Glorieta, New Mexico, a small Union force under Major John Chivington maneuvered behind their lines and destroyed the entire Confederate supply train, thus effectively ending Confederate efforts in New Mexico. According to a March 1881 Las Vegas *Daily Optic* newspaper account, Chivington's guide for part of that daring raid, which included using a secret mountain pass, was Alexander Grzelachowski, who knew the area well. He was familiar with it from his work as a priest, and had used the same trail to go to Santa Fe and to visit his Polish countryman Martin Kozlowski, who had a ranch nearby which became the Union headquarters. Though little is written of it, Kozlowski and Grzelachowski were undoubtedly friends, as Kozlowski would in the years ahead often frequent the prosperous merchant Grzelachowski's store in Puerto de Luna.

Perhaps the best proof of Grzelachowski's involvement in the raid was his August 1862 letter to the Union command requesting repayment for the loss of his horse, which died in carrying out that raid. It was signed "your obdt servant, A. Grzelachowski, late chaplain 2nd N.M. Vols." There is no evidence he was ever reimbursed for that loss, though it does show his presence at the battle and role in the destruction of the supply train which caused the Confederate retreat to Texas. Thus, though technically a formal Union chaplain, it seems clear that the greatest contribution of this unique priest to the war effort was not his spiritual efforts but his reconnoitering skills.[31]

Following the war, any "return" to whatever formal priestly ministry he may have had in 1861 was put aside, as Grzelachowski went wholeheartedly into the mercantile business. He joined together with other businessmen, opening stores first in Sapello (1863) then Las Vegas

(1867), and finally Puerto de Luna, New Mexico (1874), becoming very successful and prosperous in the process. The immigrant Grzelachowski would have stood out in a frontier territory marked by high illiteracy, because of his integrity, education, amiability, Old World polish, and intellectual capacity. He became the leading citizen of Puerto de Luna—the highly respected "Don Alejandro"—whose store was visited several times by no less than Billy the Kid. (According to legend, Billy the Kid was served his last Christmas meal there in 1880 while being transported to jail by Pat Garrett.)[32]

Grzelachowski became politically active in the state, becoming the first probate judge of the new county, the area postmaster, and a prominent rancher with livestock, orchard, and a vineyard. He entered into a "recognized common law marriage" early in the 1870s, and eventually had nine children with his wife Secundina Baca, raising them all Catholic. He maintained his ties to his Polish heritage, corresponding with his two brothers, and inculcating his love for Poland in his children. In 1896, this fascinating Renaissance man, who had been in declining health, died when thrown from a wagon on the way to his Puerto de Luna ranch. His biographer (Daniel Flores) remarks that a priest came to him on his deathbed, wanting him to renounce his relationship with Secundina and receive the Last Rites of the church. However, one of his daughters later reported that "he had been buried outside the cemetery," meaning he had refused to do so. But in the 1980s, his previously unmarked grave got a tombstone when the cemetery was expanded, thereby including him entirely within Nuestra Senora del Refugio Catholic cemetery in Puerto de Luna.[33]

However, the question remains—was Grzelachowski technically a valid priest when he became a Civil War chaplain? In Catholic theology, the mark of ordination is permanent, although permission to function publicly as a priest (called "faculties") must be granted by the local bishop or religious superior. It appears that although he had clearly begun the transition out of active ministry to a secular life by 1861, he still considered himself a priest—particularly when that fact could be to his advantage, as with accepting a chaplain's position. Likewise, there seems to be no existing evidence that his priestly faculties had been formally revoked by Bishop Lamy at the time of his Civil

War service. Therefore, like Germain and Blied before me, I too include this memorable man (with his confusing priestly "pedigree") on the official chaplains list.[34] Although his spiritual contributions as a Civil War chaplain may not have been the equal of a Corby, O'Hagan, Hubert, or Sheeran, Grzelachowski's distinctive role at Glorieta and amazing postwar success make him perhaps the most unusual Catholic chaplain of this entire book.

CHAPTER 11

UNCONVENTIONAL CHAPLAINS IN UNIQUE SITUATIONS

For those unfamiliar with churches, pastors, or denominational life, there may be a presumption that religious people are a pretty dull and traditional group, rarely deviating from acceptable rules and norms. Since much of Catholic priests' life *is* focused on religious matters, Scripture, and church issues, some assume their personalities reflect the same—a certain stuffy blandness, a boring otherworldliness that distances itself from the mundane realities of everyday life. In reality, this could not be farther from the truth, and the Catholic chaplains we have pondered thus far should easily begin to dispel that myth. In this chapter and the next, I will feature several Catholic chaplains whose lives are quite distinctive, whose temperament and work stands out both from normative church ministry, and who depart from the "usual" wartime chaplain's service.

JOSEPH BIXIO SJ: THE JESUIT TRICKSTER

One of the most colorful characters—priest or military—connected to the Civil War was the Italian Jesuit Joseph Bixio (1819–1898). Born in the Savoy region of Italy, Bixio was the brother of Nino Bixio—Giuseppe Garibaldi's right-hand man in the struggle for Italian unification. Always a somewhat restless soul, Bixio entered the Jesuits in Italy and came to the United States as a student after the Jesuits were expelled from the kingdom of Sardinia in 1848. He was ordained in 1851, and then worked in Virginia, Maine, and California as a circuit rider for a number of years. Leaving California with "some bad feelings towards his superior" (his restless independence frequently led to tensions with his order), Bixio returned to the East, apparently intrigued and attracted by the energies and issues surrounding the looming war.[1]

As the Civil War began, Bixio was serving in a parish that bordered on two states, Virginia and Maryland. At the Battle of First Manassas, the smooth-talking Bixio may have played some helpful (though not totally verifiable) role in assisting the Confederacy, by giving information about the Union to the Confederates under General Joseph Johnston. However, after that battle ended, Bixio found himself stranded on the Southern (Virginia) side of his parish, unable to return to the Northern (Maryland) side of his church. But, according to a January 1862 letter from fellow Jesuit Hippolyte Gache (who had just met Bixio in Richmond), "this didn't bother him a bit; he has simply volunteered as a Confederate chaplain." Though his exact activities are unknown, by the spring of 1862 it seems that Bixio had developed a curious knack of "slipping back and forth across the Federal lines," using his Italian charm, Roman collar, and religious identity as "passports." As Jesuit historian Cornelius Buckley coyly noted, "It is fairly certain, too, that Bixio did not sneak back empty-handed."[2]

In the spring of 1862, James Sheeran (14th Louisiana) noted in his journal that Bixio had sneaked over the lines and "gained the hearts of officers and soldiers" in the Union army. But by June 1862, the Jesuit was apparently back with the Confederates at the Battle of Gaines Mill, being referred to (not by name) in the journal of a captain of the 11th Alabama whose wound had been dressed by a priest "who had a great deal of experience in the Italian army," which could only have been Bixio. In September 1864, Sheeran again refers to Bixio as a pastor in Staunton, Virginia, noting that he was "now playing Yankee chaplain" and drawing federal rations and supplies. This time however, Bixio's "dual identity" games finally had some serious consequences, although he personally did not pay the price for his deceptions.[3]

The story of what happened has been related several times already in this text, but now it will be shared more fully from Bixio's perspective. In the fall of 1864, Bixio was posing as the Franciscan chaplain of the 9th Connecticut, Leo Rizzo de Saracena, whose credentials and uniform he had taken from Rizzo's tent when he was hospitalized with typhoid, "near to death at one point," as one biographer remarks. Using this "disguise," Bixio tricked Union General Philip Sheridan into obtaining rations, transportation, and several wagonloads of Union supplies, alleging he could distribute them to better advantage than hospital nurses. Bixio then brazenly transported these supplies into Staunton (at that point within Confederate lines) "for purposes best known to himself." Although Bixio got away with this, when the deception was discovered, other people suffered. Leo Rizzo himself was first accused of espionage and treason by an enraged Union general, but was able to provide witnesses as to his serious medical issues at the time (he had been "unconscious and writhing with fever"). But James Sheeran of the 14th Louisiana was not so lucky—a furious General Sheridan had Sheeran arrested after catching him as he ministered to the wounded of both sides after the battle of Cedar Creek (October 19, 1864). Without being told why he had been arrested (until his final contentious interviews with Sheridan in December 1864 after his release), Sheeran was imprisoned for several months under horrible conditions in two Baltimore Federal prisons.[4]

After great personal troubles, and with his physical condition rapidly failing, Sheeran managed to use his connections with the Redemptorists (his religious order) and James McMaster (editor of the *New York Freemans Journal*) to finally secure his release. Yet the sly Bixio evaded all consequences, after receiving a "polite" message in Staunton, Virginia, from an unidentified Union general (perhaps General Benjamin Butler) that Bixio would be "hanged from the first tree" if he was caught again. The devious priest had the common sense to stay away from the Valley and Sheridan, and never was caught. After the war ended, he traveled to Georgetown with a trunkful of useless Confederate money expecting to found a college there, but again left the east for California in October 1866.

To the end, Bixio retained his cunning and charisma. He charmed Archbishop Joseph Alemany (San Francisco), became his confidant, worked at the Jesuit college in Santa Clara, and even founded a number of parishes there. But his restless spirit still not quieted, Bixio left for Australia in 1878 in a failed effort to teach there, only to return to California two years later. Ironically praised in his final years for "his incredible nobility, coming and going about the town and valley, familiar to all and liked by all," Bixio remained at Santa Clara College until his death in March 1899. Joseph Bixio certainly had a colorful history as an unofficial Civil War chaplain, whatever his true nature and intentions. Perhaps this most idiosyncratic of all the Civil War Jesuits was best summarized by one historian of the order who called him "every bit as ingenious and resourceful as he was double-dealing and cunning."[5]

JEREMIAH TRECY:
CHAPLAIN FOR BOTH SIDES

While every Catholic chaplain was connected to either the North or the South in their ministry, only one priest could boast of being a recognized chaplain for both sides. That man was Jeremiah Trecy (1822?–1888), a native of County Louth, Ireland, who immigrated with his family to America in 1836, and lived in Pennsylvania until beginning his seminary studies in Emmitsburg, Maryland. He was ordained in 1851 for the Dubuque Diocese (Iowa), and for most of the next decade served outposts in Iowa and Nebraska, gathering congregations together and building churches. Bishop Mathias Loras (1792–1858) of Dubuque and Trecy were always interested in western expansion and Catholic colonization, with Trecy first ministering in the Irish settlement "Garryowen" near Dubuque, then building the first Catholic church in Nebraska, called "St. John's City" in the Dakota Territory (present-day Jackson, Nebraska).[6]

While laboring in his travels to scattered Catholics in middle America, Trecy also visited many military forts, and ministered to indigenous tribes in the area, even attempting to represent them (unsuccessfully) in Washington, DC, on the governmental injustices regarding their financial affairs. Despite being a great favorite among the tribes, after about ten years Trecy's physical condition began to suffer from exposure and long hours on horseback. He went south in 1860 with letters of recommendation, settling in the Mobile Diocese under Bishop John Quinlan. In late 1860 he was assigned to the Catholic community in Huntsville, Alabama, promptly laying the cornerstone for St. Mary of the Visitation Church there, although its construction was suspended when the Civil War broke out.[7]

Following Alabama's secession in January 1861, Huntsville became a Confederate camp, and Trecy's Confederate chaplaincy began. He volunteered to minister to the Catholics in that camp, and also at the Confederate Forts Jones and Morgan near Mobile, on the opposite side of the state. After the battle of Fort Donelson (February 11–16, 1862), Trecy was asked by Dr. David Yandell, the surgeon on General Albert Johnson's staff, to meet help the sanitary needs of wounded soldiers then in Huntsville. Though initially reluctant, Trecy consented and, with the help of parish members, quickly cleaned up the medical facility, tightened up visiting passes, and withstood accusations of Catholic proselytism (by obtaining support from area Protestant ministers, thus enabling Trecy and his Irish assistants to continue working). He was then tasked by Yandell to gather and bring much-needed medical supplies to Corinth. When he arrived with the supplies, he found Bishop John Quinlan there, and discovered that his Huntsville parish had been occupied by Union troops. He was allowed by Quinlan to attempt to return to his parish, and received a pass from Yandell to cross whatever Confederate lines he needed to do so.

It was then, however, that Trecy's true adventures began. He started out on foot along the railroad, but before the day was done, he had been shot at several times, had his pass questioned repeatedly, hid in thickets to avoid troops, and forded a river when finding the bridge burned. Staying with a friendly man that night, the next day his adventures resumed when he quite easily entered Union lines to return to his parish, but was soon stopped again and severely questioned about his Confederate pass and presence in the *Union* camp. After a rather heated dialogue, General Ormsby Mitchel became convinced of the priest's sincerity, gave him a Union pass, and Trecy set off for a nearby Confederate hospital. There was great rejoicing when he arrived, with one Louisiana non-Catholic soldier raising himself off his bed with tears rolling down his cheeks, and exclaiming, "Thank God our friend is allowed to visit us!" Trecy baptized the man a few days later, give him the sacraments of the Church, and buried him shortly after that.[8]

About an hour later that same day, Trecy was called to perform a Union soldier's funeral, and his ministry over the next days was so effective and impressive that he continued working throughout both armies until the end of August 1862. Soon though the Union army was moved back into Kentucky, and when they left, some of Trecy's old Huntsville parish members began to resent his nonpartisan ministry, considering him a traitor for ministering to Federals. He was soon advised by friends to leave the area for a while, and so in early September 1862 set out for Tuscumbia, Alabama. But at a river crossing there, Trecy was again stopped and questioned, this time by a rude and suspicious Union sergeant, who then brought him to his non-Catholic post commandant, a man from Wisconsin who did little but demean and insult the priest.

But in the midst of this officer's vituperations, Trecy's fortunes changed dramatically. General David Stanley suddenly entered the tent to learn of the whereabouts of Buell's army, and Trecy told him that the army had already left northern Alabama, speaking as well of other general Union troop movements that he had seen. Stanley at once telegraphed all this information—and Trecy's presence—to the Catholic General William Rosecrans at Iuka, who asked that Trecy be sent to him there. While these dispatches were being sent, Stanley and Trecy fell into conversation, and the general was so impressed with Trecy that he asked him to spend the night in his own tent.

The very devout Rosecrans was overjoyed to meet Trecy at Iuka, and immediately set up a headquarters for him, gave him an orderly and a large tent, and put the word out about having a Catholic priest in his army. Trecy heard confessions and ministered for five days, instructing and receiving General Stanley himself into the Catholic faith on September 12, 1862, at a Mass celebrated in the public square of Iuka. General Rosecrans was Stanley's sponsor, and because a large part of the army was in attendance, the news of Stanley's conversion spread quickly throughout the troops. Trecy was next at the battle of Iuka (September 19, 1862), where he ministered with future bishop John Ireland (5th Minnesota). When Rosecrans took charge of the Union 14th Corps in October 1862, he gave Trecy formal authority to visit all the 14th Corps camps, hospitals, and garrisons to "allow Catholics an opportunity of fulfilling their religious obligations." In May 1863, after having again dealt with illness and in response to problems with being paid for his ministry, he accepted a specific appointment as chaplain of the 4th US Cavalry.[9]

From the fall of 1862 through much of 1863, no less than seven Catholic priest-chaplains ministered in Rosecrans's Army of the Cumberland (Trecy, Ireland, Cooney, Fusseder, Christy, O'Higgins, and Stephan)—the most at one time in any comparable Civil War unit. Interacting with Rosencrans but also with troops throughout the Army, and ministering himself until the very end of the war, Trecy's wartime career was one of the longest and most fascinating of any Catholic chaplain. As mentioned in chapter 3, at Stones River (and all subsequent combat) he carried canteens of whiskey and water. The whiskey was used as a "reviving draught" to enable a dying soldier to make his last confession, and the water was "for purposes of Baptism, for members of the protestants in the army were never baptized, and a great many of them required the services of the priest on the battlefield." On one occasion, a Union deserter was captured fighting for the South in a Confederate uniform. He was sentenced to death, and refused to see any chaplain, though he did say, "If I were to have any preacher, it would be that old man Trecy. He is the damndest sensible one among them."[10]

The nonpartisan Trecy gave general absolution on several occasions, was a powerful and effective preacher, and became conspicuous for his battlefield presence and courage among the troops. He was active at Stones River, Chickamauga, the Atlanta Campaign, Nashville, and Franklin, being described as "incessant in his ministrations to the sick, the dying, the wounded, and was as well known, and in a manner as much respected by the troops as 'Olde Sherman' himself." When the war concluded, Trecy returned to his Huntsville church, where he set about repairing his damaged parish, and journeying (at his bishop's request) throughout the North raising funds for the war-ravaged Mobile Diocese. After serving there and at a parish in Bayou LaBatre, Alabama, for several years, he had a stroke in 1879 and was sent to the Alexian Brothers Hospital in St. Louis. It was there that this well-traveled priest, whose ministry truly knew neither North or South allegiance, nor any ethnic or racial distinction, died in March 1888.[11]

ABRAM JOSEPH RYAN:
POET-PRIEST OF THE CONFEDERACY

The most famous unofficial chaplain of the Civil War was Abram Joseph Ryan (1838–1886). Beloved by many, a priest both fascinating and captivating yet enigmatic and troubled, Ryan was born in Maryland to Irish immigrant parents. He and his brother David grew up with strong southern-leaning influences, likely due to their father, a Maryland plantation overseer for a time. Ryan entered seminary in 1851, heavily influenced by his mother's expectations (which became a lifelong resentment), and developed a rather self-absorbed, melancholic temperament, given to brooding as well as chronic complaining. He became a poet at an early age, was always interested in politics and writing, and showed a tremendous gift of oratory even during his seminary days. Ordained as a member of the Vincentian order at only age twenty-two (for which he needed a dispensation) in September 1860, Ryan was sent to teach for a while (supposedly to "humble" him), then went to a LaSalle, Illinois, parish, the first of no less than five geographic areas of the country he attempted to establish a ministry in. In September 1862, after months of dissension, Ryan was allowed by the highest Vincentian superior (Father Mariano Maller in Paris) to leave his order and join the Chicago Diocese.[12]

In Illinois, a pattern emerged that followed him the rest of his life. Ryan's captivating speaking style and skills as a fundraiser attracted many people and bishops initially, but sooner or later his strong Southern leanings, chronic complaints, illnesses, moody temperament, and problems with authority figures (real or imagined) torpedoed any long-term effectiveness and prompted him to move on. After being dismissed by his religious order, Ryan spent most of 1862 and 1863 in Illinois before going to Tennessee (Nashville Diocese, Bishop James Whelan) for five years, Georgia (the Savannah Diocese, Bishop Augustin Verot) for two years, Mobile (Bishop John Quinlan) for thirteen years off and on, and finally the Milwaukee Diocese (Bishop John Henni) for the last years of his life. Throughout this entire time, Ryan was rarely still—he was constantly on the move, speaking before rapt congregations, writing highly popular Lost Cause poetry, editing two separate Catholic papers, and finding ways to stir up controversy in most places he went. While his life is quite enthralling and includes brushes with celebrity (e.g., he received James Longstreet into the Catholic Church in March 1877, is mentioned in Margaret Mitchell's *Gone with the Wind*, and was a much-in-demand unreconstructed Confederate postwar speaker), for the purposes of this book on Catholic Civil War chaplains, I will include only two prominent elements of his life.

First was the April 1863 death of his brother David, a Confederate soldier who served for only seven months, while in action in Monticello, Kentucky. Though Abram only found this out a month later, the event shocked and galvanized him. The war then became no longer an abstract ideological cause for him. Ryan made his way south to find his brother's grave, going to Kentucky in an unsuccessful search for what he later called (in his poem "Our Southern Dead") the "sacred dust" of his brother's remains. Returning to Peoria, Illinois, soon thereafter, his sermonizing and pro-Southern temperament got him in further trouble, and that—along with a nasty *Chicago Tribune* article accusing him being a rebel spy and visiting a house of ill-repute—led to his leaving Illinois in November 1863. His whereabouts were unknown until he reappeared in the spring of 1864 in the Nashville area, where he ministered to small Catholic communities before becoming a pastor in Clarksville in November. He spent the next twenty-one years of his life in the south.[13]

Many myths were created, and continue to be rife, about Ryan's mysterious activities during the war years, and his supposed chaplaincy in the Confederate army. Several make him a fully commissioned chaplain in Virginia (though no records prove that), with Charles Pitts (*Chaplains in Grey*) saying he visited Confederate prisoners in St. Louis, and LaSalle "Sallie" Corbell Pickett adding that Ryan both confronted General Benjamin Butler and ministered to epidemic patients in 1862 New Orleans. Two other authors wrote that Ryan was at Fredericksburg watching the Irish Brigade being slaughtered in their futile charge. A 1929 *Commonweal* article inflates a false claim by Vincentian priest Joseph McKey and claims Ryan was at Lookout Mountain in November 1863. Finally, Father Ed Gleeson (*Erin Go Gray!*) attests to Ryan having both a military and spiritual role at Chattanooga, firing a rifle, and then ministering to soldiers.[14]

The actual facts about Ryan being a Confederate chaplain are far more mundane, highly informal and always somewhat inflated. It seems during his time in Tennessee, he did visit some Confederate units in the field, perhaps in late 1863 and the summer of 1864, among them some Louisiana troops, as one Confederate veteran of Cheatham's Tennessee Division would later recall. In early 1865 he wrote to his mother and sister that he had been at the battles of Franklin and Nashville, remarking that "we have had awful times, but I escaped unhurt. . . . I have worked harder in the last months than ever before. I am always on the go." Whatever priestly ministry Ryan did perform for Confederate soldiers, it was always in an unofficial, freelance capacity, for as his biographer David O'Connell remarks, "he preferred to serve whenever and wherever *he* felt he could do some good and did not want to have his freedom restricted by a direct military command."[15]

While ministering in Tennessee and gaining a reputation there as an outstanding speaker, the second important element of Ryan's life came into full bloom—his career as a poet. He had been visiting troops in the field in early 1865, but the Palm Sunday surrender of Lee at Appomattox devastated the twenty-seven-year-old priest. Soon after, from his Knoxville parish, Ryan penned one of his most famous poems, "The Conquered Banner," publishing it under the pseudonym "Moina" three months later in the *New York Freemans Journal*. He later wrote that "in expressing my own emotions at the time, I echoed the unuttered feelings of the Southern people; and so 'The Conquered Banner' became the requiem of the Lost Cause." In the years ahead, the poem would be cited constantly, memorized by countless southern students, and appear on many memorial stones and statues.[16] Its first stanza reads:

Furl that Banner, for tis weary;
Round its staff 'tis drooping dreary;
Furl it, fold it, it is best;
For there's not a man to wave it,
And there's not a sword to save it;
And there's not one left to lave it;
In the blood which heroes gave it;
And its foes now scorn and brave it;
Furl it, hide it—let it rest![17]

The years 1866 and 1867 would be Ryan's most prolific writing years—ten of his twelve most Southern-leaning poems were written in Tennessee in that time, including his immensely popular "The Sword of Robert E. Lee." (Jubal Early invited Ryan to personally recite that poem in June 1880 at the dedication of Lee's statue at Washington College.) Ryan's poems were reprinted in newspapers all over the south, and were first published as a book in 1879 (selling six thousand copies immediately), with a second edition in 1880 receiving rave reviews even from poets like Henry Wadsworth Longfellow, sparking a widespread promotional tour.

As his fame grew, Ryan felt increasingly isolated in pro-Union Knoxville, so he moved on to Georgia, quickly becoming the editor of Bishop Augustin Verot's Catholic paper there. But once again, in that state, Ryan's rabid Lost Cause passions, opposition to Reconstruction, and continual health complaints led to his removal after just two years. From there, it was on to Mobile for his longest stretch of ministry in one place (nearly eleven years), and where he entered into semiretirement at Biloxi on the Mississippi coast. But his preaching was so spellbinding that he was sent by Bishop Quinlan to preach and raise money all over the country—until yet again his brooding, independent, and outspoken personality did him in. His final years were spent in ministerial "wandering" through several states, including Wisconsin and Ohio, where he continued to write and speak. Though he hoped to return to Mobile to die, Ryan's health finally broke down completely while he made a Lenten retreat in Louisville, Kentucky. He died there in April 1886, and was buried in Mobile at a funeral reputedly attended by four thousand people.

To the end, Abram Ryan remained one of America's most notable Civil War–era priests. He was an outspoken, unreconstructed Confederate, a sometimes chaplain (on his own terms), a melancholy spirit, an inveterate nonconformist, and thorn in the side of nearly every bishop and clergyman with whom he served. Yet he was a spellbinding orator; and his poems (characterized by nostalgia, loss, and religious faith) went through forty editions by 1929. He was a personal friend of Longstreet, Davis, Beauregard, and Early, as well as being a household name in the South for generations. A monument to him was dedicated in Mobile in 1913, with similar monuments honoring him in other southern cities. "He lived in a world of dreams and imaginings . . . his vocation was simply 'the poet-priest of the south.'"[18]

PETER WHELAN AND
THE ANDERSONVILLE PRIESTS

In May 1864, the Irish-born Father William John Hamilton (1832–1883), a pastor in Macon whose mission included all of southwest Georgia, happened to be passing through the small town of Americus when he was told that there were Catholic prisoners at a military prison nearby. When he came to Andersonville, Hamilton was immediately aghast at what he saw. He later testified that the place was filthy: "The men all huddled together and covered with vermin . . . the heat was intolerable; there was no air at all in the stockade . . . a great many men [were] perfectly naked, walking about through the stockade . . . [seemingly having] lost all regard for delicacy, shame, morality or anything else." To minister to them, a person would have to "creep on [his] hands and knees into the holes that the men had burrowed into the ground and stretch [himself] out alongside of them to hear their confessions." Receiving a pass from the prison commander, Captain Henry Wirz, Hamilton remained only several hours that day, but returned for three days later both to minister and send a report to his bishop (Augustin Verot, Savannah Diocese). Listing the details of the horrific situation, he stated that a priest was needed full-time for the thousands of prisoners languishing there. (Hamilton later stated at the postwar trial of Henry Wirz that he visited the prison twice, but "had to curtail much of the service Catholic priests minister to the dying because they were so numerous—they died so fast.")[19]

It was into this hellhole that a native of County Wexford, Ireland, the sixty-two-year-old Peter Whelan (1802–1871) was assigned. Ordained in 1830, and the oldest of all Catholic chaplains who served during the Civil War, Whelan had already compiled a long ministry career as a pastor in several places, administrator of the diocese for two years before Verot arrived, and chaplain at Fort Pulaski (also imprisoned there for three months after its 1862 capture). In 1864 he was serving as vicar general and pastor at the Savannah cathedral, as well as ministering in nearby Confederate camps. He arrived at Andersonville on June 16, 1864, to find more than twenty-five thousand men penned up in a 26-acre stockade designed for ten thousand. Whelan remained there for more than four months until October 1864, staying in a 12-by-8-foot wooden hut a mile away, ministering in the humidity of a Georgia summer in which temperatures routinely hit the nineties. He walked to the stockade daily, staying from 9:00 a.m. to sundown, then ate a small meal, prayed his night prayers and fell asleep exhausted, "full of sorrow for what he had seen all day."[20]

Described by fellow chaplain James Sheeran as being "nearly six feet tall, with drab hair, coarse ill-shaped countenance, long arms, short body and long legs, and feet of more than ordinary size," Whelan had little concern for his personal appearance, but was an immensely compassionate and dedicated pastoral leader. As he walked the stockade, prisoners would gather around and ask him questions, since there was no outside news except what new arrivals brought or the guards or doctor might offer. He would crawl on his hands and knees into the improvised shelters called "shebangs" to hear muttered confessions or provide words of comfort or prayer. Every day the priest would meet the wagons coming from the so-called Dead House piled with corpses, arms and limbs dangling from the sides. In July, six prisoners ("armed robbers") were sentenced to death for murder in the camp, and Whelan ministered to the five who were Catholic, trying in vain to gain a stay of execution. No wonder the priest would later say that "no amount of salary could induce me to stay at Andersonville for one week ... not all the gold in the treasury.... It was to allay misery, and gain souls for God."[21]

Though Whelan was at Andersonville the longest, other Catholic priests also joined him in ministry for shorter periods of time (as did one Protestant minister, a Methodist named E. B. Duncan, who came twice). Savannah Bishop Augustin Verot (1804–1876) himself came several times, writing that "without advancing more than twenty steps, I confessed and administered nine sick men and I only stopped at the most urgent cases. The continuous sight of death ... finally dulled all human feelings." When the numbers of prisoners in the camp swelled to nearly thirty-three thousand, Whelan requested more help, and other priests arrived to assist in the overwhelming task at hand. He was joined first by John F. Kirby (?–1872), who was stationed at Augusta, Georgia, and then by the multilingual Jesuit priest Anselm Usannez (1819–1895), stationed at Spring Hill College near Mobile. Usannez was a fellow novice of the above-mentioned Joseph Bixio and was described as returning from his work at Andersonville "covered with merits and with lice." (Usannez is discussed in chapter 5.) Both Usannez and Kirby remained there for only about two weeks before leaving.[22]

On July 15, 1864, the French-born Henry Clavreul (1835–1923) arrived to assist, and he remained until August 20, 1864. Not yet thirty years old, Clavreul was a scholar and writer, and truly unprepared for what he found. He wrote later that he "was taken sick with continual vomiting. Father Whelan decided that I should leave, and so I took the train back to Savannah while the heroic old priest retraced his steps to the stockade." However, Clavreul left behind a truly remarkable document—a short personal diary and record of the names of all the soldiers to whom he had ministered confession and last rites. The list includes three hundred ninety prisoners, complete with names, sacraments, age, units, and nationalities (if known). "The comfort I brought them were the consolations of religion, and these, I may truly say, I gave with all the zeal and energy God's grace enabled me to impart.... I shall not attempt a description of the sufferings we witnessed, whatever may be said or written about it, will always remain below the stern reality."[23]

In August 1864, prison transfers commenced and numbers began to decline, but Whelan felt there was one more thing he could do. Contacting a successful Catholic restaurant owner in Macon (Henry Horne), he borrowed $16,000 in Confederate currency ($500 in Union money) to purchase ten thousand pounds of wheat flour, and had bread baked and delivered to the remaining prisoners. It lasted several months, and Dr. John Bates (the prison physician) said that this much-needed food became known as Whelan's Bread. The prisoners never forgot that event or Whelan's incredible work, with one later writing: "kneeling down by the side of decaying bodies, in the stench and filth of gangrene wards . . . many a time I have seen him thus praying. . . . His services were sought by all, for in his kind and sympathizing looks, his meek but earnest appearance, the despairing prisoners read that all humanity had not forsaken mankind."[24]

When the elderly Whelan returned to Savannah in October 1864, despondency was everywhere as the end of the Confederacy drew near. He himself was beset by a lung ailment that would plague him until the end of his life. He was still vicar general of the diocese and worked diligently to protect churches and cemeteries as new Confederate trenches disturbed graves, and Federal prisoners arrived from the camp and had to be looked after. When the war ended, he regularly visited Jefferson Davis at Fort Monroe, and attempted to get the $400 he had borrowed for bread back from the Federal government. After Edward Stanton asked for proofs of purchase, Whelan replied that he "had neither the health or strength . . . to run over Georgia to hunt up vouchers and bills. . . . Fool-like, I knocked at the wrong door. . . . Did I solicit the President or Mr. Grant, I have no doubt either of them would have refunded me."[25]

News of the horrors of Andersonville soon spread, and with the commander of the camp dead (General John H. Winder), blame fell on the Catholic Captain Henry Wirz (1823–1865). In May 1865 Wirz was arrested and brought to Washington to stand trial, where he was convicted and sentenced to death by hanging. Whelan and Hamilton were called as witnesses for the trial, and both described the horrific conditions they had seen, but spoke well of Wirz, who had seemed anxious for their help, and who to their knowledge had never personally inflicted harm on prisoners. Both priests (also Henry Clavreul and Anselm Usannez) strongly felt that Wirz was merely a symbolic scapegoat made to pay the price for all crimes committed during the war. The two priests visited and ministered to Wirz in prison, appealing unsuccessfully for a brief respite from the long trial he endured. Whelan actually accompanied him to the scaffold on the day of his November 1865 death.[26]

Peter Whelan went on to become pastor of St. Patrick's in Savannah, serving until 1868, but his physical weakness and lung condition continued to plague him. One member said the sick pastor sang the Latin Mass (the norm of the day) "so worn and debilitated . . . that he rather hung from than stood by the altar." His last recorded baptism was in mid-January 1871, and on February 6, 1871, he passed away. This humble, pastoral man reportedly "never wore on his person an ornament or a superfluous article of clothing . . . never uttered an untruth or did a foolish act," never drank nor "partook of a second dish at a meal." The *Savannah Evening News* recorded that his funeral procession four days later was the longest ever seen in the city, and that seldom was so large a gathering of people found in the streets of Savannah.[27]

PATRICK J. R. MURPHY
(58TH ILLINOIS AND CAMP DOUGLAS)

Many chaplains had multiple duties and unique experiences, but few had more of both in his short life than Patrick J. R. Murphy (1824–1869). Born in County Limerick, Ireland, in 1824, he initially studied at an Irish seminary. Murphy was recruited for the now defunct Vincennes Diocese (Indiana) and came to America in September 1846, finishing his studies for priesthood there. He was ordained in March 1848, and after serving in Indianapolis briefly, was named pastor of two churches in Daviess County, Indiana. Murphy was very zealous and dedicated during his ten years of ministry in Indiana, was an excellent speaker, much beloved and highly esteemed even outside Catholic circles. He was twice chosen to be a trustee of Indiana University, and received an honorary doctorate from there in 1865.[28]

In 1858, he left Vincennes for the Chicago Diocese (founded 1843), and was soon organizing the Irish Catholic railroad workers of Mendota, Illinois, into a new church (Holy Cross). By 1862 or 1863 he had become the pastor of St. Patrick's Church in St. Charles, Illinois, and it was from there that his Civil War career began. When the 58th Illinois (also known as the Lyon Color Guard) was organized at Camp Douglas in February 1862, he enrolled as chaplain, perhaps because parts of three companies of the 58th came from Kane County, where St. Charles was located. No reports exist of his activities with the regiment through their engagements at Fort Donelson, Shiloh, Iuka, Vicksburg, and the Meridian Campaign, but on March 17, 1864, while on the Red River Campaign, he was captured by Confederates around Markville, Louisiana. A doctor captured the same day (Elisha P. Clarke, 31st Massachusetts), recorded later that the two of them were taken to General Richard Taylor's Confederate headquarters and assigned a tent together. "Father Murphy proved to be a whole-souled comrade who gave and received sympathy in our mutual misfortunes in a manner that endeared him to me for all time. He was sent through the lines and released on the second or third day, bearing a letter to my wife from me."[29]

After his capture and parole, Murphy was sent to Alexandria, Louisiana, and then returned to the Chicago Diocese, formally resigning with an amusing but lengthy letter dated July 4, 1864. In it he gives five reasons for his decision, including his impaired medical condition and rheumatism brought on by "the hardship of sleeping on the ground," inability to endure "the intense and oppressive heat of this semi-tropical climate," and "never having been allowed to transport a tent for Religious duties." Returning to Chicago, he was named pastor in October 1864, but his zeal for ministering to soldiers was not quenched, for in that same month, his bishop (James Duggan) appointed him "as chaplain to Catholic inmates of Camp Douglas of whom there are now many destitute of all spiritual aid." That same month, Colonel Benjamin Sweet, Commander at Camp Douglas, formally authorized Murphy to "visit Camp Douglas and such soldiers as may desire his services; also prisoners of war of his faith . . . when [he] desires to visit the Prison Hospital he will be allowed to do so by reporting to the Surgeon in Charge."[30]

Often called one of the "Andersonvilles of the North," Camp Douglas became known for its appalling conditions and death rate: about 17 percent, with some 4,275 known Confederate prisoners being buried at the Chicago City Cemetery. (Between 1865 and 1867, all Confederate dead from the cemetery and prison grounds were reinterred into Chicago's Oak Woods Cemetery.) Ten of the camp's sixty acres were known as Hospital Square and served as the hospital quarters. It was there that Murphy spent much of time in his eleven months at Camp Douglas. Thanks to highly accurate church record-keeping, the name "P. J. Murphy" is listed on the baptism records of some 250 Confederate prisoners of war at Camp Douglas who were received into the Catholic Church, though Murphy admits the names of many "may have accidentally been lost." From the detailed church records of 136 of those Confederates baptized by Murphy, 79 are also recorded as dying between October 1864 and May 1865. Surely Patrick Murphy at Camp Douglas must have agreed with his Southern compatriot at Andersonville, Peter Whelan, who regularly fell asleep exhausted, "full of sorrow for what he had seen all day."[31]

Murphy endured until August 1865 in his prison and hospital chaplaincy at Camp Douglas, being formally mustered out on August 21, likely with health issues as a result of his work. He would remain pastor at St. James in Chicago until December 1866, when yet again he made another ministry move—this time into the Dubuque Diocese, where he became pastor at St. Mary's in Waverly, Iowa. (The 1862 Homestead Acts had attracted settlers to the state, including Irish Catholics.) In 1868 Murphy completed the first church building there, and built several others in area communities, all the while ministering to numerous Catholic mission "stations" in surrounding counties. From parish histories of the time, his energy, esteem, and skills had certainly not diminished, as he continued to give talks and lectures in the area.

But on August 31, 1869, on his way to visit family and friends in Vincennes, Indiana, he attempted to step off the train platform to retrieve some forgotten baggage. In doing so, Father Murphy's feet got caught and he was dragged under the wheels, horribly mangling his body and head. Two hours later, the young Irish priest died at the railroad junction house, was carried to the Catholic cathedral, then waked and buried the next week in Daviess County. Just the Sunday before, Murphy had confirmed no less than three hundred children connected to his parish in Waverly, Iowa. This author presumes that the much-traveled Irish priest found his final destination to be his last and best.[32]

MINISTRY TO GERMANS:
FRANCIS FUSSEDER AND GUSTAV MIETTINGER

It is estimated that as much as a quarter of the Union army was made up of men not born in America. Of these, the largest group were the Germans, who comprised nearly 10 percent of the Union army—with perhaps as many as 216,000 being native-born Germans, and another 250,000 being first-generation German-Americans. (Only a few hundred served in the Confederacy, and those were primarily third- and fourth- generation men descended from earlier immigrants.) Commonly referred to as "Dutchmen" by Union soldiers, and "lop-eared Dutch" by Confederates, several prominent Germans did become highly influential officers in the Union army. Major General Franz Sigel was the highest-ranking German-American officer, with Carl Schurz, August Willich, Louis Blenker, Max Weber, and Max Schimmelfennig also rising to the rank of general.[33]

While Germans did indeed faithfully bring their heritage, institutions, and customs to America, they did not bring religious unity. Roughly half of German-Americans were Roman Catholics and half were Protestants (mainly Lutheran, Evangelical, or Reformed), and centuries of old-country enmities between them did not disappear when they arrived in America. Likewise, the vociferous and radical "Forty-Eighter" immigrants (named after the failed 1848 national revolution in Germany) also caused division in the German-American community (especially old stock Americans). They tended to be atheists harshly critical of all organized religions and clerics—particularly Roman Catholics.[34]

Wisconsin supplied the second largest number of native-born Germans for the Union (some thirty thousand), with the heavily German city of Milwaukee being a major recruiting center (along with Cincinnati and St. Louis). In the late summer of 1862, recruiting in the German-American community was taking place in Milwaukee County, and thirty-three young men from Port Washington enlisted to "fight mit Sigel." The pastor of the Catholic church (St. Mary's) in Port Washington at the time was a native Austrian named Franz (Francis) Fusseder (1825–1888), who had come to American in 1847 after being recruited by Milwaukee Bishop John Henni (1805–1881). After his 1850 ordination, Fusseder had served in numerous diocesan parishes before taking the pastorship in Port Washington in January 1860. As the story goes, Fusseder saw the heavy recruiting from his own parish, and reputedly said to his members, "Boys, if you are all going to the war, I'll go too."

He then applied to the Prussian-born Governor Edward Salomon for a commission as chaplain of the 24th, received it, and was with his "boys" as they became Company H of the 24th Wisconsin, a heavily German regiment. They trained at "the city of beer and pale bricks" (as dubbed by one soldier), at a camp on Milwaukee's east side named after Franz Sigel, the German immigrant popular among Milwaukee's burghers. In his book on the 24th Wisconsin, William Beaudot remarks that "also traveling to Milwaukee with the volunteers from Port Washington was a Catholic priest named Franz Fusseder, prepared to provide religious sustenance to the soldiers. The regimental chaplain was an immigrant from Austria, and the first graduate of the new Saint Francis Seminary on Milwaukee's southern fringe. The 36-year-old blue-eyed clergyman became quite popular with the men as much for his card-playing as for his fractured way with the English language."[35]

The colonel of the 24th Wisconsin was Charles Larrabee, but the adjutant was a man whose family would become well-known in American military history—Arthur MacArthur (whose son was Douglas MacArthur). The regiment left the state for Louisville, Kentucky, on September 5, 1862, and from Kentucky moved through Indiana, Ohio, Tennessee, Georgia, Alabama, and back to Tennessee. While stories about Fusseder's ten months of service with the 24th Wisconsin are scarce, Beaudot does relate that the Austrian priest fractured the English language fairly frequently. In fall of 1862, an officer satirically cited God's providential care for the regiment before their tents very belatedly arrived, remarking that, as their "worthy chaplain" Father Fusseder would say, "God Almighty, he dakes care mit de Dwenty-Fort Regiment." It was noted that Fusseder "would take umbrage with the officer's representation of Teutonic-accented words."[36]

At the Battle of Stones River (December 1863), Fusseder was cited for confronting two cowardly officers.

During the battle, the portly & fun-loving Father Fusseder had accompanied wagons of wounded trundling to Nashville during the battle. On an early return trip to Murfreesboro, he encountered a 24th Wisconsin officer, likely [the politician] Cam Reed. The 'Captain crawled on his hands and knees to the hospital, was taken prisoner there, and with a red string around his arm, and was paroled as a hospital nurse. The same officer, Fusseder attested, had earlier urged Major Hibbard to "march the regiment to Nashville." Reed's brief military career came to an end ingloriously when he was cashiered from service for cowardice.

The good cleric also encountered [Company B's Capt. Bill] Eldred on one of his trips back to Murfreesboro for wounded soldiers. . . . The Captain had gotten himself out of harm's way, and was "sitting by the wayside when the Chaplain came riding along." Eldred hailed the priest, asking if he could carry any mail to Nashville. The Chaplain replied that it was no time to talk upon such a subject, and that he ought to be ashamed of himself, and had better return to his regiment and fight for his country. During the cleric's denunciation, another regiment marched past, overhearing the two Wisconsin men. "They gave three cheers for the Chaplain, and three groans for the Captain." . . . Bill Eldred was permitted to resign his commission, and leave the regiment.[37]

Fusseder served faithfully with the 24th Wisconsin until July 1863, when some unstated medical issues prevented him from continuing in service with the regiment. He resigned his commission and returned to Milwaukee for a year to recover his health. However, his interest in the chaplaincy apparently had been piqued, because when he recovered a year later, he decided to return to the Union armies in the western theater, which at the time were in the trenches at Atlanta, Georgia. He was again commissioned as chaplain, this time of the 17th Wisconsin, replacing Joseph "Napolean" Mignault (1826–1895), whose two-year service had been cut short by serious health issues brought on by the Vicksburg Campaign, forcing his resignation in February 1864. (Cf. chapter 7 for further information on Mignault.)

In July 1864, Fusseder mustered in with the 17th Wisconsin in the Army of the Tennessee, a group sometimes called the "Irish Regiment," although it seems it was actually not an ethnic regiment but one of far more of mixed national heritages. The Austrian cleric served with them through Sherman's March to the Sea, the Carolina Campaign, and ultimately the Grand Review in Washington. Fusseder mustered out with the regiment in Louisville, Kentucky, on July 14, 1865, and returned to the Milwaukee Diocese to resume his pastoral ministry. He served in several parishes before becoming pastor in Beaver Dam (St. Peter's Church), where he ministered until his death in July 1888.[38]

The second German priest who worked with German Union troops, or at least briefly attempted to do so, was Gustav Miettinger (1812–1869). Born in Germany, Miettinger first came on the American church scene around 1860 as a priest working in the Albany Diocese. He was pastor in a church in Nassau, New York, then at St. Lawrence Church in Troy, where he was the first pastor of the new Catholic community. It was in that area that soldiers for the 2nd New York Infantry (which became known as the Troy Regiment) were recruited when the war began, and the regiment was subsequently mustered in for two years in May 1861. The records indicate that on June 14, 1861, Miettinger was also mustered in as one of two regimental chaplains, and that he served until March 1862. There is scant information on his time there, but apparently issues arose relating to his language skills and his desire to transfer elsewhere.

Aidan Germain writes about Miettinger's ten-month service, stating that "the good will of our German citizens toward the Union cause is amply attested . . . here is a case of a German priest who, with the best will possible, was unable to give effective service because of the limitations encountered by the authorities in making assignments." It appears that after six months service with the 2nd New York, Miettinger decided that his situation there was unsatisfactory, as the soldiers were mostly Irish and Protestant. He then expressed his preference to serve a German regiment with many Catholics, stating that he was a professor, and spoke three languages (English, French, and German). The implication therein appears to be that he felt his English was good enough for confessional purposes, but not for sermon preaching and general chaplain duties. Also, it seems his confidence in the English language didn't allow him to write to Departmental Headquarters in any other language than German. There was no such German regiment available, and therefore Miettinger was discharged on March 3, 1862.[39]

The facts of his short wartime service fit the profile of his nonwartime ministry as well. Between 1859 and 1869, aside from his Civil War chaplaincy, Miettinger ministered entirely to largely Germanspeaking congregations in at least five different dioceses around the country, rarely remaining in one diocese for more than several years. While his language skills made him a valuable asset for bishops (hence his ability to find work), it seems clear he had some personal shortcomings as well. In his book *Excommunicated from the Union*, Will Kurtz refers obliquely to Miettinger (his oft-misspelled name is not mentioned), remarking that Albany Bishop John McCloskey "allowed" him to serve in the 2nd New York, but "did not want him to return, [and] quickly agreed to allow him to leave for another diocese." In his next "stop," the Fort Wayne Diocese, Bishop John Luers wrote in November 1865 to Bishop John Purcell (Cincinnati) that "what [was said] of Father (Gustave) Miettinger is true. Miettinger is a fine worker but no pastor."[40]

Miettinger then went on to serve at a parish in the Alton Diocese in Illinois, where in July 1867 he was "relieved of his charge" of a New Berlin, Illinois, church by that bishop. Finally, he made his way to what was then the Milwaukee Diocese (now Green Bay) in Wisconsin, where he ended his priestly career at the German Roman Catholic immigrant community at St. Ann's Church in Holstein, Wisconsin. After ministering as pastor for two years, Miettinger died there in August 1869 and was buried in the parish cemetery. Whatever the personal challenges were that kept this German priest on the move in ministry, it certainly would seem that his energy was never wanting, nor his desire lacking to serve his fellow German Catholics wherever he found them.

PART 4

FROM THE VANTAGE POINT OF HISTORY

Religion was central to the meaning of the Civil War,
as the generation that experienced the war tried to understand it.
Religion should be central to our efforts to recover that meaning.

—JAMES MCPHERSON

CHAPTER 12

IN RETROSPECT

Consequences, Challenges, and Changes

In 1865, America's most deadly war ended—concluding with poignancy at Appomattox Courthouse (April 9), anti-climax in the Carolinas (April 26), and a last gasp effort by the Confederates at Palmetto Ranch, Texas (May 12–13). What was this most deadly American war all about? Why did soldiers fight and die, enslaved persons dream and rejoice, chaplains preach and comfort, politicians scheme, and everyone suffer? What were the ultimate results and consequences of these four historic years?

Certainly death—as many as 750,000 were dead total, with an estimated 30 percent of the Confederate army dead from wounds or disease. Certainly destruction—the South was devastated in property, buildings, politics, economy, and political structure, and would take decades to recover. Certainly political and military defeat—one side finally surrendered, the side that had been in rebellion, supporting states' rights and race-based chattel slavery.

From the broadly religious perspective, the following consequences could also be added:

- the "religion" of the postwar Lost Cause (e.g., the near "saintly" status later given to Confederate warriors like Lee and Jackson),
- the massive and seemingly deliberate destruction of southern churches and property by some Union soldiers,

- Black religious self-determination (the meteoric postwar rise of independent African American churches and educational institutions),
- role changes brought on by the war (the increased "masculinization" of postwar Christianity, women's increased visible roles in society, emergence of the "social gospel" in the North), and
- the rise of American "civil religion" (with new nationalistic symbols representing America's "soul"—national monuments, texts like the Declaration of Independence, the American flag, and patriotic "holy days" like Independence Day and Memorial Day).[1]

What of all the Catholic priest-chaplains who ministered, comforted, and struggled right along with their troops? From our historical vantage point over a century and a half removed from the Civil War, we can identify and reflect upon the deeper meaning of several consequences from a war that not only impacted the priest-chaplains, but also the faith and culture of which they were a part.

THE PHYSICAL TOLL: SICKNESS AND DEATH

As mentioned in chapter 3, Catholic priests had advantages in camp and on campaign which, in some measure, helped spare them some of the worst problems that befell regular troops. They often had more physical "resources" available to them while on campaign—friendly Catholic homes where they could visit and take in a meal, as well as area Catholic churches or religious houses where they could sleep in a real bed, clean up, and rest for a few days. Some Catholic chaplains also had orderlies assigned to them, Catholic soldiers who helped care for the mundane things (e.g., horses, Mass materials, tents, food) if these troops were not needed for military purposes. Lastly, because of the nature of their military commitment (they were commissioned and not draftees or volunteers, as soldiers were) priests could more easily take leaves if seriously sick or in need of supplies, or even resign without penalty if they were called back to their diocese or if they faced serious health issues.

But like all soldiers and officers of both armies, Catholic priests were not exempt from facing the physical challenges rampant in the grueling everyday life of Civil War armies. The first and most obvious consequence was one affecting all soldiers—the rigors of traveling on campaigns, lack of nourishing food, sickness, and death. The death toll of the Civil War was long recorded as about 623,000; although one demographic historian, Dr. J. David Hacker, recently offered a recalculation of that amount, raising it to perhaps 750,000 dead on both sides. Disease was the primary killer of combatants—twice as many soldiers died of disease than bullets (with diarrhea and dysentery being the leading killers, and malaria next).[2]

This certainly held true for Catholic chaplains as well; the major elements impacting their length of service were their health issues. The average term of service for all Catholic chaplains in general was eighteen and a half months (cf. chapter 13). Of the seventy-six official Catholic chaplains identified in this book, only fourteen though served three years, and thirty-seven served less than twelve months. Forty-nine priests are considered occasional or situational chaplains (meaning they had other ministries, but served troops off and on for whatever time they could give). In my research, I have found only a handful of Catholic chaplains who made it through the war without *some* health or sickness issues (which led to leaves of absences or resignations for medical reasons). The lists below will briefly outline the chaplains whose military careers were cut short—either literally (by death) or militarily because of health issues.

CHAPLAINS WHOSE TERMS OF SERVICE WERE AFFECTED OR SHORTENED BY SICKNESS

The following Catholic chaplains had terms of service who were severely affected by the personal health issues that occurred during their time of ministry among the troops.

- Thaddeus Butler (23rd Illinois): a Chicago priest, he resigned in March 1863 "on account of infirmity incident to the service."[3]
- Richard Christy (78th Pennsylvania): this beloved three-year chaplain in the Army of the Cumberland "was in delicate health as the

war broke out," and was sent home four times at least because of illness, but always returned. His 1878 death was partially attributed to sickness incurred while on military duty.[4]

- Peter Paul Cooney CSC (35th Indiana): another beloved chaplain of the Army of the Cumberland, Cooney was "worn out by fatigue and almost a wreck" by 1864 according to one biographer, but was convinced to remain by the heartfelt petitions of his soldiers.[5]

- Edward P. Corcoran (61st Ohio): he caught tuberculosis after being captured by Confederates on his way to Washington, DC, was forced to resign early, and died shortly after the war (December 1866).

- Pierre Felix Dicharry (3rd Louisiana): after being captured and then imprisoned in bad circumstances, his weakened health led to an early resignation in August 1862.

- Joseph Dillon CSC (63rd New York): resigned after a year in the Irish Brigade, his lung issues exacerbated by his service. He never quite regained his health, and died in December 1868.

- Frances Fusseder (24th Wisconsin): ill health terminated his ten-month chaplaincy, and greatly affected his priestly life after the war.

- Paul Gillen CSC (170th New York): his resignation in August 1864 was based on "my advanced age, and the arduous duties that have devolved upon me . . . my health has been effectually undermined . . . I append the certificate of the Surgeon-in-chief of the Brigade."[6]

- Darius Hubert SJ (1st Louisiana): after three years of field service, he was diagnosed with tuberculosis and other debilitating medical conditions. He never resigned his chaplaincy, but while recovering in Richmond, he was reassigned to the Richmond hospitals and continued in that role until his parole in April 1865.[7]

- John Benjamin Ireland (5th Minnesota): according to his March 1863 resignation letter, he resigned because of reduced numbers in his regiment and clergy shortages in his diocese, but other documentation speaks of some health issues as well.[8]

- Thomas Kelly (90th Illinois): resigned after nine months of service, stating "my health is so bad that I am unable to discharge my proper duties, and therefore, in justice to the regiment and Govt., I tender my resignation." He died in 1864, weakened by the sickness he picked up in Yazoo City.[9]

- Michael Martin (69th Pennsylvania): after only eight months with his regiment, especially in the Peninsula Campaign, he was "discharged for disability" in June 1862.[10]
- Edward McKee (116th Pennsylvania): "wounds received or sickness contracted at the battle of Fredericksburg seems to have terminated the military career of Edward McKee." The subsequent surgeon's report of December 1862 states that McKee was "incapacitated for the performance of his duties as chaplain."[11]
- Laurence McMahon (28th Massachusetts): was forced to resign in May 1863 due to "disability incurred in the line of duty." Upon then journeying to his Bishop's house, this twenty-eight-year-old priest collapsed on the floor, and did not get out of bed for eleven months.[12]
- Napoleon Mignault (17th Wisconsin): the "vicissitudes of the strenuous Vicksburg campaign told on him," and he was honorably discharged due to physical disability in February 1864.[13]
- Daniel Mullen (9th Connecticut): his regiment was also in the Vicksburg Campaign, where he was diagnosed with "typhoid Fever and diarrhoea [*sic*] contracted while in camp opposite Vicksburg." He was deemed "unfit for duty, the prospect of recovery while in a Southern climate being distant and uncertain," and was discharged in August 1862.[14]
- Patrick J. Murphy (58th Illinois): another victim of the Vicksburg Campaign, he resigned on July 4, 1864, giving five reasons for his action, three of which pertained to his health ("sufferings and privations of the campaigns . . . rheumatism because of exposure and sleeping on the ground . . . the intense and oppressive heat").[15]
- Laurence P. O'Connell (Confederate post chaplain): after about sixteen months as chaplain in Virginia, he was present at the February 1865 burning of Columbia, South Carolina, before being relieved by his bishop due to his weakened condition ("two winters in the mountains have pretty much broken him down"). His 1894 death was partially attributed to the "inflammatory rheumatism" contracted during his chaplaincy.[16]

- Leo Rizzo (9th Connecticut): although on military records as serving for three months, the scholarly Rizzo was unable to get a horse and had trouble with the physical strain of marching and being in the field. He was hospitalized about a month after joining the regiment, and likely had typhoid fever, all of which wore him down "near to death at one point." Due to his weakened condition, Rizzo was discharged in October 1864 while on a twenty-day leave.[17]

- Patrick Ryan (post chaplain, Charleston): a native Irishman, Ryan endured prewar prejudice, insults, and even an attack on his life. After ministering most of the war in camps and hospitals, he seems to have been weakened both physically and emotionally, because in 1867 he was granted a long leave of absence in Rome. He returned refreshed, but transferred to the Baltimore Diocese.[18]

- Thomas Scully (9th Massachusetts): not only was he captured during the Peninsula Campaign, but he also needed a medical leave of absence after it was over "to recruit my health which for some weeks before the late battles was very infirm, and greatly impaired by the recent hardship."[19]

- Damaso Taladrid (1st New Mexico): his August 1863 letter of resignation commented that he "took this step on account of ill health—my bodily age and infirmities are such that I cannot bear the many exposures incident to the active service . . . and perform my active duties." As stated in an earlier chapter, his disapproval of his regiment's new orders to pursue Navajos may also have motivated his decision.[20]

- Peter Tissot SJ (37th New York): despite prewar health concerns, he was an effective chaplain for two years, although he required several military leaves to recover from various health issues ("derangements of stomach, liver and bowels"). Those issues, and his ongoing fragile health led to his retirement and death in 1875.[21]

- Joseph Titta (Gombitelli) OFM (13th Pennsylvania Cavalry): resigned after six months not because of health but because "three-fourths of the members of the Reg't. are of a different Religious denomination from my own."[22]

- Charles Truyens SJ (12th Kentucky): former missionary to indigenous tribes in Kansas Territory. Though not in any official Union records, Truyens served for about six weeks in Kentucky with Union troops before his health broke down, and he resigned in March 1862.

- Peter Whelan (post chaplain; Andersonville): in 1861, he was the oldest of all Catholic chaplains (fifty-nine years old in 1861) and was running the Savannah Diocese in the absence of his bishop. Imprisoned for three months in 1862 when Fort Pulaski was captured, his months at Andersonville further weakened him, giving him lung congestion in 1866. Although one parish member said he "hung from rather than stood by the altar," Whelan persevered in ministry until his death in 1871.[23]

An incident from the life of William Corby himself, as related in his *Memoirs*, illustrates the personal side of contracting an illness while serving. While the Irish Brigade was in the unhealthful Chickahominy River swamps of Virginia (where malaria killed far more soldiers than bullets), Corby wrote that he became extremely sick. His Holy Cross compatriot, James Dillon, and Catholic nuns serving in the hospitals helped care for him, as his *Memoirs* relate.

June 17: I felt queerly, and being usually healthy I complained to my friends, particularly Father Dillon . . . about June 18, I reeled and fell to the ground. I was put on board a steamer, bound for Washington. Father Dillon saw that I was placed on a berth on board, with my coat for a pillow. . . . [in Washington] under the care of the good Sisters of Charity, I lay insensible with a burning fever for three days. Persons were placed to watch me day and night. Thanks to the good medical treatment and excellent care of the Sisters, I soon recovered. Being removed in good time from the malarial camp, no doubt helped . . . Poor Father Dillon, who so kindly assisted me in that sickness, contracted the [same] disease that carried him to an early grave in 1868. . . .[24]

Four priests have just been mentioned who were greatly weakened during their Civil War service and died within a few years after having been weakened by those illnesses: Richard Christy, Thomas Kelly,

James Dillon, and Peter Whelan. However, the following priest-chaplains also died during or shortly after the war as a direct result of their Civil War service:

- Emmeran Bliemel OSB (10th Tennessee): Bliemel was killed by a cannon ball while giving the sacrament of the sick (extreme unction) to his commanding officer during battle at Jonesborough on August 31, 1864.
- Thomas Brady (15th Michigan): his health weakened while ministering to the sick at Chattanooga hospitals in early 1865. He marched with his regiment in the Grand Review in Washington on September 3, 1865, but died a week later in a Washington hospital.
- Ghislaine Boheme (16th Mississippi): suffering previously from dysentery, this fifty-nine-year-old chaplain (one of the oldest Catholic chaplains) suffered a massive stroke and died within minutes on June 27, 1862. (Another source has the death date as June 23, with a letter noted in the Notre Dame Archives saying he died in the tent of Stonewall Jackson.)[25]
- Julian Prosper Bourget CSC (hospital chaplain): only newly arrived from France, he was sent by Notre Dame president Father Sorin to work in the military hospital at Mound City, Illinois. His stay was not long; he contracted malaria while caring for the soldiers and died at the hospital on June 12, 1862.
- Basil Elia: an unofficial chaplain, this Mississippi pastor was allowed to minister at Young's Point, Louisiana, during the Vicksburg Campaign. He had only been there three weeks when he caught one of the many diseases rampant in that swampy environment and died on April 2, 1863.
- Julian Guillou (Corinth, Washington Artillery): although not listed in Confederate records, Guillou was at Corinth attending the wounded in the Tishomingo Hotel. During the first week in May, when most of the sick and wounded had been evacuated, a much weakened and ailing Guillou returned to his church, dying of consumption on February 7, 1863.
- Zepherin Joseph Lévêque CSC (New Jersey troops?): this Canadian priest of the Holy Cross community was very zealous, but

also sickly. Serving for only a few months, he died in a state of exhaustion in New Jersey on February 13, 1862.

- John McCosker (55th Pennsylvania): despite his scant formal history, it is recorded that he served his troops faithfully until hardship and disease weakened him, and he died in June 1862 while on a leave of absence to procure more supplies for Mass.

- John Nealis OP: while a pastor in Chattanooga, Tennessee, and an occasional chaplain during the war, he was attacked in that city by three "ruffians" in mid-1862. They beat him up and shot him, and although he survived the attack, the resultant perennial fainting spells led to him falling to his death from an upper window at the Nashville cathedral in March 1864.

- Francis Pont (13th Louisiana): after serving at Corinth and with Louisiana troops, he was a victim of the 1867 yellow fever epidemic, dying on September 27, 1867.

- Isadore Turgis (30th Louisiana): in poor health after several years of service, he died in 1868 in New Orleans, having been further weakened by the 1867 yellow fever epidemic.

Many Civil War accounts contain stories of near misses—soldiers escaping death or serious injury because of some purely random even inconsequential reason. Several Catholic priests also avoided death by the closest of margins. Darius Hubert was wounded at Gettysburg, and also survived a near fatal shot during the Battle of Second Manassas; the Union bullet that hit his kit is today held in New Orleans's Confederate Memorial Hall. Isadore Turgis reputedly narrowly escaped death at Shiloh when a grape shot hit and killed the wounded Union officer he was carrying off the battlefield. As related earlier (chapter 7), John Bannon survived two near misses from artillery shells (and being incapacitated with diarrhea for two weeks) during the long Vicksburg siege.[26]

The Dominican Joseph Jarboe became vicar general of the Nashville Diocese postwar but had two wartime close calls. A bullet shattered a knife he was holding as he labored at Shiloh over a wounded soldier; at that same battle he was captured by Union pickets, brought before General William "Bull" Nelson, and almost shot as a spy, until he was recognized by the provost marshal. Jeremiah Trecy too was captured in September 1862, but was fortunate to be brought to the Catholic General William Rosecrans. Trecy then was doubly blessed when three bullets passed harmlessly through his coat at the September 1863 Battle of Chickamauga.

A Bible passage says that death comes like a thief in the night (Matthew 24:42–44). The priests who served amidst the horrible uncertainties of battle certainly knew that passage well. Though not spared from the reality it described, perhaps because of their own faith and belief, they were better prepared to meet the "thief" when it showed up unexpectedly on their own doorstep.

INTERDENOMINATIONAL CHALLENGES AND CONSEQUENCES

In chapter 1, we cited religious historian Sydney Ahlstrom about the prejudice against Catholics latent in American history. Ahlstrom remarks that in fact "a fierce tradition of anti-Catholicism, both visceral and dogmatic, is one of Puritanism's most active legacies to Anglo-American civilization."[27] Those prejudices were carried into the Civil War world, where Catholics ("Papists") were mistrusted for theological and nativist reasons, and for so-called allegiance to the foreign power of a pope.

The 1865 memoirs of a young Confederate soldier (Philip Stephenson, 13th Arkansas) seem to reflect this bias, referring as it does to the "debauched Irish soldiers" in his company. He writes that they not only drank to excess but engaged in "deeds of secrecy and violence . . . to satisfy immediate lusts, such as marrying green country girls and deserting them when the army moved away." Stephenson then comments that "a wicked little priest, Father Carius, would come to them periodically, erect his tent, and absolve them all, they confessing with the greatest outward reverence. The afterward he would gamble and drink with them." Although deeper research into the veracity of these strong accusations is needed, Stephenson's comments aptly reflect the overall tone of prejudice against Catholics that existed among many Protestants in the war.[28]

But on a positive note, other Confederates—wounded and recovering in hospitals—reflected prejudice both spoken and yet overcome, thanks to the work of Catholic hospital nuns. Hippolyte Gache wrote that when many Confederate wounded were asked by a priest in the hospital if they wanted to be baptized Catholics, they would respond, "Oh no . . . I don't like that church a bit! I never seen a Catholic, but I've heard a lot about them. The sisters' church is the church for me!' . . . And the next thing you know, they'd be asking on their death beds to be baptized in the Catholic church." The powerful and positive influence of Catholic sister-nurses in the Civil War is well captured in the words of two contemporary authors. In *Excommunicated from the Union*, William Kurtz says that "the selfless devotions of these women . . . did more to rehabilitate the church in the eyes of Protestant Americans than did the actions of Catholic chaplains or soldiers." Gracjan Kraszewski remarks in his 2020 book, *Catholic Confederates*, that the sister-nurses "in the end proved to be the Civil War's most evangelically effective Catholics."[29]

It was in this turbulent environment of nativism and bigotry that Catholic priest-chaplains had to minister as America's deadliest conflict unfolded. Some priest-chaplains had immediate challenges with bias when they began their work. Richard Christy (78th Pennsylvania) faced initial resistance from his mainly Protestant regiment, yet won them over by his dedicated and selfless service. When Michael Nash (6th New York) joined his regiment, he had no trouble working with the Catholic Colonel William Wilson, but winning over the predominantly Protestant officers took considerably longer. They freely admitted they had never spoken with a Catholic priest before, and had been leery of having him.

Paul Gillen clearly perceived religious prejudice in October 1861 when a colonel stopped Catholic troops on the way to Mass, claiming they were simply going to get drunk. Peter Paul Cooney and four other Catholic chaplains of the Army of the Cumberland (Christy, Trecy, Fusseder, and O'Higgins) banded together in the summer of 1863 to counteract the divisive proselytizing efforts of the United States Christian Commission (USCC, founded by Protestant evangelicals). Cooney later happily recorded that the USCC had little effect on the soldiers after their appearance, and their failure there offered "the clearest proof of the impotency of Protestantism which has no power over the heart."[30]

As related earlier in chapter 1, Louis Lambert (18th Illinois) experienced immense resistance from the regiment's predominantly Protestant officers who petitioned for his removal in December 1861. After stating bluntly they wanted a Protestant chaplain, they began a litany of possibly dubious criticisms against Lambert (claiming he did not hold religious services, never visited the sick, nor filed a report), then demanded he be withdrawn as chaplain. Deeper research would be needed to determine the veracity of each of these specific charges, but all things taken together, in Lambert's case, it is not a surprise that he resigned from the predominantly Protestant regiment four months later.[31]

Catholic priests themselves were not exempt from looking down on their Protestant counterparts, however, nor from being strong Catholic apologists amidst the polarized, non-ecumenical attitudes of their day. The First Vatican Council of the Catholic Church would happen shortly after the war (June 1868), and its controversial doctrine of "infallibility" (the pope cannot err when speaking on matters of faith and morals) captured well the "fortress mentality" that permeated the Catholic Church of the late nineteenth century. A number of Catholic wartime chaplains regularly expressed negativity toward their Protestant counterparts, focusing mostly on lazy Protestant chaplains who were not spiritually motivated (and did not place themselves in danger during the war) but were eager for the pay. Typical of the times, this frequently got expressed as a kind of Catholic "we are better than Protestants" attitude.

This triumphalistic mentality can be seen in the strong comments made toward Protestants by Catholic chaplains such as Peter Cooney (see his comment above), Thomas Scully, and perhaps most frequently in James Sheeran's diary and Hippolyte Gache's letters. Though motivated by slightly different personal reasons, that innate Catholic apologetical attitude so common to many Catholics of the day clearly shines through this pair's wartime writings.[32]

Although Sheeran never refused ministry to any soldier, when the issue of faith did emerge, he was not shy about speaking out in favor of Catholicism. In March 1864, when told about a Virginia soldier sentenced to be shot, Sheeran wrote that "he was not a Catholic, yet I resolved to try and save his soul. . . . I reminded him I was a Catholic priest and consequently believed that in order to save his soul it was necessary to become a member of the Catholic Church; and I gave him some reasons for so believing." Sheeran was successful in this conversion, writing that even the soldier's strongly Protestant mother was grateful he had been baptized. He then went on to comment on a "nasally sound of a Protestant minister singing a hymn," writing that "he resolved not to be disturbed by him . . . [and I] soon had the whole regiment, Protestants as well as Catholics, around me."[33]

He also wrote of a more contentious encounter with the wife of a landlord where he was spending the night. She was "extremely pious and in her own opinion well versed in Scripture," and Sheeran described their dialogue. "'Don't the people think that you are their saviour?' 'No, ma'am, they're not such fools.' 'Well, don't you pretend to forgive sins?' 'No, ma'am, we make no pretensions at all, but we do actually forgive them, because God has given us the power and authority to do so.'" Sheeran then took the offensive, remarking, "I perceive ma'am, that you are very ignorant to the Catholic religion, I would advise you then to act reasonably and suspend your judgment about the Catholic Church, until you make yourself acquainted with its doctrines." He then went on to explain Catholic teaching on confession, saying that "she became somewhat reasonable in as much as she acknowledged her own ignorance." He left the next day, having met another woman who had never seen a Catholic priest, and "after a few minutes conversation, I think I left her under the impression that priests were at least not devils."[34]

Though always outspoken, Sheeran seemingly did at least make sincere efforts to maintain a public civility when confronting religious differences. The Jesuit priest Hippolyte Gache, on the other hand, was not so reserved in expressing his sentiments to his fellow Jesuits. (Though, in his defense, Gache likely never suspected his letters would be published for the world to see.) The sharp-tongued, outspoken Frenchman was an ultra-orthodox Catholic apologist, already ready to quibble with any perceived "threat" demeaning Catholicism. His English was never great, but he always found words to express his displeasure and intolerance of Protestants.[35]

In a September 1861 discussion with the Confederate General John Bankhead Magruder, Gache's attitude is clearly seen. In talking about his experiences thus far, Gache writes, "Tis curious how much more esteem educated and intelligent men have for Catholicism than they seem to have for the Protestant sects. This is particularly evident where there are two chaplains—the Catholic receives all the attention and respect and the Protestant is forgotten. This is my opinion is a sign that a great harvest is ripening in America." Two months later, Gache couldn't resist commenting on how well people at Mass listened to his Catholic preaching, as opposed to area Protestants. "The Protestants there . . . were delighted to hear Christian doctrine presented with such clarity, precision, and economy—qualities which they have never observed in their own ministers."[36]

The Jesuit Gache frequently took issue with "privileges" given to Protestant chaplains. In June 1863, he expressed his displeasure with a new policy for celebrating military funerals at cemeteries. He disagreed with the decision that allowed "Protestant chaplains to take turns in conducting a daily funeral service for all the military dead brought to the cemetery. So as not to violate the laws of the [Catholic] church they recite not the prayers of the Latin ritual, but other prayers, and in English. They also insist they do not read the prayers for the dead, but rather for those who are present at the funeral service. They have asked me to cooperate too." Gache would not go along with this, because for him, it violated the rituals of proper Catholic funeral services.

Writing from the Lynchburg hospital he was ministering at in December 1864, Gache spoke of confronting an "upstart" Protestant chaplain who had just arrived. He wrote that there had been assigned a "ministerial individual who had the impertinence to establish himself right here at the college." The letter describes how this man (Gache didn't even call him a "minister") got his comeuppance, much to Gache's undisguised glee. The hospital surgeon had allowed the man to hold religious services in the hospital yard, but a scheme to disrupt it had been made. Gache wrote that at the man's initial homily "eloquence was gushing forward in great torrents from his Presbyterian lips . . . when behold! A naughty refectorian, a wily rogue from Erin's green shores . . . suddenly sounded the supper bell. Before the clock had struck five, all the congregation was at the table and the preacher left alone, his arms outstretched and his mouth gaping, still standing on the grassy mound. You ought to have seen the dismay and astonishment of that disciple of Calvin. . . . You may be sure that his humiliation tended to tame his zeal, and not once since then was he ever seen on the accursed little grass mound."[37]

The mid-nineteenth century was truly a polarized, partisan time of denominational bias in the United States. While Catholic priests felt the brunt of this on a regular basis during the Civil War when they interacted in "mixed" settings, it is certainly clear that many of them were themselves not immune from its divisive tensions. The days of true Christian ecumenical cooperation were still far off, and would not truly materialize until well into the twentieth century.

INTERDENOMINATIONAL CAMARADERIE

Transforming entrenched denominational attitudes always begins on the grassroots level, in the words and actions of individuals. While prejudice and bias did not disappear from the political and social post–Civil War American stage, it certainly seems that some "thawing" in the hard ice of prejudice began on the small stage of individual wartime experiences. In the close quarters of Civil War regiments, Catholics and Protestants constantly intermingled as they fought, camped, traveled, and worked together; at times chaplains did support each other in their mutual ministries. One example of this mutuality is seen in what happened with Jeremiah Trecy as he was encouraging soldiers to attend his Masses in northern Alabama in September 1862. In an incident paralleling what other priests occasionally witnessed, Trecy tells of a non-Catholic regimental chaplain very supportive of his Catholic ministry. "During the whole morning before Mass, it was both pleasing and praiseworthy to see the Protestant chaplain of one of the regiments going around among the Catholic soldiers, urging them to their religious duties."[38]

Occasionally, those wartime relationships developed into some close and lasting friendships, despite the differing theologies. One of the clearest examples of this is the friendship of the Jesuit Joseph

O'Hagan (73rd New York) and Congregationalist minister Joseph Hopkins Twichell (71st New York), both chaplains in General Dan Sickles's predominantly Catholic Excelsior Brigade. The two met when O'Hagan became chaplain in October 1861, then twenty-three-year-old Twichell writing that he was "most pleased" with the young priest, describing him as a "young man, affable, a godly person. . . . We concluded a treaty of amity, peace and cooperation at our first introduction and I have no doubt that we shall be friends. . . . Through O'H I hope to get at the rum drinking although I observe he is not averse to a little tipple on his own account." The two men ministered and collaborated for two years, one example being that when they toured Fredericksburg together, they bought a huge amount of tobacco, and gave it away to the soldiers. They even bunked together on several occasions, one of which elicited this comment from Twichell: "Some of my Protestant brethren were considerably amused that Father and I occupied the same stateroom, seeming to think that somehow or another Popery was of a gaseous or odorous nature calculated to hinder sound sleep."[39]

Their other experience of bunking together occurred in the Battle of Fredericksburg (December 11–15, 1862), and is another humorous and poignant story. The two men were exhausted after a long and terrible day ministering to Union wounded, and lay down to sleep beneath their thin blankets on a very cold December night. Twichell reported what happened next.

Presently there came a call out of O'Hagan's blanket, "Joseph," and the answer was "Well Joseph." "I'm cold," said one and "I'm cold," said the other. "Then let's put our blankets together." And so they did, lying close with blankets doubled. Presently there was a movement as of one struggling with suppressed laughter. "What are you laughing at?" demanded Twichell. "At this condition of things," was the reply. "What? At all this horrible distress?" "No! No! But at you and me; a Jesuit priest and a New England Puritan minister of the worst sort—spooned close together under the same blanket. I wonder what the angels think." And after a moment, he added, "I think they like it."[40]

O'Hagan's September 1863 resignation filled Twichell with sadness. "We were both merry and sad, for our two years of acquaintanceship furnished many a pleasing reminiscence, while the thought of parting for good tinged our conscience with a real regret. I shall always remember him with tender emotion, as a gentleman, a charming companion and an honest-hearted friend. It would fill me with gratitude to feel that he is a true Christian. Today a letter came from him beginning 'My own dear boy.'" The relationship that began in denominational differences and wartime death would conclude in a lifelong friendship that saw the two men frequently visit and spend time with each other in the years ahead.[41]

Another example of the respect that sprang up between chaplains was that of Thomas Quinn (1st Rhode Island) and the Unitarian minister Augustus Woodbury. Woodbury wrote of their relationship in his narrative of the campaigns of the 1st Rhode Island.

> It is well known that a Catholic chaplain, Rev. Thomas Quinn, was associated with me in our regiment, and our intercourse was always of the most cordial and friendly nature. It was yet another example of the obliteration of ecclesiastical lines by the influence of patriotic feeling. I was no less a Protestant. He was no less a Catholic. Yet we could most heartily join hands in this great enterprise of freedom, which we both felt to be thoroughly Christian. The feeling is which prevailed is well illustrated by an interview which Father Quinn had once with a chaplain of a New York regiment. After some conversation on unimportant topics, the chaplain asked Father Quinn, "But how do you, a Catholic, get along with that Unitarian?" "I have yet to learn, Sir that religious differences are to be allowed to interrupt that intercourse which is becoming to scholars and gentlemen!"[42]

Darius Hubert (1st Louisiana) is another striking example of a far more conciliatory approach toward Protestant chaplains than, for example, his Catholic chaplain-brothers James Sheeran and Hippolyte Gache. While Sheeran and Gache regarded Protestant chaplains with fairly undisguised disdain and condescension, Hubert developed very good relationships and maintained them with a number of Protestant chaplains both during the war and after. He befriended and mentored a young soldier named Robert Hardie, a Methodist and an aspiring preacher, who eventually became chaplain of the 2nd Louisiana Infantry. Hubert was also close to other Protestant wartime chaplains such as Andrew Jackson Witherspoon (Presbyterian, 21st Alabama), Alexander Bakewell (Episcopalian, 38th Mississippi), Thomas Markham (Presbyterian, 1st Mississippi Light Artillery), and Benjamin Morgan Palmer, a prominent Presbyterian churchman in New Orleans.[43]

Thus, as one can see, the issue of wartime prejudice could have many facets and faces. The letters of Peter Tissot (37th New York), found now in the Jesuit in-house journal *The Woodstock Letters*, capture his own mixed experiences around those prejudices and attitudes. On the one hand, speaking of his imprisonment in Richmond, Tissot remarked that many Catholics in the capitol of the Confederacy refused to attend Mass on Sunday simply because it was being said by a Northern chaplain (other Catholic chaplains had similar experiences). Yet, of his contacts with soldiers themselves, he later wrote:

> It is unbelievable how high the war has lifted the Catholic priest in the eyes of observing men, and, on the other hand into what discredit the Protestant ministers have fallen. It is a staring truth, witnessed to by all the army, that Protestant Chaplains show very little devotion to their work, and are thereby possessed of little influence over their co-religionists. The following incident serves well.
>
> One day as they were setting out on a dangerous move, the general of a brigade, a Protestant, rode up while I was taking off my mass-vestments. "So, there you are, Father, eh!" was his cheery exordium, "you're coming along with us, aren't you?" When the Chaplain had returned a hearty "to be sure," the general went on, "because, you know, not only your men but I myself should feel very easy in mind if I knew you were around."[44]

While prejudicial attitudes may not have been changed on a national level, clearly a significant number of interactions between Catholics and Protestants softened on individual levels, and this had long-lasting ramifications. A final anecdote illustrating this comes from a Protestant Confederate officer commenting on Father Charles Heuze's courage in continuing his public ministry and soldier/hospital visits during the Vicksburg siege. "The Catholic religion may and perhaps does place too much hope . . . in Works—but I tell you that I would rather see Works of charity . . . and courage to go among the sick and wounded and attend them as brothers—than all the boast of faith that is unseen."[45]

The changed impressions, and the individuals who were touched by priests, were many—from people of other denominations, to wounded in hospitals and camps, to soldiers who became professed religious (Notre Dame's cemetery holds about a dozen such former soldiers), to leaders like General Winfield Hancock at Gettysburg (who removed his hat when William Corby gave absolution) and Reverend Beverly Tucker Lacy (who lavished praise upon James Sheeran), to Catholic converts like Generals David Stanley and James Longstreet (postwar). A few comments from some of these prominent Civil War figures about the impact of Catholic priests and nuns will be shared in the final chapter of this book; David Powers Conyngham's *Soldiers of the Cross* has numerous citations in this regard.

TOWARD A NEW FUTURE

Did the wartime work of Catholic priests have any effect on the pervasive anti-Catholic prejudice of their day? Were they able to break down the old prejudices—both within their own Faith and in the larger society—which had been so endemic in American history? As William Kurtz conveys in *Excommunicated from the Union*, as psychologists will attest, and as American history reveals, changing deeply held prejudicial attitudes is not an easily accomplished feat. "During Reconstruction, nativism and anti-Catholicism in national politics and society remained as strong as ever. Republican attacks on Democrats as the party of 'Rum, Revolution and Romanism' and a resurgence of post-war nativism outweighed any instances of religious toleration resulting from the patriotism of Catholic soldiers."[46]

In his 2023 book, *American Catholics*, Robert Emmett Curran gives an example of how Catholics themselves, along with much of the country, continued to be caught up in the prejudices of their day. When speaking of race-based bias, he remarks that "Catholics, as a community, had known, for generations, the consequences of being treated inequitably. But when the moment came to be part of a revolution to right the historic imbalance for everyone, most white Catholics could not rise above their tribal instincts to treat equality as something more than a zero-sum commodity."[47]

Yet there are other criteria we can use to evaluate the ecumenical impact of priests' wartime work. There is a well-known Christian hymn (based on Scripture) that contains the words "they will know we are Christians by our love, by our love." In the end, if long-term attitudinal change begins with individual actions, then the selfless actions done by many Catholic priests, and the nonbiased support offered by some Protestant ministers, certainly helped to begin to crack a few walls of historic prejudice. The best of the Catholic chaplains confronted denominational prejudice and religious apathy not by frontal assaults, but by flank attacks—personal courage shown in combat, a willingness to share the ordinary soldier's sufferings, spiritual outreach beyond prejudice, and individual priest's special gifts of "connecting" with soldiers in personal and deeply meaningful ways.

Not only because of the bias they faced, but also because of the inherent structure of the church (a hierarchical organization with the pope in Rome), the Catholic Church in America took no public stand on the Civil War. Bishops, priests, and laity were left to follow their own hearts and choose their own particular side. Yet clergy on both sides saw the Civil War as an opportunity—a chance to promote acceptance of Catholicism by perhaps undermining prejudice, and by showing a predominantly Protestant country that Catholics could be just as patriotic, and just as loyal as anyone else. Having Catholic priest-chaplains in the armies (and over six hundred nuns in hospitals) not only proved they could be both Catholic *and* American, but it helped begin to promote a different opinion of Catholicism by Protestants.

In retrospect, many of the priest-chaplains themselves—and the Catholic religious sisters who served in hospitals—strongly believed that their dedicated wartime service had helped change the minds of many Protestants they had interacted with during the war. Peter Paul Cooney, for example, wrote that at his 1864 Easter services, thousands of non-Catholics attended, and "prejudice against the Church is gone almost entirely." William Corby wrote that the "common danger" soldiers had faced helped them give up their religious prejudice against one another. From diaries, letters, and journals of priests like these, and soldiers as well, it is clear that countless individual lives were touched and attitudes changed during the war, even if the prevalent anti-Catholic and nativist attitudes were not significantly transformed on a postwar national scale.[48]

CLERGY IMPACTING POSTWAR AMERICA AND THE CATHOLIC CHURCH

It was a challenge to simply be a Catholic in a largely Protestant America, and it was equally difficult to be both Catholic and American in the nineteenth century. The Catholic clergy who wrestled with the challenges of the Civil War also faced challenges from the Vatican-based leadership of their own church. Simply put, Rome (as archetype of the institutional Catholic Church) simply didn't "get" American democracy. Concepts such as democratic government, individual freedoms, and the "liberty, equality, fraternity" espoused by French revolutionaries in 1789 were considered truly radical ideas by a Catholic Church leadership more acclimated to the "divine right" leadership style of the Middle Ages.

Historian Anthony Gilles summarizes the situation succinctly when he remarks that in the mid-nineteenth century,

> Rome was horrified by the revolutionary ideas spreading throughout the world. It placed all such ideas under the heading of "liberalism," and condemned liberalism as anti-Catholic. To the popes of the day, revolutionary ideas were nothing less than Protestant reform doctrines dressed up in different garb. Rome detested most the concepts of popular democracy and separation of church and state.

Rome wanted society to be run the old way, with aristocrats protecting the Church's interests, and the lower classes humbly submitting to the authority of prince and prelate. . . . People in the new democracies asked themselves "Can democracy and the Catholic Church coexist in the same country?"[49]

Thus, the bishops and priests who emerged from the Civil War had to fight a battle on two fronts—against the anti-Catholic animus of the United States, but also "appeasing" Rome and defending America's unique vision of Divine freedom, as enshrined in its founding documents. In short, it was a struggle to not only preserve Catholic identity, but to prove one could be both American and Catholic at the same time. In many ways, this struggle was as difficult as any Civil War battle. It was not easy for Catholic clergy to represent a church mired in Vatican One ecclesiology (i.e., hierarchical, defensive, and reactive stances against change in the world), while at the same time living and ministering in an America founded on Enlightenment era principles (liberty, equal rights, and separation of church and state).[50]

Added to these attitudinal roadblocks within the Church, the belief that Catholics in general were a "foreign culture" of outsiders in America only grew stronger after the war ended. The waves of Irish and German immigrants who had entered America before the war had instinctively formed strong ethnic Catholic enclaves, particularly in the North. Following the war, events occurred both nationally and beyond which increased the sense of Catholic alienation and separation. Broader divisive issues such as the contentious public school debates, the rise of Italian nationalism and control of the Papal States, and Reconstruction anti-Catholicism only exacerbated the cultural divide between American Catholics and the prevailing culture in which they lived.[51]

Just as Catholic chaplains had fought to preserve Catholic faith and values *during* the war, so many of these same men continued working *postwar* to bridge the gap between Catholicism and the American culture. In the last half of the nineteenth century, some Catholic leaders, including former chaplains, helped create a unique Catholic subculture in the United States—a culture centered around churches, schools, and institutions that would preserve Catholic identity in a biased, nativist national culture. Catholic clergy and immigrants alike began to insist that their rights in public American life be respected, most notably in realms like public education, where, as Will Kurtz explains, "their criticism of explicitly Protestant teachings made them anathema to many educational reformers."[52]

Thirty of the forty-seven Catholic wartime bishops were themselves immigrants, making them especially sensitive to the challenges of being both Catholic and American. Many of these bishops were English-speaking Irishmen who became very influential leaders in the country as well by the early twentieth century. It was the active, outspoken postwar ministry of some of these bishops and Catholics activists on many levels of public and civic engagement that slowly created a new subcultural "refuge" for American Catholics. Several priests who had served as Civil War chaplains made significant contributions to the creation of this Catholic subculture. Let us delve briefly into four areas in the postwar public realm of American life and culture in which chaplains continued their Civil War promotion of Catholic faith and values.

In the "Public Eye": The Catholic Schools Issue (Wiget and Scully)

The most contentious postwar issue for American Catholic leaders took place on the stage of public-school education. The nativist sentiment of the country had led to a general feeling that Catholic children—especially Irish immigrants—should be educated in public schools to become "truly American." The Blaine Amendments of the 1880s (eventually adopted in thirty-eight states) legally forbade government tax monies to be used to fund parochial schools. Fearing the influences of biased Protestant public school systems, and led by strongly Irish Catholic church leaders, Catholics began to build a network of parish-based schools staffed by religious sisters, especially in the urban north. Protestants responded with even stronger efforts to oppose any funding or support of these non-public schools. With its unique history of anti-Catholicism dating from colonial days, Boston, Massachusetts, was a prototypical example of this struggle, and two Civil War chaplains figured prominently in that contentious issue—the Jesuit Bernardin Wiget (hospital chaplain, Washington) and Thomas Scully (9th Massachusetts).

As a member of a religious order that boasted twelve colleges in the country by 1861, Bernardin Wiget had a deep commitment to Catholic education. He had himself begun a Catholic school in 1854 at St. Thomas Manor, Maryland, the oldest Jesuit establishment in the United States. On March 14, 1859, he was ministering at St. Mary's Church in Boston when the infamous Eliot School incident occurred. On that day, a ten-year-old Catholic boy was severely whipped for over thirty minutes at that school for refusing to read a King James version of the Bible. Boston law required the Ten Commandments and Bible passages to be recited daily, but Wiget had told the Catholic parents and children in his parish not to recite Protestant prayers, lest they fall into "infidelity and heresy." Immediately following this incident, some three hundred boys left the school, with others returning to use the Catholic Vulgate translation instead of the King James, although they were refused permission to do so.

An intense public debate on the issue arose almost immediately, which led Wiget (despite some opposition from his order and the bishop) to create the first parochial school in Boston with those who had withdrawn from Eliot School. First called St. Mary's Institute, and later named in honor of Father Wiget himself, the school enrolled 1,150 boys in the 1859–1860 school year. As historian John McGreevy notes, Wiget often "enjoyed marching the boys 2 by 2 from the school to the church on religious holidays, in view of startled non-Catholics." Wiget went on to serve at St. Aloysius Church in Washington, DC, where he became a wartime chaplain of the hospital on that Jesuit property, and served as president of Gonzaga College from 1861 to 1868. His life and educational achievements were later lauded with these words: "[We] remember Fr. Wiget's genial face and whole-souled enthusiasm, which fired all who came in contact with him. And these living witnesses of his zeal and labor will be the first to acknowledge that his name is still a household word in many a home in Washington."[53]

However, Puritan Boston's anti-Catholic animosity only intensified as immigrants flooded into and around the city in the postwar years, resulting in frequent clashes between native Bostonians and the waves of Irish immigrants. It was in this setting that Thomas Scully was ordained in 1860, served his eighteen months Civil War chaplaincy, then began forty years of parish ministry. His first four years were at a Malden, Massachusetts, church, but then in May 1867 he became pastor of St. Mary's Church in a heavily Irish area of Cambridge, where he served for thirty-five years until his 1902 death. Not only was the colorful native Irishman active in veteran's affairs and Catholic temperance issues, but he also became an outspoken figure in the Catholic education debates which broke out in the Boston area in the 1880s and 1890s.

A strong supporter of Catholic schools, Scully had begun a school at his heavily Irish parish, taking a hard line against members who did not did not attend it. He denounced them from the pulpit, calling them "scoundrels, hypocrites, and cowards," and refused the sacraments to parents whose children attended the "infidel public school system." This did not sit well with those parents (who saw public schools as not only free, but better educationally and a good way to assimilate), and they appealed to Archbishop John Williams (who was the third bishop of Boston, from 1866 to 1907).

At first Williams took a rather noncommittal approach to the issue, trying to moderate it, but when the entire issue became a national one with letters going to the Vatican from both sides, he was forced to intervene. In the end, Williams quietly stepped in and simply let it be known that he was establishing a parochial school system in the entire Boston Archdiocese, thus undercutting the efforts of Catholic school opponents. That decision, plus an 1884 Catholic bishops' directive mandating pastors to do all they could to erect parish schools, resulted in Boston Catholic schools growing quickly—from sixteen in 1879 to thirty-five in 1884. Ultimately this helped lead to a national Catholic school system in the United States which by 1900 had some 3,500 schools, all under the control of local parishes and bishops.

All of this caused shock waves among non-Catholic Bostonians, and it sent a clear signal that Catholic immigrants, especially the Irish, were there to stay. Partly inspired by the efforts of the Jesuit Bernardin Wiget and the "healthy hornet" Thomas Scully, the Irish Catholics of Boston no longer saw themselves as mere guests among their "Boston

Brahmin betters," but as equal citizens with rights and an independent voice of their own.[54]

"Liberal" Bishops on the National Stage
(Ireland and Gibbons)

When it came to proving one could be both patriotically American and truly Catholic, no two Civil War chaplains were more influential in the late nineteenth century than Archbishop John Ireland of Minnesota, and Cardinal James Gibbons of Baltimore. Both were members of what was deemed the more "liberal" branch of late nineteenth-century American Catholicism, meaning they promoted a greater "Americanizing" of the Catholic Church at home and abroad. Both supported America's core political principles, such as separation of church and state, adopting democratic procedures, and progressive social ideals. But both also had to "fight the good fight" within their own church, confronting immense Vatican mistrust of the American Church's loyalty, as well as resistance of their agenda from many fellow American bishops and Vatican clergy.

Introduced in chapter 7, the Irish-born John Benjamin Ireland (5th Minnesota) was appointed bishop in 1875, and archbishop in St. Paul, Minnesota, in 1888. A glib, affable, classically trained priest, Ireland became renowned for many things, including being a religious leader, builder, politician, colonizer, orator, writer, diplomat, and a friend to presidents. One of Minnesota's most prominent citizens, he recruited thousands of Irish immigrants to settle in the state, believing that the countryside was the ideal locale for Irish to settle in and practice their faith. He was also known for his significant influence on America's public and religious stage, as well as his international diplomatic connections (especially in France and the Vatican).[55]

Ireland was active in the political arena, campaigning against Tammany Hall and the Democrats, and supporting the 1896 election of William McKinley. He was an outspoken Republican and intimate of McKinley, Roosevelt, and Taft at a time when the sympathies of American Catholics rested largely with the Democratic Party. As a leader of the modernizing element in postwar Catholicism, he became associated with the Americanism movement, which encouraged Catholics to become assimilated and take an active role in public society. To that end, Ireland supported Catholic higher education, strongly advocating for the building of The Catholic University of America in Washington, DC, and promoting a unique but short-lived plan for Catholic schooling in Minnesota called the Faribault School Plan.[56]

For his public efforts in these areas, Ireland frequently met with resistance from more conservative-minded prelates like Michael Corrigan (New York) and Bernard McQuaid (Rochester). Partially because of fears of prelates like Ireland and his supposed "modernist" leanings (i.e., undermining the divinely instituted social order and Church structure), Pope Leo XIII in February 1899 issued a papal brief (*Testem Benevolentiae*) condemning what was termed "the heresy of Americanism." It was specifically addressed not to Bishop Ireland though, but to only one American churchman—Cardinal James Gibbons of Baltimore.[57]

James Gibbons (1834–1921) was a Baltimore-born priest, an informal Civil War chaplain at Fort McHenry, and the youngest of more than one thousand bishops in the world when raised to the episcopacy in 1868. In less than nine years, he rose from being a bishop in North Carolina, then Richmond, to the prominent archdiocese of Baltimore (1877), and became only the second-ever American cardinal in 1887. Gibbons was an ardent proponent of American civic institutions, calling the Constitution the finest instrument of government ever created. As a champion of the working class, he played a key role in securing papal permission for Catholics to join labor unions. In 1887, he helped found The Catholic University of America in Washington, DC, and served as its first chancellor.

Like Ireland, Gibbons was also active politically. He knew every president from Andrew Johnson to Warren Harding and frequented the White House as a visitor. President Taft honored him for his humanitarian work at Gibbons's 1911 golden jubilee, and in 1917 President Theodore Roosevelt hailed Gibbons as "the most venerated, respected and useful citizen in America."[58]

James Gibbons, John Ireland, and several other prominent American Catholic leaders were seen as leaders in the liberal wing of American Catholicism, and had been promoting a greater reconciliation of

American culture and Catholic faith when the furor of the Pope Leo's stern 1899 letter occurred. Gibbons was instructed to repudiate the heresy of Americanism. Instead, he wrote back to the Pope, stating that no Catholic in America believed the supposed doctrines underlying that false charge. "I do not believe there is a bishop, priest, or even a layman who knows his religion and utters such enormities. No, this is not, has never been, and will never be our 'Americanism.'" The controversy eventually died down, although Rome continued to remain somewhat suspect of American Catholicism.[59]

In their combined ninety-six years of episcopal ministry, the two old Civil War chaplains Gibbons and Ireland developed a close bond on many issues—supporting the same programs, promoting Catholic assimilation in the public culture, worker's rights, and their national, political, and ecclesial connections that advanced the "cause" of Catholicism in America. The legacy they left on the national Catholic scene was great, as were the accolades at their passing.

Bishop John Ireland was dubbed the "Consecrated Blizzard of the Northwest" for his robust personality and vision, and in a 1918 obituary he was called "one of the most distinguished churchmen of this or any other country during the past 100 years." After Cardinal James Gibbons's 1921 death, praise arrived from an unlikely source, Baltimore journalist H. L. Mencken (who often heaped scorn on Christian leaders): "More presidents than one sought the counsel of Cardinal Gibbons: He was a man of the highest sagacity, a politician in the best sense, and there is no record that he ever led the Church into a bog or up a blind alley. He had Rome against him often, but he always won in the end, for he was always right."[60]

Controversial Priests on the Public Stage
(McGlynn and Lambert)

As we have seen, the process of being both a patriotic American and a faithful Catholic was not easy, and achieving that goal many took different forms for different people. Two priests who took a more outspoken approach to that ideal, and impacted their country and church by their writing, publishing, and speaking were the former chaplains

Edward McGlynn (hospital chaplain, New York City) and Louis Lambert (18th Illinois). The strong political opinions of these two would ultimately result in the Vatican getting involved after both ran afoul of their respective bishops.

Introduced briefly in chapter 8, McGlynn was an imposing figure. Aside from being over six feet tall and two hundred pounds, he was a charming man and a powerful orator whose speeches drew large crowds of people. After being ordained in 1860, he was a wartime hospital chaplain from 1863 to 1865, before becoming pastor of St. Stephen's in New York City in 1866. There McGlynn refused to open a Catholic school (supporting public schools instead), was openly friendly with Protestant clergymen (speaking at Henry Ward Beecher's church), and became heavily involved in politics. McGlynn actively promoted the political goals of Henry George and the "single tax" movement (intended to be a remedy for poverty), even campaigning for George when he ran for mayor in 1886.

McGlynn was a leader in a clergy group that questioned the conservative attitudes of their local church, under Archbishop Michael Corrigan (New York). Though hated in many quarters for his views, he always had his supporters. He espoused social reforms, worker's rights, and land reform at a time when the Gilded Age and rapid economic growth in America were creating great poverty and inequality. McGlynn was suspended by the conservative Corrigan in 1886 for his views on Henry George and for speaking at a mayoral canvas, and was excommunicated by Corrigan in 1887.

Though declining to go to Rome at that time to defend himself, McGlynn was ultimately supported by Cardinals James Gibbons (Baltimore) and Henry Manning (Westminster, England). He was restored to the priesthood by the Vatican through an Apostolic Delegate sent to review the case in December 1892. Then in 1894, McGlynn was allowed to transfer out of New York City to upstate New York (St. Mary's Church in Newburgh), where he continued his outspoken ways. After a six-week illness reduced his robust frame greatly, he died on January 7, 1900.[61]

Louis Aloysius Lambert, the short-term Civil War chaplain of the 18th Illinois, also faced off with one of America's most conservative

Gilded Age–era bishops, Bernard McQuaid (Rochester). Though he never faced excommunication like Peter McGlynn, Lambert had his priestly faculties severely restricted, and he too wound up appealing to Rome. Born in Pennsylvania in 1835, Lambert had attended seminary in the St. Louis area, and was ordained for the Alton, Illinois, Diocese in 1859. After his short and troublesome wartime chaplaincy (described earlier in chapter 1), he settled in as pastor at two small southern Illinois towns, serving there until around May 1868. At that time, he resigned his parish and diocese and went to New York to assume the chair of moral theology for the Paulist Fathers (a Catholic religious order founded by Father Isaac Hecker), then established their house of studies at New York.[62]

Lambert was formally accepted into the new Rochester, New York Diocese (created in 1868 under Bernard McQuaid), and became a pastor in Waterloo, New York, in October 1869. It was there that Lambert's prolific writing career began, and he became a Catholic editor, apologist, and promoter of Catholic press. Lambert founded and edited Buffalo's *Catholic Times* (1874–1880), later being connected with the Catholic *Philadelphia Times* (1880–1882) and prestigious New York *Freeman's Journal* (1894–1910). His most well-known work was a series of articles (later a popular book) titled *Notes on Ingersoll*, which was written against the teachings of Robert Ingersoll, a prominent American agnostic of that time. Lambert was much in demand as an essayist, lecturer, and literary editor. In 1892 the University of Notre Dame bestowed on him an honorary doctorate of laws (LLD).

Though a truly influential figure in the burgeoning world of Catholic press, it was his outspokenness in print that got Lambert in trouble. Bishop McQuaid initially supported the priest-editor, but in the early 1880s he began to take issue with Lambert's veiled attacks upon his policies, and was especially angered by an article attacking diocesan officials who had refused to financially support a needy but controversial priest. McQuaid felt that Lambert was writing in opposition to church leadership, was the leader of a group of "rebellious" priests seeking undue control in the diocese (a clergy fund, specifically), and was antagonistic toward episcopal authority (especially in regards to certain Irish patriotic demonstrations).

McQuaid made these allegations against Lambert in a February 1888 letter to Rome, adding that he had been deceived by his character when Lambert first entered the Rochester Diocese; McQuaid claimed that Lambert had been dismissed from his prior Alton Diocese because of misconduct. Described by some as the "tyrant of Rochester," the legendary McQuaid seemed to thrive on controversy, and his role in the Lambert case was a classic example. The allegations against Lambert were not true, as later facts would show, but the autocratic McQuaid had trouble working with "recalcitrant," outspoken priests like Lambert. For his part, Lambert's literary and oratorical successes may have emboldened him to speak more freely, and perhaps to neglect to show his bishop due respect.

At any rate, both clergymen brought their cases to Rome, making journeys there to defend themselves. Rome at first upheld McQuaid, saying Lambert was still bound to Alton, but later in 1888 when McQuaid tried to formally remove him as pastor of the Waterloo parish, Lambert again appealed to Rome (through a lawyer) and this time the bishop was overruled. It was decided in 1890 that Lambert would remain in the Rochester Diocese, but be transferred to a new parish in Scottsville, New York. During his subsequent two decades there, Lambert's popularity only increased, his writing and editorial work continued, and great crowds gathered to hear him speak. Shortly after celebrating his golden jubilee as a priest, he died in September 1910 and was buried in Scottsville.[63]

Renaissance Men in Service to God and Country (Vahey and Stephan)

Two final Civil War chaplains who left a significant postwar mark on parts of America are John William Vahey (prison and hospital chaplain, Alton) and Joseph Andrew Stephan (hospital chaplain, Nashville). The most apt phrase to describe both these uniquely gifted priests is Renaissance men. The native Irishman John Vahey (1830–1903) came to the United States in 1848, went through seminary in St. Louis but did not get ordained, and then taught Latin, Greek, philosophy, and Scripture in that area for three years. From there he went to Buffalo, New

York, where he studied law before returning to Missouri and being admitted to the practice of law there, plying his profession for about four years in the Ninth Judicial District of Missouri.

In the 1850s Vahey went to Dubuque, Iowa, where after nine months of teaching philosophy, he was ordained a priest by Bishop Mathias Loras in June 1854. He founded the Fort Dodge Catholic colony, built a church and residence, and engaged in missionary-type ministry traveling around the diocese (all of Iowa at the time). During the Civil War, Vahey became a chaplain at the Alton, Illinois, hospital and prison (from November 1863 to June 1864); very little is known of his service during that time. He next went to Wisconsin to teach in the seminary there, but due to the scarcity of priests, he was appointed pastor in Waukesha, Wisconsin, serving there and in five other parishes over the next forty years. A truly energetic, effective yet peripatetic priest for five decades of ministry, Vahey ministered in dozens of Midwest parishes, building in the process eighteen churches, five parish residences, and two large schoolhouses.

Besides his parish ministry, Vahey was a writer whose pen was never idle. He wrote five books in all, and several of them became bestsellers, including a novel, letters, and discussions with a controversial Episcopal minister (Rev. H. W. Spaulding), and some lectures on scientific subjects. Vahey had a wide range of knowledge from his broad life and studies, was Republican in his politics, supported universal freedom and tolerance, and won many friends and admirers both Catholic and Protestant by his warm personal qualities. In his last years, he became disabled, and bought a farm near Elkhorn, Wisconsin, where he was cared for by his sister Margaret until his death in June 1903. Having served faithfully in four states and two dioceses, there was no one more beloved and respected in Wisconsin at the time of Vahey's death than this highly gifted, Renaissance man from Ireland.

Joseph Andrew Stephan (1822–1901) was born in Germany to a Greek father and Irish mother, and was briefly a carpenter and a soldier in Germany before entering civil engineering and philology studies. It was then that he turned to God during a two-year period of blindness, pledging to become a priest if he recovered. True to his word, he immigrated in 1847, and was ordained in March 1850 for the Cincinnati

Diocese (Bishop John Purcell). After pastoring several scattered churches, he moved to northern Indiana in the late 1850s to the newly formed Ft. Wayne Diocese (1857). There he began a Catholic colonization project, purchasing thousands of acres of land around Jasper County, and encouraging Catholic settlers to move in. He then used his engineering background to assist the government in surveying the valley to ensure the settlers got proper titles for their new homes. As a priest, he assisted at numerous area missions, and established new churches in several counties.

An excellent administrator and inspirational person, the energetic Stephan was described as a "remarkable if not eccentric individual"—a talented musician and cook, he could also be impatient and contentious when difficult issues arose. Some parish members felt he was rather odd because he occasionally wore blue suits or clothing that was thought to be inappropriate for Catholic clergy of the time. Even more interesting, it seems Stephan occasionally missed his Sunday Mass; he was an enthusiastic hunter, and several times he strayed too far to return in time to say Mass![64]

In 1863 Stephan volunteered to serve in the Union army and was assigned to the Army of the Cumberland. Though listed among the commissioned officers of the 47th Indiana, it appears Stephan served more as a post and hospital chaplain in Nashville in the Army of the Cumberland as one of seven Catholic chaplains there. Described by one surgeon as "a zealous and exemplary man who has rendered universal satisfaction," even as a chaplain Stephan found a use for his engineering skills by helping to construct a pontoon bridge, which so impressed his commanders that they offered him a promotion and a permanent military assignment. Stephan refused both offers, and instead in July 1865 he returned to his missionary work in the Ft. Wayne Diocese.[65]

After the war Stephan was drawn into the Church's mission to Native Americans, becoming an agent of the government-supported Bureau of Catholic Indian Missions (BCIM) to the Sioux tribe in the Dakota Territory. The story of Catholic involvement with Native Americans is a nuanced conversation and beyond the scope of this work, but Stephan's decades-long ministry in the Dakota Territory reflected the immense difficulties this work presented—financial struggles, governmental challenges, anti-Catholic resistance, general prejudices of the day, and more. It was his responsibility to distribute government monies, regulate trade, and promote civilization among the Sioux; but maintaining the delicate and very difficult balance between the Sioux, the army, frontiersmen, and the US government was extremely difficult. The outspoken Stephan fought until his dying days for Catholic Indian missions, winning some small victories, but in the end he was unable to halt the closure of many of his schools due to financial struggles and politics.[66]

Stephan remained in the Dakotas working with Native Americans and white settlers for nearly thirty years, always passionate about the existence of Native American schools in the Catholic tradition. However, worn down by years of struggling with the military, government, and Protestant reform groups, in 1899 he retired to Cornwall Heights, Pennsylvania (the motherhouse of Katherine Drexel's *Sisters of the Blessed Sacrament*). Stephan was named a monsignor during his years in South Dakota, and after a 1900 trip to Europe in hope of restoring his health, he died suddenly in September 1901 while in Washington, DC, for a conference. He is buried in the cemetery next to the motherhouse in Pennsylvania. Stephan—along with the multitalented John Vahey—joined the long list of Catholic Civil War chaplains who left a large and significant mark on the American landscape long after their wartime service had ended.[67]

CHAPTER 13

REFLECTIONS
AND LESSONS

As our review of Catholic Civil War chaplains concludes, what wisdom might be drawn from this unique lens into Civil War historiography? Presenting an organizational history of these men, updating the numbers of those who served as Catholic religious professionals, and telling their unique Civil War stories—these certainly are valuable additions to the Catholic and Civil War history fields. However, there are other important insights and lessons which have emerged from our decades of research in this field which are important to consider.

Some of these insights are readily apparent, while other lessons may not be quite so obvious. All contribute to a broader picture and meaning than simply detailing an accurate accounting of names, places, and activities of the priests identified here. It is my belief that there is *meaning* in history, and *wisdom* that emerges from the study of history—thus also consequences from people's failures to learn these lessons of history. The theme of Lord Acton's 1877 lecture on the history of freedom was the fact that religion and liberty have been the greatest source for good and evil throughout time. Let us examine whether these men of religion might have something of value to give us "moderns" in this twenty-first century.

DIFFERENT MEN LINKED
BY A COMMON FAITH

Catholic priests have been rather of an enigma in America from its beginning. From the colonial period on, in a predominantly non-Catholic country, Americans were unfamiliar with Catholic theology, the rites and routines of Catholic worship, and especially the clerical lifestyle. The mandatory practice of priestly celibacy (and living together in community, for religious orders) made priests even more mysterious, distant, and highly suspect to some people. A final sense of alienation came from the traditional, hierarchical Catholic Church structure of having its highest spiritual leader in another country: the pope in the Vatican (Pius IX at the time of the Civil War). These differences led to a sense of mystery and skepticism at best about priests, and suspicion, mistrust, and prejudice at worst.

But the simple truth is that Catholic priests at their core—then and now—are basically as *alike* as all men in emotions and temperaments, and yet as *unique* in the expression of their gifts as everyone is. Those men who became priests, who served willingly in the American Civil War, were normal men, with very human weaknesses and fears, with perspectives born out of their countries of birth, and with attitudes shaped by their upbringing, education, and religious training.

To begin with, the 126 Catholic Civil War chaplains were an incredibly diverse ethnic group, literally from all over the globe. A surprising 80.4 percent of all Catholic Civil War chaplains were born overseas, with fifteen different countries being represented in that group. In terms of their general ethnicity and range of ages, a few statistics are worth reiterating:

- 37.3 percent of the priests whose ethnicity is clearly known (123 in my list) were Irish.
- 19.5 percent were American-born.
- 17.8 percent were of French background, with Italy, Germany, and Canada rounding out the next highest ethnic backgrounds.
- Ages at the time of service ranged from the very young John Ireland (twenty-two years and seven months old in 1861) to the Charleston

legend Peter Whelan (fifty-nine years old in 1861). Six chaplains were in their fifties, and eleven in their twenties.[1]

The priests' ethnic diversity reflected that of white Americans on the eve of the Civil War. The 1860 census counted 34,513,000 people in the United States, with 13 percent (over four million) being foreign-born. About half resided in the Mid-Atlantic and New England states, with only 10 percent living in the South. Predictably, the American Catholic Church reflected the same diversity. The Catholic population of the United States in 1860 was about 3.1 million, or roughly 10 percent of the population. About 90 percent of those Catholics lived in the states remaining in the Union. The Catholic Church's astounding growth since 1830 had been largely driven by overwhelmingly Irish and then German immigration as the war broke out (with postwar growth coming from Italy and Poland). Of the fifty-one wartime archbishops or bishops, thirty-five were foreign-born (seventeen were Irish, and twelve were French); only fourteen of the prelates were born in America.[2]

More wartime priest-chaplains were connected to Union troops (58.7 percent) than to Confederates (41.3 percent). Although some were quite partisan, the majority of priest-chaplains were fairly apolitical, more focused on caring for the troops they served or met. All were connected either to religious orders (33 percent of chaplains) or individual geographic dioceses (66 percent) in the Catholic institutional church they were part of.

Humanly speaking, the priest-chaplains covered the spectrum of personalities. United by their commitment to God, the Church, and theology, still they differed widely in life histories, political views, temperaments, mannerisms, attitudes toward authority, styles of dress, and approaches to ministry. They and their individual issues were as varied as any human being in the nineteenth century United States. Let us briefly recall a few examples, and then draw some lessons:

- The irascible and outspoken Confederate chaplain, James Sheeran (who ironically ended up in a New Jersey parish after the war).
- The "stuffy" traditionalist, who wore his Jesuit habit in camp, Hippolyte Gache.

- The "one-of-the-guys" priests who played cards or chess with soldiers: John Ireland, Damaso Taladrid, and Francis Fusseder.
- The common-man, "all things for all people" clergy: John Bannon, Richard Christy, and Jeremiah Trecy.
- The intellectuals and scholars: William Corby, Joseph Carrier, John Vahey, and many Jesuits (such as Joseph O'Hagan, Bernardin Wiget, and Joseph Carrier).
- The multitalented Renaissance men priests: John Mouton (architect), Paul Gillen (scientist), Louis Lambert (editor, writer, and pastor), and John Vahey (lawyer).
- The French immigrants trying to figure out American democracy: Henri Georget, Julian Guillou, John Mouton, and Henry Picherit.
- Those wrestling with their priesthood or place in the Catholic Church: Alexander Grzelachowski (left the priesthood eventually), Charles Lemagie (four separate dioceses), and Peter McGrane (from the Redemptorists to Philadelphia to Kentucky).
- Those who were strong Irish-American patriots: Thomas Mooney, William O'Higgins, and Thomas Brady.
- Those with authority issues, like William O'Higgins (nearly expelled from Cincinnati) and Thomas Brady (had multiple run-ins with his Detroit Bishop).
- Those who were rabid Southern partisans who were never afraid to share their thoughts: John Finucane, John Bannon, James Sheeran, John Teeling, and Claude Chambodut.
- Those who were quiet, unpretentious, faithful, apolitical, and unselfish in their priestly service: Peter Whelan, Egidius Smulders, and Darius Hubert.

We gain two insights about these Catholic chaplains from this list (a microcosm of all priests of this book). First, despite all their individual differences, these 126 men were spiritually and personally more connected than any other group of wartime clergy. They were linked by the only things that could *ever* unite such a temperamentally and ethnically divergent group of men—their common spirituality and Catholic heritage, their desire to put their spiritual faith into concrete practice at a liminal point of American history, and a deep zeal for the spiritual and personal welfare of dying and wounded soldiers.

A further reality uniting these disparate men was the shortage of Catholic clergy for wartime service. The lack of priests forced those serving to work longer hours, travel farther in the pursuit of their duty, and endure unique deprivations and challenges (cf. chapter 1). It made their workload and its accompanying stresses far more overwhelming, and also unfortunately deprived many Catholic soldiers, especially the sick and wounded, of badly needed sacramental and spiritual care. The faith life of the ordinary Catholic soldier suffered because of this dearth.

Without the sacramental availability of priests, religion for lay Catholics tended to become far more devotional and "peripheral." Instead of building upon a solid theological context of Trinity, God's presence in Word and sacrament, and regular preaching, Catholic troops easily fell back upon the mere devotional "externals"—peripheral and ritual Catholic faith practices like sacramentals (medals, scapulars, Agnus Dei medallions), rosaries, statues, and so on. Given this situation, it is not surprising then that some Catholic soldiers became easily susceptible to being pulled away from Catholicism by so-called sheep-stealing preachers of other denominations.

Second, by looking at the above list, another insight emerges: the unique bond that most Catholic priests developed with their flocks (or at least had the potential to develop). Of all the factors keeping Catholic soldiers in the fold and close to their faith, certainly the Church's teachings and sacraments were foundational, but perhaps even more crucial were the informal human connections with priests that developed outside traditional ministry. It was these numerous nonclerical human connections that had the potential to make the campground and the battlefield sacred spaces, and encourage soldiers to carry on their faith long after the war was done.

Many of these non-ministerial functions are listed above and throughout the book, but let us highlight some of them here to underscore this point: card-playing (Taladrid and Fusseder), prewar parish connections (Boheme, Christy, Bannon, Pont, Sheeran, and Hubert), a good sense of humor (Mouton, Bliemel, Trecy, and Brady), sending money home (Ouellet and Scully), willingness to share a drink (Taladrid and Carrier, who shared a drink with General Sherman), defending soldiers facing trials (Corby, Cooney, Whelan, and Trecy), writing letters for soldiers (Irish Brigade chaplains), calling out "offending" officers (Sheeran and Fusseder), going selflessly beyond the call of duty (Nash, Cooney, Christy and O'Higgins), being shot at and almost killed (Trecy, Bannon, Cooney, Nash, Jarboe, Christy, Ouellet, and Hubert), and of course, simply sharing the hardships of marches and camp life. Faith and the sacraments did link all wartime Catholics together, but what made those wartime bonds deeper, more lasting, and even sacred over time was the poignant commonness shown by these simple men of God.[3]

All nineteenth-century Catholic priests had been solidly and deeply formed over many years by the Catholicism of their day. They followed its laws and guidelines faithfully (a few even obsessively), and were fired by a zeal and passion to serve Catholic soldiers far from their homes. In the end, perhaps only the Good Book best captures this disparate and effective group of Catholic wartime chaplains: "There are different kinds of working, but in all of them and in everyone it is the same God at work" (1 Corinthians 12:6 NIV).

PAYING THE PRICE OF CIVIL WAR CHAPLAINCY

Perhaps the one word that best captures the reality of the Civil War is "overwhelming." The war years of 1861 through 1865 and the years of Reconstruction that followed were an utterly shattering experience for anyone connected to them. Nothing before in American history had prepared people for the amount of destruction, tragedy, death, suffering, and social upheaval that resulted. Nearly as many men died in Civil War captivity (prisons and jails) as were killed in the entire Vietnam War. An estimated 1.5 million total casualties were reported during the Civil War (people killed, wounded, captured, or missing). For every three soldiers killed in battle, five more died of disease. The primitive nature of Civil War medicine, both in its intellectual underpinnings and its practice in the armies, meant that many now treatable wounds and illnesses were unnecessarily fatal.[4]

Drew Gilpin Faust's marvelous 2008 book, *This Republic of Suffering*, explored the overwhelming aspect of the war's death toll from a number of angles—material, political, intellectual, and spiritual. She describes how survivors mourned during the war years, and how a deeply religious nineteenth-century culture struggled to reconcile the slaughter with its belief in a good God. "It is work to die, to know how to approach and endure life's last moments . . . to worry about how to die . . . to manage death . . . to deal with the dead. . . . The work of death was Civil War America's most fundamental and most demanding undertaking." Specifically speaking, the *ars morienda* (work of death) of which Faust speaks eloquently was the fundamental moral task of primarily one group during the Civil War—its religious professionals, the chaplains of both armies.[5]

It was the 3,400 chaplains who had to confront this overwhelming "culture of death" in camps, battlefields, and hospitals. They were the ones who regularly paid the spiritual price of the *ars morienda*—thus enabling others to better cope with the shock of sudden death or permanent disfigurement on a massive scale. But in doing so, they paid their own personal price for the shattering experiences of war. Together with chaplain shortages, the episodic nature of their work (moving suddenly from the religious routines of camp life to the sudden terrors of a battlefield)—the religious work of life and death in wartime took a mental, physical, and even spiritual toll on chaplains as well.

The task of the understaffed Catholic chaplains specifically was to officiate and concretely deal with the spiritual and moral price tag that the *ars morienda* demanded of Catholics in a bleeding country. Thankfully, the innately sacramental and ritual nature of Catholicism meant that priests had more spiritual tools, rituals, and resources to assist soldiers than most chaplains. However, it also meant that as a consequence, more was required of priests' time and energy to perform those rituals and prayers on a regular, systematic basis. Almost to a man, Catholic chaplains—especially those in regiments—worked incredibly long hours and pushed themselves almost beyond endurance, often going without food and sleep in order to perform their sacramental and spiritual duties.

They celebrated Masses (in Latin) as often as possible, led public rosaries and prayers for Catholic troops, passed out Catholic literature (if available), preached publicly to crowds of soldiers (which many non-Catholics frequently attended), and met with soldiers one-on-one as needed. Using Catholic rites, they baptized the dying, anointed the battlefield's sick and wounded, and performed countless funerals. Going beyond mere Catholic rituals, priests began temperance societies, ministered and moved about on bloody battlefields, visited hospitals (field and general), brought soldiers' pay to posting stations, consoled family or friends with letters or prayer, passed out religious articles (medals, scapulars, etc.), and gave spiritual guidance.

Most Catholic regimental chaplains traveled many miles on horseback to perform their duties, particularly among the widely scattered and encamped regiments or brigades of their respective armies. Yet, despite their years of seminary training, spiritual maturity, and strong sense of dedication and faithfulness, Catholic priests were also affected by the traumas they faced. They too became overwhelmed emotionally by the all-pervasive work of death, and examples of the personal and emotional price they paid abound in the diaries and letters of those who chronicled their wartime careers.[6]

The Jesuit Joseph O'Hagan's diary entry for February 19, 1863, reveals his spiritual struggles in dealing with the overwhelming human brokenness he had faced all around him since becoming a chaplain in the predominantly Catholic Excelsior Brigade. "The experience of the past eighteen months in the army [has been] with some exceptions, everywhere corrupt, low vulgar and debasing [as] our corrupt nature is rampant. Would that I were out of it altogether, but it cannot be yet. I may still do some good where I am and I will make the sacrifice of my feelings for that object. God grant that this unhappy war may soon terminate."[7]

In November 1864, having been arrested after being unjustly blamed for another priest's self-serving activity, James Sheeran vented his feelings after three years of challenging ministry. "How many of the world's miseries have I not seen! What phase of human misery have I not witnessed. Hunger and hardship, fatigue and privations, sleepless nights and days of dreadful anxiety; the excesses of cold and the burning rays of the sun, the wild shouts of victory, the groans and lamentations of the wounded and the piteous sighs of the dying, who with their expiring lips, pronounce the name of a fond mother, wife, or perhaps dear sister; now it may be some thousands of miles away."[8]

Less than a month later, an extremely depressed Sheeran wrote again from Fort McHenry (Baltimore) in what was the lowest point of his priestly career. In a letter of Wednesday, November 30, 1864, he remarked that "I think much of death, but care little about it, could I but receive the benefits of the sacraments. I could not murmur against Providence, for I knew I deserved much more severe punishment at the hands of God, though I was conscious I did not deserve it from man." Although eventually released from prison, Sheeran never returned to ministry as a Confederate chaplain after this experience, finishing the war in Richmond, recovering partly through the care of Catholic nuns there. The combined stress of three years of endless travel and crushing loads of human misery culminated in an unjust imprisonment, which deeply affected one of the war's most successful chaplains. Within three years he had left the South, had three assignments in one year (1868), departed from his religious order, and was searching for a new home, eventually joining the Newark Diocese (1871), where he finished his priestly career (remaining as feisty as ever).[9]

The long-serving Hippolyte Gache, who spent much of the war's final years ministering in Southern hospitals, also had a combat experience that touched him deeply. While with the 10th Louisiana at Cedar Mountain in August 1862, Gache initially expressed great pleasure at the rout of "an insolent enemy who had come to slaughter us. . . . I think this was the greatest thrill of my life." But later that same afternoon, as he walked a battlefield strewn with dead and mangled soldiers, his attitude quickly changed. "Faced with this carnage I quite forgot the joy I had experienced . . . all at once I was overwhelmed with a profound sadness." His sadness turned to disgust when he then saw Confederate soldiers stripping corpses of their clothes and other valuables.[10]

The bookish Notre Dame priest-scientist Joseph Carrier was entirely unused to the grim realities of war. Having been sent by his superior to Vicksburg in June 1863, soon after his arrival he witnessed a Union soldier being shot dead by a Confederate sniper. As described previously in chapter 4, Carrier was so shaken by this death that he left the scene to be by himself and went to lay down in his tent. To his credit, he soon returned to the line of battle and resumed ministering to soldiers wounded in the famous mine explosion at Vicksburg on June 25, 1863. Yet by the end of 1863, he had returned to Notre Dame, where he began placing the school's science program on a solid foundation for the future.[11]

As related in chapter 12, fifteen of the war's 126 Catholic chaplains died early because of events or situations directly connected to the Civil War. Of the war's seventy-six full-time Catholic chaplains, at least twenty-five had their terms of military service unexpectedly shortened, all except one due to death, sickness, or disease. Being in the swamps of Louisiana was particularly deadly—no less than four priests were seriously affected by issues like typhoid fever and diarrhea (Thomas Kelly, Napoleon Mignault, Daniel Mullen, and Patrick J. Murphy), and one died (Basil Elia). A final recounting of some of the medical reasons why certain Catholic chaplains left the service shows the price paid for their chaplaincy:

- "Worn out by fatigue and almost a wreck" (Cooney, though he returned to finish the war)
- Lung issues exacerbated his already weakened health, and he never recovered (Dillon)
- "Advanced age and arduous duties have devolved upon me . . . my health has been affected" (Gillen)
- "Discharged for disability" (Martin)
- "Resigned on account of infirmity" (Butler)
- "Disability in the line of duty" (MacMahon spent eleven months in bed after collapsing on the floor of his bishop's house)
- "Inflammatory rheumatism" (O'Connell)
- "Derangements of the stomach, liver and bowels" (Tissot)

THE ELITE VANGUARD
OF ALL WARTIME CHAPLAINS

Chaplains from many denominations served faithfully, courageously, and with great success, and were deservedly remembered and honored for their work. However, it is safe to say that no clergy of any denomination stood above Catholic priests in providing regular worship, being an edifying presence in both battlefield and camp, in quantity and quality of spiritual care, moral standards upheld, absence of moral issues, and in winning deep, hard-earned respect. By virtue of all these factors, as well as their extensive seminary training, spiritual traditions and practices, youthful ages, and longer time of wartime service on average, Catholics priests can be considered the vanguard, the elite of all Civil War chaplains of both sides (in the eyes of this author, at least).

This fact in no way denigrates other chaplains who served either side, many of whom rendered excellent, faithful, and deeply moving ministry to soldiers under their care. However, the unique background of Catholic priests, what statistics reveal about their length of service, and the distinctive features of their service set them apart from others. The Catholic seminary formation process was the most rigorous and thorough of any religious denomination. Seminarians were monitored by priests as both teachers and spiritual directors, and studied a broad curriculum of Scripture, history, canon law, and theology. Their spiritual and moral development was closely supervised. A missionary spirit was strongly encouraged (as mentioned above, 80 percent of Civil War chaplains were born overseas), and virtues of charity, faithfulness, and unselfish dedication were considered absolutely paramount.[12]

As a result, those priests who successfully matriculated the rigorous Catholic seminary training and ultimately were approved for ordination were among the best educated, and most dedicated, clergy in the United States at the time. To a person, the priest-chaplains of the Civil War were erudite men, dutiful worship leaders, faithful spiritual men, and deeply committed to their ministries. So, the moral and theological training of Catholic priests clearly set them apart from most other ministers at the war's outset, putting them in the vanguard of those ministering.

Several other aspects of Catholic priests' training and wartime experience bear mentioning in some detail, further illustrating why, denominationally speaking at the least, it is reasonable that Catholic priests be considered the elite of all wartime chaplains. These factors are their average age and length of time served in the military, the quality of their priestly ministry, their moral standards, and faithfulness to duty.

Age and Length of Service

Considering age and length of service is a helpful perspective from which to view the ministries and appointments of all Civil War chaplains. Selecting older men as chaplains would potentially bring the benefits of pastoral experience to troops, but could also lead to problems with enduring the rigors of camp life (as it indeed did). Younger men, if well trained and mature morally and personally, could adapt more easily to the physical stresses of wartime ministry, and perhaps relate better to troops who, on average, would likely be younger that they. However, younger chaplains could lack the pastoral experience and emotional wisdom that older clergy could bring.

In regard to average age and length of service, we look to the comments of Bernard Maryniak in the multiauthored *Faith in the Fight*. In that excellent study of chaplains, he remarks that "the average regimental chaplain in the Union army was a Methodist, thirty-eight years and eight months of age, who served thirteen and a half months." Maryniak remarks that his calculations of Union regimental chaplains need to be taken with a grain of salt, because of incomplete data and the small numbers of regiments for some states. But, his research of Union regimental chaplains' average ages and length of service is insightful, especially because of what it reveals about Catholic chaplains. His statistics on Union chaplains by denomination are as follows:

- Congregational: averaged 37.8 years of age, 13.7 months of service
- Methodist: averaged 38.3 years of age, 15 months of service
- Baptist: averaged 39 years of age, 14.7 months of service
- Presbyterian: averaged 39 years of age, 15.2 months of service
- Episcopal: averaged 40.6 years of age, 13.3 months of service
- Catholic: averaged 34.9 years of age, 16 months of service[13]

The age difference between Catholic and Protestant regimental chaplains in the Union army shown here is quite significant, revealing a potential advantage in the relative youthfulness of Catholic chaplains (in terms of health, stamina, energy, and ability to endure harsh wartime conditions). Maryniak's research, and my own, shows that Catholic priests on average served longer in wartime ministry than other chaplains—a fact likely connected to their relatively younger average age. The forty-one full-time Union Catholic regimental chaplains I have outlined in this book averaged 34.3 years of age (younger by six months than Maryniak's number), and less on average by more than three and one-half years than the next closest denomination, the Methodists. Catholic priests in the Union served on average 17.6 months in regimental chaplaincy—longer by more than two years than the denomination with chaplains closest in length of service, the Presbyterians.[14]

- The oldest Union chaplain was Paul Gillen (fifty years and five months old in April 1861).
- The youngest Union chaplain was John Ireland (twenty-two years and seven months old in April 1861).
- The longest serving Union chaplain was Thomas Brady (forty-four months); three priests served only three months at most (Doane, N. O'Brien, and Truyens).[15]

The seventeen full-time regimental chaplains of the Confederate armies averaged an astounding 40.9 average years of age, which is six years older on average than Catholic Union chaplains. Yet these regimental chaplains served on average 20.8 months each during the war—a full five months *beyond* the already longer Union chaplains' longevity. (Unfortunately, statistics on the denominational breakdown of all Confederate chaplains are not yet available.) Consider the following:

- The oldest Confederate chaplains were Peter Whelan (age fifty-nine in 1861), and Ghislaine Boheme (age fifty-eight in April 1861).
- The youngest Confederate chaplain was Emmeran Bliemel (twenty-nine years and seven months old in April 1861). (Ironically, both Boheme and Bliemel died during the war.)
- The longest serving Confederate chaplains were Darius Hubert and Egidius Smulders (four years each); the shortest term belonged to Henry V. Browne (four months).[16]

Thus, if all seventy-six Catholic regimental chaplains are considered together, the average Catholic chaplain would have been of Irish heritage, 36.1 years of age, and served 18.5 months in the chaplaincy. The remaining fifty part-time Catholic chaplains (i.e., those with at least three months of sustained service) averaged 16.8 months of service per chaplain. Looking at these statistics, it is clear that Catholic priests as a group were the longest serving chaplains of the war. Their dedication to the troops, despite their own issues, health concerns, and the travails of war, is truly commendable.

Moral Quality and Faithfulness to Duty

Other critical factors in averring that priests were among the elite Civil War chaplains in general are the quality of their ministry, their moral standards, and faithfulness to duty. In reviewing the 126 priest-chaplains' lives, these factors are clearly evident in nearly all. I refer once again to the well-written description of a "successful chaplain," as given in the unpublished thesis of Charles Edward Smith, "The Work of Civil War Chaplains." He writes there that "a good chaplain was one who (1) was not neglectful of his duties, temporal or spiritual, in favor of lighter pleasures; (2) never failed to observe the highest moral standards; (3) preached sermons appropriate to the battlefield situation; (4) was mindful of his military bearing and dress, (5) adopted his religious faith to the exigencies of battle, and (6) proved his physical courage in battle."[17]

Catholic priests as a denomination were exemplary in how they fulfilled all these categories. Rarely if ever were they accused of neglecting or slacking in their duties, and on the rare occasion when such an accusation was made, other extenuating circumstances—not moral turpitude—must be taken into account (e.g., the tensions around Louis Lambert and the Catholic colonel of the heavily non-Catholic 18th Illinois, described in chapters 1 and 12). In my two decades of research, except for the deceitful practices of Joseph Bixio, no other circumstance has been discovered involving a Catholic priest-chaplain of the Civil War where any truly serious accusation of moral impropriety was ever leveled against them. Indeed, if "promoting the highest moral standards" is considered a chaplain's norm, priests were, in general, the officers perhaps most responsible for promoting such standards, whether by attending and encouraging worship, moderating alcohol use among the troops, helping soldiers avoid "near occasions of sin," and so on. Their sermons were always well-received (where we find references), inspiring large Protestant attendance on many occasions as well. Their battlefield courage has been mentioned repeatedly in earlier chapters of this book.

Countless people noticed the extraordinary work of priest-chaplains noticed frequently during the war, and was intentionally commented upon afterward. Two such comments from prominent wartime leaders will suffice to encapsulate the unique status that Catholic Civil War chaplains emerged from the war with. At a congressional committee in January 1862, Benjamin Butler declared: "A good chaplain is a very good thing, but a poor chaplain is much worse than none at all. . . . I am bound to say that I have had never seen a Roman Catholic chaplain who did not do his duty. . . . They have always been faithful, so far as my experience goes. They are able men . . . responsible . . . this is not always the case with other chaplains." Later in 1870, Winfield Scott Hancock asserted: "Having the good fortune during the war to have in my command . . . troops with chaplains who were Catholics, I had favorable opportunities of observing the manner in which the chaplains performed their duties and I can safely and with pleasure assert than none were more useful or more devoted to their duties under all circumstances on the service. . . . They too had the respect of the troops, without regard to their religious views, from the general down to the drummer boy."[18]

BELIEVE IN BELIEF

An important social lesson can be drawn from the lives and work of Catholic wartime chaplains (and indeed all wartime chaplains). The dedication of the men described in this book is a challenge to our postmodern culture to recognize a possibly discomforting truth—the need to believe in belief. Religious beliefs and practices have had an incredibly profound and powerful role in shaping world history and countless cultures. This concept should not be a surprise to any true student of either world or American history.

Today, the United States is considered a philosophically and spiritually postmodern culture, a place where skepticism and relativism reign about overarching values, grand narratives, or life-encompassing spiritual worldviews. Cynicism, apathy, or outright hostility are now commonplace in public and private forums when addressing historic religious practices, traditional spiritual beliefs, or the foundational religious perspectives that motivated people to live good and productive lives. However, from a broad global perspective, religion and faith have always been some of the most profound motivators of human beings in all of history.

Thus, reckoning with belief and realizing that religion was a vital factor in the Civil War era (certainly to the greater number of soldiers and citizens) are crucial to accurately representing that time. It is a serious mistake, historically speaking, to allow one's (post)modern attitudes (or personal beliefs) toward religion and faith to subconsciously infect one's studies of the Civil War era. The mid-nineteenth century was a vastly different cultural and religious landscape from that of the twenty-first century. For example, the culture of unbelief so widespread today was virtually unthinkable in mid-nineteenth century America. There would have been virtually no one in America—even if they did not attend church (and many did not on a regular basis)—who denied that God existed and that his commandments were central guidelines for culture and life. Of the actions and attitudes of the soldiers themselves during the war years, James McPherson remarked that "Civil War armies were, arguably, the most religious in American history," estimating that at least one-half of Civil War soldiers took religion very seriously.[19]

Religious historian Mark Noll writes that in 1861 "religion was much more important than any other center of value at work in the country. As a promoter of values, a generator of print media, a source of popular music and artistic endeavors, and as comforter of America's internal life, religion and faith had long united the country—but now contributed heavily to its division." It was not that churches, believers, or clergy were more numerous or widespread in 1861, but rather because all other cultural and educational institutions, as well as government agencies, were far smaller and more limited in their reach. Cultural institutions of the day tended to *reinforce* the values of churches rather than oppose them. Furthermore, the impact of overarching governmental institutions on most citizens was negligible. As an example, there were no truly national newspapers or agencies, and there were no national stores; indeed nothing you could buy in New York could you also buy, for example, in New Orleans or Charleston.[20]

On the sociocultural level, the Second Great Awakening had just rolled across the country, creating a surge in religious enthusiasm, generating thousands of evangelical converts, reviving interest in Christian social reforms, and birthing Protestant nondenominational churches. As mentioned in an earlier chapter, the number of Catholics (particularly Irish) was growing rapidly as well. Catholic places of worship had risen from about 1,200 in 1850 to over 2,500 in 1860. The Catholic presence in America was expanding at an incredible pace and continued to do so after the war. Thus, put simply, in the nineteenth century, there was no other cultural or voluntary organization who could (and did) bring together more people on a regular basis than America's religious institutions.

There was also no group in America with as much power to influence the great numbers of people on a regular basis than the clergy. They were better educated and more broadly well-read than most of their congregations, hence they often became extremely influential leaders in the community. In fact, churches were among American citizens' chief sources of information in mid-nineteenth century. In the decisive 1860 election, at least three (and maybe four) times as many people as the 4.7 million males who voted in that election were regularly in church on any given Sunday. During the tumultuous antebellum years and heated debates about slavery, America's clergy were more politically active, contentious, and outspoken than perhaps at any other time in history. When the deadly Civil War finally broke out, it was the clergy of the country who helped soothe shell-shocked souls, brought peace to troubled minds and spirits, inspired a measure of hope and healing to horribly mangled soldiers, and offered a broad existential sense of purpose and vision to the specter of death hovering everywhere in the wounded country.[21]

The dedication of Catholic Civil War chaplains and their compatriots, in the inherently secular, "profane" public spaces of battlefields and hospitals, is a living lesson that religious factors are central and vital, and cannot be ignored when studying America's most deadly conflict. Religion played an enormously influential role in the founding of the country (the Puritans were English religious dissidents), and in the development of nearly every colony; religious attitudes and values continued to be preeminent in the country that stumbled into the Civil War. Believing in belief—in the power of strongly held faith beliefs and religious practices to motivate people and societies—is an essential and too often overlooked factor in analyzing historical events.[22]

George Rable opines that "historians have yet to write a religious history of the Civil War . . . [they] must address this reality. . . . The grand and sweeping narratives of the sectional crisis and Civil War . . . have seldom paid attention to religion much less tried to create a religious narrative." James McPherson as well challenges historians to seriously study the religious history of the Civil War. "Religion was central to the meaning of the Civil War, as the generation that experienced the war tried to understand it. Religion should also be central to our efforts to recover that meaning." The dedication, faithfulness, courage and humor of the 126 Catholic priests who served during those dismal and deadly four years is a stark reminder of the critical role that belief and religious values have played throughout our nation's history, and in people's personal histories.[23]

POSTWAR REMEMBERING
AND MEMORY-MAKING

People remember. How people remember, and what they choose to remember, though, are always open to debate. The Athenian historian Thucydides perhaps captured it best: "the people made their recollections fit in with their sufferings." What is termed "Lost Cause" writing dominated Southern accounts of the Civil War until well into the twentieth century. Supposed facts about Ulysses Grant's butchery, or James Longstreet's having "lost" Gettysburg, and other such suppositions float through Civil War history to this day. Historians, social commentators, and aficionados will long continue to debate what is important to remember. David Blight's 2001 book, *Race and Reunion: The Civil War in American Memory*, especially explores how no other historical event has left as deep an imprint on America's collective memory as the Civil War. He outlines in detail the perilous American path of both remembering and forgetting, speaking in a powerful way about its tragic costs to race relations and America's national reunion.[24]

The North

Postwar Catholic writers and veterans wrestled with remembering the war from their own vantage points (and forgetting its "inconvenient" aspects) when they reported the roles and contributions of their co-religionists. It will be no surprise that memory-making in the Catholic community differed between the North and South in the postwar years. In the North, the work of remembering the contributions of Catholics had a highly apologetic purpose, began very shortly after the war, and was undertaken mostly by the Irish. In his excellent 2016 book, *Excommunicated from the Union*, William Kurtz writes of these Catholic efforts, remarking that "Catholic apologists and veterans believed that their wartime sacrifices could be publicized to promote religious tolerance . . . these efforts attempted to lionize Catholic soldiers such as those of the Irish Brigade, to celebrate the devotion of Catholic chaplains. . . . and to remember the contributions of prominent Catholic heroes such as General Rosecrans to the Union cause."[25]

After the war, prominent Catholic laymen quickly began the commemoration process. Convert and writer Orestes Bronson argued in 1866 that Catholics should be accepted as equals into American society "because of their Civil War contributions." Louis Garesche's biography of his father Julius memorialized his death at Stones River, speaking of his "martyred father's devotion to his duty, country and God." In 1898, George Barton wrote *Angels of the Battlefield* as the first full presentation of the labors of the Catholic nuns in Civil War hospitals.

Journalist and veteran David Power Conyngham's nineteenth-century manuscript, *Soldiers of the Cross*, compiled the stories of fourteen Catholic chaplains and six female religious communities serving both North and South. (This work was finally published in 2019.) Irish veterans were among the most prolific promoters of the Church's role. In face of some early barriers to joining from the predominantly Protestant and Republican Grand Army of the Republic (GAR), Catholic veterans formed their own religious groups (e.g., the Irish Brigade Association). Over time, as the GAR became less partisan and more focused on pensions and memorializing, more and more Catholics did join.[26]

Union veterans were also ready and willing to attempt to make heroes of some of their own Catholic wartime leaders: for example, Archbishop John Hughes (New York), Irish nationalist General Thomas Francis Meagher, as well as General Philip Sheridan (only a nominal Catholic). However, General William Rosecrans became the greatest postwar Catholic Civil War hero, and a symbol of Catholic patriotism across the west and north. His 1898 death brought a huge outpouring of support from Catholics but also from previous detractors, with a St. Louis Catholic paper describing him as "one of the greatest generals . . . one of the purest and best men living." Interestingly, Rosecrans's somewhat mediocre wartime reputation, which had previously been seen mostly through the eyes of Ulysses Grant in his memoirs, has now begun to be reevaluated in a more positive light through the writing of several recent authors.[27]

More than any other place, the spiritual center of northern Catholic efforts at remembering was the University of Notre Dame. "The university's contribution to the Civil War did not end with Lee's surrender . . . [its] postwar contribution nearly equaled in importance its actual role during the war. The university constructed a memory of the Civil War past that emphasized Catholic patriotism and loyalty rather than divisions and anti-war sentiment within the community." William Corby and Peter Paul Cooney were the most prominent postwar chaplains connected to Notre Dame. Cooney traveled extensively on the temperance circuit, remarking in 1887 to veterans of the 35th Indiana that Catholic Americans were "the safest bulwark for the nation's preservation." Corby began collecting priceless Civil War relics, became president of Notre Dame twice, and in 1893 wrote his immensely popular *Memoirs* in order to "silence the vituperation" of "bigots."[28]

As mentioned previously, St. Clair Mulholland worked for years promoting the "cause" of Corby (and the wartime nuns), trying to establish Catholic heroes as American heroes. The unveiling of William Corby's statue at Gettysburg in 1910 was the result of a long and successful financial and marketing campaign, although Mulholland himself had died in 1900. The unveiling of its exact copy on the Notre Dame campus thirteen years later was well attended by members of the GAR, who heard several people deliver stirring patriotic addresses in honor of Corby. In 1897, Cooney and Corby helped found the unique Notre Dame Post 569 of the GAR, composed entirely of priests and brothers who had served in the Union army. Perhaps Bishop John Ireland's August 1888 panegyric on the occasion of founder Father Edward Sorin's golden jubilee best captures the postwar import of northern "remembering" that centered on Notre Dame. In that talk, the former chaplain of the 5th Minnesota proclaimed aloud, "Father Sorin, you saved the honor of the Church!"[29]

However, at least two caveats need to be mentioned about these Northern apologetic efforts, which were mainly carried out by Irish and American-born Catholics. First, northern remembering was in many ways a "heroic and sanitized version of their contributions. . . . directed at a receptive Catholic audience." It conveniently ignored issues such as slavery, Catholic opposition to the war, the draft riots, political divisions, and the role that race-based thinking played in the Reconstruction era. Over the next century, northern Catholics in particular and all Americans in general would wrestle with attempting to broaden their perceptions of people different from themselves, whether by race, religion, geography, or politics.[30]

Secondly, in the end, the pervasive national bias against Catholicism was not truly diminished in any major way by postwar Northern memorializing efforts. Anti-Catholic attitudes in mainstream America continued to be reflected not only in the decades immediately following the war, but also over the next century in issues like the Catholic Schools crisis in the late nineteenth century, restrictive immigration policies in the 1920s, the rise of the Ku Klux Klan, and the inflamed rhetoric of the 1928 presidential race around the Catholic Democrat Al Smith. However, it can be said that at least these Northern apologetic efforts did help Catholics—especially the Irish—to better remember the brave deeds of their ancestors, for as Kurtz opines, "[Today] the story of the Catholic Church during the war has become almost an exclusively Irish Catholic one."[31]

The South

Catholic memory-making in the Southern states after the war was a very different phenomenon. The same apologetic emphasis that predominated in the postwar North did not occur in the South, due to what Gracjan Kraszewski calls "the confederatization" of Southern Catholics. "Southern Catholics learned to balance their Catholicism and Confederatism. . . . for the vast majority, these identities were not in tension, rather they reinforced each other, making it possible for one to be a devout Catholic and a devoted Confederate." Catholics had long been a smaller percentage of the Southern population, but Catholicism also had a longer cultural history and deeper roots there (New Orleans being but one example). As an institution, the Catholic Church has tended historically to stand against "progressive" causes (e.g., the Enlightenment, overturning monarchies, the Reformation) on the basis on "defending tradition," whether ecclesiastical or cultural. Thus, being part of the world's oldest hierarchical and most traditional institution, and having a longer time to live and work in a larger predominantly Protestant milieu, led to different perceptions both about Catholics and by Catholics themselves when it came to perceptions of the Civil War and its causes.[32]

In many ways, mid-nineteenth-century Catholics in the South fared better socially than their northern counterparts because they were less alienated from their Protestant neighbors. For the majority of Southern Catholics, their religion and politics did not become points of conflict with their neighbors; instead, they made themselves virtually indistinguishable from their Protestant neighbors. The two largest immigrant groups in the South—the Irish and French—were "widely reputed to be the most pro-Confederate." Both groups tended to be supportive of slavery and the Confederacy and outright opposed to abolition. Also, since Democrats were the majority political party in the Confederacy (as opposed to being the minority in the North), the Democratic Protestant majority "saw Catholics as 'sound on the slavery question.'"[33]

In general, Catholics found "broad support from a combination of non-Catholic southerners who genuinely respected Catholics and Catholicism, with other southerners who—whatever their views about Catholics . . . found alliance with Catholics politically expedient." Although some anti-Catholicism certainly existed, an overly simplistic retelling of its role in the South "omits the significant private sincerity of pro-Catholic southern Protestants, and the public story also largely ignores women." Although a minority in both the North and South, Catholics had deeper cultural and historical roots in the South (particularly in urban areas). A number of Southern Catholics, particularly some born there, had achieved significant prosperity, community stature, and political influence in the South by 1861. Finally, New Orleans's simultaneous prominence as the largest Confederate city and the nation's "most Catholic" city, reflected a unique urban culture in the South that was "marked by greater religious diversity and tolerance."[34]

The actions and attitudes of Catholics during the Civil War years further promoted the creation of positive postwar memories, and an increase in toleration and respect. The wartime service of Southern-born Catholics (like the Irish of Louisiana), fostered further favorable view toward them, as did the ministry of Catholic nuns and priest-chaplains. Despite facing occasional prejudice, Catholics' dedicated work gained approval and respect among many non-Catholic Confederates. Leaving aside the multiple witnesses of non-Catholic soldiers regarding the care and concern shown by Catholic nuns in this regard, some Catholic chaplains became almost legendary in the postwar memory making of the South (e.g., Peter Whelan in Savannah and Isadore Turgis in New Orleans). Some of this may have been caught up in the overarching Lost Cause movement, but the postwar written accounts of these men leave no doubt about the impact they had on people nostalgically remembering their unique contributions to the Southern cause.[35]

The poet-priest Abram Ryan is the classic example of the "confederatization" process that drew Catholics more smoothly into the

Southern social milieu. Despite ambiguities around Ryan's actual wartime chaplaincy and his vagabond clerical lifestyle (moving through five dioceses and one religious order in twenty-six years), he became a household name in the South following the war due to his poetry and eloquent preaching. His book, *Father Ryan's Poems*, went through forty editions until 1929. He received frequent requests for his Lost Cause poetry, speaking in 1883 at both the University of Virginia and Lee College (at the unveiling of a new Robert E. Lee statue there). He was adored in Lexington, Virginia; churches were packed for his unique emotion-filled homilies, and all the leaders of the Confederacy knew him personally. Ryan's Catholicism and priesthood was never an issue for the Southern people or leaders—he was praised and adulated because he remembered and venerated the "heritage" of the Confederacy. Just as the North left out of their remembering various "inconvenient" factors, so the South left aside Ryan's theology and personal issues. As Thucydides said so well: "the people made their recollections fit in with their sufferings."

Thus, Southern Catholics became "acceptable in southern society, and for many proslavery politicians, useful as well" because of their wartime support and contributions, their "politically acceptable" attitudes toward slavery, and their support for postwar Confederate "redemption." There was no overarching need to apologetically prove anything through postwar remembering to a society and a political structure that largely supported them. All this might have been more of an extension of Southern courtesy, hospitality, and toleration than true acceptance or religious equality, but then again, Catholics never really posed any integral or doctrinal threat to slavery, Reconstruction, or "the Southern way." As their prewar status in the Confederacy had long been well established, remembering chaplains, nuns, and Catholics positively in the postwar years was far easier, more acceptable, and even expedient.[36]

FINAL THOUGHTS ON REMEMBERING

In both the North and South after the Civil War, many well-known leaders expressed their deep appreciation for the work that the Catholic priest-chaplains had done. However, due to space, I will not list here their written remarks on the impactful role that priests and nuns had during the war. Many of these comments have already been compiled by journalist and Civil War veteran David Conyngham (1825–1883) after the war in his *The Soldiers of the Cross*. This fascinating history of the contributions of the war's priests and nuns was thankfully annotated and published in 2019 by William Kurtz and David Endres.[37]

I feel obliged one final time to note the powerful influence in postwar remembering played by the six-hundred-plus Catholic sisters, and their incredible nonpartisan care for the war's wounded and sick. Almost beyond recounting are the stories of wounded soldiers who were shocked at meeting these "strange" women with "Papist" faith and strange headgear ("God's geese," one order was called). But in the writings by Northern and Southern troops, there is virtually no account of those hospital encounters that did not in the end result in attitudes being radically transformed, and indeed even hearts being converted—both spiritually and even religiously. Many went on to be baptized as Catholics. Indeed, I would concur with the word of Mary Denis Maher in her study of these amazing women, that "in the end, it was the selfless devotion of these women and their careful neutrality in terms of religious faith and politics that did more to rehabilitate the church in the eyes of Protestant Americans than did the actions of Catholic chaplains or soldiers."[38]

CATHOLICISM AND SLAVERY

In closing, one cannot write about the Civil War and not talk at least briefly about its primary cause, slavery, at least within the context of this book's content. The Catholic position on slaveholding is complex and fraught with nuance. But in theory and practice, for centuries the Church did embrace slavery, authorize the slave trade, and allow members to keep enslaved persons. After some four centuries of its operation, in 1839 Pope Gregory XVI condemned the slave trade (in the decree *In Supremo Apostolatus*). However, he did not speak on whether slaveholders in the Americas should free their enslaved people. Catholic slaveholding was thus able to continue in the United States and else-where, arguably without disobedience to the letter of the Church's teaching. Pope Leo XIII formally changed the Church's teaching in May 1888 with his encyclical letter *In Plurimis*, which publicly opposed slavery. All subsequent popes have continued that tradition, also op-posing slave-like economic practices and human trafficking.[39]

During the Civil War, Catholic chaplains ministered to people of all nationalities, although none of them primarily focused on African Americans in their ministry. Catholic chaplains did routinely and will-ingly minister to people of color when the situation arose, or when en-slaved or formerly enslaved persons crossed their paths. Bishop William Elder (Natchez Diocese) is an example, as his wide-ranging ministry in-cluded frequent work with freed Blacks, enslaved persons, and Black troops—going to their houses, visiting hospitals and camps, teaching catechism, and so on. He tried to recruit other bishops to baptize and catechize freed Black people, but his wartime efforts came to nought, as did postwar institutional Catholic efforts to evangelize freed Blacks or create a position in the Church to oversee such evangelization. Though the 1866 Second Plenary Council of Baltimore spoke often about giving more attention to this area, no coherent plan formed, and disagreements led to nothing of substance being decided or acted upon. (Of note, no formal wartime chaplains participated in that council.) Thus, in the Re-construction era and beyond, except for the isolated efforts of certain religious orders (e.g., the Josephites, Spiritans, and Mill Hill Fathers) and individuals (e.g., Father Francis Weninger, Mother Katherine Drexel), the American Catholic Church, generally speaking, dropped the ball on offering humanitarian aid or offering spiritual welcome to African Americans.[40]

LET US REMEMBER GREAT MEN

Despite faults, the Catholic Church feeds, houses, clothes, cares for, and educates more people than any other institution in history, or in-deed on the face of the earth. In the Church's two-thousand-year his-tory, Catholic clergy have stood in the vanguard of their Church's greatest spiritual and social achievements. They have defended humanity, sheltered the defenseless, encouraged education and scientific discovery, guided people to faith, and trod bravely on countless battlefields. While remaining very human men themselves—with both strengths and weaknesses, virtues and vices (perhaps more obvious now than at any previous point in history)—still as a group, Catholic priests have contributed in untold and unrecognized ways to the civilization and progress our world now enjoys.

The 126 nineteenth-century priest-chaplains who walked the bloody battlefields of Vicksburg, Antietam, and countless other Civil War campaigns; those who baptized and anointed the wounded in hospitals like Chimborazo and Satterlee; those who buried soldiers in innumerable graves across the county—these men, veterans all, deserve to be known and recognized for their accomplishments. Too long have not only the religious professionals of the Civil War been ignored in the retellings of written histories and battlefield museums, but Catholic priests as a subset have been even more relegated to mere footnotes or one-line mentions. This work has been an attempt to tell their stories and honor them for their contributions.

This author prays that their faithful service, dedication, humor, and accomplishments will continue to be recounted in the decades ahead. For indeed, countless wounded, suffering, and dying Civil War soldiers thanked their Creator "for the men who stood their ground when their numbers dwindled and their days darkened. . . . For the many quiet and gracious sanctifiers who strengthened and took the sting out of life's sorrows; whose blessing brought solace, whose presence dried tears, whose words quenched the fires of revenge, whose anointed touch healed soul-wounds. . . . For so many men of heroic heart . . . and may the long line never be broken."[41]

Indeed, may the long line of America's dedicated Catholic chaplains never be broken!

EPILOGUE

In the introduction, I described *Faith of the Fathers* in several ways—as a reference work of Catholic wartime chaplains, as a much-needed updated historical record of the places and people Catholic Civil War chaplains served, and as a collective biography of these 126 men. In this epilogue, I offer a reflection on where the work might go from here, pointing the way for further research opportunities which might flow from and build upon this text.

With these newly updated Catholic chaplains' listings, the door is open for academics, scholars, and historians to expand upon this information, specifically by developing what might be called thematic reflections and trajectories. These are themes with broader and more encompassing connections beyond the scope of this manuscript—areas such as the social and ecclesial impact of chaplains' experiences, the effects of the war upon them and the Church, reactions to their ministry from both Catholic soldiers and Catholics on the home front, and so on. It is my hope that further contextualizing of the larger historical and social aspects of their work will indeed result, particularly from those in academic settings.

To facilitate and better organize such potential thematic trajectories, I would like to outline some possible directions, all flowing naturally from the four sections of this book.

PART ONE:
TROUBLED TIMES, WILLING MEN, FAITHFUL WORK

This first section laid out the critical foundational components and "anchoring concepts" of *Faith of the Fathers* before delving into specific details of the 126 Civil War Catholic priest-chaplains. Chapter 1 spoke to the central issues confronting and challenging Catholic clergy even before they *became* chaplains, and which continued to influence them throughout the war. Chapter 2 is the heart of this book: using a new system of classifying Catholic chaplains as full-time or occasional/situational in the Civil War (never done previously), a thoroughly updated and comprehensive listing of the priests who served between 1861 and 1865 has been completed. Chapter 3 described the actual ministry and work Catholic chaplains performed and undertook during the war.

Several thematic trajectories present themselves for development in this section. First, the impact on chaplains of America's prevailing anti-Catholicism, before and during the war, is a fruitful area to pursue. I discuss in chapters 1 and 12 how some Catholic chaplains experienced this challenge personally, reflected that bias in their own wartime ministry, and yet how others built bridges beyond denominational lines that lasted well past 1865. The wartime work of the Irish Brigade chaplains, as well as James Sheeran, Hippolyte Gache, Joseph O'Hagan, and Thomas Quinn could be analyzed further for deeper analysis of the multivalent impacts of anti-Catholicism in and beyond the war years. Discussion continues to this day on what overall impact the work of Catholic chaplains and nuns had on the prevalent anti-Catholic prejudice in America as a whole. Other religious historians and chroniclers have already begun to develop this theme further (William Kurtz and Robert E. Curran are two examples).[1]

A second interesting expansion of chapter 3 would be a fuller development of the tasks undertaken by wartime Catholic chaplains. Aside from required spiritual and sacramental duties, priests performed tasks similar to other chaplains. They served as informal postmaster and amanuensis for soldiers' letters, handled pay, conducted classes for troops, and so on. Several works delve into this area in general terms, but enumerating in fuller detail these and other unique tasks

Catholic chaplains undertook could be a fascinating study. Also, what were the expectations of their bishops and superiors, troops, or even area residents regarding Catholic priests? How did the ministry of Catholic chaplains compare with that of their Protestant compatriots? The starting point here could be a deeper analysis of the two Catholic chaplains' diaries (Corby and Sheeran) and wartime letters and journals available (e.g., Tissot, Bannon, Gache, Nash, and Cooney), as well as painstaking archival footwork. Some inroads have already been made along this line.[2]

A third future trajectory, requiring a deep dive into archival materials, is the content of the Catholicism about which wartime chaplains preached. Chapter 3 speaks about the importance of preaching in nineteenth-century America, reflecting as it did the predominantly Protestant environment of the day, where the preached Word of God was of utmost importance. However, it is clear from reading letters and journals that some Protestants did attend the sermons of "good" Catholic preachers during the war, and vice versa. Thus, the content of the "best" of Catholic preachers did appeal to a broader Christian audience, and appears to have been free from more overt and specifically Catholic "nuances" which might alienate some. Sadly, the wartime sermons of Catholic priests were not in general written down or preserved at all, excepting occasional summaries mentioned in diaries or letters. Deeper research into the diaries and letters of religious soldiers and various others could reveal some of the specific thematic content of Catholic wartime preaching.[3]

A final worthwhile topic for deeper analysis and research is what Catholic chaplains thought about the politics of the day—volatile issues such as secession, emancipation, Abraham Lincoln, chattel slavery, the war's aftermath, and more. Clearly many priests and bishops had strong opinions on these issues, and some of them do emerge in greater or lesser degrees from the speeches, letters, and the few wartime diaries left behind. Some priests were outspoken in public ways—such as James Sheeran and Abram Ryan, as well as bishops like John Purcell (Cincinnati) and John McGill (Richmond). Readers received a taste of some of these opinions throughout the chapters of the second section especially, but this is an area well deserving future expansion and research.

PART TWO:
THE GIANTS OF CATHOLIC CHAPLAINCY

This second section introduced the men deemed the giants of Catholic wartime chaplaincy—priests whose longer tenure, dedication, scope of work, and ability to connect with troops set them apart both then and now. Not without reason, most of these priests were connected to Catholic religious orders, as their primary commitment was to their order and not to a specific diocese or parish, thus giving them greater freedom to serve the troops as needed. Chapter 4 introduces the near-legendary men of the University of Notre Dame—undoubtedly the most well-known Catholic wartime chaplains, both because of William Corby's *Memoirs*, as well as Notre Dame's ongoing reputation as perhaps the country's leading Catholic university.

Chapter 5 fleshed out the contributions of arguably the leading Catholic order both in America and the worldwide Church—the "men of Loyola," the Jesuits—who had far more men (twenty-one) serving in Civil War chaplaincy on both sides, in all time spans, and at all levels (regimental, hospital, prison, and post). No other Catholic religious order or individual diocese in the entire war comes close. Chapter 6 covered other prominent religious order chaplains, including two temperamentally different but very effective Redemptorists (Sheeran and Smulders), as well as Dominicans (five), Franciscans (two), and Vincentians (five). Chapter 7 turned to priests connected to specific geographic Catholic dioceses who were allowed by their bishops to serve in the war. Two of the longest serving and most outspoken Catholic chaplains, John Bannon and William O'Higgins, are featured.

Once again, thematic trajectories present themselves here. First, the vowed commitments of the religious order chaplains raise interesting perspectives regarding the unique Catholicism and spirituality that animated their service. Possible tangents to be explored are the specific spiritualities of various religious orders that may have affected their wartime commitments, any ethnic-related views or backgrounds that may have motivated them, the deeper bonds of religious priest-chaplains flowing from their shared vowed backgrounds, and the potentially different ways in which Catholic religious priests preached and celebrated than did their diocesan compatriots. The unfortunate dearth of postwar diaries and letters from Catholic priest-chaplains opens up another possible field of inquiry. The writings of men like Cooney, Sheeran, Corby, Bannon, O'Hagan, Gache, Nash, Tissot, and several others could be interesting jumping off points in analyzing the chaplains of religious orders and those of specific dioceses.[4]

Second, how these chaplains dealt with being called back from wartime service (i.e., transition times), for whatever reason, is an intriguing thematic trajectory. This occurred frequently, primarily due to the shortage of priests in the rapidly expanding nineteenth-century American Catholic Church. Several priests did fight to return to service after their initial term of service ended (Smulders, O'Hagan, and Mignault, for example), feeling the deep need for assistance that their war-weary and spiritually starved troops had. Continuing to explore and flesh out their feelings and thoughts at times of both leaving military service and then returning to "normal" priestly life could be insightful.

Third, when the Civil War ended, Catholic chaplains headed back home, bringing with them deep, lasting, and powerful memories. By all accounts, priests' lives (like soldiers') were radically transformed by their experiences in four years of war. While I endeavor here to briefly outline what happened to them postwar, room does not permit me to delve more deeply into their postwar attitudes, reactions, and beliefs. (Chapter 12 is somewhat of an exception, though, as I review briefly the impactful postwar work of several chaplains.) But probing more thoroughly and deeply into the postwar worlds of a few chaplains could potentially yield some interesting insights as to how the Civil War impacted the remainder of these chaplains' years both on earth and in their postwar ministries.[5]

A final trajectory is motivated by the Jesuits priest-chaplains: a contemporary review of their contributions is sorely needed. For example, many Jesuits came to America in response to the Jesuit suppression in Europe (mid-eighteenth and nineteenth centuries); one wonders how that experience affected their subsequent American ministry. Unfortunately, despite the prolific intellectual achievements and writings of Jesuits in the past century, there is no single clear resource detailing the twenty-one Jesuit Civil War chaplains and the remarkably varied wartime work they did. The next largest group of religious—the men and women of the University of Notre Dame—have ample written and online materials about their contributions. Surprisingly, the Jesuits do not. It is my hope that someone take up the task of researching and writing a comprehensive work about the amazing work of these men often termed "God's Marines."[6]

PART THREE:
DIFFICULT SITUATIONS AND UNIQUE MEN

The third section of *Faith of the Fathers* explored the unique circumstances that distinguished the ministry of Catholic chaplains, introducing several who were quite singular in their temperaments or motivations. Aside from making up only 3 percent of all Civil War chaplains, Catholic priests were also set apart by the groups they worked with and places where they ministered. Chapter 8 reviewed the world of hospital chaplaincy in the Civil War, introducing the priests who served the sick, wounded, and dying—about nineteen full-time priest-chaplains out of the approximately two hundred hospital wartime chaplains (i.e., nearly 10 percent of all chaplains who served in the hospitals).

Chapter 9 focused on a popular Civil War subtheme—the role of the Irish, and the chaplains who served the nearly two hundred thousand heavily Catholic Irish soldiers on both sides. (It is no surprise that 60 percent of the priest-chaplains were of Irish descent or birth.) In contrast to this "popular" focus on the Irish, chapter 10 addresses a rarely discussed theater of the war—the chaplains who served in the general area of Trans-Mississippi and further west, and Bishop William Elder's unique Natchez Diocese. Chapter 11 is deals with unconventional priests who broke the mold of traditional priestly or chaplaincy roles. Nineteenth-century bishops struggled to find priests for the burgeoning workload of their territories, so often some rather "colorful" men were accepted out of these needs; partially because of this, some truly unique and distinctively different priests went on to minister and bring faith to soldiers.

At least four fascinating thematic trajectories emerge from this section as areas for development. The topic of priest-chaplains' interactions inside Civil War hospitals cries out for archival perusal. This includes their relationships with nurse-nuns, staff, and patients, but also with administrators of hospitals that had a significant US Sanitary Commission or United States Christian Commission presence. Those two Protestant groups posed a special challenge to Catholic priests because of their conscious efforts to proselytize and distribute Bibles and religious tracts to soldiers. Few resources are available in this field of study (since only nineteen priest-chaplains were full-time), except the excellent firsthand accounts of some of the Catholic nuns who worked in hospitals. But during wartime, where the nuns were, so priests were as well—thus the existent records of groups like Daughters of Charity, Sisters of Mercy, and Sisters of the Holy Cross are very helpful starting points. The fact that hospital chaplains were required to file reports of their work, many of which are now available online, is likewise helpful, though many are of a more routine nature.[7]

The ethnic backgrounds and influences of the 126 priest-chaplains are a second fertile field for exploration, though the topic is being addressed to some degree both online and in written form. With thirteen different countries of birth represented by priest-chaplains, it is interesting to reflect how those different backgrounds and national issues influenced priests' wartime or postwar ministry. For example, the French priests (18 percent of all Catholic chaplains) who served in the south and west came from the far more traditional Catholic environment of France, and generally found the rough and tumble frontier conditions and ministry quite a challenge. Language difficulties and frequently being misunderstood by American church members was an issue that arose often. On the other hand, chaplains of Irish heritage had the distinct advantage of sharing the English language, and many became postwar advocates for national pride, education issues, and so on. Exploring how the so-called devotional revolution of the nineteenth century, especially in Ireland, affected these chaplains might be a worthwhile topic for deeper analysis.[8]

A third line for potential research centers around priests and nuns being representatives of the Catholicism they practiced, thus bringing their unique histories to the fields in which they labored. Many Catholic priests, nuns, and laymen made great societal contributions to politics and culture out of their educational heritage and spiritual sensibilities. Clergy like Bishop Sylvester Rosecrans (Cincinnati) and John Ireland (St. Paul), chaplains like Bernardin Wiget and Thomas Scully, laymen like General William Rosecrans and Orestes Brownson, and the six hundred-plus Catholic nursing nuns of the war are excellent examples of how individual Catholics greatly impacted America by their faith, work, and influence. Chapter 12 expands on this theme, but there is ample room for future development around this nexus of Catholic pastoral ministry and the broader American culture, which is beyond the scope of this book.[9]

A final trajectory arising here is the balance that Catholic chaplains struggled with when representing and speaking *for* the Catholic Church *in* the United States of America. The mid-nineteenth-century Catholic Church was a highly authoritarian, hierarchical structure, yet the American political system is based on individual freedoms and liberties (some of which were condemned by the Vatican at the time). At least indirectly, Catholic chaplains were forced to "defend" the papacy and structure of the Church at times, but their primary pastoral focus was always to transmit and celebrate Catholic faith and values. Maintaining and managing these two often conflicting pastoral energies during the Civil War must have been an extremely difficult balancing act for chaplains, particularly in close quarters like hospitals, heavily Protestant areas (such as the Natchez Diocese), encampments, and the like. Expanding further on this issue, and indeed pondering and reflecting on the balancing challenges of both Catholics in general and wartime clergy would be a very worthwhile project.[10]

PART FOUR:
FROM THE VANTAGE POINT OF HISTORY

This final section of *Faith of the Fathers* presented a summary of the work of Catholic wartime chaplains from the vantage point of history. These closing chapters attempted to situate the lives, wartime work, and faith of these Catholic chaplains within larger historical and social contexts. For example, connections with other Civil War chaplains, overall issues of health and death, postwar issues involving Catholic faith and American society, and postwar efforts in both North and South at memory-making and remembering.

Chapter 12 offered a macro view of the consequences, challenges, and changes that confronted Catholic chaplains both during the war and after. Two major issues detailed here were the immense physical health toll that confronted all troops and chaplains, and the necessity of working interdenominationally with non-Catholic ministers (which had both unifying and divisive elements). Chapter 13 offered some personal reflections from decades of research in this field, and spelled out some important lessons that emerge from the Civil War ministry of Catholic priests—the most important of which was the common faith bonding them together amid the horrors and division of the war, and the importance of "believing in belief" (acknowledging the central historical role that faith has played in world and American history).

As with previous sections, intriguing thematic trajectories for future development present themselves from these reflections. A review of Catholic priests' wartime relationships with Protestant ministers is discussed in Chapter 12, but a deeper analysis of this area might yield further interesting fruit (if resources can be found), especially with regard to friendships that developed. Examples here are the collaboration of Joseph O'Hagan and Joseph Twichell (Congregationalist), Thomas Quinn and Augustus Woodbury (Unitarian), and Darius Hubert's broader approach to working with non-Catholics. But aside from wartime camaraderie, the challenges which some Catholic clergy (Sheeran and Gache come to mind) had getting along with non-Catholics would be worth researching, particularly how the inherent religious bias of the time predisposed them to respond the way they did, also how wartime experiences impacted their postwar ministry.[11]

The transcendent centrality of ever-present death was also a unifying factor for chaplains from the North and the South, impacting them deeply and personally. An excellent field for future development is expanding upon the Chapter 12 theme of Catholic chaplains' deaths, using archival research to pursue how wartime death impacted their personal lives and work. The existent writings of chaplains are filled with references to death on battlefield and hospitals, and funerals they conducted, and are nearly always marked by powerful emotions. Without a doubt the most poignant parts of all priest-chaplains' writings are stories of executions they attended or ministered at. William Corby, Jeremiah Trecy, and Peter Whelan all attended these rare and tragic occasions, with Corby and Whelan later describing them with immense pathos. Continuing to pursue this theme of omnipresent death and dying with evidence from the letters, diaries, and period accounts of priests (and soldiers) would certainly deepen our appreciation for the immense emotional burden that the unending *ars morienda* had upon priests in our most deadly war.[12]

In closing, there are a plethora of other issues that could be teased out of this section and indeed the entire book for further development, despite not being directly related to this book's biographical focus on Catholic chaplains. Examples here include the Reconstruction-era Church, Catholic priests' role in the "religion" of the Lost Cause, the rampant destruction of Southern churches, the increasing Civil War "masculinization" of Christianity, and the transition to an increased civil religion in the United States that emerged in postwar decades. The majority of these have been briefly explored in my previous book on religion and faith in the Civil War, *Both Prayed to the Same God*, but could benefit from further research.[13]

Finally, as mentioned in the introduction and at the end of chapter 13, while not a direct focus in this book, the issue of slavery must not be far removed when discussing mid-nineteenth-century America and Catholicism, and is worth a longer review elsewhere. The Church's overall attitude toward slavery is fraught with nuance, but in terms of the Civil War, no Catholic chaplains worked primarily with African Americans, but neither was there any occasion when priests refused ministry to *anyone* who sought spiritual help. As their diaries reveal, clergy like Bishops William Elder and Augustin Verot frequently ministered to enslaved persons and free Blacks. Sadly though individual priests made efforts to evangelize freed Blacks continued after the war, the Catholic Church in America did not make this a focused outreach.

Black religious self-determination became one of the significant results of the Civil War, but the Catholic Church missed this opportunity to welcome new members, and did not gain any significant foothold in the Black community at that time. Although it had ample reason to be proud of the priests and nuns who served faithfully in the war, the American Catholic Church continued to wrestle with ethnic changes and challenges well into the twenty-first century.[14]

CATHOLIC DIOCESES AND BISHOPS IN THE UNITED STATES, 1861–1865

FACTOTUMS OF THE AMERICAN CATHOLIC CHURCH FROM 1861 TO 1865

- Pope Pius IX led the Catholic Church at the time of American Civil War (June 16, 1846–February 7, 1878)
- There were 43 archdioceses or dioceses and 4 vicariates (which eventually became dioceses):
  - 26 of the 47 (55 percent) of the archdioceses, dioceses, and vicariates sent chaplains to the Civil War.
  - The Baltimore and New York Archdioceses each had two wartime bishops (due to deaths).
  - The dioceses of Albany, Little Rock, and Louisville had episcopal vacancies for the remainder of the war after their bishops either died, resigned, or were transferred.
- There were 51 archbishops or bishops, 35 of which were immigrants (33 percent from Ireland; 29 percent from US; 21.5 percent from France)
- The list below includes (a) bishop's name and terms of service (if known), (b) archdiocese/diocese, (c) religious order (if applicable), (d) country of birth (if known), and (e) any Civil War chaplains (official or unofficial) from that archdiocese/diocese.

Province of Baltimore

Baltimore	Archbishop Francis P. Kenrick (August 1851– July 1863) (Ireland)
	Archbishop Martin Spaulding (May 1864– February 1872) (Kentucky)
	Chaplains: Boyle, Gibbons, McCarthy, O'Keefe
Charleston	Bishop Patrick N. Lynch (Ireland)
	Chaplains: Croghan, O'Connell, P. Ryan
Erie	Bishop Josue Young (Maine)
Philadelphia	Bishop James Wood (Pennsylvania)
	Chaplains: Martin, McCollum, McCosker, McGrane, McKee
Pittsburgh	Bishop Michael Domenec (Vincentian; Spain)
	Chaplain: Christy
Richmond	Bishop John McGill (Pennsylvania)
	Chaplains: Plunkett, Sears, Teeling
Savannah	Bishop Augustine Verot (Sulpician; France)
	Chaplains: Clavreul, Hamilton, Kirby, O'Neill, T. O'Reilly, Whelan
Wheeling	Bishop Richard Whelan (Dominican; Ireland)
Vicariate of E. Florida	Bishop Augustine Verot (Sulpician; France)

Province of Cincinnati

Cincinnati	Archbishop John Purcell (Ireland)
	Chaplains: Corcoran, O'Higgins, Stephan
Cleveland	Bishop Amadeus Rappe (France)
Covington	Bishop George Carrell (Jesuit; Pennsylvania)
Detroit	Bishop Peter Lefevre (Belgium)
	Chaplain: Brady
Fort Wayne	Bishop John Luers (Germany)

Louisville	Bishop Martin Spaulding (February 1850–May 1864) (Kentucky) Bishop Peter J. Lavialle (July 1865–May 1867) (France)
Sault Ste. Marie	Bishop Frederick Baraga (Austria)
Vincennes	Bishop Maurice de St. Palais (France) Chaplain: P. J. R. Murphy

Province of New Orleans

New Orleans	Archbishop Jean-Marie Odin (Vincentian; France) Chaplains: Carius, Lemagie, Turgis
Galveston	Bishop Claude Dubuis (France) Chaplain: Chambodut
Little Rock	Bishop Andrew Byrne (November 1843–June 1862) (Ireland) Bishop Edward Fitzgerald (September 1866–February 1907) (Ireland)
Mobile	Bishop John Quinlan (Ireland) Chaplains: Coyle, Manucy, Pellicer, Trecy
Natchez	Bishop William Henry Elder (Maryland) Chaplains: Boheme, Guillou, Leray, Mouton, Pont; Elder's "Clerical Legion": Elia, Finucane, Georget, Huber, Picherit
Natchitoches	Bishop Augustus Martin (France) Chaplain: Dicharry

Province of New York

New York	Archbishop John Hughes (December 1842–January 1864) (Ireland) Archbishop John McCloskey (May 1864–October 1885) (New York) Chaplains: McCrossin, McGlynn, Mooney

Albany   Bishop John McCloskey (May 1847–May 1864)
      (New York)
      Bishop John J. Conroy (July 1865–October 1877)
      (Ireland)
      Chaplain: Miettenger

Boston   Bishop John Fitzpatrick (Massachusetts)
      Chaplains: MacMahon, N. O'Brien, Scully

Brooklyn   Bishop John Laughlin (Ireland)

Buffalo   Bishop John Timon (Vincentian; Pennsylvania)
      Chaplain: Moore

Burlington   Bishop Louis de Goesbriand (France)

Hartford   Bishop Francis McFarland (Pennsylvania)
      Chaplains: Mullen, Quinn

Newark   Bishop James Bayley (New York)
      Chaplains: Doane, McQuaid

Portland   Bishop David Bacon (New York)

Province of Oregon

Oregon City   Archbishop Francis X. Blanchet (Canada)
Nesqualy   Bishop Augustine M. Blanchet (Canada)
Vancouver Island   Bishop Modest Demers (Canada)

Province of St. Louis

St. Louis   Archbishop Peter Kenrick (Ireland)
      Chaplains: Bannon, J. P. Ryan

Alton   Bishop Henry Juncker (France)
      Chaplain: Lambert

Chicago   Bishop James Duggan (Ireland)
      Chaplains: Butler, Kelly, Vahey

Dubuque   Bishop Clement Smyth (Cistercian; Ireland)

Milwaukee   Bishop John Henni (Switzerland)
      Chaplain: Fusseder

Nashville	Bishop James Whelan (May 1860–September 1863) (Dominican; Ireland)
	Bishop Peter Feehan (July 1865–September 1880) (Ireland)
	Chaplains: Bergrath, Browne
Santa Fe	Bishop John Lamy (France)
	Chaplains: Fialon, Grzelachowski, Taladrid
St. Paul	Bishop Thomas Grace (Dominican; South Carolina)
	Chaplain: John Ireland
Vicariate of Indian Territory	Bishop John B. Miege (Jesuit; France)
Vicariate of Nebraska	Bishop James O'Gorman (Cistercian; Ireland)

Province of San Francisco

San Francisco	Archbishop Joseph Alemany y Conill (Dominican; Spain)
Los Angeles and Monterey	Bishop Thaddeus Amat (Vincentian; Spain)
Vicariate of Marysville	Bishop Eugene O'Connell (Ireland)

Religious Orders and the List of Chaplains Who Served

Benedictine	Bliemel
Dominicans	Egan, Jarboe, McGrath, Nealis, Orengo
Franciscans	Rizza, Titta
Holy Cross	Bourget, Carrier, Cooney, Corby, Dillon, Gillen, Leveque
Jesuits, official	Bruehl, de Chaignon, Gache, Hubert, McAtee, Nash, O'Hagan, Ouellett, Prachensky, Tissot, Truyens, Wiget
Jesuits, unofficial	Bixio, Brady, Cornette, Nachon, O'Callaghan, O'Reilly, Pacciarini, Roccofort, Usannez

Redemptorists	Sheeran, Smulders
OMI (Missionary Oblates of Mary)	Mignault
Vincentians, unofficial (all)	Boglioli, Burke, Burlando, A. Ryan, Smith

Civil War Chaplains Who Became Bishops (Year, Diocese)

Union

John Ireland	(1875, St. Paul Diocese)
Laurence McMahon	(1879, Hartford Diocese)
Bernard J. McQuaid	(1868, Rochester Diocese)

Confederate

Francis Xavier LeRay	(1877, Natchitoches Diocese; 1883, New Orleans Archdiocese)
Dominic Manucy	(1874, Brownsville Diocese; 1884, Mobile Diocese)
Anthony D. Pellicier	(1875, San Antonio Diocese)

APPENDIX 2

RATIOS OF CATHOLIC CHAPLAINS TO CIVIL WAR SOLDIERS

CAVEATS

- Statistics assume all chaplains and soldiers would be in the field at the same time.
- Unless noted, statistics pertaining to Catholic chaplains do not distinguish between official chaplains (76) or unofficial chaplains (50).
- Numbers of soldiers and chaplains used are generally accepted numbers, and may not be completely accurate.
- The number of Catholic Confederate soldiers is an educated supposition since accurate accounting is difficult.

SOLDIERS ESTIMATES

- An estimated 2.1 million Union soldiers
- An estimated 750,000 to 1 million Confederate soldiers
- Total: 2.85 million to 3.1 Civil War soldiers

CHAPLAIN ESTIMATES OVERALL

- 2,398 Union chaplains, and 1,308 Confederate chaplains (3,706 total chaplains)

- 126 total Catholic chaplains
  - 76 Catholic official chaplains (meaning they served at least 3 months, with some official recognition)
    - 51 official Union Catholic chaplains; 25 official Confederate Catholic chaplains
  - 50 Catholic unofficial chaplains (no official recognition; occasional or situational work only)
    - 23 unofficial Union Catholic chaplains; 27 unofficial Confederate Catholic chaplains

RATIOS OF CHAPLAINS TO SOLDIERS

- 1 chaplain for every 769 to 836 Civil War soldiers (3,706 chaplains for 2.85 to 3.1 million soldiers)
- 1 Catholic chaplain for every 22,800 to 24,800 Civil War soldiers (126 Catholic chaplains for 2.85 to 3.1 million soldiers)

RATIOS OF UNION CHAPLAINS TO SOLDIERS

- 1 Union chaplain for 876 Union soldiers (2,398 chaplains for 2.1 million soldiers)
- 1 Catholic chaplain for 28,378 total Union soldiers (74 Catholic chaplains for 2.1 million soldiers)
- 1 Catholic chaplain for 2,702 Catholic Union soldiers (74 Catholic chaplains for an estimated 200,000 Catholic soldiers)

RATIOS OF CONFEDERATE CHAPLAINS TO SOLDIERS

- 1 chaplain for 573 to 765 Confederate soldiers (1,308 chaplains for 750,000 to 1 million soldiers)
- 1 Catholic chaplain for 14,423 to 19,230 Confederate soldiers (52 Catholic chaplains for 750,000 to 1 million soldiers)
- 1 Catholic chaplain for 480 to 769 Catholic Confederate soldiers (52 Catholic chaplains for the unverified suppositions of 25,000 to 40,000 Catholic Confederate soldiers)

NOTES

INTRODUCTION

1. The collective stories of the 126 Catholic chaplains in this book have been compiled largely from their own writings and other accounts directly concerning them. A broader sweep of materials from soldiers' accounts, diocesan archives, women religious and even non-Catholics could potentially be mined in the future for even more expanded perspectives of their wartime work and its effectiveness.

2. Cf. chapter 2 of this book for specific and important distinctions in this area, including details of places of birth, diocese or religious order, Civil War unit, and length of service.

3. It is worth mentioning here that, as referenced in the prologue, there were slight differences in chaplain appointment styles between the North and the South (in wartime hospitals, for example), and this had impacts on the later ministries of some Catholic chaplains.

4. Ellis, *Documents of American Catholic History*, 385.

5. Kraszewski, *Catholic Confederates*, 27. Also, Katherine Jeffrey does point out that in *Faith in the Fight* there are errors in chaplain records beyond those of the Catholic chaplains. Cf. Jeffrey, *First Chaplain*, 153.

6. From the private correspondence of the author and Father David Endres.

7. Cf. Robert Miller, *Both Prayed to the Same God*. For the sake of transparency, for four decades the author has been actively involved in Civil War Roundtables (including being president of the prestigious Chicago Civil War Roundtable), reenacting groups, and in giving innumerable talks nationally on various aspects of Civil War religion and related wartime issues.

PROLOGUE

1. A more fully developed history of chaplaincy can be found in Honeywell, *Chaplains of the United States Army*; Germain, *Catholic Military and Naval Chaplains: 1776–1917*; the anonymously written *American Army Chaplaincy: A Brief History*; Norton, *Struggling for Recognition: The United States Army Chaplaincy, 1791–1865*; Brinsfield, "Military Chaplains: A Historian's View from the American Revolution to Iraq"; and O'Malley, "Providing Shepherds for Soldiers: A History of Catholic Military Chaplaincy in the U.S."

2. Honeywell, *Chaplains*, 2–5.

3. Germain, *Chaplains*, iii–iv; see also Steve O'Brien, *Blackrobe in Blue: The Naval Chaplaincy of John P. Foley, S.J. 1942*. In regard to Wellington and his chaplains, cf. Roy David Burley, "An Age of Negligence? British Army Chaplaincy 1796–1844," https://etheses.bham.ac.uk//id/eprint/4329/1/Burley 13MPhil.pdf. Two ministers in particular, Müller and Monrad, despite having the chaplain title, were arguably more colonial/missionary ambassadors than military chaplains, although they were attached to the local Danish fort.

4. Daryl Densford, *The Chaplain Kit (blog)*, "George Washington's Christian Influence," December 26, 2015, https://thechaplainkit.com/history/chaplains-at-war/revolutionary-war/george-washingtons-christian-influence/.

5. Germain, *Chaplains*, 10; Honeywell, *Chaplains*, 30–53; Brinsfield, "Military Chaplains"; O'Malley, "Providing Shepherds."

6. Germain, *Chaplains*, 17.

7. Germain, *Chaplains*, 39. Cf. the anonymously written *American Army Chaplaincy*, 22–23.

8. Germain, *Chaplains*, 40–41. De Smet, *Life, Letters, and Travels*, 715–19. Though Germain and several others speak of Milley being a Catholic, the 1946 anonymous work, *American Army Chaplaincy: A Brief History*, indicates he may have been Presbyterian. Nineteenth-century military records did not always indicate a chaplain's religion, so confusion sometimes exists over the faith of certain individuals.

9. Brinsfield et al., *Faith in the Fight*, 9.

10. This was amended in July 1862 to include spiritual representatives from other prominent religious denominations, most notably, Jewish rabbis.

11. Woodworth, *While God Is Marching On*, 145–46.

12. Shattuck, *Shield*, 52–63; Brinsfield et al., *Faith in the Fight*, 9.

13. Pitts, *Chaplains in Gray*, 39.

14. "Congress of the Confederate States," *New Orleans Daily Picayune*, May 5, 1861; 3; and Brinsfield, *Spirit Divided – Confederacy*, 10.

15. Cf. C. Smith, "Work of the Civil War Chaplains," 19–20; Brinsfield et al., *Faith in the Fight*, 54–55. Gardiner Shattuck states that in the Confederacy "many aspects of the political and military life were either poorly organized or left intentionally to individual initiative." Thus, the confusion surrounding Confederate chaplains fell into a much larger confusion that plagued the entire Southern bureaucracy. (Cf. Shattuck, *Shield*, 63–64.) Three reasons why the Confederacy did not place emphasis on chaplains are as follows: the de-emphasis on the role of chaplains in the military in the years immediately preceding the Civil War (especially at West Point), Jefferson Davis's own ambivalent attitudes toward chaplains, and the higher priority the Confederacy placed on filling their ranks with properly equipped soldiers than finding Bible-toting chaplains.

16. Brinsfield, *Spirit Divided – Confederacy*, 10.

17. Norton, *Struggling for Recognition*, 132; Brinsfield, *Spirit Divided – Confederacy*, 7–11.

CHAPTER 1. Prewar Challenges to Catholic Chaplains

The part epigraph is from the letter of Archbishop John Ireland to Father Peter P. Cooney, May 24, 1892; cf. Shannon, "Archbishop Ireland's Experience," 304.

1. The size of the prewar Catholic Church in America vis-à-vis other denominations remains a somewhat uncertain figure. Cf. Ahlstrom, *Religious History*, 541–42; and Hennessey, *American Catholics*, 117. Cf. also the website of the Catholic Education Resource Center, https://www.catholiceducation.org.

2. Perko, *Catholic and American*, 135–37.

3. Germain, *Chaplains*, 71.

4. James Titta (from Gombitelli, Italy) served only a little over five months, partly because his cavalry unit (13th Pennsylvania) only fought minor engagements, but also because, as he stated in his discharge request, "three-fourths of the members of the Reg't are of a different Religious denomination from my own." Cf. Germain, *Chaplains*, 70–71; Brinsfield et al., *Faith in the Fight*, 156; Blied, *Catholics*, 122. Cf. also Shannon, "Ireland's Experiences," 298–305.

5. From the online archival records of Augustus Woodbury, *Second Rhode Island*, 34.

6. Germain, *Chaplains*, 49.

7. Further details on the distinctions employed in this book between official and unofficial chaplains, as well as full-time and part-time, will be elaborated in chapter 2.

8. John Purcell, "Army Chaplains," *The Catholic Telegraph*, January 15, 1862.

9. There were never enough chaplains of any denomination on either side. In the Confederacy, each regiment was intended to have an active chaplain, but in reality the Confederate Chaplains Association reported in 1863 that half of the units were without a minister. Even the great chaplain proponent General Thomas "Stonewall" Jackson lacked sufficient chaplains for his troops. The Northern War Department announced in June 1862 that of 676 regiments in the field, only 395 had chaplains on official assignment. Of those, twenty-nine were absent on detached service while another thirteen were absent without leave; one third of all Union regiments had no chaplains. Cf. Shattuck, *Shield*, 47.

10. Chaplain figures are based on the 2003 roster of Civil War chaplains found in Brinsfield et al., *Faith in the Fight*, 129–256. Other rosters do exist, but this list is the largest, most contemporary, and well-researched, making it is the best statistical base for my calculations. Their roster is not without some errors, such as four chaplains who are erroneously called Catholic, but these have been taken into account.

11. Brinsfield et al., *Faith in the Fight*, 129–256. In some locations, fluctuations in the ratio of priests to troops occurred. For example, for twelve months between November 1862 and 1863, Rosecrans's Army of the Cumberland actually had seven priests serving simultaneously. (Jeremiah Trecy, Peter Cooney, John Ireland, Francis Fusseder, Richard Christy, William O'Higgins, and later Joseph Stephan). A more normative example, though, was the spring of 1862 in the East, when only twenty-two priests served among the 472 Union chaplains then on duty—a ratio of one in twenty-one, when ratio of Catholic to Protestant soldiers was one to nine. Catholic chaplains. Cf. Gary Sheftick, "Chaplain Corps Turns 236 with New Strength," July 29, 2011, https://army.mil/article/62568/chaplain_corps_turns_236_with_new_strength.

12. Accurate numbers of Confederate soldiers are difficult to determine, given the incomplete and destroyed enlistment records. Cf. Hieronymus, "For Now and Forever," 3.

13. Gracjan Kraszewski states that about 97,300 Irish fought for the Confederacy, and were "the region's largest Catholic ethnic group." However, his estimates are rather an outlier compared to other far smaller estimates. Kraszewski, *Catholic Confederates*, 26 and 156n7.

14. Budd, "Ohio Army Chaplains," 3–6.

15. The German paper *Der Wahrheitsfreund* of April 30, 1862, is cited in Blied, *Catholics*, 112–13.

16. The War Department was responsible for the draft, with the Provost Marshall Generals Bureau "enforcing" it. Draft quotas were established by dis-

tricts but rarely followed. Registration was left to Federal initiative, with no community or individual role or responsibility. The system was slow and complicated, and aroused much hostility. The Confederacy had three conscription measures between 1862 and 1864, using mostly the same system as the Union, with similar results. However, in the act of April 21, 1862, Christian ministers (along with other "reserved occupations") in the Confederacy were exempted from the draft. Cf. Brinsfield et al., *Faith in the Fight*, 60; and the April 5, 1864, letter from Bishop William Elder to Bishop John Purcell on Confederate exemptions, found at https://www.archives.nd.edu/calendar/cal1864d.htm.

17. Garraghan, *Jesuits*, 161. Ministers and divinity students in the United States have legally had an automatic and special exemption to the military draft since the draft law of May 18, 1917. This status has been retained in all subsequent draft statutes with only minor variations. Cf. J. L. Smith, *Ministerial Draft Exemption*, passim.

18. The commutation fee was dropped in July 1864, leaving hiring a substitute the only escape from the draft. June 15, 1863, letter from Bishop Henry Juncker (Alton) to Bishop John Purcell (Cincinnati), summary available at www.archives.nd.edu. Slawson, "Vincentian Experience," 54; Miller, Stout, and Wilson, *Religion and the Civil War*, 281.

19. De Smet actually had a previous acquaintance with Colonel Hardie, which proved very beneficial in this case. Garraghan, *Jesuits*, 159–62.

20. Bell, *Civil War Stories*, 73–74.

21. Wimmer, *Letters*, February 7, 1863.

22. The fact that there were no clergy exemptions from the national draft is one of the reasons why, as historian Will Kurtz avers, Catholics grew to dislike the war in 1864. Kurtz, *Excommunicated*, 108–28.

23. B. Miller, "When 'Good Father Seelos' Met 'Good Father Abraham,'" 13.

24. Founded by St. Alphonsus Liguori in 1732, and formally known as the Congregation of the Most Holy Redeemer, the Redemptorist seminary had just been moved to Annapolis from Cumberland, Pennsylvania, the previous year. Cf. B. Miller, "When 'Good Father Seelos' Met 'Good Father Abraham,'" 10–14.

25. Ahlstrom, *Religious History*, 114, 124. Cf. also Kurtz, *Excommunicated*, 2–3.

26. Ahlstrom, *Religious History*, 555. Cf. also Curran, *American Catholics*, 24–26, for a fine summary of challenges facing Irish immigrants in the antebellum era.

27. The Know Nothing platform opposed citizenship for any new immigrant until after twenty-one years, and wanted to ban foreign-born citizens from holding political office. Know Nothings were strong in New York for a

time; they became the "American" political party in 1854, taking control of the Massachusetts legislature and electing several members of Congress. However, they splintered over disagreements over slavery and were already fading in strength by the 1856 elections, when—although gaining over 20 percent of the vote in that election—they lost many adherents to the newly formed Republican party.

28. Moorhead, *American Apocalypse*; and Randall Miller, "Catholic Religion, Irish Ethnicity," 264–65.

29. Norton, *Struggling*, 94; Blied, *Catholics*, 112–13; Randall Miller, "Catholic Religion, Irish Ethnicity," 265. Richard C. Christie, elected as chaplain by the overwhelmingly Protestant 78th Pennsylvania, was one exception to Catholics being elected for Protestant regiments.

30. Tom Emery, "Gettysburg Hero Buford Grew Up in Rock Island," *The Dispatch-The Rock Island Argus*, July 6, 2013.

31. Germain, *Chaplains*, 73–77.

32. Germain, *Chaplains*, 73–74.

33. Anonymous, "Obituary of Fr. Joseph B. O'Hagan," 178.

34. I am grateful to Dr. Mark Noll for his insights on this "uniquely American way of interpreting Scripture." The people of the United States "had done it our own way"—reading the Bible fervently, relying upon its wisdom, confident of our own ability to interpret it, and using it to shape our own lives and the structures of our churches and nation. Cf. Noll, *Civil War*, passim; and Robert Miller, *Both Prayed*, 43.

35. Attitudes such as these appear to have affected the decreased Confederate emphasis on having chaplains at the outset of the war. See C. Smith, "Civil War Chaplains," iv, 27–32; Norton, *Struggling*, 22–42; Honeywell, *Chaplains*, passim.

36. Ambrose Bierce is amusingly described by Maryniak as "America's favorite posttraumatic shock casualty." Brinsfield et al., *Faith in the Fight*, 27–28. Cf. also Robertson, *Soldiers*, 179, and Shattuck, *Shield*, 47.

37. *The Cincinnati Daily Enquirer* (1852–1872), April 3, 1862, 1. The author is grateful to Father David Endres for finding this newspaper article.

38. Dr. W. H. White to J. Harlan, June 12, 1865, file of Chaplain M. Carr, RG 94, 679, National Archives; see also C. Smith, "Civil War Chaplains," iv. The humorous story is told of a Confederate chaplain who tried to improve his condition by commandeering a horse from a Virginia farmer. When the chaplain rejoined his commander and was asked where the horse was from, he responded, "Down the road there." The colonel promptly told him to return it, but the chaplain protested, "Why, Jesus Christ, when he was on earth, took an ass to ride to Jerusalem." The colonel snapped back, "You are not Jesus

Christ; that is not an ass; you are not on your way to Jerusalem; and the sooner you return that horse to its owner, the better it will be for you." Cf. Robertson, *Soldiers*, 177–78.

39. C. Smith, "Civil War Chaplains," 66. Gardiner Shattuck Jr. states that of the overall 2,398 Union chaplains, less than six hundred were in service at any one time. Most were regimental (2,154), but others served in hospitals, prisons, and the navy. He claims the Confederacy had 938 known chaplains—14 percent of all eligible Southern clergy. However, Bernard Maryniak in *Faith in the Fight*, a more recent accounting of chaplains (2003), lists 3,708 total chaplains: 2,400 Union and 1,308 Confederate. Cf. Brinsfield et al., *Faith in the Fight*, 128–256; and Shattuck, *Shield*, passim.

40. Endres and Kurtz, *Soldiers*, 129–30.

41. Endres and Kurtz, *Soldiers*, 149–50.

CHAPTER 2. Toward a Roster of Catholic Civil War Chaplains

1. Letter of Archbishop John Ireland to Father Peter P. Cooney, May 24, 1892, as provided in Shannon, "Archbishop Ireland's Experience," 304.

2. Germain, *Chaplains*, passim.

3. Endres and Kurtz, *Soldiers*, passim.

4. Prior to the Council of Trent in 1545 to 1563, the requirements for priestly ordination were somewhat loose and subject to abuse. Beginning with that council, every diocese was required to have a seminary and to give its students professional education in preaching, sacraments, theology, etc.

5. This list of occasional chaplains is not intended to be comprehensive or complete in any way. Unnamed priests by the score were involved with troops in some way, far beyond enumeration or available records. In major cities where troops were consistently present or battles were fought (for example, Richmond, Savannah, Washington, DC, Richmond, and the upper Mississippi by Corinth), one would not be far off the mark in saying that nearly *every* priest and bishop in the vicinity would have ministered in some way, shape, or form.

6. I am aware that in many ways, choosing three months and three years as delineating factors in Civil War chaplaincy ministry is arbitrary. However, qualifying a chaplain's actual length of military service is a critical organizational factor in understanding the dedication and commitment of these men, let alone the challenges and struggles they had to endure (which would have been very different the longer one served). Three months was chosen because, before conscription was used by both armies, it was the first (and shortest) enlistment period used, whereas three years was the longest. As will be shown, some Catholic

chaplains' length of service did not fall under either of those standards—a few served less than three months, and several for more than three years. The Confederate army initially authorized one hundred thousand volunteers for a one-year period, while US president Abraham Lincoln initially called for seventy-five thousand men for three months, and later for five hundred thousand volunteers for a three-year enlistment.

7. Their names were Abraham Frankel (hospital chaplain), Bernard H. Gotthelf, and Ferdinand Sarner (54th New York). Honeywell, *Chaplains*, 107–8.

8. Dr. Stanley Burns was the medical, historical, and technical advisor to the PBS special *Mercy Street*. This citation is from Burns, "Civil War-Era Hospitals." The names and stories of the Catholic hospital chaplains will be recounted in chapter 8.

9. The eight post chaplains were: Charles Lemagie (Carrolton, Louisiana) and Joseph Fialon (Ft. Sumner, New Mexico) for the Union, and in the Confederacy, Charles Croghan and Laurence O'Connell (Montgomery White Sulphur Springs, Virginia), Francis Leray (Oxford, Mississippi), Dominic Manucy (Montgomery, Alabama), John Mouton (along the Mobile-Ohio railroad in Eastern, Mississippi), Anthony Pellicer (Montgomery, Alabama), Patrick Ryan (Charleston, South Carolina) and Peter Whelan (Ft. Pulaski, Georgia).

10. Germain, *Chaplains*, 58–59.

11. For those unfamiliar with these terms, a diocese is a specific geographical district, administered by a Catholic bishop, where a priest's primary pastoral responsibility for ministry lies. A Catholic religious order is a community of priests and brothers (or nuns and sisters) who have formally vowed to follow their founder's religious practices, and who are not bound by specific geographic boundaries.

12. I am grateful to Robert Worden, the archivist of the Redemptorist house in Annapolis, Maryland, for his information on the Civil War Redemptorists who belonged to what was then their Eastern province. Their anonymously published *History of the Redemptorists at Annapolis 1853–1903* offered great insight (especially pages 38–39).

13. Listing specific references for each occasional chaplain would be too burdensome a process. Interested readers should know that all information here is from the records of various religious orders, period Catholic almanacs, local parish records, reliable internet resources, historical books, general Civil War materials, and military records. All information here is based upon solid collaborative sources, not merely hagiographic or anecdotal sources. The author may be contacted for further details.

14. Slawson, "Vincentian Experience," 48.

15. McQuaid, *Life and Letters*, 348.

16. O'Reilly's heroic picking up of the fallen green flag of the 69th New York militia at First Bull Run was cited in the July 28, 1861, entry of Maria Lydig Daly's diary. Cf. Randall Miller et. al. *Religion and the American Civil War*, 289.

17. Cf. Barton, *Angels*, 32–33.

18. Randall Miller et al, *Religion and the American Civil War*, 271.

19. Fortin, *Faith and Action*, 143–44.

20. Gannon, *Rebel Bishop*, 94–96.

21. Cf. Jeffrey, *First Chaplain*, 163–64. Teeling is referred to in Barton, *Angels*, 74, though with a misspelled name.

22. Carroll, *Catholic History*, 326.

23. Blied, *Catholics*, 39.

24. The story of Elder's life, with special focus on his Civil War career, is recounted in Ryan Starrett's *Mississippi Bishop William Henry Elder and the Civil War*.

25. The interesting story of Verot's life, containing much of his diary, is told in his biography by Peter V. Gannon, *Rebel Bishop*.

26. For these cases of "mistaken identity," cf. Germain, *Chaplains*, 110, 115, 122, and 124.

27. Visit www.findagrave.com to search for the memorial to William Clarkson Meredith.

CHAPTER 3. The Wartime Ministry of Catholic Priests

1. An encompassing summary of the chaplains' work is captured in Charles Edward Smith's thesis, "The Work of the Civil War Chaplains." His list includes "managing libraries, conducting schools, certifying mail, keeping the history of the regiment/hospital, arranging banquets and civic events, conducting bands, glee clubs, literary clubs, collecting money for patriotic causes, examining prisons, superintending contrabands and national cemeteries, helping soldiers with finances, keeping medical records, publishing newspapers, and serving as postmasters." C. Smith, "Civil War Chaplains," 23. Cf. also Armstrong, *Courageous Fighting*, 14–15.

2. Brinsfield et al., *Faith in the Fight*, 5 and 76; Germain, *Chaplains*, 45. The Higginson quote can be found in Eastman, "Army Chaplain," 339.

3. In Catholic theology, the revelation of God to his people (also known as the "deposit of faith") is transmitted to people through both the Word of God and tradition. "Tradition" refers to the teaching authority of Catholic leadership (the bishops in union with the pope as the chief shepherd), as expressed through

Church doctrines and dogmas, usually generated from the synods and ecumenical councils in the long history of the Catholic Church. The Second Vatican Council of 1962–1965 marked an enormous change in how much of this was expressed and lived out in our contemporary world.

4. William Kurtz emphasizes this point as well in *Excommunicated from the Union*. As one might guess, the central role priests played in Catholic prayer life was both a blessing and a challenge, especially given the relative paucity of priests to Catholics in the armies. Catholic soldiers needed priests to fulfill their religious duties, thus could be strongly bonded to them as father figures and authority symbols, especially if they were of the same ethnicity. But they could also more easily fall away from regular practice of the faith without a priestly presence or regular reception of the sacraments.

5. A sacrament defined in its classic Catholic form is an outward sign, instituted by Christ, that gives grace. All seven sacraments are rooted in specific words and actions of Jesus during his earthly ministry. The Latin words for sacrament (*sacra* and *mentum*) reflect the purpose and power of these ritual prayers—they are celebrated at the critical holy moments of a human life—birth, death, life commitments, failure and sin, eating, and nourishment.

6. May 7, 1864 quote in Sheeran, *Diary*, 359.

7. Sheeran, *Diary*, 359; Tissot, "Year," 65.

8. Gache, *Frenchman*, 124.

9. Endres and Kurtz, *Soldiers*, 175 and 92.

10. Brinsfield et al., *Faith in the Fight*, 124.

11. Endres and Kurtz, *Soldiers*, 266–67.

12. "General absolution" refers to a priest giving absolution for a person's sins in a general and therefore not individual way to a large number of people at the same time. This differs from the customary form of a penitent speaking or confessing one's sins individually and privately to the priest. Cf. Tissot's 1861 diary, "Year," 87. Father O'Hagan also gave the last rites to General Dan Sickles, the original commander of the Excelsior Brigade, when he was badly injured at Gettysburg. (Sickles later lost a leg, which he "visited" proudly where it was and is displayed at the National Museum of Health and Medicine.) A somewhat notorious character who was involved in many postwar scandals, Sickles lived until 1914. One can only hope that the hardened sinner gained some spiritual benefits from the ministrations of Father O'Hagan!

13. Cooney quote from McAvoy, *War Letters*, 152. Egan quote from McKenna, *Under the Maltese Cross*, 109.

14. Endres and Kurtz, *Soldiers*, 59–60. The convert William Stark Rosecrans (1819–1898), the most prominent Catholic general officer in the Union

army, attracted numerous Catholic chaplains into his Army of the Cumberland, including John Ireland (5th Minnesota), Francis Fusseder (17th and 24th Wisconsin), Richard Christy (78th Pennsylvania), Peter Paul Cooney (35th Indiana), William O'Higgins (10th Ohio), and Joseph Stephan (Nashville US Hospital). The confiteor is a traditional penitential prayer, usually said at Mass, to acknowledge one's sinfulness. The act of contrition is the traditional prayer said by the person asking for forgiveness in confession just before they are absolved of their sins.

15. Peter Tissot mentions the difficulty he had of getting such a "chapel tent." "The government makes no provision for [saying Mass], gives him a tent only for his personal use. He may say Mass in this, but only about a dozen men can be inside. He may sometimes get a large hospital tent . . . but if he gets one it is only through fervor. He may say Mass in the open air, but if the wind blows this is hardly possible." Tissot, "Year," 55.

16. Corby, *Memoirs*, 37–38.

17. Corby, *Memoirs*, 302–3.

18. Tissot, "Year," 62; Corby, *Memoirs*, 36; and Germain, *Chaplains*, 68. There are at least three well-known images of priests vested for Mass with Civil War troops. One is the Matthew Brady picture of Bernard O'Reilly standing with Catholic troops in June 1861, another shows Thomas Scully getting ready to celebrate with the 9th Massachusetts, and the last is part of a large 1864 lithograph focusing on Peter Paul Cooney of the 35th Indiana.

19. Germain, *Chaplains*, 67; Rooney, *Father Nash*, 191.

20. In his diary entry of October 17, 1861, Tissot described Colonel Romaine Lujeane (99th Pennsylvania) as "a hot Garibaldian. 'I am going to hell,' he said to me, 'all gentlemen go to hell. Nobody goes to heaven but priests and old women. . . . I know but one text of the Scriptures, 'Cain murdered Abel'; go do likewise." He was odd and was much disliked by his regiment, who got rid of him shortly after." Lujeane resigned his command of the 99th Pennsylvania in November 1861. Tissot, "Year," 47 and 52.

21. Sheeran, *Diary*, 146.

22. Corby, *Memoirs*, 100–101.

23. Corby, *Memoirs*, 168–69; Turgis, "Turgis to Odin," April 16, 1862.

24. From the diary of John Bannon of May 16–17, 1863, as cited in Tucker, *Fighting Chaplain*, 125–26.

25. From the Catholic newspaper of the Diocese of Nashville, *Tennessee Register*, May 4, 1962.

26. "Neither Blue nor Gray."

27. Gache, *Frenchman*, 119–20.

28. William Corby describes executions of soldiers in great detail no fewer than seven times in his *Memoirs*; these deaths always touched him profoundly. Six of Tissot's letters are reprinted in *The Woodstock Letters* 43 (1914), 169–80.

29. Philip Tucker, *Fighting Chaplain*, 36–37.

30. Cooney, *War Letters*, July 5, 1864; Tissot letter of April 20, 1863, as recounted in Tissot, "Letters," 175.

31. Tissot, "Year," 86.

32. Tissot, "Letters," 172.

33. Sheeran, *Diary*, 233. Sheeran's lengthy diary is unique in that it is a little less spiritual than others, and focuses on more military details. Much of the time he was within yards of the battle, thus his comments about the real-time impact of fighting are powerful. For example, in writing about the deadliness of the mini-ball (bullet), he says, "It was a killing machine because it could rip through flesh; when infection set in, it could kill people within a day or two." His simple, terse description of Gettysburg is among the best ever written: "Had Hell itself broken its boundaries, it would not have presented a more terrifying spectacle." Sheeran, *Diary*, 197.

34. Sheeran, *Diary*, 249–50.

35. Father Aegidius Smulders to Reverend John DeDucker, private letter, written from Fort Jennings, Ohio, on September 26, 1865. Cf. also the in-house Redemptorist publication "Let Us Praise Great Men - Egidius Smulders," by Edward Cosgrove (privately published).

36. Tissot, "Year," 68–69; Endres and Kurtz, *Soldiers*, 166.

37. Letter from Charles J. Murphy, cited in Endres and Kurtz, *Soldiers*, 200–201.

38. Endres and Kurtz, *Soldiers*, 60.

39. Endres and Kurtz, *Soldiers*, 51–52.

40. Honeywell, *Chaplains*, 96; Endres and Kurtz, *Soldiers*, 136–37. One non-Catholic chaplain, Milton Haney (55th Illinois), was even awarded the Medal of Honor for his conspicuous bravery in helping retake Union entrenchments near Atlanta after the death of General James McPherson.

41. Endres and Kurtz, *Soldiers*, 126–27.

42. Tissot, "Letters," 174.

43. As mentioned already, Tissot's diary captures the different ministry styles that priests used. In addition to the quote mentioned above in this chapter, in May 1862 Tissot surprisingly remarked that "there is not much good to be done the day of a battle. Most of the wounded are left scattered on the ground. . . . The first thing they want is a nurse or surgeon, someone to attend to their wounds. . . . he place for the chaplain to do good is in the camp. If he does no good there, he had better stay at home." Tissot, "Year," 69. Yet in

Conyngham's manuscript, the regimental surgeon Dr. William O'Meagher reveals that Tissot put himself frequently in the thick of the fight. (Cf. Endres and Kurtz, *Soldiers*, chapter 11.)

44. Norton, *Rebel Religion*, 73.

45. McAtee, "Reminiscences," 77. Endres and Kurtz note that Cooney "on three different occasions sent home the round sum of forty thousand dollars," and experienced at least one adventure being accosted by thieves while bringing $23,000 to post on another occasion. Endres and Kurtz, *Soldiers*, 216–19; Honeywell, *Chaplains*, 145.

46. Philip Tucker, *Fighting Chaplain*, 44; Faherty, *Exile in Erin*, 87; Curran, *John Dooley's Civil War*, 163–79. Whiskey was used frequently for medicinal purposes during the Civil War (to ease pain, soothe nerves, and clean wounds).

47. Gache, *Frenchman*, 96 and 223.

48. McQuaid, *Life and Letters*, 348.

49. Quintard, *Doctor Quintard*, 58. Twichell first mentions O'Hagan in October 1861, writing that "through O'H I hope to get at the rum drinking although I observe he is not averse to a little tipple on his own account." He wrote of his March 3, 1862, visit to Georgetown that he enjoyed the visit, but Catholic priests "in view of the great physical mortification involved in celibacy [appear] to regard all the other fleshy indulgences their purchased right." Cf. Twichell, *Civil War Letters*, 73 and 95.

50. There is an entire chapter devoted to Catholicism and Confederate overseas diplomacy in Kraszewski, *Catholic Confederates*, 105–31. Cf. also Robert Miller, *Both Prayed*, 113–14.

51. Gallagher, *Union War*, 57–58.

52. Nash, "Letters," 12–29, 139–49, 269–87, and 269.

53. Tissot, "Year," 67. Corby's record book of monies he brought to post for soldiers is now kept in the University of Notre Dame Archives. Cf. also the Joseph O'Hagan papers, which are held in the Maryland Province Archives of the Society of Jesus, Box 10, Folder 10, Washington, DC, Georgetown University Library.

54. For a picture of Wiget in his white stole next to Mary Surratt, visit https://www.thoughtco.com/trial-and-execution-of-mary-surratt-4123228.

55. Armstrong, *Courageous Fighting*, 80.

56. Jeffrey, *First Chaplain*, 47–49.

57. Barton, *Angels*, 96–108.

58. The Emmitsburg convent of the Daughters of Charity was founded in 1809 by Saint Elizabeth Seton, the first American Catholic saint. The convent supplied one-third of all Catholic nurse-nuns who served during the war,

and its property included the convent itself, an orphanage, and school for Catholic girls. See Lydia Strickling, "The Daughters of Charity and the Battle of Gettysburg," *Gettysburg National Military Park* (blog), August 22, 2019, https://npsgnmp.wordpress.com/2019/08/22/the-daughters-of-charity-and -the-battle-of-gettysburg/.

59. Endres and Kurtz, *Soldiers*, 29.

CHAPTER 4. The Original "Fighting Irish"

The part epigraph is from the letter of Archbishop John Ireland to Father Peter P. Cooney, May 24, 1892, as provided in Shannon, "Archbishop Ireland's Experience," 304.

1. Hope, *Notre Dame*, http://archives.nd.edu/hope/hope09.htm.

2. One member of the order at that time, Father E. B. Kilroy, was certified by Indiana Governor Oliver Morton for chaplaincy to the navy, but he turned it down, backing out just before the appointment was made. On January 18, 1863, Kilroy was appointed by Governor Morton to visit the Indiana regiments in the Department of the Cumberland as his special agent. Kilroy subsequently became a priest in Lafayette, Indiana. Sixty-three nuns from the Sisters of the Holy Cross in total served as Civil War nurses in ten hospitals. Cf. Germain, *Chaplains*, 143; Blied, *Catholics*, 119; Schmidt, *Notre Dame*, 41–50.

3. Dr. John Dwyer, former surgeon of the 182nd New York, commented on the unique nature of Gillen's "creative" vehicle. "In the twinkling of an eye his establishment was converted into a chapel, and he was never at a loss for a covering or a place for his altar wherever he travelled. [If] a large barn or building was to be had, well and good, or if the large chapel tent was up with the Quartermaster's stores, he used it BUT if not, no matter, whether we were on a march or a scout, the Holy Sacrifice of the mass was always offered every morning at Father Paul's establishment." As cited in Endres and Kurtz, *Soldiers*, 199.

4. Endres and Kurtz, *Soldiers*, 199.

5. Corby, *Memoirs*, 286 and 297; Schmidt, *Notre Dame*, 33–34.

6. Armstrong, *Courageous Fighting*, 28. Cf. also Corby, *Memoirs*, 291; Schmidt, *Notre Dame*, 34.

7. In a humorous aside, the copy of the famed Gettysburg statue of Corby at Notre Dame today has been dubbed "Fair-Catch Corby" in honor of the university's later football prominence! The well-known painting of Corby's general absolution at Gettysburg (called *Absolution Under Fire*) was done by Paul Wood in 1891, and hangs today in the Snite Museum at Notre Dame.

8. Corby, *Memoirs*, 72.

9. Corby, *Memoirs*, 99–102, 140–44, 207, 264.

10. Corby, *Memoirs*, 27.

11. Corby, *Memoirs*, 112–13.

12. The statue was created by Samuel Aloysius Murray and unveiled in 1910. The captain's quote is in Corby, *Memoirs*, 165.

13. The Mound City Hospital that the Holy Cross nuns staffed was an enormous complex of about two dozen crude warehouses, which were numbered alphabetically and called wards by the sisters. None other than Mary Livermore herself described the site as "the best military hospital in the United States. . . . A Shaker-like cleanliness and sweetness of atmosphere pervaded." Three of the sister-nurses that served there died of disease. Cf. Schmidt, *Notre Dame*, 45–47.

14. Schmidt, *Notre Dame*, 45–47.

15. In retrospect, Ellen Ewing may have been mistaken. Napolean Mignault (17th Wisconsin) was also with the Union troops in front of Vicksburg, although he was in poor health for part of that time. Also, Daniel Mullen (9th Connecticut) and Patrick J. Murphy (58th Illinois) appear to have been there with their regiments, as both were seriously affected by sickness as well at that very time.

16. Endres and Kurtz, *Soldiers*, 89 and 264.

17. Schmidt, *Notre Dame*, 36–37.

18. Hope, *Notre Dame*, https://archives.nd.edu/hope/hope09.htm.

19. Cooney to Owen Cooney, December 30, 1861, as cited in McAvoy, "War Letters," 55.

20. McAvoy, "War Letters," 54.

21. Cooney quotes the colonel's citation in a January 12, 1863, letter to his brother, Owen Cooney. McAvoy, "War Letters," 152.

22. McAvoy, "War Letters," 152.

23. Germain, *Chaplains*, 63.

24. From a December 1964 letter to Owen Cooney after the Battles of Franklin and Nashville. As cited in Robert Miller, *Both Prayed*, 111.

25. As cited in Schmidt, *Notre Dame*, 113. Members of the GAR Post 569 included not only the priest-chaplains, but also former soldiers who had subsequently joined the order after the war. They are as follows: Brother Richard (William Stoney), 38th New Jersey; Brother Sebastian (Thomas Martin), 1st Pennsylvania Volunteers, Cavalry; Brother Polycarp (James White), US Navy; Brother Leander (James McLain), 15th US Infantry; Brother John Chrysostom (Mark Wills), 54th Pennsylvania; Brother Cosmas (Nicholas Bathe), 2nd US Infantry; Brother Eustachius (John McInerny), 38th Ohio; Brother Benedict (James Matele), 1st Pennsylvania Heavy Artillery; Brother Ignatius (Ignatz

Mayer), 75th Pennsylvania; and Brother Raphael (James Maloy), 133rd Pennsylvania. Most are buried in the order's cemetery on the Notre Dame campus. Cf. Brother Aidan O'Reilly's online diary, found at http://archives.nd.edu /aidan/aidan276.htm.

26. O'Reilly, "Brother Aidan's Extracts," https://archives.nd.edu/aidan/.

27. O'Reilly, "Brother Aidan's Extracts," https://archives.nd.edu/aidan/.

28. Schmidt, *Notre Dame*, 113–17. Barton's *Angels of the Battlefield*, 287–90, has a detailed list of every member of GAR Post 569 as of 1897 (the date of the book's original publication).

29. The statue was dedicated in 1924, and was the result of the long work of Ellen Joly, head of an Irish Catholic fraternal group.

30. Brosnahan, *King's Highway*, 253.

31. See the December 12, 1941, edition of the *Notre Dame Scholastic*, https://archives.nd.edu/Scholastic/VOL_0075/VOL_0075_ISSUE_0011.pdf.

CHAPTER 5. "God's Marines"

1. As cited in George Reimer, *The New Jesuits* (Boston: Little, Brown and Company, 1971), xiv, xxxvi.

2. The extensive Jesuit formation process is well explained in an article by James Martin SJ, in a 2013 article in *America* magazine (cf. Martin, "Novice?"). The twelve Jesuit colleges in 1861 were in these places: Cincinnati, Ohio (Xavier), St. Louis, Missouri (St. Louis University), Bardstown, Kentucky (St. Joseph College), Baltimore, Maryland (Loyola), New York, New York (Fordham), Washington, DC (Gonzaga and Georgetown), Worcester, Massachusetts (Holy Cross), Boston, Massachusetts (Boston College), Mobile, Alabama (Spring Hill College), Grand Coteau, Louisiana (St. Charles College), and Santa Clara, California (Santa Clara College).

3. Some well-known Jesuits missionaries are Francis Xavier, Peter Claver, Matthew Ricci, and Pierre-Jean De Smet. Well-known Jesuit martyrs include Isaac Jogues and companions (in upstate New York), Edward Campion (England), Paul Miki (Japan), Miguel Pro (Mexico), and Jean de Brebeuf (New France or Canada).

4. In the Revolutionary War, these were Pierre Floquet and Louis Lotbinière, and in the Mexican-American War, two Jesuits were asked to minister—Anthony Rey and John McElroy—as result of conversation between President James Polk and Bishop John Hughes of New York. As mentioned in the prologue of this book, Anthony Rey became the first chaplain working for American troops to be killed while on duty.

5. Germain, *Chaplains*, 48. Sixty-seven of the 126 Catholic chaplains (53 percent) were members of religious orders. The breakdown in terms of other religious orders are as follows: Holy Cross of Notre Dame had seven (Corby, Cooney, Dillon, Carrier, Gillen, Bourget, and Leveque); the Dominicans had five (Jarboe, McGrath, Egan, Orengo, and Nealis); the Lazarists (also known as Vincentians) had five (Boglioli, Burke, Burlando, Ryan, and Smith); the Redemptorists had two (Sheeran and Smulders); the Franciscans had two (Gombitelli and Rizzo); and the Benedictines just one (Bliemel).

6. At an amazingly high number of major battles, Jesuits apparently "faced" each other across battle lines. This includes Battle of First Manassas, the Peninsula Campaign, Antietam, Chancellorsville, Gettysburg, and others. Whether they were aware of it at the time is unclear, though it appears one poignant Jesuit reunion did occur in Richmond at the end of the war. As mentioned above, former Confederate chaplain Hippolyte Gache recognized and welcomed Union chaplain Joseph O'Hagan when he arrived at Stuart Hospital with the victorious Union troops into the fallen capital.

7. "Obituary of Father Joseph O'Hagan," 178–79. The Zouaves became part of General Dan Sickles's newly organized Excelsior Brigade, and became well-known for their colorful French-influenced uniforms, which included red pants and unique hats.

8. O'Hagan, *Obituary*, 173–83.

9. Corby, *Memoirs*, 302–3.

10. Corby, *Memoirs*, 306.

11. McAtee, "Reminiscences," 71–77.

12. George Hogg's letter with this comment was published in the New York *Irish-American*, on February 2, 1862; also cf. Lonn, *Foreigners*, 316.

13. McAtee, "Reminiscences," 74.

14. The eleven Civil War letters of Father Michael Nash were published in the Jesuit journal *The Woodstock Letters*, volumes 14–19, between the years of 1885 and 1890.

15. Schroth, *Fordham*, 77.

16. Rooney, "Father Nash, S.J.," 191.

17. Schroth, *Fordham*, 76.

18. Rooney, "Father Nash S.J.," 191–93.

19. Cf. Tissot, "Year," 39–87; Faherty, *Exile*, 88.

20. Tissot, "Year," 78.

21. Gache, *Frenchman*, 124.

22. Germain, *Chaplains*, 103–4; Gache, *Frenchman*, 124–25.

23. O'Callaghan's supposed mustering in and out dates correspond nearly exactly to the unit history of the 69th Infantry Regiment, the New York State

Militia of the National Guard for the same period. More information about this regiment can be found searching the New York Veteran's Research Center records online at https://dmna.ny.gov/historic/reghist/.

24. St. Inigoes, in St. Mary's County, Maryland (also known as St. Thomas Manor), was the oldest continually operating Catholic church in America, having been in existence since the 1640s. The Jesuits who came to Maryland with the first settlers created their first farms and mission there and brought with them indentured servants. They also soon established a tobacco plantation in St. Inigoes in order to fund their mission. According to his obituary in the Jesuit *Woodstock Letters*, Pacciarini was pastor at St. Inigoes from 1854 to 1874. Bernardin Wiget SJ, also a Civil War chaplain, served two terms there as well, one before the Civil War and the other toward the end of his life.

25. Usannez's fellow Jesuits Peter Tissot and Joseph Bixio were also from the Savoy region.

26. Local priest William Hamilton (from Macon, Georgia) spotted Andersonville accidentally while on his rounds, though he spent little actual time there. He reported the camp to his Bishop, Augustine Verot, who asked sixty-two-year-old Peter Whelan to minister there. Other priests joined him briefly—Verot himself, John Kirby (Augusta, Georgia), and Henry Clavreul. See chapter 11 for more of the Andersonville story.

27. "Obituary of Father Anselm Usannez," 484–85.

28. Gache mentions in one letter that to his knowledge his fellow Jesuits Darius Hubert and Joseph Prachensky were the only Catholic chaplains in the war who did not wear priestly garb. Cf. Gache, *Frenchman*, 62. The editor of Gache's letters, fellow Jesuit Cornelius Buckley, comments extensively on Gache's choice to wear his Jesuit habit. In December 1861 Gache requested that his superior Father Jourdan send him a new cassock since the one he had brought to camp in Virginia was showing its wear. Buckley writes that "such clerical attire was entirely proper 'for the perfect country priest' who in January 1862 purchased a bell so that the village church in the middle of the camp would be yet more authentic." Among the men of the 10th Louisiana, Gache's habit would have caused no wonder, but another soldier from a Virginia regiment noted in his diary a description of the "old country priest clad in a black gown hanging down to the ground with a singular hat on his head and with his beads around his neck and with a face representing the Virgin Mary, etc." When traveling, Gache clearly sought to dress "in a guise so humble and so indicative of another calling" than that of a Confederate officer. Gache, *Frenchman*, 76.

29. Barton, *Angels*, 77; Gache, *Frenchman*, 223. This letter was actually written from Charleston, South Carolina, in July 1865.

30. Gache, *Frenchman*, 234. The Culinary Institute of America (once a Jesuit house), where Gache is buried, is still operating in Hyde Park, New York, as of this writing.

31. Truyens's challenging wartime experiences are captured in two of his letters, this one from January 1862, and in a postwar 1867 letter to a Jesuit superior. Cf. Garraghan, *Jesuits*, 156.

32. Webb, *Centenary*, 438.

33. There were two 1st Louisiana regiments in the Confederacy. Hubert served in the one commanded initially by Albert Blanchard and finally by James Nelligan in the eastern theater, whereas the 1st Louisiana Infantry Regulars (Strawbridge's) served in the western theater of the war. I am grateful to Katherine Bentley Jeffrey for her insights about Gache and Darius Hubert, captured in her excellent 2020 biography of Hubert, entitled *First Chaplain of the Confederacy*.

34. Gache, *Frenchman*, 60.

35. Volume 43 of *The Woodstock Letters* (page 170) describes this incident more fully, though perhaps not entirely accurately. Cf. Jeffrey, *First Chaplain*, 46–49.

36. Entry for April 16, 1865, in Garidel, *Journal*, 379.

37. Here is how Gache weighed in on Prachensky's "pretensions": "I had heard rumors about this nonsense. . . . I regarded the whole business as a joke. But I was wrong. Fr. Prachensky is dead serious when he puts on that he is a major, and the proof of it is that he wears a uniform with all of the accessories . . . no amount of reasoning will make him give it up. I scoffed at his pretensions . . . but to it all Prachensky merely answered 'I'm wearing this uniform and I'm going to continue to wear it. I couldn't care less for those who criticize me for it.'" Cf. Gache *Frenchman*, 61–62.

38. Schmandt and Schulte, "Civil War Chaplains," 59.

39. Gache mentions meeting him in the summer of 1865 while Prachensky was at Fordham, remarking simply that he "has grown monstrously fat." Gache, *Frenchman*, 75–76, 78, and 226. Cf. also Schmandt and Schulte, *Civil War Chaplains*, 59; and Brinsfield et al., *Faith in the Fight*, 243. Prachensky's obituary is located in *The Woodstock Letters* 20, no. 1 (1891), 120–21.

40. Germain, *Chaplains*, 115.

41. Germain, *Chaplains*, 115; Giblin, "American Jesuits," 106–8; Widman, "Grand Coteau," 38.

42. De Chaignon's exact birth date is unclear; it is listed as between 1823 and 1825, which would put him between forty-two and forty-four years old at the time of his death.

43. As cited in Brueske, *Last Siege*, 51.

44. Gache, *Frenchman*, 97. Cf. also Buckley's footnote 73 on page 251, which gives the title of the Englishman's book, but not his name, only stating was that he was a "lieutenant of artillery on the field-staff."

CHAPTER 6.   Other Religious Who Served as Chaplains

1. As a reminder, the term "religious" refers to priests and brothers who belong to a specific religious order or community, and not to a specific geographic Catholic diocese. Obvious examples of religious orders would be the Society of Jesus (Jesuits), the Franciscans, and Benedictines.

2. Cf. chapter 12 for a more detailed explanation of the Catholic Schools issue, which involved conflict about government funding being used for private schools, which was an idea strongly opposed by the predominantly Protestant public school leadership structure.

3. One writer mentions that at the time, there were not many options for a single father other than remarriage or placing children in an orphanage to be reared. Sheeran would later say that deciding to leave his two children behind "was like tearing the heart from [his] bosom."

4. Cf. Sheeran, *Diary*, passim. Reverend Joseph Durkin had in 1960 published an abridged version of Sheeran's letters. I am grateful to Patrick Hayes for being allowed to collaborate on the unabridged, newly released version of Sheeran's diary. John Bannon's diary, along with his wartime papers are held at the University of South Carolina, and remain unpublished.

5. Sheeran, *Diary*, 341.

6. Sheeran, *Diary*, 307–8.

7. Sheeran, *Diary*, 258–60.

8. Much of Sheeran's life and adventures, like (for example) his pastoral work while on extended leave in 1863 and 1864 is also spoken of in several chapters in *Soldiers of the Cross*, the authoritative text of David Power Conyngham's nineteenth-century manuscript. Cf. Endres and Kurtz, *Soldiers*, 269–320.

9. Sheeran, *Diary*, 2.

10. Cf. Rev. Edward Cosgrove CSsR., "'Let Us Praise Great Men," privately published by the Redemptorists of the Denver Province. "Missions" refers to extraordinary preaching events done by two priests together in parishes for periods of two weeks or more in length. Cosgrove mentions in the above document that mission-preaching was the hallmark of Redemptorist

ministry, and that this was Smulders's forte. He continued giving missions in the American West until he was seventy-three years old, supposedly giving the first English mission in the Redemptorist format in the United States in 1848.

11. Sheeran, *Diary*, 113, 227, 363, 416–17.

12. Sheeran, *Diary*, 155. A photocopy of the General Pass which Lee gave Sheeran can be seen in Joseph Durkin's abridged version of Sheeran's journal, entitled *Confederate Chaplain: A War Journal.*

13. Cf. the anonymously written *Seelos Newsletter* of August 2011, privately published by the National Shrine of Blessed Francis Xavier Seelos CSsR (in New Orleans, Louisiana).

14. As a personal sidebar, I confess a bias concerning the Redemptorists, as I was a member of the order for twenty years before joining the Archdiocese of Chicago. Their preaching focus and fraternal camaraderie has shaped my life and ministry to this very day.

15. Cf. Gache, *Frenchman*, 179–80, 186. For a general history of the American Dominicans, see the online history available at www.domlife.org /BeingDominican/History.

16. Jarboe was president of Sinsinawa Mound College for about three years. The college is still in existence, now known as Dominican College in River Forest, Illinois, after having been moved there in 1922 and named at first Rosary College. The Dominican Sisters remain in Sinsinawa to this day.

17. In his book on Catholic chaplains, Aidan Germain notes of Jarboe that "his name appears on the register containing rosters of Commissioned Officers, Provisional Army, Confederate States. His appointment is dated 1861." Cf. Germain, *Chaplains*, 122.

18. Another version of his capture was written in 1909 by Jarboe's relative and lifelong friend, Miss Lulu Timmons. In that version, it was General Philip Sheridan who happened along and recognized Jarboe from having served at his Mass while a child in Somerset, Ohio. However, while both *were* in Somerset in the 1840s, Sheridan was not at the Battle of Shiloh, but rather in Chicago buying horses for the cavalry at the time. I thank Father John Vidmar, the historian of the Dominicans, for supplying the correct facts on this incident.

19. King, "Dominican Chaplains."

20. Germain, *Chaplains*, 53–54.

21. Many of the details on McGrath's life can be found in the history of the American Dominicans. Cf. O'Daniel, *Dominican Province*, 243–44.

22. Information about the incident which began Egan's chaplaincy comes from Conyngham's late nineteenth-century manuscript, and is related in Endres and Kurtz, *Soldiers*, 184. The previous chaplain of the 9th Massachusetts

had been Thomas Scully, but he had resigned on account of bad health following his capture and release in June 1862.

23. His hospital chaplaincy was authorized by presidential appointment on July 28, 1864. Cf Germain, *Chaplains*, 55.

24. I am grateful for the support of Father John Vidmar in this section, and for the book he authored in this area, entitled *Fr. Fenwick's "Little American Province" – 200 Years of Dominican Friars in the United States* (Dominican Province of St. Joseph, 2005).

25. O'Daniel, *Dominican Province*, 197. Cf also McGreal, *Dominicans at Home*, passim.

26. McGreal, *Dominicans at Home*, chapter 9, 1–16.

27. O'Daniel, *Dominican Province*, 197.

28. As an example of Tennessee's wartime tensions, after Nashville's Bishop Richard Miles died in 1860, another Dominican (James Whelan) succeeded him, but lasted only two years in the job before resigning in 1862. He eventually left the episcopal residence for good in July 1863. The struggles and sufferings of the war had a very detrimental effect on Whelan, including the Nashville cathedral becoming a hospital, accusations of Union partisanship, and a vague "scandal" report concerning him that went to Rome. For more details, cf. McGreal, *Dominicans at Home*, 13.

29. Endres and Kurtz, *Soldiers*, 73–74.

30. Cf. http://www.ninthregimentcv.com/soldiers/chaplain-leo-rizzo.html; Belmonte, *Rizzo*, 37–45; the history of Leo (Rizzo) de Saracena found at https://stjoseph-winsted.org/about-us/history/; and Hogan, "Historic Men," 1, 5–6.

31. Cf. the biographies of the presidents of St. Bonaventure College, found at http://jmc.sbu.edu/Biographies/Presidents.htm. See also Belmonte, *Roaring Lion*.

32. The description of Titta is from an old website of his former St. Brigid Church in Meadville, Pennsylvania, now merged to become Epiphany Church (https://www.epiphanymeadville.org/history). Unfortunately, the new parish did not transfer Titta's personal information to their new website. Cf. also the 1878 *Sadliers' Catholic Almanac*, at https://archive.org/details/SadliersCatholicDirectory1878.

33. Germain, *Chaplains*, 70–71. See the history of the 117th Pennsylvania, found at http://www.pacivilwar.com/regiment/117th.html.

34. Germain, *Chaplains*, 70–71.

35. As a reflection of the respect the order had in the Catholic Church, four of America's forty-seven Catholic dioceses of the Civil War era were

headed by members of the Vincentians. John Mary Odin was in New Orleans, John Timon in Buffalo, Michael Domenec in Pittsburgh, and Thaddeus Amat in Monterey, California.

36. Cf. the July 29, 1882, edition of *The Assumption Pioneer*, from Napoleonville, Louisiana.

37. Cf. Dicharry, "Leper Priest," 175.

38. Slawson, "Vincentian Experience," 46. Burke is also referred to in Barton's *Angels of the Battlefield*, 29–30.

39. Barton, *Angels of the Battlefield*, 78–79; McNeil, *Balm of Hope*, 73–74.

40. Barton, *Angels of the Battlefield*, 96, 134–36, 141, 143, and 336.

41. Barton, *Angels of the Battlefield*, 106–8.

42. McNeil, *Balm of Hope*, passim; Barton, *Angels of the Battlefield*, 66 and 262–67. The latter pages include a short biography of his life. Cf. also Mc-Neil's "Daughters of Charity."

CHAPTER 7.   Prominent Diocesan Chaplains

1. Kurtz, *Excommunicated*, 71.

2. As a postwar bishop, John Ireland (see chapters 7 and 11) criticized the hierarchy for not sending enough chaplains to the war effort. Bishop John Purcell (Cincinnati) lamented that he wished he could "manufacture" an adequate number of priests to meet General Rosecrans's 1863 request for more chaplains.

3. Though unclear, it seems Mignault had become a member of the Quebec Diocese, and was sent by the bishop on this "detached" missionary ministry to French-speaking immigrants in the United States. He was joined in New England for a time by Zepherin Leveque, another priest of the Quebec Diocese and later a member of the Holy Cross priests at Notre Dame. Leveque was also very briefly a wartime chaplain—his story is told in chapter 4. One author describes the results of their ministry as Cf. Petrin, *French Canadians*, 75.

4. Theriault, *Diamond Jubilee Souvenir and History*, 26.

5. Blied, *Catholics*, 132–33. Cf. also Germain, *Chaplains*, 85.

6. Perhaps surprisingly, Wisconsin had the second greatest percentage of Catholics in the North at the time of the Civil War (24 percent), following Minnesota (28.7 percent). Rousey, "Aliens in the WASP Nest," 156–161, quote is on 156. Cf. also Ryan, *History of Outagamie County*, 386; Bates, *History of Crawford County*, 1096; and Barton, *Melting Pot*, 151.

7. As mentioned previously, David Conyngham's journal of Catholic priests and nuns who served during the war, was released in book form in 2019. Cf. Endres and Kurtz, *Soldiers*, 102.

8. An *O* had been added to the surname "Higgins" by his bishop-uncle shortly after William's birth, as a nod to the royal branch of their family. William O'Higgins's subdeaconate ceremony was August 13, 1853, the deaconate August 14, and ordination to priesthood on August 15.

9. A strong Unionist, Purcell allowed three Cincinnati priests to serve as chaplains: O'Higgins (10th Ohio), E. P. Corcoran (61st Ohio) and Joseph A. Stephan (who served as a hospital chaplain in Nashville for a time). In March 1862, Bishop Sylvester Rosecrans (1827–1878)—the brother of General William Rosecrans—became Purcell's auxiliary bishop.

10. Endres and Twobig, "With a Father's Affection," 120–23; Pollard, *The Glories of War*, 388. The shooting incident was related in a letter from his sister to William H. Lytle dated September 14, 1862.

11. Endres and Twobig, "With a Father's Affection," 125. I am also grateful to the private writings of Reverend David Endres, PhD, especially one entitled "An Ohio 'Holy Joe': Chaplain William T. O'Higgins' Wartime Correspondence with Archbishop Purcell of Cincinnati, 1863."

12. See the regimental history at https://civilwarindex.com/10th-ohio-infantry-3-years.html.

13. Reflecting the relative scarcity of Catholics in the South outside of Louisiana, the Little Rock Diocese had in 1862 only nine priests, thirteen churches, thirty mission stations, and twelve schools, though it comprised all of Arkansas and the Indian Territory.

14. The Brigidine Order was founded by Bishop Daniel Delany in Tullow, Ireland, in February 1807, for the specialized work of Catholic education. The nephew of Father Thomas Brady, John Brady (1837–1914), immigrated in 1855, following him first to upstate New York then to Grand Rapids, where he practiced medicine until 1862. He became an assistant surgeon for the Union army from 1862 to 1866, serving in Michigan and Tennessee until joining the 45th Illinois in 1863 for the Vicksburg Campaign. According to an undocumented family source, Dr. Brady was literally with General Grant when a blindfolded messenger arrived with the letter of surrender from the Vicksburg garrison.

15. A priest-historian of the Grand Rapids Diocese remarked to the author that Brady didn't appear to be a very well-educated man, and had clear troubles with his bishop. In a January 16, 1861, letter, Bishop Lefevere wrote to Brady that "we have, on two different occasions, forbidden you to give lessons or to teach any worldly science to any sister, novice or postulant of the institution of St. Bridget established in Grand Rapids." He threatened to suspend him

if he did not cease his work. When Brady was approved by the bishop as a chaplain, all his "faculties"—permissions to minister as a Catholic priest—were revoked *except* for his military work.

16. Endres and Kurtz, *Soldiers*, 227.

17. Endres and Kurtz, *Soldiers*, 227. Jeremiah Trecy had previously been the pastor in Huntsville, Alabama, before becoming a Union chaplain. His unique story is related in chapter 11.

18. Endres and Kurtz, *Soldiers*, 227.

19. Endres and Kurtz, *Soldiers*, 231.

20. This description of Christy was taken from the now defunct website and parish of St. John the Evangelist in Fenelton, Pennsylvania (www.stjohn theevangelistparish.org, site discontinued). There is today a state historical marker to Father Christy on the grounds of St. John's in Coylesville. Cf. https://www.hmdb.org/m.asp?m=42641.

21. Gibson, *History of the Seventy-Eighth Pennsylvania Infantry*, 22–24.

22. Endres and Kurtz, *Soldiers*, 136–37.

23. Mohney, *History of Butler County*, 238. The Corby quote is from Corby, *Memoirs*, xvi.

24. At the youthful age of 23 years and 4 months, Ireland was the youngest of all Catholic chaplains. He later described his appointment as somewhat anomalous, because it was a state and not a federal appointment. The officers of the 5th Minnesota had elected a Methodist named Chaffee as chaplain in May 1862, but the governor had been asked by Bishop Thomas Grace (St. Paul) to send a Catholic chaplain to serve the many Catholics in the Minnesota regiments. Thus Ireland was appointed as "chaplain to all MN units serving in the Western theater." Cf. Shannon, "Archbishop Ireland's Experience," 298–305.

25. Shannon, "Archbishop Ireland's Experience," 304.

26. Germain cites Ireland's actual resignation letter, which says "I have received a letter from my Bishop . . . the clergyman who has taken my place is sick and is totally unable to attend the spiritual wants of a large congregation." Cf. Germain, *Chaplains*, 72; Shannon, "Archbishop Ireland's Experience," 305.

27. Bannon kept a diary of his chaplain's experiences, which he gave to an American historian in 1907. It is now at the University of South Carolina, and forms the basis of Philip Tucker's *The Confederacy's Fighting Chaplain: Father John B. Bannon*. Bannon also wrote "Experiences of a Confederate Chaplain" (published in *Letters and Notices of the English Jesuit Province*). In 1861, the Irish population of St. Louis was second only to that in New Orleans, if compared to the Confederate states. It was one of five "seats" of Catholic archbishops in the United States in 1861—the others being New York, Baltimore, Cincinnati, and New Orleans.

28. Gallen, "John B. Bannon."

29. Faherty, *Exile in Erin*, 55; Brinsfield et al., *Faith in the Fight*, 74; Curran, *American Catholics*, 76–78.

30. Cited in Philip Tucker, *Fighting Chaplain*, 83.

31. Faherty, *Exile in Erin*, 78; see also Faherty, *Fourth Career*, which brings in Bannon's postwar career as a prominent Jesuit orator in Ireland.

32. Bannon's abhorrence of Yankees was not softened as the war went on. Soon after Vicksburg surrendered, after promising the assistant pastor he would say a High Mass and preach, Bannon refused to because the church was filled with Yankees. Endres and Kurtz, *Soldiers*, 114.

33. Faherty, *Exile in Erin*, 114–15, citing Bannon's July 4, 1863, diary entry. Charleston Bishop Patrick Lynch was also asked by the Confederate government to go to Europe and Rome as an emissary, and did so in April 1864. However, he wound up getting stranded there when the war ended, and was only able to return through the active intercession of Baltimore Bishop Martin Spaulding. Cf. Curran, *American Catholics*, 230–32, 279–80.

34. For a succinct summary of Bannon's propagandist work for the Confederacy, cf. Curran, *American Catholics*, 227–28. Pope Pius IX's attitude toward the American Civil War, and his supposed "support" for the Confederacy, has been a subject of other writings, and is beyond the scope of this book. In short, despite letters written to Catholic leaders, visits from American Bishops like Patrick Lynch (Charleston), John Hughes (New York), Michael Domenec (Pittsburgh), Joseph Fitzpatrick (Boston), and self-appointed ambassadors like Bannon, the Pope's attitude was to support immediate peace, but take no sides in the struggle. Some have argued after the war that the Pope recognized the Confederacy by addressing "His excellency Jefferson Davis" in an 1863 response to the Confederate president, but that letter is best viewed as mere formality, with no deeper political meaning. Cf. Robert Miller, *Both Prayed*, 113; Kurtz, *Excommunicated*, 120–21; Kraszewski, *Catholic Confederates*, 105–31; and Curran, *American Catholics*, 220–33.

35. Turgis was not counted by Aidan Germain or Benjamin Blied as a formal chaplain, but I have included him in the registry of full-time chaplains despite a lack of formal documentation, based on his length of service (albeit much of it informally).

36. Cf. the April 7, 2021, blog entry of Michael Pasquier, which can be found at www.almostchosenpeople.wordpress.com/2021/04/07/.

37. McClarey, "Father Turgis."

38. It should be noted that it is highly doubtful there were 18,000 to 20,000 French-speaking Catholics at Shiloh. I am grateful to Civil War historian

and researcher Bruce Allardice for pointing this out. This April 16, 1862, letter from Turgis to Bishop Odin is cited in Pasquier *Fathers on the Frontier*, 192. Quote is from McClarey, "Father Turgis."

39. Cf. Pasquier, *Fathers on the Frontier*, 193. See also the University of Notre Dame online archives for a copy of Turgis's letter to Archbishop Odin, which can be found at www.archives.nd.edu/calendar/cal1862d.htm.

40. Richey, *Tirailleurs*, 52.

41. Pasquier, *Fathers*, 200–202.

42. Pasquier, *Fathers*, 200–202.

43. The author is personally familiar with this cemetery and grave.

44. O'Reilly was appointed chaplain by Secretary Seddon on March 16, 1864, to date from February 9, 1864. However, a letter from December 1863 by Confederate officers says that "he has been performing the duties of Chaplain to the Catholic soldiers at this post, and also visiting the sick and dying soldiers at Kingston, LaGrange, Marietta, Newman and Griffin since Hospitals were established at the above-named places. He is a highly educated gentleman, and a Christian in every sense of the word, and we feel and know he would discharge the duties of the position he desires with the greatest alacrity and promptness." Cf. Germain, *Chaplains*, 127.

45. Cf. the online history at https://www.catholicshrineatlanta.org/about-3.

46. An Atlanta Irish group called the Hibernian Rifles was prepared to protect their church with arms, if needed. Some Federal soldiers actually helped protect Father O'Reilly's Catholic church by preventing fires being set too near the building. Although Atlanta's churches were saved, many were heavily damaged, and most were occupied for various uses by the Union soldiers.

47. Cf. Germain, *Chaplains*, 127; Blied, *Catholics*, 123; and the website of Atlanta's Catholic Shrine, found at www.catholicshrineatlanta.org.

48. Endres, *Bicentennial History*, 94–95; Germain, *Chaplains*, 65–66.

49. Germain, *Chaplains*, 67–68.

50. Germain, *Chaplains*, 81–86. Cf. also the letter of July 7, 1858, from Father Edward Joos (Monroe, Michigan) to Bishop Peter Paul Lefevere, (Detroit, Michigan), in the online archives of the University of Notre Dame. http://www.archives.nd.edu/cgi-bin/author.pl?c185807.xml+26.

51. Germain, *Chaplains*, 83.

52. There is confusion over Quinn's birthplace. The 1870 Federal Census notes it as Maine, while other sources say Canada. Cf. Germain, *Chaplains*, 92–93, and the online history of the Providence (Rhode Island) Diocese at https://dioceseofprovidence.org/history.

53. Germain, *Chaplains*, 113–14.

CHAPTER 8. Catholic Hospital Chaplains

The source of the part epigraph is Endres and Kurtz, *Soldiers*, 69.

1. As mentioned previously, many Civil War hospital chaplains were essentially post chaplains since they served in one general geographic location, even though they may have ministered in several hospitals. Pfab, "American Hospital Chaplains," 5.

2. Adams, *Doctors in Blue*, 150; Moss, *Christian Commission*, 546.

3. Pfab, "American Hospital Chaplains," 7–8. The other five chaplains were Reverend G. G. Goss, John G. Butler, Henry Hopkins, John C. Smith, and William Y. Brown. Cf. also Armstrong, *Courageous Fighting*, 3–4, 127–28.

4. Maryniak and Brinsfield, *Spirit Divided – Union*, 183–84.

5. Norton, *Struggling*, 116. John Ireland, for example, rode from hospital to hospital seeking out wounded Catholic men. Kurtz, *Excommunicated*, 77.

6. Carrington, "Chimborazo Hospital." Regarding Southern medical care during the war, the opinion of H. H. Cunningham in *Doctors in Gray* is worth noting, "Southern medical development on the eve of the Civil War was at least as far advanced as that in the Northern states."

7. Cf. the letter of October 9, 1863, from Moore to McCaw, as cited in Green, *Chimborazo Hospital*, 192. Cf. also Brinsfield et al., *Faith in the Fight*, 211–56.

8. Protestant chaplains routinely passed out Bibles, pamphlets, and religious tracts, a practice not common among Catholic chaplains due to differing theologies. Many Catholics, though, sought to obtain rosaries, medals, crosses, or special sacred pendants called *agnus dei*. There were some Catholic reading materials and pamphlets available as well.

9. McNeil, "Daughters of Charity," 148–49. Catholic nuns were highly desired in many dioceses, particularly to start Catholic schools. But after being invited to Civil War ministry by a bishop, and being approved by their religious superiors, the nuns had to travel great distances (in full traditional nineteenth-century habit) to get to their fields of ministry, hence the need for priests to accompany them. For more on the nuns in the Civil War, cf. Maher, *To Bind Up the Wounds*, and Oakes, *Angels of Mercy*.

10. Philip Tucker, "Fr. John Bannon," 202–6. Cf. also Faherty, *Exile in Erin*, 79–80.

11. Winthrop, "War Hospitals." The Sisters of Mercy staffed both Stanton and Douglas General Hospitals in Washington. Bernadin Wiget's life will be described a bit further in this chapter and also in chapter 12. He and other Jesuits from the area tended to the spiritual needs of both the nuns and hospitalized Catholics.

12. "Stone General Hospital," Civil War Washington (website), https://civilwardc.org/data/places/view/164. For information about all other hospitals during the Civil War, explore the database available at https://civilwardc.org/data. The Catholic Sisters of Mercy also served at Stanton Hospital during the war.

13. Adams, *Doctors in Blue*, 150–73; and Burns, "Civil War-Era Hospitals."

14. According to local lore, the famous doctor Mary Walker served at Seminary Hospital, and became the first woman to receive the Medal of Honor. Miss Lydia English, though, was an ardent secessionist, and could not stand to see the flag flying over her building, so she moved out of its sight to the house of the widow of Stephen Decatur just around the corner. (Stephen Decatur was a prominent navy officer in the Revolutionary War, and later led daring raids in the Barbary Wars and the War of 1812.)

15. Though some chaplains began doing this in July 1862, it was only in 1864 that the Surgeon General ordered all Union hospital chaplains to submit monthly reports of their hospital duties. There are nine boxes of these reports presently housed at the National Archives in Washington, DC.

16. Cf. https://www.fold3.com/image/300924178.

17. Many of McCarthy's monthly reports and a multitude of other great Civil War resources can be found at www.Fold3.com.

18. S. Smith, "Notes on Satterlee," 399–49. Cf. also "St. Patrick's Day," *The Daily Age*, Philadelphia, Pennsylvania, March 16, 1864, 1.

19. Adams, *Doctors in Blue*, 155.

20. Over one hundred Daughters of Charity nuns staffed Satterlee and cared for thousands of wounded and dying soldiers. Mother Mary Gonzaga Grace kept a diary of her wartime work, which gives a fuller account of both the nuns' and chaplains' work, and was remembered fondly after the war as a "ministering angel" and a calm presence. The distinctive headdress of this order included a large, winged cap called a cornette, based on traditional French peasant clothing. Because of their distinctive headwear, the sisters were often called "God's Geese." The hats were an object of wonder to many. Cf. S. Smith, "Notes on Satterlee," 399–49; and McNeil, "Daughters of Charity as Civil War Nurses," passim.

21. S. Smith, "Notes on Satterlee," 403. One soldiers of the 142nd Pennsylvania later recalled the work of Mother Mary Gonzaga, writing that "no matter what their creed, her devotion was the same ... her silent steps after 'Taps' and in the dim gaslight were listened for, and with her white-winged head-dress she flitted from bed to bed to soothe and cheer the wounded soldiers. She was one of the purest and loveliest of women." Cf. Michael Mahr, "The Story of Satterlee Hospital," National Museum of Civil War Medicine (website), November 30, 2022, https://www.civilwarmed.org/satterlee-hospital/.

22. I am grateful to Redemptorist archivist Robert Worden for his accurate records on McGrane, whose early years were spent in the Redemptorist Order.

23. Barton, *Angels*, 174–75. The nun's mention of Bruehl being "sixty years of age" is incorrect; Jesuit archival records state his birth year as being March 1811, making him only fifty at the time. Fordham is the oldest Catholic and Jesuit university in the northeastern United States. It was given to the Jesuits in 1841 by Archbishop Hughes and originally called St. John's College. Every Fordham president since 1846 has been a Jesuit priest, and its curriculum remains strongly influenced by Jesuit educational principles.

24. US War Department, Official Records, Serial 009, 411.

25. Barton, *Angels*, 174–75.

26. Barton, *Angels*, 213–15; Hannings, *Every Day*, 194. Also Herron, "Sisters of Mercy," 216–37.

27. St. Aloysius was one of only six Catholic churches in Washington in 1860. Cf. chapter 12 for the details of this controversy. Cf. also McGreevy, *Catholicism*, chapter 1.

28. The Daughters of Charity ministered at Eckington, Providence, Lincoln, and Cliffburn Hospitals in Washington, DC, and the Sisters of Mercy at Douglas and Stanton Hospitals. Cf. www.Fold3.com for its excellent records on Wiget here. Cf. Anderson, "Bernardin Wiget," 734–64.

29. Hill, *Gonzaga College*, 87.

30. Walt Whitman's account of his hospital volunteer efforts in Washington makes for marvelous reading to capture the picture of area hospitals, wounded, medical staff, and more. Originally published in 1875, it is available now as *Memoranda During the Civil War*.

31. Reilly, "Medical and Surgical Care," 139.

32. Cunningham, *Doctors in Gray*, 286–90; Johns and Page, "Chimborazo Hospital," 190–200; Reilly, "Medical and Surgical Care," 138–42.

33. Barton, *Angels*, 77.

34. Cf. "Montgomery White Sulphur Springs," *Virginia Center for Civil War Studies*, https://civilwar.vt.edu/montgomery-white-sulphur-springs/.

35. Jeremiah O'Connell, *Catholicity*, 477.

36. Germain, *Chaplains*, 125–26.

37. J. O'Connell, *Catholicity*, 281.

38. The burning of Columbia is controversial to this day. Despite allegations of rampant drunkenness among Union soldiers before the rampage started, General William Sherman maintained the fires were started by evacuating Confederates and fanned by high winds. He claimed he never ordered it, though: "I have never shed any tears over the event, because I believe it hastened what we all fought for, the end of the war" (Kagan, *Eyewitness*, 358).

39. Jeremiah O'Connell, *Catholicity*, 281. O'Connell offers a deeply compelling and moving description of the burning and its impact on the citizens. Laurence's newspaper article comments are contained in his brother's 1879 book.

40. Apparently, Charleston Bishop Patrick Lynch asked the Vatican to make North Carolina a Vicariate Apostolic so he could focus on rebuilding South Carolina. Lynch was gone so much raising money and support for his diocese that his sister (herself a nun) is said to have remarked, "When can you cease to be a carpet-bagger bishop?"

41. Jeremiah O'Connell, *Catholicity*, 156. Croghan studied at St. John the Baptist Seminary in Charleston, founded by Bishop John England in 1824 (it closed in 1851).

42. Barton, *Angels*, chapter 23.

43. Jeremiah O'Connell, *Catholicity*, 158. Bishop Lynch did subsequently go to Ireland, London, Paris, and Rome in 1864. Although he was always greeted warmly by the nations' leaders, he received little active support for the Confederate cause.

44. Notable descendants of this Minorcan community were the famed poet Stephen Benet and his brother William, 1930s Hollywood star Judy Canova, and the two cousin-bishops, Pellicer and Manucy.

45. Although it was founded in 1830, Spring Hill College was not authorized by the state to grant degrees until 1836, which likely became the motivation for their attendance. One member of the class of 1837 was Stephen Russell Mallory, a Catholic and later a US senator from Florida, and the Confederate Secretary of the Navy during the Civil War.

46. Cunningham, *Doctors in Gray*, 62. Known as "the cradle of the Confederacy," Montgomery remained virtually untouched by conflict during the Civil War. It was only on April 12, 1865, following the Battle of Selma, that Major General James H. Wilson captured the city for the Union.

47. "Sisters of Mercy" was a generic term for many nuns in the war, thus the exact religious order being referred to here is somewhat unclear. Cf. "*Cives Miles*" letter in the *Montgomery Daily Mail*, March 1, 1865, page 1.

48. Germain, *Chaplains*, 128–29.

CHAPTER 9. Chaplains for the Irish

1. Cf. appendix 1 for the ethnic origins of America's bishops. Cf. also Connor, *Faith and Fury*, 214–15; Loughery, *Dagger John*, 185; and Curran, *American Catholics*, 24–26.

2. Rousey, "Catholics in the Old South," 6. Robert Curran remarks that "fewer than 7% of Irish-born lived below the Potomac, but like their northern counterparts, they were concentrated in urban areas." Cf. Curran, *American Catholics*, 68.

3. *Chicago Tribune*, February 26, 1855, as cited in Connor, *Faith and Fury*, 215. Approximately 85 percent of Ireland at the time was Catholic, and this religious pattern generally continued in the North. The South did have a greater number of Irish Protestants due to immigrations in the colonial period, but also a good number of Irish Catholics in the South drifted into other religions because of the dearth of Catholic clergy and churches there. Connor, *Faith and Fury*, 225; Patrick Tucker, *Irish Confederates*, 14–15.

4. Perko, *Catholic and American*, 135–37.

5. Randall Miller, "Catholic Religion," 265–66. Cf. also Patrick Tucker, *Irish Confederates*, 12–14. Gracjan Kraszewski's statement on page 26 in *Catholic Confederates* that 70 percent of the 139,000 Irish in the South fought for the Confederacy (i.e., 97,300 men) differs widely from the accepted norm.

6. The Irish Brigade consisted of five regiments: a reconstituted 69th New York, the 63rd and 88th New York, and the 28th Massachusetts and 116th Pennsylvania, which were added in August 1862. According to Fox's *Regimental Losses*, only the 1st Vermont Brigade and the Iron Brigade suffered more combat dead than the Irish Brigade during the Civil War. The Irish Legion was comprised of the 69th New York (later reconstituted as the 182nd New York), and the 155th, 164th, and 170th New York. Another regiment, the 175th New York was also raised but never saw service with the Legion. Cf. Endres and Kurtz, *Soldiers*, 458–59.

7. In Philip Tucker's 2006 book, *Irish Confederates*, he goes into extensive detail about large numbers of Confederate Irish serving in companies from places like Charleston, Mobile, Montgomery, Savannah, Augusta, north St. Louis, Kentucky, Memphis, and rural Louisiana. Unfortunately, he refers in depth to only one Catholic chaplain, John Bannon, in his whole book. See Philip Tucker, *Irish Confederates*, 23–46.

8. Of the seventy-four known Union priest chaplains, both official and unofficial, twenty-nine were native Irish (39.1 percent), sixteen others were born in America or Canada and have names clearly indicating Irish ancestry (21.6 percent). All other Union chaplain nationalities (including French, German, and Italian), and those whose ancestry is unknown, combined to total only 39 percent.

9. A good description of this event is found online. Cf. McClarey, "Matthew Brady."

10. Kurtz, *Excommunicated*, 73; Connor, *Faith and Fury*, 151–52.

11. Corby, *Memoirs*, 85.

12. Corby, *Memoirs*, 114–22; Germain, *Chaplains*, 82–83.

13. The chancellor of a Catholic diocese keeps the official diocesan archives, manages the administrative offices, and sometimes finances and personnel as well. Corby, *Memoirs*, 82; Germain, *Chaplains*, 81.

14. Germain, *Chaplains*, 82–83.

15. Germain, *Chaplains*, 89. The Irish Catholicity of the 28th Massachusetts must have been strong. The story is told of Irish soldiers in the regiment marching past a Catholic church who saluted the church with their colors, upon being ordered to do so by their commander. Cf. Callaghan, *Thomas Francis Meagher*, 57.

16. This could have been the June 16 assault of the 28th Massachusetts on Fort Johnson (also known as the battle of Secessionville), an inconclusive battle which did, however, win the 28th commendations for their poise and bravery. Cf. the Boston College newspaper, *Sacred Heart Review*, vol. 46, no. 1, June 24, 1911, https://newspapers.bc.edu/?a=d&d=BOSTONSH19110624-01.2.3.1.

17. Germain, *Chaplains*, 84.

18. Endres and Kurtz, *Soldiers*, 198–200.

19. Germain, *Chaplains*, 60–61. Cf. C. J. Kirkfleet's article on St. James Parish in the Rockford, Illinois, Catholic paper, *The Observer*, December 19, 1935, https://obs.stparchive.com/Archive/OBS/OBS12191935p02.php?tags=december|19,|1935.

20. In a curious sidebar, the 90th Illinois apparently had a disguised woman named Frances Elizabeth Quinn in their ranks on two occasions. Discovered and dismissed once, she rejoined with a different name a year later, and was successful until captured by the Confederates a year later. Cf. Blanton and Cook, *They Fought Like Demons*, passim.

21. Germain, *Chaplains,* 72–73; Swan, *Chicago's Irish Legion*, 21, 41, 47, 50.

22. Curran, *American Catholics*, 100.

23. Cf. his obituary published in the New York *Irish American Weekly* on March 16, 1878.

24. Belmonte, *Rizzo*, 37–44. More details are available in the online archives of St. Bonaventure College, found at http://archives.sbu.edu.

25. Cass is reputedly the other person standing with Father Scully in the often-seen picture of a vested Scully standing outside the tent preparing to say Mass. Cass was mortally wounded at Malvern Hill, and died several days later on July 12, 1862.

26. Endres and Kurtz, *Soldiers*, 157–59.

27. Germain, *Chaplains*, 94–95; Endres and Kurtz, *Soldiers*, 157–59; and Gache, *Frenchman*, 125–26. Cf. also Scully's death notice in the *Cambridge*

Tribune 25, no. 28, September 13, 1902, http://cambridge.dlconsulting.com /cgi-bin/cambridge?a=d&d=Tribune19020913-01.2.4.

28. From Father John Vidmar's history of the province, *Fr. Fenwick's "Little American Province."*

29. Endres and Twobig, "With a Father's Affection," 105.

30. Quote taken from Charles Pollard Jr., as cited in Endres and Twobig, "With a Father's Affection," 115–25.

31. Durney, "Kildare Rebels." In his excellent 2020 book *Catholic Confederates*, Gracjan Kraszewski estimates that some 97,300 Irish fought for the Confederacy (see note 5 above). Without more evidence to bolster that statistic, however, I have chosen to go with the standard numbers here.

32. Rousey, "Aliens," 161.

33. E. Gleeson, *Rebel Sons*, 23–25, 40, 72, 100.

34. Germain, *Chaplains*, 112, and E. Gleeson, *Rebel Sons*, 146.

35. Meaney, *Valiant Chaplain*, 43–44.

36. Meaney, *Valiant Chaplain*, 45.

37. The first priest-chaplain killed was the Jesuit Father Anthony Rey, shot by Mexican guerrillas on January 19, 1847, during the Mexican-American War. Ed Gleeson in *Rebel Sons of Erin* erroneously mentions that "there were at least two other Catholic chaplains associated with the Army of the Tennessee at that time." He refers to Darius Hebert "of the 1st Louisiana regulars" and the better-known Abram Ryan, who Gleeson says "did the Lord's work at Missionary Ridge with his musket." Unfortunately, Gleeson is wrong on both accounts: Hubert spent his entire service in the eastern theater with the "other" 1st Louisiana, and the validity of Abram Ryan's chaplain career is highly debatable. Cf. Gleeson, *Rebel Sons*, 277.

38. Curran, *American Catholics*, 69.

39. French-born bishops in the South and West at the time of the Civil War included the legendary Jean-Baptiste Lamy (Santa Fe); three successive French bishops in New Orleans: Antoine Blanc, Jean-Marie Odin, then Napolean Perche; Auguste Martin (Natchitoches); and Augustine Verot (Savannah and Florida). The chaplains' information that follows is compiled primarily from Germain's work, but also from reliable internet resources such as the blog of James Durney, *Kildare Rebels, Irish Confederates*, at https://kildare.ie/ehistory /index.php; Romero, "Louisiana Clergy"; and the insightful book *First Chaplain of the Confederacy*, by Katherine Jeffrey, who was of great assistance personally on this section.

40. Cf. the blog of J. C. Sullivan, especially the article "Irish Units in the Confederacy," now found at https://www.authentic-campaigner.com/forum /military-forums/the-sinks/28846-irish-units-in-the-confederacy. There is an

excellent book about Father Darius Hubert by Katherine Bentley Jeffrey entitled *First Chaplain of the Confederacy*. She is also the author of *Two Civil Wars: The Curious Shared Journal of a Baton Rouge Schoolgirl and a Union Sailor on the USS Essex*.

41. Gannon, *Rebel Bishop*, 90.

42. Kinsella, "Holy Trinity in Paola."

43. Carius's "French connections" may have helped him as he traveled from diocese to diocese. Bishop Jean-Marie Odin (New Orleans), Napoleon Perche (later a bishop himself), and Bishop Antoine Blanc (Natchitoches) were all French prelates and helpful to his career.

44. Ferguson, "History of Diocese Excerpt."

45. McCall, "God of Our Fathers," 23.

46. Germain, *Chaplains*, 115–16; McCall, "God of Our Fathers," 25. Cf. also D'Antoni, *Abbe Pierre Felix Dicharry*, passim.

47. McClarey, "Father Turgis."

48. Richey, *Tirailleurs*, 52. His reference here to twenty thousand Catholics at Shiloh seems, however, to be an exaggerated number.

49. Chick, "Supposed Enigma."

50. Widman, "Grand Coteau," 34–49.

51. Letter from Pont to Bishop Odin in the University of Notre Dame online archives is available at http://archives.nd.edu/calendar/cal1862d.htm; and see Widman, "Grand Coteau," 38.

52. In a curious sidebar, in October 1855, Teeling was at the center of an interesting "Catholic seal of confession" conflict in a legal case. When called to testify against a Catholic whose confession he had heard after the man had wounded his wife in a fit of jealousy, Teeling followed standard Catholic canonical practice and refused to divulge the details of what he had heard. In what later became known as the "Teeling Law," the judge upheld the Catholic practice, saying that "to encroach upon the confessional . . . would be to ignore the Bill of Rights, so far as it is applicable to that Church." Cf. Magri, "Virginia," 457.

53. *The Richmond Times Dispatch*, April 22, 1861, https://dispatch.richmond.edu/1861/4/22/1/15.

CHAPTER 10. Chaplains in the West

1. Miller and Wakelyn, *Catholics in the Old South*, 45.

2. Cf. Starrett, *Mississippi Bishop*, 41–44. The Emmitsburg, Maryland, seminary would ironically become a prominent part of Civil War lore

(mentioned frequently in diaries of the period), as it was regularly visited by troops of both sides, particularly during the Gettysburg campaign.

3. The second group of people most bishops immediately sought out were Catholic women's religious orders. Starting Catholic schools was of paramount priority for most bishops, but especially those in priest-poor areas where Catholics influence was lacking. Catholic nuns were essential not only for forming and running schools, but also for providing critical care of the many orphans and sick in the communities they lived in.

4. The priests serving troops after Shiloh were the Jesuit Anthony de Chaignon; two priests from the New Orleans Diocese, Isadore Turgis and Francois Bertrand; and six priests from Natchez, Francis Pont, John Mouton, Julian Guillou, Francis Leray, Philip Huber, and Henry Picherit.

5. Elder's diary is available in book form, or online at https://archive.org /details/39020017676308-civilwardiaryof/ (cited hereafter as Elder, *Civil War Diary*). Cf. also Curran, *American Catholics*, 236–37.

6. The University of Mississippi ("Ole Miss") had been founded in 1844 in Oxford. Its Lyceum building, three dormitories, and other buildings were used as a Civil War hospital for soldiers of both sides eventually. Some 250 or more soldiers who died in the campus hospital were buried in a cemetery on the grounds of the university. For a short history of the hospital in Shelby Springs, Alabama, see "The Old Shelby Hotel Was the First in Alabama to Have Running Water," https://www.al.com/strange-alabama/2012/06/the_old_shelby _hotel_was_first.html; for the use of the Oxford, Mississippi, university buildings as hospitals for wounded soldiers from both sides, see "Oxford's Olden Days: The Civil War Hospital, Purposes for University," https://www.hotty toddy.com/2015/04/21/oxfords-olden-days-the-civil-war-hospital-war -purposes-for-university/.

7. Elder, *Civil War Diary*, 78.

8. A "coadjutor bishop" in Catholic parlance is a bishop whose main role is to assist the diocesan bishop in the administration of the diocese. In essence, a coadjutor acts as vicar general but is co-head of the diocese in all but ceremonial precedence.

9. Price, "Reverend John B. Mouton," 104.

10. Price, "Reverend John B. Mouton," 102–6.

11. Bishop Elder to Rev. John Mouton, September 14, 1866, in Natchez-Jackson Diocesan Archives. Cf. also Price, "Reverend John B. Mouton," 105.

12. Pillar, *Catholic Church*, 211–12.

13. Germain, *Chaplains*, 128–29.

14. These quotes are from the April 8, 1862, letter of Francis Pont (at Corinth) to Archbishop John Mary Odin (in New Orleans, Louisiana), as

found in the online archives of the University of Notre Dame, http://archives
.nd.edu/calendar/cal1862d.htm.

15. Starrett, *Mississippi Bishop*, 77; Maryniak et al., *Faith in the Fight*, 243;
Germain, *Chaplains*, 129; and the websites of both St. Paul Church and Cemetery in Pass Christian, Mississippi, http://cemeteries.passchristian.net/st_paul
_catholic_cemetery.htm.

16. Patrick Tucker, *Irish Confederates*, 31.

17. Elder, *Civil War Diary*, 16. A fascinating note is connected to Father
Guillou in the *Metropolitan Catholic Almanac of 1851*, and it reflects the true
multiracial nature of Catholicism, despite the social situation of the South. It
was said of Guillou's Yazoo City ministry that he cared for "four stations in
Yazoo, among them three plantations for the benefit of the negroes; one station
in Holmes county, and one in Panola." Cf. the *Metropolitan Catholic Almanac
of 1851*, which can be found online.

18. Elder, *Character Glimpses*, 48.

19. Lamy's Santa Fe Diocese was immense, comprising all of New Mexico and Arizona, as well as part of Nevada at the time the Civil War began. The
new Arizona Territory was formed in 1863. Cf. Garett, "French Missionary
Clergy," 292.

20. Most of the French priests who served under Bishop Lamy came from
his home region of Auvergne in France. A comprehensive list of all the French
priests who served in the Santa Fe Diocese can be found at https://frenchin
newmexico.com/surnames-of-french-families/thematic-lists/church/list-of
-french-priests/. Lamy himself became the subject of a famous 1927 award-
winning book by Willa Cather, entitled *Death Comes for the Archbishop*.

21. The two battles of note in this four-month campaign were Valverde
(February 20–21, 1862) and Glorieta Pass (March 26–28, 1862)—the latter being
described with tongue-in-cheek humor as the "Gettysburg of the West." A
number of small skirmishes took place between April 8 and May 1, 1862, before
the Confederates abandoned New Mexico.

22. According to one source, Taladrid was a lieutenant in the Spanish military before being captured by the French. However, as the French and Spanish
hadn't fought since 1823, this remains unverified. Cf. Thompson, *New Mexico
Volunteers*, 25.

23. Ceran St. Vrain (1802–1870), the son of a French aristocrat, lived in
Mora and ran a well-known trading post in the Taos area. He became the
supplier for Fort Union in northeastern New Mexico, the main guardian of
the Santa Fe Trail, and began the recruiting of the 1st New Mexico Infantry.
Christopher "Kit" Carson (1809–1868), the legendary frontiersman, was a fur
trapper, Indian agent, and military officer. In 1861 the two men organized the

1st New Mexico Volunteer Infantry, which fought at Valverde, and in March 1862 was consolidated with other units to form the 1st New Mexico Cavalry Regiment, with Carson as its colonel.

24. Thompson, *New Mexico Volunteers*, 25 and 134. Cf. also Germain, *Chaplains*, 95–102, for an in-depth discussion of why Taladrid was also associated with the 1st New Mexico Cavalry after it was formed from a consolidation of three regiments in May 1862.

25. Cf. Thompson, *New Mexico Volunteers*, 246. Aidan Germain has a long reference to the letter (originally in Spanish) that Taladrid defiantly wrote in response to the charges made against him. The priest closed by saying, "If it is thought . . . that I am no longer useful or competent for the service . . . I would immediately present my resignation. . . . I assure you that I shall never be found wanting, should ever again the enemy invade this Territory, but will be ready physically and morally to assist in the triumph [*sic*] of liberty and union." Germain, *Chaplains*, 97–99.

26. Germain, *Chaplains*, 100–101.

27. Rebekha C. Crockett, "Carleton Visits," New Mexico Historic Sites, Facebook, April 16, 2020, https://www.facebook.com/profile/100064731758933 /search/?q=carleton%20visits.

28. R. E. Twichell, *New Mexico History*, 421.

29. Grzelachowski's life is documented by two authors: an article by Francis Kajencki, and two fascinating, privately published volumes by his great-grandson Daniel Flores (see the bibliography for details). Grzelachowski spoke several languages, including Latin, Polish, and Greek, which made him quite a fascinating conversationalist throughout his life. The spelling of his Polish name was always troublesome—written at times as Garelousky, Grzelausky, and Gregelowski, among other variations.

30. Grzelachowski was officially commissioned on February 3, 1862, and mustered out with his regiment at Santa Fe on May 31, 1862.

31. The accounts of the Polish priest's crucial role at Glorieta are taken from Daniel Flores's book and Frank Kajencki's article, both of which present supporting evidence for his role.

32. Kajencki, "Alexander Grzelachowski," 250–59.

33. Secundina was thirty years his junior, as shown by the 1880 census: "Alexander Grzelachowski: 55, single, farmer and stockraiser; Secundina: female, 25, mother of Adelina (age 10), Adolfo (9), Amelia (4), Emilia (4 months)." Cited in Kajencki, "Alexander Grzelachowski," 255. For the stories about his deathbed encounter and the cemetery he is buried in, cf. Flores, *Grzelachowski*, book 2, pages 121 and 143.

34. Existing records verify that by 1860 or 1861, Grzelachowski was making the transition out of active ministry into the secular life. The 1861 *Sadlier's Catholic Almanac* does not include his name at all among the twenty-nine priests listed as serving in the Santa Fe Diocese at the outbreak of the war. The 1860 Federal census reflects well the ambiguity of his situation, stating that "he was thirty-six years old, a Roman Catholic clergyman, valued his real estate at $400 and personal estate at $18,000." In today's economy, that estate would be worth nearly $560,000—an indication that his personal financial resources were far more what he could have acquired from ministry alone while in New Mexico. It is my personal speculation that while becoming a priest may have been a highly esteemed "career choice" in his traditionally Catholic Polish culture, when he came to the wilds of New Mexico his wealth, temperament, and business acumen eventually led him to (as we used to say in the seminary) seek his sanctity elsewhere.

CHAPTER 11. Unconventional Chaplains in Unique Situations

1. Buckley, "Joseph Bixio," 14–25.

2. A letter from visiting British artillery officer is the source for the statement about Bixio's possible role in that battle as an "informant" to the Confederate leadership. Cf. Gache, *Frenchman*, 97–98.

3. Sheeran, *Diary*, 468–69; Belmonte, *Rizzo*, 39–40.

4. In his diary, Sheeran writes that Bixio wanted to get himself and his "purchased, presented, or begged merchandise" back to his parish in Staunton. He comments that Rizzo had already resolved to quit the 9th Connecticut (he was "disgusted with those barbarians"), and Bixio had agreed with Rizzo to act as chaplain in his place. But Sheeran is undoubtedly mistaken—he was told that story by Bixio himself, whose self-serving, opportunistic, and fraudulent motives even he was not fully aware of (and would condemn in Sheridan's presence three months later). Cf. Sheeran, *Diary*, 468–69, 548–49; Belmonte, *Rizzo*, 37–44, 63–64; and Buckley, "Joseph Bixio," 14–25.

5. Cf. Gache, *Frenchman*, 97–99.

6. It should be noted that Innocent Bergrath also worked for troops of both sides in Tennessee during the war, albeit in an unofficial way, unlike Trecy. Trecy's name was often misspelled as "Tracy," "Tracey," or simply "T." He is described at length in David Conyngham's nineteenth-century unpublished manuscript, which was edited and published in 2019 as *Soldiers of the Cross:*

The Authoritative Text (Endres and Kurtz). Three chapters in that book are devoted to Trecy.

7. There is an amusing story about Trecy when he worked in the area known then as Indian Territory. He found himself suddenly addressed in perfect Gaelic by a person who appeared to be a war-paint covered Native American. He discovered these men were two Tipperary Irishmen who had taken refuge among that tribe after killing their landlord in Ireland in 1838, fleeing to and all across America, until finally joining trappers in the Fort Union area, between Montana and North Dakota. They hunted buffalo with the Native Americans, distinguished themselves among them by their bravery, married Native American women, and even became chiefs. After he got over his astonishment, Trecy then baptized the women and their children, and forty other Native Americans there. Cf. Endres and Kurtz, *Soldiers*, 40.

8. Endres and Kurtz, *Soldiers*, 46.

9. Cf. the postwar description of Bishop John Ireland about the faith of General David Stanley, as cited on the 22nd US Infantry webpage, at http://122 infantry.org/commanders/stanleypers.htm.

10. Endres and Kurtz, *Soldiers*, 60 and 69.

11. Cf. the 2023 documentary film on the seven chaplains of Rosecrans's Army of the Cumberland, also entitled *Faith of the Fathers*, produced by the author and Tim Frakes. It is available for viewing at www.faithofthefathers.net or https://www.historyfix.com.

12. Abram Ryan bypassed his local provincial, Father Stephen Ryan, in getting a dispensation to leave his order, though his self-will and insubordination was long known to his local province. Much has been written on Ryan through the years, but I have used David O'Connell's excellent biography as a primary information source. Cf. O'Connell, *Furl That Banner*, published 2006.

13. Cf. O'Connell, *Furl That Banner*, 43–53. Some say that Ryan freelanced as a chaplain with Longstreet's troops, while Longstreet's Army was in Tennessee in late 1863.

14. Cf. O'Connell, *Furl That Banner*, 53; Pitts, *Chaplains in Gray*, 126–28; Pickett, *Literary Hearthstones*, 211–12. McKey is cited in Friedel, "Intimate Study," 39. For further comments on Ryan, see E. Gleeson, *Erin Go Gray*; Beagle and Giezma, *Poet of the Lost Cause*, and Jeffrey, "Contrasting Legacies."

15. O'Connell, *Furl That Banner*, 54–59.

16. Browne, *Bugle Echoes*, 278.

17. O'Connell, *Furl That Banner*, 204–5.

18. O'Connell, *Furl That Banner*, 202–4. Cf. also E. Gleeson, *Erin Go Gray*, passim.

19. William Hamilton was erroneously called (even by William Corby in his *Memoirs*) "the only Catholic priest" at Andersonville, citing the journal of one Union prisoner (Sergeant S. S. Boggs, 21st Illinois). Hamilton's testimony is found in US Congress, The Trial of Henry Wirz, 277–78, 291, 294. His story is also related in Gannon, *Rebel Bishop*, 95–96.

20. Meaney, "Father Whelan," 1–20. In 1861, the Savannah Diocese covered the entire state of Georgia, and had only eleven priests and six churches covering the whole state. Cf. Gannon, *Rebel Bishop*, 91–92.

21. James Sheeran (14th Louisiana) visited Whelan on his own extended leave in 1863 and 1864 from the Army of Northern Virginia. Sheeran, *Civil War Diary*, 286; Whelan to Townsend, May 21, 1866; *Savannah Daily News Herald*, June 4, 1866.

22. Cf. Meaney, "Father Whelan," 14. Whelan wrote little about his prison work, but Clavreul, Verot, and Hamilton all recorded more extensive memories. Cf. *Annales*, Report of the Diocese of Savannah, 397–401; also Gannon, *Rebel Bishop*, 93–104 (for the description of Usannez returning from Andersonville).

23. The quotes are from pages 5–6 of Clavreul's diary, which was privately published in 1910 and is available online. *Diary of Rev. H. Clavreul: With the Names of Dying Federal Soldiers to Whom He Ministered at Andersonville, Ga., During July and August, 1864*, https://www.google.com/books/edition/Diary_of_Rev_H_Clavreul/k_JDAAAAYAAJ?hl=en&ggbp=1.

24. At least five Union soldiers later mentioned this or bread in their accounts of Andersonville. Whelan later told the postwar court that the quality of the daily diet was so poor that many prisoners could not eat his bread. Gannon, *Rebel Bishop*, 101–2; Davidson, *Fourteen Months*, 224; and US Congress, The Trial of Henry Wirz, 426.

25. *Savannah Daily News Herald*, June 4, 1866.

26. Clavreul, for example, did not blame Wirz for the horrors at Andersonville. "He was boorish, profane, although never, to my knowledge, guilty of the acts of violence and cruelty that were afterward laid to his charge, being himself the sufferer of conditions he could in no way help." *Annales de la Propagation de la Foi*, Report of the Diocese of Savannah, 398.

27. *Savannah Evening News*, February 11, 1871. Meaney, "Father Whelan," 23–24.

28. The Vincennes Diocese began in 1834 and comprised all of Indiana and the eastern third of Illinois. It was led by French-born bishops, including the second bishop, Celestin de la Haliandiere (1798–1882), who was responsible

for recruiting the Irish-born Murphy to work in the diocese with Catholics of English origin.

29. Dr. Clarke's letter is available at the website of the 31st Massachusetts Infantry, https://31massinf.wordpress.com/narratives-letters-diaries/dr-e-p -clarke-my-capture/.

30. Germain, *Chaplains*, 87. Cf. https://www.fold3.com/image/304979224 /murphy-p-j-r-page-8-us-letters-received-by-commission-branch-1863-1870; also https://www.fold3.com/image/304979217/murphy-p-j-r-page-5-us-letters -received-by-commission-branch-1863-1870. Murphy was pastor at St. James on Prairie Avenue, a church literally just blocks away from the infamous prison compound. He was officially appointed on February 27, 1865, follow-ing a slew of interesting letters recommending him, including two from General Nathaniel Banks.

31. Baker and Larzalere, "Baptisms in St. James' Catholic Church," 39–48. Exact records of how many died at Camp Douglas remain unclear; some esti-mates are around six thousand soldiers.

32. Cf. "St. Patrick Catholic Church," Cerro Gordo County webpage, https://www.iagenweb.org/cerrogordo/church/cg_ch_stpatricks_dougherty.ht m. The article about his death was published in the *Vincennes Weekly Western Sun* on September 4, 1869.

33. In *Melting Pot Soldiers*, William Burton cites Ella Lonn's research, and estimates the total number of Germans fighting in the Union as in the range of 176,817 to 216,000, though the exact number is unknown. He also estimates that 36,000 of these Germans fought in ethnic regiments. Cf. Burton, *Melting Pot Soldiers*, 109–10.

34. Cf. Reinhart, "Germans in the Civil War," website http://sites.roots web.com/.

35. Only New York provided more native Germans to the Union army than Wisconsin, with their contribution being 36,000. Cf. the 24th Wisconsin website, at http://genealogytrails.com/wis/military/cw/24thWIInfReg.html; see also Beaudot, *24th Wisconsin*, passim.

36. Beaudot, *24th Wisconsin*, 118.

37. Beaudot, *24th Wisconsin*, 185–86.

38. For further details about the 17th Wisconsin's ethnic heritage, see Bur-ton, *Melting Pot*, 151.

39. Germain, *Chaplains*, 85. Miettinger's name is spelled many different ways, making tracing his already scant history more difficult. Different records spell it as "Meittenger," "Mietinger," "Mettinger," and "Meithenger."

40. Kurtz, *Excommunicated*, 73. The Bishop John Luers letter is found in the University of Notre Dame online archives at http://archives.nd.edu /calendar/cal1865k.htm.

CHAPTER 12. In Retrospect

The part epigraph is from James M. McPherson, afterword to *Religion and the American Civil War*, ed. Randall M. Miller, Harry S. Stout, and Charles Reagan Wilson (New York: Oxford University Press, 1998), 412.

    1. The numbers of Confederate dead come from James McPherson's estimates of Confederate troop strength. A fuller description of these religious consequences of the Civil War, as well as a bibliography that expands these topics, can be found in my previous book on religion and the Civil War. Cf. Robert Miller, *Both Prayed*, 177–85.

    2. Gugliotta, "Death Toll," 18. Craig L. Barry authored an excellent article delving into the poor diets of Civil War soldiers and nutritional deficiencies leading to poor health conditions among many. See Barry, "More on Rations: Nutritional Deficiencies."

    3. Germain, *Chaplains*, 61.

    4. Endres and Kurtz, *Soldiers*, 122 and 133. The now defunct website of his former Coylesville, Pennsylvania, church also spoke about Christy's wartime sicknesses leading to an early death.

    5. Hope, *Notre Dame*, 23.

    6. Germain, *Chaplains*, 69–70.

    7. Jeffrey, *First Chaplain*, passim.

    8. Germain, *Chaplains*, 71–72; also cf. McClarey, "Father John Ireland."

    9. Germain, *Chaplains*, 73.

    10. Germain, *Chaplains*, 81.

    11. Germain, *Chaplains*, 84.

    12. Germain, *Chaplains*, 84.

    13. Germain, *Chaplains*, 85.

    14. Germain, *Chaplains*, 85.

    15. Germain, *Chaplains*, 87.

    16. Germain, *Chaplains*, 125–26.

    17. Belmonte, *Rizzo*, 39–44.

    18. O'Connell, *Catholicity*, 162 and 243.

    19. Germain, *Chaplains*, 94.

    20. Germain, *Chaplains*, 94.

    21. Germain, *Chaplains*, 104.

    22. Germain, *Chaplains*, 70.

    23. Meaney, "Father Peter Whelan," passim.

    24. Corby, *Memoirs*, 82–84.

    25. Cf. Notre Dame, "Calendar for January 1940," http://archives.nd.edu /calendar/c1940.htm.

    26. Philip Tucker, *Fighting Chaplain*, 146.

27. Ahlstrom, *Religious History*, 114–15 and 124–25.

28. Stephenson refers here to Father Anthony Carius, chaplain of the 1st Louisiana Regulars, who operated in the western theater. It is perhaps relevant that Stephenson was only fifteen or sixteen years old when he observed these "interactions," wrote the memoirs when he was twenty, and did not revise and publish them until much later when he was then a Presbyterian minister. Cf. Stephenson, *Civil War Memoir*, 20.

29. Gache, *Frenchman*, 147; Kurtz, *Excommunicated*, 68; Kraszewski, *Catholic Confederates*, 103. Although it is not my purpose here to discuss the role of Catholic nuns in the war, I again recommend the book *To Bind Up the Wounds*, by Sister Mary Denis Maher. Gracjan Kraszewski's *Catholic Confederates* also has a marvelous chapter on the nuns' influence, especially in the Confederacy.

30. All examples taken from original documents are cited in Endres and Kurtz, *Soldiers*, 78–79, 194.

31. From the files of the 18th Illinois, as cited in Germain, *Chaplains*, 73–77.

32. As related previously in this book, Scully once had an amusing response after listening to ministers pontificating about the need for higher pay, and even striking to get it. He said simply, "I cannot join you in your movement upon the government. . . . I am sorry to learn she has foes within. . . . I labor in the service of God. He is my paymaster. . . . I hope you all may be generals and be paid as such!" Cf. Endres and Kurtz, *Soldiers*, 149–50.

33. Sheeran, *Diary*, 335–36.

34. Sheeran, *Diary*, 124–15.

35. Gache's letters to his Jesuit confreres are fascinating reading. Filled with what his editor calls "teasing" of them, they appear to an outsider as pompous, bombastic, and even rude in places. Cf. Gache, *Frenchman*, passim.

36. Gache, *Frenchman*, 51, 143.

37. Gache, *Frenchman*, 210–13.

38. Endres and Kurtz, *Soldiers*, 49. In another gesture of wartime ecumenism, one Union Protestant chaplain, Reverend Fredric Denison, once returned from his leave with three hundred Douay Bibles for the Catholic men of his regiment.

39. Though he ministered as chaplain during the war, Twichell was only formally ordained in January 1863, following the July 1862 ruling that chaplains had to be "regularly ordained members of a denomination." Cf. J. Twichell, *Civil War Letters*, 73, 170.

40. J. Twichell, *Civil War Letters*, 204; and retold in Brinsfield et al., *Faith in the Fight*, 124. Sadly and poignantly, just before the battle of Fredericksburg, O'Hagan had written to a fellow Jesuit remarking that "if [Burnside] attempts it

here, it will be at a terrible sacrifice of life" (O'Hagan to Wiget, November 30, 1862, published in *Woodstock Letters* 15 (1886), 111–12).

41. Joseph Twichell mustered out with the regiment in July 1864, married shortly after the war, and went on to pastor one Connecticut church for forty-seven years. He became a well-known figure in the religious and cultural life of New England and New York in the late nineteenth century, also becoming friends with Mark Twain, a postwar neighbor in Hartford, Connecticut. Increasing deafness led him to retire from pastoring in 1912, and after a debilitating illness in his later years, he died in Hartford on December 20, 1918. J. Twichell, *Civil War Letters*, 261–64.

42. Woodbury, *First Rhode Island*, 44–45.

43. Jeffrey, *First Chaplain*, 154 and 164; Brinsfield et al., *Faith in the Fight*, 212 and 235.

44. Tissot, "Letters of Civil War Chaplains," 171–72.

45. Pillar, *Catholic Church in Mississippi*, 288.

46. Endres and Kurtz, *Soldiers*, 129.

47. Curran, *American Catholics*, 380.

48. Schmidt, *Notre Dame*, 103. On this topic, I am grateful to William Kurtz. In his fine book *Excommunicated from the Union* (especially pages 77–88), he offers a detailed, multifaceted summary of the issue of prejudice in America, and how it impacted clergy, religious, and ordinary soldiers during the war.

49. Gilles, *People of God*, 154. It was only in the twentieth century that Vatican attitudes toward the United States began to change. In 1984 the Vatican transitioned from the position of Apostolic Delegate to the United States to a formal Apostolic Nuncio post, with ambassadorial power. America's embassy in Rome began that same year, born out of the friendship of Ronald Reagan and Pope John Paul II. What helped greatly in this changed attitude were the strong social commitments of the American Catholic Church—educational institutions, hospitals, charities, work for the poor, and financial support for the Vatican.

50. Kurtz opines that this "battle on two fronts" fought by Catholic clergy postwar applied as well to the relationship with American Protestants. The struggles of Catholic conservatives to relate to their non-Catholic counterparts in open, ecumenical ways continued well into the twentieth century, with more conservative Catholic leaders in the Vatican resisting the foundational *Decree on Ecumenism* (*Unitatis redintegratio*), which emerged from the Second Vatican Council in November 1964.

51. Gracjan Kraszewski maintains that postwar southern Catholics seemed to be caught up in a "Confederatization" process where they "were fully integrated . . . and believed the same things as and acted in similar fashion

to their Protestant neighbors." Yet their unique Catholic beliefs only further put them at odds with the victorious North's anti-Catholic nativism after the war. Endres and Kurtz, *Soldiers*, 3–5; Kraszewski, *Catholic Confederates*, 140–41.

52. In *Excommunicated from the Union*, Will Kurtz has an excellent summary of the struggles that Catholics had with America's public education system. Cf. Kurtz, *Excommunicated*, 136–41; quote is on 136.

53. McGreevy, *Catholicism*, chapter 1. The entire chapter elucidates the prewar struggles within the Church about education, in which Wiget played a prominent role. Cf. also the Wikipedia page on the Eliot School rebellion, https://en.wikipedia.org/wiki/Eliot_School_rebellion. See also the Catholic newspaper *The Arkansas Catholic*, June 11, 1911, page 7, which contains the young boy's account of the incident. Quotation is from Hill, *Gonzaga College*, 77. For a fuller history of this whole issue, see also Dennis Ryan's doctoral dissertation, "Beyond the Ballot Box: A Social History of the Boston Irish, 1845–1917" (University of Massachusetts, 2014).

54. Hippolyte Gache used those words to describe Scully in Gache, *Frenchman*, 125–26. See also O'Connor, *Boston Catholics*, 137–38. This book has an overview of the whole controversy between Scully and O'Hagan, and how Archbishop John Williams quietly intervened by starting a parochial school system in Boston. Also cf. Candal, "'Be Not Afraid,'" passim.

55. The former chaplain of the 35th Indiana, Peter Paul Cooney, collaborated with Bishop Ireland on temperance work after the war. Both even worked and corresponded with the liberal Women's Christian Temperance Movement (WCTU), founded in 1874, demonstrating an ecumenical outreach typical of Ireland's career. For more on Ireland's Civil War experiences, see M. O'Connell, *John Ireland*, and Shannon, "Archbishop Ireland's Experience."

56. Under Ireland's 1890 Faribault School Plan, the local board of education rented the Catholic school building, but after school hours it reverted to the parish, and the same teachers taught the children catechism. Most Catholic bishops were against the plan, though Pope Leo XIII gave it his blessing (likely only because Ireland and his plan were popular in some Paris circles where the Vatican, at the time, was seeking to improve relations with the French). Agreements made with the local Faribault school board, however, soon collapsed, and the plan fell apart.

57. These "modernist" fears were part of what is termed the "fortress mentality" of the institutional Catholic Church, which dominated their approach to the world between the time of the Reformation and the early twentieth century. This mindset in many Church prelates led to fears of such "radical" ideas as freedom of the press, democratic models of government, social progress movements, and laity receiving too much power in what was seen as a divinely

instituted Church and social structure. Bernard McQuaid (1823–1909) himself was very briefly a Civil War chaplain in 1864, when he went to Fredericksburg to determine the status of Catholic chaplaincy there. Finding only one chaplain to serve the five general hospitals there, he remained for an undetermined (although short) time until another priest arrived. Named the first bishop of Rochester, New York, in 1868, McQuaid is considered an occasional chaplain for the purposes of this book.

58. In 1862, when he was pastor of St. Brigid Church in South Baltimore, Gibbons crossed the harbor each Sunday at 6:00 am to hear confessions and say Mass at Fort McHenry. At the time, the fort was a prison for captured Confederate soldiers and Maryland civilians who were suspected of being Confederate sympathizers. Cf. the online parish history of Our Lady of Good Counsel Church, found at https://www.southbaltcatholic.org/our-lady-of-good -counsel; see also William J. Shepherd, "The Archivist's Nook: Silent Sentinel of Catholic University," July 9, 2015, https://www.lib.cua.edu/wordpress/news events/6157/.

59. Other Catholic leaders who were considered more liberal at the time were Bishop John Keane of Richmond, and Denis O'Connell, the rector of North American College. Gilles, *People of God*, 166.

60. Ellis, *Cardinal Gibbons*; Hannum, "Rerum Roots"; and the Baltimore Archdiocese history of Gibbons, available at https://www.archbalt.org/his -eminence-james-cardinal-gibbons/.

61. Curran, *McGlynn Affair*, 197–200; McGreevy, *Catholicism*, 133–37.

62. Mustered in shortly after the war began, Lambert is said to have seen action with the 18th Illinois at Forts Henry and Donelson and at Shiloh before his resignation on April 16, 1862. As mentioned above, he got caught up in contentious regimental politics around the Irish Catholic commander of the 18th Illinois, Michael Lawler. While pastor in Cairo, Illinois, he hosted Father Joseph Carrier CSC, who was at that time heading south to join Grant's army around Vicksburg. Cf. Germain, *Chaplains*, 73–77.

63. Janus, "Bishop Bernard McQuaid," 53–76; K. McKenna, *Battle for Rights*, passim.

64. Abing, "Catholic Indian Missions," passim.

65. The surgeon was George E. Cooper, a doctor in the Army of the Cumberland at Nashville. Abing, "Catholic Indian Missions," 3.

66. Like most Americans of the time, Stephan believed no indigenous person could be truly "civilized" unless they were educated and embraced Christianity; thus he devoted much energy to establishing schools and recruiting Catholic missionaries to staff them. Trying to do his work impartially as both priest and civilian Indian agent, Stephan wrote that if, as a Catholic priest, he

422 Notes to Pages 326–332

failed to carry out his duties in an impartial manner, "the whole of Protestantism from the great grandfather Martin Luther down to Susan B. Anthony would squeal like the hogs, which jumped into the sea, when our Lord drove the devils in them." Letter from Stephan to Ewing, November 14, 1878, cited in Abing, "Catholic Indian Missions." The small town of Stephan, South Dakota—today only containing a Native American school and a post office—was named after Monsignor Stephan in 1878.

67. In 1884 Stephan was named director of the Bureau of Catholic Indian Missions (BCIM) at the Standing Rock Agency, and worked for seventeen years to advance that cause. However, in 1900, the negative politics of Catholics running Native American missions (much of them stemming from Protestants) led to all governmental appropriations ending. Stephan commented that agency Native Americans were "peaceable, industrious and good, with only few exceptions. Our mutual relations [were] of the most amicable and friendliest kind." According to his observations, it was white settlers who were the "troublesome element . . . the constant harassing, backbiting and lieing [sic] from those men, makes me disgusted with the place." At the time of his 1901 death, the existence of Catholic Indian schools was still in doubt—but many endured thanks to his zeal and his successor's renewed financing. Cf. letter from Stephan to Charles Ewing, March 31, 1881, and letter from Stephan to Father Brouillet of the BCIM, May 3, 1881; both are cited in Abing, *Catholic Indian Missions*, 6.

CHAPTER 13. Reflections and Lessons

1. The fifteen countries of the chaplains' birth are Ireland, the United States, France, Germany, Austria, Prussia, Italy, Canada, Belgium, Holland, Hungary, England, Switzerland, Spain, and Poland (listed in order of the number of chaplains born there, from most to least). John Ireland was not ordained until December 1861.

2. Four European regions account for the bulk of America's immigrants: Ireland, the many German states, Great Britain (including Scotland and Wales), and Scandinavia. Burton, *Melting Pot Soldiers*, 15–16; Kurtz, *Excommunicated*, 3; Perko, *Catholic and American*, 131–45.

3. William Kurtz has three pages of marvelous short chaplain anecdotes which help illustrate the wartime bonds of Catholic priest-soldier "connectedness." Kurtz, *Excommunicated*, 74–76.

4. The American Battlefield Trust has done excellent research in this area, and their numbers are used here. Cf. "Civil War Casualties," American Bat-

tlefield Trust, https://www.battlefields.org/learn/articles/civil-war-casualties; M. Smith, *Smell of Battle*. The number of wartime casualties remains an open discussion, though more historians of late are augmenting the number beyond the "traditional" 623,000 wartime deaths.

5. Faust, *Republic of Suffering*, 3–31.

6. The term post-traumatic stress disorder (PTSD) would not enter the medical lexicon until 1980, but its symptoms turn up frequently in accounts of Civil War soldiers, and clergy would not have been unaffected. The subject of historic wartime trauma has received more attention in recent years, e.g., Tony Horwitz, "Did Civil War Soldiers Have PTSD?," *Smithsonian Magazine*, January 2015, https://www.smithsonianmag.com/history/ptsd-civil-wars-hidden-legacy-180953652/, and Diane Miller Sommerville, "Post Traumatic Stress Disorder and the American Civil War," National Museum of Civil War Medicine, May 2, 2019, https://www.civilwarmed.org/ptsd/.

7. Lucey, "Diary of Joseph B. O'Hagan," 402–9.

8. Sheeran, *Civil War Diary*, 501, entry from November 5, 1864.

9. Sheeran, *Civil War Diary*, 528.

10. Gache, *Frenchman*, 130–33.

11. Schmidt, *Notre Dame*, 36–37.

12. Protestant seminary training of the time often ran the gamut depending on the denominational affiliation. As a general rule, more liturgically oriented religious denominations tended to have rigorous education or qualification standards for their ministers. The more evangelical denominations (e.g., Baptists and Methodists) had no established seminaries at the time of the Civil War, and their chaplains relied far less on formal theological training than on charisma to bring the gospel message to people, or (as one author phrased it) "to make an impression."

13. Brinsfield et al., *Faith in the Fight*, 43–45.

14. My own statistics on the average age of Catholic hospital and post chaplains (with one Confederate chaplain excluded due to lack of information): ten Union chaplains (36.8 years), nine Confederate chaplains (37.7 years), all Catholic hospital and post chaplains (37.2 years).

15. The estimates given by William Kurtz are closer to the actual number of Catholic chaplains that my own research has determined. While using his figure of fifty-three Catholic chaplains (with no distinctions made between official or occasional), Kurtz remarks that "the average length of service lasted for only eighteen months . . . limiting their ability to serve adequately Catholic soldiers, let alone dispel nativist tendencies." Cf. Kurtz, *Excommunicated*, 68.

16. Accurate numbers for Confederate chaplains are harder to determine. A number of men who became Protestant chaplains did not enter as such, but were "promoted" or chosen later by their regiment for chaplain duties. Also, the denominational breakdown and length of service for Confederate chaplains who were not Catholics have been difficult to track down. The Civil War Chaplains Museum in Lynchburg is presently working on such a database.

17. C. Smith, "Civil War Chaplains," 66.

18. Both the Butler and Hancock quotes are from a series of letters solicited between 1868 and 1870 from leading Union and Confederate generals by David Power Conyngham for his late nineteenth-century manuscript on Catholic priests and nuns of the Civil War. Unpublished for a century, Conyngham's work was released in 2019 as *Soldiers of the Cross: The Authoritative Text*, edited by David Endres and William Kurtz. Cf. Endres and Kurtz, *Soldiers*, 23–24 and 442.

19. Interested readers can look for online versions of Moses Stuart, *Conscience and the Constitution* (1850), and Alexis de Tocqueville, *Democracy in America* (1835). See also Woodworth, *While God Is Marching On*; McPherson, *Cause and Comrades*, 63; Marsden, "New Old-Time Religion," 34.

20. As an example, criminal law of the day was indebted to the Ten Commandments, a fact accepted by everyone in the 1860s as entirely sensible because of the need for "moral absolutes" in life. Cf. Noll, *Civil War*, 11–13. The rest of Mark Noll's book is an excellent source on the argument that religion was the most important cultural and social factor at work in the country at the outbreak of the war.

21. Noll, *Civil War*, 12. Cf. also Shattuck, *Shield*, 14; Ahlstrom, *Religious History*, 672–74.

22. The omission of religion in recounting the Civil War is clearly seen in National Park exhibits and films, written histories of the war or its battles and leaders, and even in the Ken Burns 1990s classic documentary on the Civil War. This acclaimed documentary quotes freely from letters of Civil War soldiers (like Elisha Hunt Rhodes) without ever revealing the frequent expressions of religious faith that ran through them.

23. Rable, *Chosen People*, 1. Cf. Robert Miller, *Both Prayed*, 6. In the second chapter of *Both Prayed*, I discuss important distinctions between "religion" and "faith," further clarifying the scope and power of "belief" in the Civil War era.

24. Blight, *Race and Reunion*, 3–5.

25. Kurtz, *Excommunicated*, 145. German Catholics apparently felt no need to promote their role in the war, for virtually no histories were written and few monuments erected by the German community. Kurtz speculates the rea-

sons for this being a possible greater degree of connection in American society, as well as a weaker sense of German identity compared to the Irish.

26. Kurtz, *Excommunicated*, 144–46.

27. *Western Watchman*, March 17, 1898. Regarding a reevaluation of Rosecrans, cf. Frank Varney, *General Grant and the Rewriting of History*; and David Moore, *William S Rosecrans and the Union Victory: A Civil War Biography*.

28. Kurtz, *Excommunicated*, 148–49.

29. Hope, *Notre Dame*, chapter 9.

30. Kurtz, *Excommunicated*, 162. As mentioned earlier in this chapter, the Catholic Church generally missed the boat of building strong connections in the African American community postwar. This was partly due to prejudice, and clergy shortages, but also it must be realistically said that Latin-based Masses and the highly structured worship of the time were unlikely to attract people of color, most of whose faith had its American origins in evangelical Baptist or Methodist backgrounds.

31. Kurtz, *Excommunicated*, 157–60.

32. Kraszewski, *Catholic Confederates*, xviii.

33. Kraszewski, from the jacket of *Catholic Confederates*; Rousey, "Old South," 16–17.

34. Kraszewski, *Catholic Confederates*, 21. The Semmes family is one example of a very influential Catholic Confederate family; they were originally from Maryland. Admiral Raphael Semmes commanded the famed raider *Alabama*, his brother, Albert, was a judge in Florida, his cousin Thomas was a Confederate senator from Los Angeles, another cousin Paul Jones was a Confederate general, and three of his children were Confederate officers or connected to the army in some way.

35. Kraszewski, *Catholic Confederates*, 25. Cf. also D. Gleeson, *Irish in the South*, passim.

36. Rousey, "Old South," 21.

37. Endres and Kurtz, *Soldiers*, 19–34.

38. Maher, *To Bind Up the Wounds*, 69–70, 120; cf. also Kurtz, *Excommunicated*, 68.

39. Some Jesuits in Maryland retained ownership of enslaved persons right to the end. In October 1864, as the end of the war loomed, Basil Pacciarini, a prison chaplain at Point Lookout (Maryland), asked his superiors for directions about what to do with the enslaved persons still in residence at their St. Inigoe's community house. Kurtz, *Excommunicated*, 106.

40. Cf. Starrett, *Mississippi Bishop*, passim; Kurtz, *Excommunicated*, 104–6; Cyprian Davis, *Black Catholics*, 116–36. By the mid-twentieth century, Chicago and New Orleans had become the preeminent Black Catholic cities. In

Chicago's case, this is in large part thanks to the heavily marketed presence of Catholic schools in inner-city areas. Cf. Matthew Cressler, *Authentically Black and Truly Catholic: The Rise of Black Catholicism in the Great Migration.*

41. Slattery; *Heroism*, 247–48. I am also grateful to Travis Wakeman for privately sharing his unpublished 2018 master of arts (history) thesis at Norwich University (Northfield, Vermont) on the impact of Catholic Civil War chaplains; his comments therein were helpful in shaping this final chapter.

Epilogue

1. For example, Sheeran considered chaplains from other faiths to have no standing, though he did welcome non-Catholics to Mass and other religious services. Cf. Sheeran, *Civil War Diary.* This trajectory has already been pursued elsewhere, such as in Kurtz, *Excommunicated*; Connor, *Faith and Fury*; Curran, "Image-Changers"; and Randall Miller, "Catholic Religion, Irish Ethnicity," 261–95.

2. Armstrong, *Courageous Fighting*; Maryniak and Brinsfield, *Spirit Divided—Union*; Honeywell, *Chaplains*; and C. Smith, "Work of Civil War Chaplains."

3. Cf. Dolan, *Catholic Revivalism*; Brownson, "Protestant Revivals and Catholic Retreats;" and Taves, *Household of Faith.*

4. Worth reviewing as well is how the unique mission or charism of a religious order (or its founder) impacted the work of the members of that order during the Civil War. For example, the Jesuits brought both a deep intellectual and missionary focus to their worldwide ministry, and their unique charism impacted many others they met along their ministry road. Resources to pursue this line of thought are these: Wright, "Transatlantic Jesuit Encounters"; Garraghan, *Jesuits of the Middle United States*; and Cubitt, *Jesuit Myth.* Also, reviewing the *Woodstock Letters* publication of the Jesuit order could be helpful. The biographies, letters, and diaries of several Jesuit wartime chaplains were outlined in this publication after the war concluded.

5. In his history of the Archdiocese of Cincinnati, Father David Endres does a bit of this, contextualizing the area's wartime chaplains and nuns within their larger archdiocese. Cf. Endres, *Bicentennial History.* Another book touching on this is Ryan Starrett's *Mississippi Bishop William Henry Elder.*

6. Burton and Wright, *Jesuit Suppression in Global Context*; and Shore, "Years of Jesuit Suppression." Twenty-one Jesuits ministered during the Civil War in some way, and thus far more thorough research into Jesuit archival ma-

terials is needed, especially the *Woodstock Letters* (the in-house Jesuit periodical published between 1872 and 1969). Within *Woodstock Letters* are articles on the Suppression, Civil War chaplains, and individual Jesuits. Likewise, Jesuit histories such as the one by Gilbert J. Garraghan (*Jesuits of the Middle United States*) contain sections on the Civil War, though unfortunately they are badly out of date.

7. Hippolyte Gache's confrontation of an "upstart" Protestant chaplain at a Lynchburg hospital (recounted in chapter 12) certainly reveals his personal reactions to Protestant proselytizing. Cf. McNeil, "Daughters of Charity as Civil War Nurses"; McNeil, *Balm of Hope*; and Maher, *To Bind Up the Wounds*. The archival records of many individual female religious orders involved in the Civil War are well-hidden gems of insight and history.

8. David Endres reflects on the Irish heritage of Civil War chaplains in his 2023 article, "Three Cheers for the Union." On the "devotional revolution," cf. Larkin, "Devotional Revolution"; and Delay, "The Devotional Revolution on the Local Level." Other resources on ethnic issues are Randall Miller, "Catholic Religion, Irish Ethnicity, and the Civil War"; Burton, *Melting Pot Soldiers*; and Ural, *Civil War Citizens*.

9. One book that speaks to the political, social, and military contributions of specific Catholics in the war years is Longley, *For the Union and the Catholic Church*. Other resources are Hennesey, *American Catholics*; Perko, *Catholic and American*; and Massa, *Catholics and American Culture*.

10. Some writers have already made headway into this thematic trajectory. Cf. Ellis, *American Catholicism*; McGreevy, *Catholicism and American Freedom*; and Hennesey, *American Catholics*. More recently, Gracjan Kraszewski makes convincing arguments for Southern Catholics' greater societal acceptance in his book *Catholic Confederates*.

11. O'Hagan is mentioned frequently and warmly throughout Joseph Twichell's Civil War letters. Cf. J. Twichell, *Civil War Letters*. Several of O'Hagan's letters in the *Woodstock Letters* also talk to a more limited degree about his relationship with Twichell. This thematic tangent also surfaces in research done by Warren Armstrong and Katherine Jeffrey. Cf. Armstrong, *For Courageous Fighting*; and Jeffrey, "Contrasting Legacies of Confederate Priests."

12. This topic has already been explored to some degree by Drew Gilpin Faust in her book, *This Republic of Suffering: Death and the American Civil War*. Benjamin Miller's 2019 work speaks from the perspective of "sacred space" in the war, and how the Civil War was an assault on nearly every aspect of the antebellum world, including death and suffering. Cf. B. Miller, *In God's Presence*; and Stout, *Upon the Altar of the Nation*.

13. Robert Miller, *Both Prayed to the Same God*. The chapter endnotes of this book, as well as related references, detail possible other sources for exploration in all these areas.

14. Cf. the February 2023 article by Kellerman, "Slavery and the Catholic Church." See also Davis, *History of Black Catholics in the United States*; and Miller, *Both Prayed to the Same God*, 178–80. For the significant flourishing of Black Catholicism in Chicago in the mid- to late twentieth century, cf. Cressler, *Authentically Black and Truly Catholic*.

BIBLIOGRAPHY

PRIMARY SOURCES

Bates, Samuel P. *History of Crawford County, Pennsylvania: Containing a History of the County; Its Townships, Towns, Villages, Schools, Churches, Industries, Etc.; Portraits of Early Settlers and Prominent Men; Biographies; History of Pennsylvania; Statistical and Miscellaneous Matter, Etc., Etc.* Chicago: Warner, Beers & Company, 1885.

Beaudry, Louis N. *War Journal of Louis N. Beaudry, Fifth New York Cavalry.* Edited by Richard E. Beaudry. Jefferson: McFarland and Company Publishers, 1996.

Cooney, Peter Paul. "The War Letters of Father Peter Paul Cooney." Edited by Thomas McAvoy. PhD diss., University of Notre Dame, 1930.

Corby, William. *Memoirs of Chaplain Life: Three Years with the Irish Brigade in the Army of the Potomac.* Notre Dame, IN: Scholastic Press, 1893. Reprinted and edited by Lawrence Frederick Kohl. New York: Fordham University Press, 1992.

De Smet, Pierre-Jean. *Life, Letters, and Travels of Father Pierre-Jean De Smet, S.J. 1801–1873.* Edited by Hiram Martin Chittenden, Hiram Martin and Alfred Talbot Richardson. New York: Francis P. Harper, 1905.

Elder, William Henry. *Mississippi Bishop William Henry Elder and the Civil War.* Edited by Ryan Starrett. Charleston: The History Press, 2019.

———. *Civil War Diary (1862–1865) of Bishop William Henry Elder of Natchez.* Edited by R. O. Gerow. Published privately by Natchez-Jackson Diocese. https://archive.org/details/39020017676308-civilwardiaryof/.

———. *Character Glimpses of Most Reverend William Henry Elder, Second Archbishop of Cincinnati.* Rome: Frederick Pustet and Company, 1911.

Endres, David, and William Kurtz, eds. *Soldiers of the Cross: The Authoritative Text.* Notre Dame: University of Notre Dame Press, 2019.

Gache, Louis-Hippolyte. *A Frenchman, A Chaplain, A Rebel—The War Letters of Louis-Hippolyte Gache SJ*. Edited by Cornelius M. Buckley. Chicago: Loyola University Press, 1981.

Lucey, William L. "The Diary of Joseph B. O'Hagan, S.J., Chaplain of the Excelsior Brigade." *Civil War History* 6, no. 4 (1960): 402–9.

McAtee, Francis. "Reminiscences of an Army Chaplain in the Civil War." *The Woodstock Letters* 44 (1915): 71–77.

McAvoy, Thomas J. "The War Letters of Father Peter Paul Cooney of the Congregation of Holy Cross." *Records of the American Catholic Historical Society of Philadelphia* 44 (1933): 50–51.

McQuaid, Bernard. *The Life and Letters of Bp. Bernard McQuaid, Prefaced with the History of Catholic Rochester before His Episcopate*. Edited by Frederick J. Zwierlein. Rochester: The Art Print Shop, 1925. Https:// archive.org/stream/MN5184ucmf_2/.

Nash, Michael. "Letters from a Chaplain in the War of 1861." *The Woodstock Letters* 17, no. 1 (March 1888): 12–29.

Ryan, Thomas H., ed. *History of Outagamie County, Wisconsin: Being a General Including a History of the Cities, Towns and Villages throughout the County, from the Earliest Settlement to the Present Time*. Chicago: Goodspeed Historical Association, 1911.

Sheeran, James. *Confederate Chaplain: A Military Journal*. Edited by Joseph T. Durkin. Milwaukee: Bruce Publishing, 1960.

——. *The Civil War Diary of James Sheeran, C.Ss.R.* Edited by Patrick Hayes. Washington, DC: Catholic University of America, 2018.

Stephenson, Philip Dangerfield. *Civil War Memoir of Philip Dangerfield Stephenson, D. D.* Edited by Nathaniel Charles Hughes Jr. Baton Rouge: Louisiana State University Press, 1998.

Tissot, Peter. "A Year with the Army of the Potomac—Diary of the Reverend Father Tissot, S.J., Military Chaplain." Edited by Thomas G. Taafe. *United States Catholic Historical Society* 3, part 1 (January 1903): 42–87.

——. "Letters of Civil War Chaplains." *The Woodstock Letters* 43 (1914): 169–80.

Tucker, Philip, ed. "Fr. John Bannon—Experiences of a Confederate Chaplain." *Letters and Notices of the English Jesuit Province*. October 1867. https://www.jesuitarchives.ie/bannon-john-1829-1913-jesuit-priest.

Turgis, Francois I. "Father Francois Turgis to Archbishop John Odin." April 16, 1862. Photostat of a manuscript in the Chancery Office of the Archdiocese of New Orleans.

SECONDARY SOURCES

Abing, Kevin. "Directors of the Bureau of Catholic Indian Missions: Reverend Joseph A. Stephan, 1884–1901." Marquette University Library, 1994. https://www.marquette.edu/library/archives/Mss/BCIM/BCIM-SC1 -directors2.pdf.

"An Account of the Bloody Battle of Shiloh." *New Orleans Crescent*. March 5, 1868.

Adams, George Worthington. *Doctors in Blue: The Medical History of the Union Army in the Civil War*. Baton Rouge: Louisiana State University Press, 1952.

Ahlstrom, Sydney. *Religious History of the American People*. New Haven: Yale University Press, 1972.

Anderson, George M. "Bernardine Wiget, S.J., and the St. Aloysius Civil War Hospital in Washington, D.C." *The Catholic Historical Review* 76, no. 4 (October 1990): 734–64.

Andrews, Rena Mazyck. *Archbishop Hughes and the Civil War*. Chicago: University of Chicago, 1935.

Annales de la Propagation de la Foi. Translated by Andrew Smith. Report of the Diocese of Savannah 37, 1893: 397–401.

Armstrong, Warren B. *For Courageous Fighting and Confident Dying: Union Chaplains in the Civil War*. Lawrence: University of Kansas Press, 1998.

Baker, Barbara, and Jeanne Larzalere. "Baptisms in St. James' Catholic Church Register of Confederate Soldiers Interred at Camp Douglas, Chicago, Illinois." *Chicago Genealogist* 40, no. 2 (Winter 2007–2008): 7–12.

Barry, Craig L. "More on Rations: Nutritional Deficiencies." *The Civil War News* (October 2020): 23–29.

Barton, George. *Angels of the Battlefield*. Philadelphia: The Catholic Art Publishing Company, 1897.

Beaudot, William. *The 24th Wisconsin Infantry in the Civil War: The Biography of a Regiment*. Mechanicsburg: Stackpole Books, 2003.

Bell, John T. *Civil War Stories, Compiled from Official Records: Union and Confederate*. San Francisco: The Whitaker and Ray Company, 1903.

Belmonte, Peter. *The Roaring Lion: Father Leo Rizzo, a Calabrian Priest in the American Civil War*. Monee: Doughboy Publishing, 2021.

Bennett, William. *Narrative of the Great Revival in the Southern Armies During the Late Civil War between the States of the Federal Union*. Harrisonburg: Sprinkle Publications, 1989.

Blanton, DeAnne, and Lauren M. Cook. *They Fought Like Demons: Women Soldiers in the American Civil War*. Baton Rouge: Louisiana State University Press, 2002.

Blied, Benjamin. *Catholics and the Civil War*. Milwaukee: Bruce Publishing Company, 1945.

Blight, David W. *Race and Reunion: The Civil War in American Memory*. Cambridge: Belknap Press, 2001.

Brinsfield, John W., Jr. "Military Chaplains: A Historian's View from the American Revolution to Iraq." *Christian Science Monitor*. October 30, 2007. https://www.csmonitor.com/2007/1030/p25s02-usmi.html.

Brinsfield, John W., Jr., ed. *The Spirit Divided: Memoirs of Civil War Chaplains— The Confederacy*. Macon: Mercer University Press, 2006.

Brinsfield, John W., Jr., William C. Davis, Benedict R. Maryniak, and James I. Robertson Jr. *Faith in the Fight: Civil War Chaplains*. Mechanicsburg: Stackpole Books, 2003.

Browne, Francis Fisher. *Bugle Echoes: A Collection of the Poetry of the Civil War, Northern and Southern*. New York: White, Stokes and Allen, 1886.

Brownson, Orestes. "Protestant Revivals and Catholic Retreats." *Brownson's Quarterly Review* 3 (July 1858): 294–322.

Brosnahan, M. Eleanore. *On the King's Highway*. New York: D. Appleton and Company, 1931.

Brueske, Paul. *The Last Siege: The Mobile Campaign, Alabama 1865*. Philadelphia: Casemate Publishers, 2018.

Buckley, Cornelius Michael. "Joseph Bixio: Furtive Founder of the University of San Francisco." *California History* 78, no. 1 (Spring 1999): 26–30.

Budd, Richard M. "Ohio Army Chaplains and the Professionalization of Military Chaplaincy in the Civil War." *Ohio History Journal* 102 (Winter-Spring 1993): 5–19.

Burns, Stanley B. "Civil War-Era Hospitals," 2016. https://www.pbs.org /mercy-street/uncover-history/behind-lens/hospitals-civil-war/.

Burton, Jeffrey D., and Jonathan Wright, eds. *The Jesuit Suppression in Global Context: Causes, Events and Consequences*. Cambridge: Cambridge University Press, 2015.

Burton, William L. *Melting Pot Soldiers: The Union's Ethnic Regiments*. New York: Fordham University Press, 1998.

Callaghan, Daniel M. *Thomas Francis Meagher and the Irish Brigade in the Civil War*. Jefferson: McFarland and Company, 2006.

Candal, Cara Stillings. "'Be Not Afraid'—A History of Catholic Schooling in Massachusetts." Paper issued by the Pioneer Institute of Public Policy Research, no. 72, March 2011.

Carrington, William A. "Chimborazo Hospital." William A. Carrington 1862 Papers. *Civil War Richmond*. October 28, 2014. https://www.civilwar richmond.com/written-accounts/archival-sources/national-archives /compiled-service-records/william-a-carrington-papers/4028-1862-10-29 -william-a-carrington-papers-inspection-report-for-marshall-spring-hosp.

Carroll, Austin. *A Catholic History of Alabama and the Floridas*. New York: Kennedy and Sons, 1908.

"Chaplains during the Civil War of 1861." *The Woodstock Letters* 14, no. 3 (November 1885): 375–80.

Chick, Sean Michael. "The Supposed Enigma of Isidore Francois Turgis." *The Emerging Civil War* (blog). April 7, 2022. http://emergingcivilwar.com /2022/04/07.

"Civil War Casualties—The Cost of War: Killed, Wounded, Captured, and Missing." American Battlefield Trust (website), updated September 15, 20203. https://www.battlefields.org/learn/articles/civil-war-casualties.

Clarke, Elisha P. "Dr. Elisha P. Clarke—My Capture." *31st Massachusetts Volunteers* (blog). https://31massinf.wordpress.com/narratives-letters-diaries /dr-e-p-clarke-my-capture/.

Connor, Charles P. *Faith and Fury: The Rise of Catholicism during the Civil War*. Irondale: EWTN Publishing, 2019.

Cormier, Steven A. "Appendices." *Acadians in Gray*. http://acadiansingray.com.

Cressler, Matthew. *Authentically Black and Truly Catholic: The Rise of Black Catholicism in the Great Migration*. New York: New York University Press, 2017.

Cubitt, Geoffrey. *The Jesuit Myth: Conspiracy and Politics in Nineteenth Century France*. New York: Oxford University Press, 1993.

Cunningham, H. H. *Doctors in Gray: The Confederate Medical Service*. Baton Rouge: Louisiana State University Press, 1993.

Curran, Robert Emmett. *American Catholics and the Quest for Equality in the Civil War Era*. Baton Rouge: Louisiana State University Press, 2023.

———. *John Dooley's Civil War: An Irish American's Journey in the First Virginia Infantry Regiment*. Knoxville: University of Tennessee Press, 2011.

———. "Image-Changers: Catholic Chaplains and Nurses Encounter Non-Catholic America in the Civil War." *United States Catholic Historian* 39, no. 4 (Fall 2021): 77–100.

——. "The McGlynn Affair and the Shaping of the New Conservatism in American Catholicism, 1886–1894." *The Catholic Historical Review* 66, no. 2 (April 1980): 185–95.

D'Antoni, Blaise C. *Abbe Pierre Felix Dicharry, Vicar General of Natchitoches 1854–1887*. Mimeographed Booklet. Loyola University (Louisiana) Library.

Davidson, Henry M. *Fourteen Months in Southern Prisons*. Milwaukee: Daily Wisconsin Printing House, 1865.

Davis, Cyprian. *The History of Black Catholics in the United States*. New York: Crossroad, 2000.

Delay, Cara. "The Devotional Revolution on the Local Level: Parish Life in Post-Famine Ireland." *United States Catholic Historian* 22, no. 3 (Summer 2004): 41–60.

DeStefano, Michael. "'We Shall Be a Catholic Country': Counting Catholics in the Antebellum United States." *United States Catholic Historian* 39, no. 4 (Fall 2021): 49–75.

Dicharry CM, Warren. "The Leper Priest of Louisiana." *Vincentian Heritage Journal* 11, no. 2 (Fall 1990): 171–82.

Dolan, Jay P. *Catholic Revivalism: The American Experience, 1830–1900*. Notre Dame: University of Notre Dame Press, 1978.

Eastman, William R. "The Army Chaplain of 1863." Speech given December 13, 1911. https://museum.dmna.ny.gov/application/files/6515/5240/0683/Eastman_Army_chaplain.pdf.

Durney, James. "Kildare Rebels, Irish Confederates: Kildaremen in the 6th Louisiana Infantry Regiment." *Kildare Rebels, Irish Confederates* (blog), March 28, 2013. https://kildare.ie/ehistory/index.php/kildare-rebels-irish-confederates/.

Ellis, John Tracy. *American Catholicism*. Chicago: University of Chicago Press, 1969.

——. *Documents of American Catholic History*. Milwaukee: Bruce Publishing, 1956.

——. *The Life of James Cardinal Gibbons: Archbishop of Baltimore, 1834–1921*. Milwaukee: Bruce Publishing, 1952.

Endres, David J. *A Bicentennial History of the Archdiocese of Cincinnati*. Milford: Little Miami Publishing, 2001.

——. "'Three Cheers for the Union': Catholic Chaplains and Irish Loyalty during the American Civil War." *The Catholic Historical Review* 108, no. 1 (Winter 2023): 92–117.

Endres, David J., and Jerrold P. Twobig. "With a Father's Affection: Chaplain William T. O'Higgins and the Tenth Ohio Volunteer Infantry." *United States Catholic Historian* 31, no. 1 (January 2013): 97–127.

Escott, Paul, Lawrence Powell, James I. Robertson Jr., and Emory Thomas, eds. *Encyclopedia of the Confederacy*. Vol. 4. New York: Simon and Schuster, 2002.

Fabiun, Sean. "Civil War Chaplains." *Catholic Historical Review* 99, no. 4 (October 2013): 1–15.

Faherty, William Barnaby. *The Fourth Career of John B. Bannon: St. Louis Pastor; Southern Chaplain; Confederate Agent; Irish Jesuit Orator*. Portland: C & D Publishing, 1994.

———. *Exile in Erin: The Life of Father John B. Bannon*. St. Louis: Missouri Historical Society Press, 2002.

"Father Michael Nash SJ." *The Woodstock Letters* 26 (December 1897): 334–36.

Faust, Drew Gilpin. *This Republic of Suffering: Death and the American Civil War*. New York: Andrew Knopf, 2008.

Ferguson, Joan, transcriber. "History of Diocese Excerpt." A Time of Hope—History of the Diocese of Natchitoches (website), September 20, 2010. http://www.scribd.com/doc/38753923/History-of-Diocese-Excerpt.

Fitzpatrick, Michael E. "The Mercy Brigade: Roman Catholic Nuns in the Civil War." *Civil War Times Illustrated* 36, no. 5 (October 1997): 34–40.

Flores, Daniel B. *Alexander Grzelachowski: Puerto de Luna's Renaissance Man*. Self-published, 2012.

———. *Alexander Grzelachowski: Puerto de Luna's Renaissance Man, Book 2*. Self-published, 2014.

Fortin, Roger. *Faith and Action: A History of the Catholic Archdiocese of Cincinnati, 1821–1996*. Columbus: Ohio State University Press, 2002.

Friedel, Robert Edward. "An Intimate Study of the Poet-Priest Abram Joseph Ryan." Master's thesis, Peabody College for Teachers, Vanderbilt University, 1930.

Gannon, Michael V. *Rebel Bishop: The Life and Era of Augustin Verot*. Milwaukee: Bruce Publishing Company, 1964.

Gallagher, Gary. *The Union War*. Cambridge: Harvard University Press, 2011.

Gallen, James M. "John B. Bannon: Chaplain, Soldier and Diplomat." Civil War St. Louis (website), June 7, 2001. https://www.civilwarstlouis.com/articles/father-bannon/.

Garidel, Henri. *Exile in Richmond: The Confederate Journal of Henri Garidel*. Edited by Michael Chesson and Leslie Roberts. Richmond: University of Virginia, 2001.

Garraghan, Gilbert J. *The Jesuits of the Middle United States*. Vol. 2. New York: America Press, 1938.

Garett, Clarke. "French Missionary Clergy Confront the Protestant Menace in New Mexico, 1851–1885." *Proceedings of the Western Society for French History* 33, (2005): 292–305.

Germain, Aidan. *Catholic Military and Naval Chaplains: 1776–1917.* Washington, DC: Catholic University of America, 1929.

Giblin, Gerald J. "American Jesuits as Chaplains in the Armed Forces: 1775–1917." *The Woodstock Letters* 91, no. 2 (April 1962): 323–482.

Gibson, J. T., ed. *History of the Seventy-Eighth Pennsylvania Infantry.* Pittsburgh: Historical Commission of the Regimental Association, 1905.

Gilles, Anthony E. *People of God: The History of Catholic Christianity.* Cincinnati: St. Anthony Messenger Press, 2000.

Gleeson, David T. *The Irish in the South, 1815–1877.* Chapel Hill: University of North Carolina Press, 2001.

Gleeson, Edward. *Erin Go Gray!* Carmel: Guild Press of Indiana, 1997.

——. *Rebel Sons of Erin: A Civil War Unit History of the 10th TN Irish Infantry, CSA Volunteers.* Carmel: Guild Press of Indiana, 1993.

Green, Carol Cranmer. "Chimborazo Hospital: A Description and Evaluation of the Confederacy's Largest Hospital." PhD diss., Texas Tech University, May 1999.

Goen C. C. *Broken Churches, Broken Nation: Denominational Schisms and the Coming of the Civil War.* Macon: Mercer University Press, 1985.

Gugliotta, Guy. "New Estimate Raises Civil War Death Toll." *New York Times.* April 2, 2012.

Haney, Milton. *Pentecostal Possibilities, or Story of My Life: An Autobiography.* LaVergne: General Books, 2009.

Hannings, Bud. *Every Day of the Civil War: A Chronological Encyclopedia.* Jefferson: McFarland and Company, 2014.

Hannum, Kristen. "Rerum Roots: A Brief History of American Support for Unions." *The U.S. Catholic,* July 20, 2011. https://uscatholic.org/articles/201107/.

Heidler, David, and Jeanne Heidler, eds. *Encyclopedia of the American Civil War.* New York: W. W. Norton and Company, 2000.

Hennesey, James. *American Catholics: A History of the Roman Catholic Community in the United States.* New York: Oxford University Press, 1981.

Herron, Mary Eulalia. "Work of the Sisters of Mercy in the United States, Diocese of New York, 1846–1921." *Records of the American Catholic Historical Society of Philadelphia* 33, no. 3 (September 1922): 216–37.

Hieronymus, Frank. "For Now and Forever: The Chaplains of the Confederate States Army." PhD diss., University of California Los Angeles, 1964.

Hill, Owen Aloysius. *Gonzaga College, an Historical Sketch*. Washington, DC: Gonzaga College, 1922.

Hill, Samuel S., and Charles H. Lippy. *Encyclopedia of Religion in the South*. Macon: Mercer University Press, 2005.

History of the Redemptorists at Annapolis 1853–1903. Ilchester, Maryland: College Press, 1903.

Hogan, Neil, ed. "Historic Men of the Cloth." *The Shanachie: Connecticut Irish-American Historical Society* 21, no. 2, 2009. https://digitalcommons .sacredheart.edu/cgi/viewcontent.cgi?article=1006&context=shanachie.

Honeywell, Roy J. *Chaplains of the United States Army*. Washington, DC. Office of the Chief of Chaplains, Department of the Army, 1958.

Hope, Arthur J. *Notre Dame: One Hundred Years*. http://archives.nd.edu /hope/hope.htm.

Janus, Glen. "Bishop Bernard McQuaid: On 'True' and 'False' Americanism." *The United States Catholic Historian 11*, no. 3 (Summer, 1993): 53–76.

Jeffrey, Kathleen Bentley. "The Contrasting Legacies of Confederate Priests Abram Ryan and Darius Hubert SJ." *United States Catholic Historian* 37, no. 1 (Winter 2019): 1–22.

———. *First Chaplain of the Confederacy: Father Darius Hubert SJ*. Baton Rouge: Louisiana University Press, 2020.

———. *Two Civil Wars: The Curious Shared Journal of a Baton Rouge Schoolgirl and a Union Sailor on the USS Essex*. Baton Rouge: Louisiana State University Press, 2016.

Johns, Frank, and Ann Page. "Chimborazo Hospital and J. B. McCaw, Surgeon in Chief." *Virginia Monthly Magazine of History and Biography* 62, no. 2 (1954): 190–200.

Johnson, Curtis D. *Redeeming America: Evangelicals and the Road to the Civil War*. Chicago: Ivan R. Dee, 1993.

Jones, John William. *Christ in Camp: The True Story of the Great Revival during the War between the States*. Harrisonburg: Sprinkle Publications, 1986.

Kagan, Neil, ed. *Eyewitness to the Civil War*. Washington, DC: National Geographic Society, 2006.

Kajencki, Francis. "Alexander Grzelachowski: Pioneer Merchant of Puerto de Luna, New Mexico." *Arizona and the West* 26, no. 3 (Autumn 1984): 243–60.

Katcher, Philip. *Civil War Source Book*. New York: Facts on File Publishers, 1992.

Kellerman, Christopher. "Slavery and the Catholic Church: It's Time to Correct the Historical Record." *America*, February 15, 2023. https://www .americamagazine.org/faith/2023/02/15/catholic-church-slavery-244703.

King, Richard. "Dominican Chaplains of the Civil War." https://www
.dominicanajournal.org/wp-content/files/old-journal-archive/vol9/no3
/dominicanav9n3dominicanchaplainsthecivilwar.pdf.

Kinsella, Thomas H. Transcribed by Sean Furniss. "Part V - Holy Trinity
Church, Paola." In *The History of Our Cradle Land*. 1921. http://www
.ksgenweb.org/miami/kinsella/ (site discontinued).

Kraszewski, Gracjan. *Catholic Confederates: Faith and Duty in the Civil
War South (The Civil War Era in the South)*. Kent: Kent State University
Press, 2020.

Kurtz, William. *Excommunicated from the Union: How the Civil War Created a Separate Catholic America*. New York: Fordham University Press,
2016.

Larkin, Emmet. "The Devotional Revolution in Ireland, 1850–75." *The American Historical Review* 77, no. 3 (June 1972): 625–52.

Larzalere, Jeanne, and Barbara Baker. "Baptisms in St. James' Catholic Church
Register of Confederate Soldiers Interred at Camp Douglas, Chicago, Illinois." *Chicago Genealogist* 40, no. 2 (Winter 2007–2008): 39–48.

Levine, Alan J. *Race Relations with Western Expansion*. Westport: Praeger Press,
1996.

Longley, Max. *For the Union and the Catholic Church: Four Converts in the
Civil War*. Jefferson: McFarland and Company, 2015.

Lonn, Ella. *Foreigners in the Union Army and Navy*. Baton Rouge: Louisiana
State University Press, 1951.

Loughery, John. *Dagger John: Archbishop John Hughes and the Making of
Irish America*. Ithaca: Cornell University Press, 2018.

Magri, Francis Joseph. "Virginia." *The Catholic Encyclopedia 15*. New York:
Robert Appleton Company, 1912. http://www.newadvent.org/cathen
/15451a.htm.

Maher, Sister Mary Denis. *To Bind Up the Wounds: Catholic Sister Nurses in
the U.S. Civil War*. Baton Rouge: Louisiana State University Press, 1989.

Marsden, George. "The New Old-Time Religion." *U.S. News & World Report*. December 8, 2003.

Martin, James Martin. "Novice? Regent? Scholastic? A Guide to Jesuit Formation (and Lingo)." *America: The Jesuit Review*, August 11, 2013. https://
www.americamagazine.org/faith/2013/08/11/novice-regent-scholastic
-guide-jesuit-formation-and-lingo.

Maryniak, Benedict R., and John W. Brinsfield, eds. *The Spirit Divided: Memoirs of Civil War Chaplains – The Union*. Macon: Mercer University Press,
2007.

Massa, Mark S. *Catholics and American Culture*. New York: Herder & Herder, 2001.

McBrien, Richard. *Catholicism*. Minneapolis: Winston Press, 1980.

McCall, Gary. "God of Our Fathers: Catholic Chaplains in the Confederate Armies." PhD diss., University of New Orleans, December 2010.

McClarey, Donald R. "Father John Ireland and the 5th Minnesota." *The American Catholic: Politics and Culture from an American Perspective* (blog), August 23, 2012. http://the-americancatholic.com/2014/05/25.

———. "Father Turgis: Preacher by Deeds, Not Words." *The American Catholic: Politics and Culture from an American Perspective* (blog), May 25, 2014. https://the-american-catholic.com/2014/05/25/father-turgis-preacher-by-deeds-not-words/.

———. "Matthew Brady, Father Thomas H. Mooney, Dagger John and the Fighting 69th." *Almost Chosen People* (blog), August 3, 2011. https://almostchosenpeople.wordpress.com/tag/father-thomas-h-mooney/.

McGreal, Mary Nona, ed. *Dominicans at Home in a Young Nation: 1786–1865—Volume 1 of the Order of Preachers in the United States: A Family History*. Strasbourg, France: Editions du Signe 2001.

McGreevy, John. *Catholicism and American Freedom: A History*. New York: W. W. Norton and Company, 2014.

McKenna, Charles. *Under the Maltese Cross, Antietam to Appomattox: The Loyal Uprising in Western Pennsylvania, 1861–1865; Campaigns 155th Pennsylvania Regiment*. Reprint. London: Forgotten Books, 2018.

McKenna, Kevin. *The Battle for Rights in the United States Catholic Church*. Mahwah: Paulist Press, 2007.

McNamara, Patrick. *New York Catholics: Faith, Attitude and the Works!* New York: Orbis Books, 2014.

McNeil D. C., Betty Ann. *Balm of Hope: Charity Afire Impels Daughters of Charity to Civil War Nursing*. Chicago: DePaul University Vincentian Studies Institute, 2015.

———. "The Daughters of Charity as Civil War Nurses, Caring without Boundaries." *Vincentian Heritage Journal* 27, no. 1, Article 7 (October 2007): 133–68.

McPherson, James M. *For Cause and Comrades: Why Men Fought in the Civil War*. New York: Oxford University Press, 1997.

Mead, Frank, and Samuel S. Hill. *Handbook of Denominations in the United States*. 11th edition. Nashville: Abingdon Press, 2001.

Meaney, Peter J. "Valiant Chaplain of the Bloody Tenth." *Tennessee Historical Quarterly* 41, no. 1 (Spring 1982): 37–47.

———. "Father Whelan of Fort Pulaski and Andersonville." *Georgia Historical Quarterly* 71, no. 1 (Spring 1987): 1–24.

Miller, Benjamin. *In God's Presence: Chaplains, Missionaries and Religious Space during the American Civil War.* Lawrence: University Press of Kansas, 2019.

Miller, Byron. "When 'Good Father Seelos' Met 'Good Father Abraham.'" *Redemptorist North American Historical Bulletin* 26 (December 2006): 10–14.

Miller, Randall M. "Catholic Religion, Irish Ethnicity, and the Civil War." In *Religion and the American Civil War*, edited by Randall M. Miller, Harry S. Stout, and Charles R. Wilson, 261–96. New York: Oxford Press, 1998.

Miller, Randall M., Harry S. Stout, and Charles R. Wilson, eds. *Religion and the American Civil War.* New York: Oxford Press, 1998.

Miller, Randall M., and Jon L. Wakelyn. *Catholics in the Old South.* Macon: Mercer University Press, 1983.

Miller, Robert J. *Both Prayed to the Same God: Religion and Faith in the American Civil War.* Lanham: Lexington Publishers, 1999.

Mitchell, Reid. *Civil War Soldiers.* New York: Penguin Books, 1988.

Mohney, Donna, transcriber. *The History of Butler County, PA 1895.* Kittanning: R.C. Brown, 1895. www.rootsweb.ancestry.com/~pabutler/1895.

Moore, David. *William S Rosecrans and the Union Victory: A Civil War Biography.* Jefferson, North Carolina: McFarland Press, 2014.

Moorhead, James H. *American Apocalypse — Yankee Protestants and the Civil War, 1860–1869.* New Haven: Yale University Press, 1978.

Moss, Lemuel Moss. *Annals of the Christian Commission.* Philadelphia: J. B. Lippincott, 1868.

Murphy, Robert Joseph. "The Catholic Church in the United States during the Civil War Period (1852–1866)." *Records of the American Catholic Historical Society* 39, no. 4 (December 1928): 272–346.

Murray, Thomas Hamilton. *History of the 9th Regiment, Connecticut Volunteer Infantry, the Irish Regiment, in the War of Rebellion, 1861–1865.* New Haven: The Price, Lee, and Adkins Company, 1903.

"Neither Blue nor Gray: Dominican Chaplains in the Civil War." *Order of Preachers: Eastern Province* (blog), November 4, 2012. https://opeast.org /2012/11/neither-blue-nor-gray-dominican-chaplains-in-the-civil-war/.

Noll, Mark A. *America's Book: The Rise and Decline of a Bible Civilization, 1794–1911.* New York: Oxford University Press, 2022.

———. *America's God: From Jonathan Edwards to Abraham Lincoln.* New York: Oxford University Press, 2002.

———. *The Civil War as a Theological Crisis*. Chapel Hill: University of North Carolina Press, 2006.

Norton, Herman. *Rebel Religion*. St. Louis: The Bethany Press, 1961.

———. *Struggling for Recognition: The United States Army Chaplaincy, 1791–1865*. Washington, DC: Office of the Chief of Chaplains, Department of the Army, 1977.

Oakes, Mary Paulinus. *Angels of Mercy: An Eyewitness Account of the Civil War and Yellow Fever*. Long Prairie: Cathedral Foundation Press, 1998.

"Obituary of Father Anselm Usannez." *The Woodstock Letters* 24, no. 2 (May 1895): 484–85.

"Obituary of Father Joseph O'Hagan." *The Woodstock Letters* 8, no. 3 (December 1879): 173–83.

"Obituary of Father Joseph Prachensky." *The Woodstock Letters* 20, no. 1 (1891): 120–21.

O'Connell, David. *Furl That Banner: The Life of Abram Ryan, Poet-Priest of the South*. Macon: Mercer University Press, 2006.

O'Connell, Jeremiah J. *Catholicity in the Carolinas and Georgia*. New York: D and J Sadlier, 1879.

O'Connell, Marvin Richard. *John Ireland and the American Catholic Church*. Minneapolis: Minnesota Historical Society Press, 1988.

O'Connor, Thomas H. *Boston Catholics: A History of the Church and Its People*. Boston: Northeastern University Press, 2019.

O'Daniel, Victor Francis. *The Dominican Province of Saint Joseph*. New York: Holy Name Society, 1942.

O'Malley, Mark Francis. "Providing Shepherds for Soldiers: A History of Catholic Military Chaplaincy in the U.S." Lecture at Seton Hall University, South Orange, New Jersey, April 21, 2010. https://www.shu.edu/documents/2010-04-21_-_Providing_Shepherds_for_Soldiers_-_Reverend_Mark_Francis_O_Malley_-_v2-2.pdf.

Paludan, Phillip Shaw. *A People's Contest: The Union and the Civil War, 1861–1865*. New York: Harper and Row, 1988.

Pasquier, Michael. *Fathers on the Frontier: French Missionaries and the Roman Catholic Priesthood in the United States (1789–1870)*. New York: Oxford University Press, 2010.

Pfab, Charles B. "American Hospital Chaplains during the Civil War, 1861–1865." Master's thesis, Catholic University of America, June 1955.

Perko, Michael. *Catholic and American: A Popular History*. Huntington: Our Sunday Visitor, 1989.

Petrin, Ronald Arthur. *French Canadians in Massachusetts Politics—1885–1915: Ethnicity and Political Pragmatism*. London and Toronto: Associated University Presses, 1990.

Pickett, LaSalle Corbell. *Literary Hearthstones of Dixie*. Philadelphia: J. B. Lippincott, 1912.

Pillar, James L. *The Catholic Church in Mississippi 1837–1865*. New Orleans: Hauser Press, 1964.

Pitts, Charles F. *Chaplains in Gray: The Confederate Chaplains' Story*. Concord: R.M.J.C. Publications, 2003. First published 1957 by Broadman (Nashville).

Pollard, Charles, Jr. *The Glories of War: Small Battles and Early Heroes of 1861*. Bloomington: Author House, 2004.

Price, Beulah M. D'Olive. "The Reverend John B. Mouton: Confederate Chaplain." *The Journal of Mississippi History* 24, no. 2 (April 1962): 102–6.

Quintard, Charles Todd. *Doctor Quintard, Chaplain C.S.A. and Second Bishop of Tennessee*. Edited by Sam Davis Elliot. Baton Rouge: Louisiana State University Press, 2003.

Rable, George C. *God's Almost Chosen Peoples: A Religious History of the American Civil War*. Chapel Hill: University of North Carolina Press, 2010.

Reilly, Robert F. "Medical and Surgical Care during the American Civil War, 1861–1865." *Proceedings (Baylor University. Medical Center)* 29, no. 2 (April 2016): 138–42.

Reinhart, Joseph R. "Germans in the Civil War." Germans in Campbell County (website). www.usgenwebsites.org/KYCampbell/germans.htm.

Richard, Joseph L. "Field and Staff: The 18th Louisiana Infantry Regiment of Orleans Parish." *LAGenWeb Archives*. August 2000. http://usgwararchives.net/la/orleans/military/18lainf.txt.

Richey, Thomas H. *Tirailleurs: A History of the 4th Louisiana and the Acadians of Company H*. New York: Writers Advantage, 2003.

Robertson, James I. *Soldiers Blue and Gray*. Columbia: University of South Carolina Press, 1988.

Romero, Sidney J. "Louisiana Clergy and the Confederate Army." *Louisiana History—The Journal of the Louisiana Historical Association* 2, no. 3 (Summer 1961): 277–300.

———. *Religion in the Rebel Ranks*. Lanham: University Press of America, 1983.

Rooney, James A. "Father Nash, S.J. Army Chaplain (1825–1895)." *The Catholic Historical Review* 2, no. 2 (July 1916): 188–94.

Rousey, Dennis C. "Aliens in the WASP Nest: Ethnocultural Diversity in the Antebellum Urban South." *The Journal of American History* 79, no. 1 (June 1992): 152–64.

———. "Catholics in the Old South: Their Population, Institutional Development, and Relations with Protestants." *U.S. Catholic Historian* 24, no. 4 (Fall 2006): 1–21.

Schmandt, Raymond, and Schulte, Josephine. "Civil War Chaplains: A Document from a Jesuit Community." *American Catholic Historical Society* 73, nos. 1–2 (March, June 1962): 58–64.

Schmidt, James. *Notre Dame and the Civil War: Marching Onward to Victory.* Notre Dame: University of Notre Dame Press, 2010.

Schroth, Raymond. *Fordham: A History and a Memoir.* Chicago: University of Loyola Press, 2002.

Shannon, J. P. "Archbishop Ireland's Experience as a Civil War Chaplain." *The Catholic Historical Review* 39 (1953): 302–10.

Shattuck, Gardiner, Jr. *A Shield and Hiding Place: The Religious Life of the Civil War Armies.* Macon: Mercer University Press, 1987.

Shore, Paul. *The Years of Jesuit Suppression, 1773–1814: Survival, Setbacks, and Transformation.* Research Perspectives in Jesuit Studies. Boston: Brill Publishers, 2019.

Slattery, William J. *Heroism and Genius: How Catholic Priests Helped Rebuild Western Civilization.* San Francisco: Ignatius Press, 2017.

Slawson, Douglas. "The Vincentian Experience of the Civil War in Missouri." *American Catholic Studies* 121, no. 4 (Winter 2010): 31–60.

Smith, Charles Edward. "The Work of Civil War Chaplains." Master of Arts thesis, University of Arizona, 1965.

Smith, Jack L. "Ministerial Draft Exemption and the Establishment Clause." *Cornell Law Review* 55, no. 6 (July 1970), Article 6. https://scholarship.law.cornell.edu/clr/vol55/iss6/6/.

Smith, Mark M. *The Smell of Battle, the Taste of Siege: A Sensory History of the Civil War.* Oxford: Oxford University Press, 2014.

Smith, Page. *Trial by Fire: A People's History of the Civil War and Reconstruction.* New York: Penguin Books, 1982.

Smith, Sara Trainor, ed. "Notes on Satterlee Military Hospital, West Philadelphia, Pennsylvania from 1862 to Until Its Close in 1865 (From a Journal Kept at the Hospital by a Sister of Charity)." *Records of the American Catholic Historical Society of Philadelphia* 8, no. 4 (December 1897): 399–449.

Stampp, Kenneth M. *The Peculiar Institution: Religion in the Antebellum South.* New York: Vintage Books, 1956.

Starrett, Ryan. *Mississippi Bishop William Henry Elder and the Civil War*. Charleston: The History Press, 2019.

"Stone General Hospital—Warren; Park; Frederick Prison Hospital." *Civil War Washington* (blog), April 16, 2012. https://civilwardc.org/data/places /view/164.

Stout, Harry S. "Baptism in Blood." *Books and Culture* 9, no. 4 (July/August 2003): 5–10.

———. *Upon the Altar of the Nation: A Moral History of the Civil War*. New York: Viking/Penguin, 2006.

"St. Patrick Catholic Church." Cerro Gordo County Iowa (website). http:// iagenweb.org/cerrogordo/church/cg_ch_stpatricks_dougherty.htm.

Stravinskas, Peter, ed. *Our Sunday Visitor's Catholic Encyclopedia*. Huntington: Our Sunday Visitor, 1991.

Sullivan, J. C. "Irish Men in the Confederacy." *Irish Units in the Confederacy* (blog), April 28, 2011. https://www.authentic-campaigner.com/forum /military-forums/the-sinks/28846-irish-units-in-the-confederacy.

Swan, James B. *Chicago's Irish Legion: The 90th Illinois Volunteers in the Civil War*. Carbondale: Southern Illinois University Press, 2009.

Talbott, John. "Combat Trauma in the American Civil War." *History Today* 46, no. 3 (March 1996): 45–52.

Taves, Ann. *The Household of Faith: Roman Catholic Devotions in Mid-Nineteenth Century America*. Notre Dame: University of Notre Dame Press, 1968.

Theriault, Marie Laura. *Diamond Jubilee Souvenir and History of Notre Dame Church, Chippewa Falls, Wisconsin, 1856–1931*. Chippewa Falls: Chippewa Printery, 1931.

Thompson, Jerry. *A Civil War History of the New Mexico Volunteers and Militia*. Albuquerque: University of New Mexico Press, 2015.

Tolson, Jay. "The Faith of Our Fathers." *U.S. News and World Report*, June 28/ July 5, 2004.

Tucker, Patrick. *Irish Confederates: The Civil War's Forgotten Soldiers*. Abilene: McWhiney Foundation Press, 2006.

Tucker, Philip. *The Confederacy's Fighting Chaplain: Father John B. Bannon*. Tuscaloosa: University of Alabama Press, 1992.

Twichell, Joseph. *The Civil War Letters of Joseph Hopkins Twichell: A Chaplain's Story*. Edited by Peter Messent and Steve Courtney. Athens: University of Georgia Press, 2006.

Twichell, Ralph Emerson. *The Leading Facts of New Mexico History: Volume 3*. New York: Nabu Press, 1911.

US Congress, House Executive Document 23. The Trial of Henry Wirz. 40th Congress, 2nd Session, 1868, 277–94. United States, War Department. *The War of the Rebellion: A Compilation of the Official Records of the Union and Confederate Armies.* Washington: [s.n.], 1894.

Ural, Susannah J. *Civil War Citizens: Race, Ethnicity and Identity in America's Bloodiest Conflict.* New York: University Press, 2010.

Varney, Frank. *General Grant and the Rewriting of History: How the Destruction of William S. Rosecrans Influenced Our Understanding of the Civil War.* El Dorado Hills: Savas Beatie, 2013.

Vidmar, John. *Fr. Fenwick's "Little American Province."* Washington: Dominican Province of St. Joseph, 2005.

Wagner, Margaret, Gary Gallagher, and Paul Finkelman, eds. *Library of Congress Civil War Desk Reference.* New York: Simon and Schuster, 2002.

Warren, Robert Penn. *The Legacy of the Civil War.* Lincoln: University of Nebraska Press, 1961.

Webb, Benjamin Joseph. *The Centenary of Catholicity in Kentucky.* 1884. https://www.google.com/books/edition/The_Centenary_of_Catholicity_in_Kentucky/UlBFAQAAMAAJ?hl=en&gbpv=1.

Whitman, Walt. *Memoranda during the Civil War.* Bedford, Massachusetts: Applewood Books, 1993.

Widman, C. M. "Grand Coteau in War Times." *The Woodstock Letters* 30, no. 1 (1901): 34–49.

Wight, Willard E. "The Bishop of Natchez and the Confederate Chaplaincy." *Mid-America: An Historical Review* 39, no. 2 (April 1957): 67–72.

———. "The Churches and the Confederate Cause." *Civil War History* 6, no. 4 (September 1960): 361–73.

Wiley, Bell Irvin. *The Life of Billy Yank: The Common Soldier of the Union.* Baton Rouge: Louisiana State University Press, 1990.

———. *The Life of Johnny Reb: The Common Soldier of the Union.* Baton Rouge: Louisiana State University Press, 1988.

Wilson, Charles Reagan. *Baptized in Blood: The Religion of the Lost Cause.* Athens: University of Georgia Press, 1980.

Wimmer, Boniface. *Letters of An American Abbot.* Latrobe: Saint Vincent Archabbey Publications, 2008.

Winthrop, R. D. "The War Hospitals: 1861–1865 in Washington, DC." https://www.pa-roots.com/pacw/hospitals/dchospitals.html.

Woodbury, Augustus. *A Narrative of the Campaign of the First Rhode Island Regiment in the Spring and Summer of 1861.* Providence: Sidney S. Rider, 1862.

——. *The Second Rhode Island: A Narrative of Military Operations in Which the Regiment Was Engaged from the Beginning to the End of the War for the Union.* Edited by Col. John S. Slocum, 1875. https://babel.hathitrust .org/cgi/pt?id=uc2.ark:/13960/fk2z31ns4b&seq=4.

Woodworth, Steven E. "The Meaning of Life in the Valley of Death." *Civil War Times* 42, no. 5 (December 2003): 55–58.

——. *While God Is Marching On: The Religious Life of Civil War Soldiers.* Lawrence: University Press of Kansas, 2001.

Wright, Jonathan. "Transatlantic Jesuit Encounters during the Nineteenth Century." *United States Catholic Historian* 36, no. 3 (Summer 2018): 65–80.

Zanca, Kenneth J. *The Catholics and Mrs. Mary Surratt: How They Responded to the Trial and Execution of the Lincoln Conspirator.* Lanham: University Press of America, 2008.

Internet Sources

Many of the churches that Civil War pastors served at have parish histories online mentioning the priests who served there. They can be found by searching for the name, city, and state of the parish itself. (Unfortunately, on a few occasions while doing research for this book, parish mergers or closures, or changes in website information or organization, have led to previously accessed information becoming unavailable for readers of this bibliography.)

Online Catholic almanacs for the Civil War years are invaluable sources of information about the locations of priests in specific places during those years. The *Metropolitan Almanac* and the *Sadlier's Catholic Almanac* are both sources here, and can generally be read most easily through the Hathitrust, found at www.hathitrust.org.

Various wartime Catholic bishops' correspondence can be found in the online archives of the University of Notre Dame, at https://archives.nd.edu/.

CATHOLIC CHAPLAINS INDEX

GENERAL INDEX

THE REVEREND ROBERT J. MILLER
is a retired Catholic priest, scholar, and former president
of the Chicago Civil War Round Table. He is author of
six books, including *Both Prayed to the Same God:
Religion and Faith in the American Civil War*.

JAMES M. MCPHERSON
is an American historian specializing in the American Civil War.
He is the George Henry Davis '86 Professor Emeritus
of United States History at Princeton University.
He received the 1989 Pulitzer Prize for *Battle Cry of Freedom*.